Beginning Build and Release Management with TFS 2017 and VSTS

Leveraging Continuous Delivery
for Your Business

Chaminda Chandrasekara

Apress®

Beginning Build and Release Management with TFS 2017 and VSTS

Chaminda Chandrasekara
Colombo, Sri Lanka

ISBN-13 (pbk): 978-1-4842-2810-4   ISBN-13 (electronic): 978-1-4842-2811-1
DOI 10.1007/978-1-4842-2811-1

Library of Congress Control Number: 2017943489

Cover image designed by Freepik

Managing Director: Welmoed Spahr
Editorial Director: Todd Green
Acquisitions Editor: Nikhil Karkal
Development Editor: James Markham / Poonam Jain
Technical Reviewer: Mittal Mehta
Coordinating Editor: Prachi Mehta
Copy Editor: April Rondeau
Compositor: SPi Global
Indexer: SPi Global
Artist: SPi Global

Distributed to the book trade worldwide by Springer Science+Business Media New York, 233 Spring Street, 6th Floor, New York, NY 10013. Phone 1-800-SPRINGER, fax (201) 348-4505, e-mail orders-ny@springer-sbm.com, or visit www.springeronline.com. Apress Media, LLC is a California LLC and the sole member (owner) is Springer Science + Business Media Finance Inc (SSBM Finance Inc). SSBM Finance Inc is a **Delaware** corporation.

For information on translations, please e-mail rights@apress.com, or visit http://www.apress.com/rights-permissions.

Apress titles may be purchased in bulk for academic, corporate, or promotional use. eBook versions and licenses are also available for most titles. For more information, reference our Print and eBook Bulk Sales web page at http://www.apress.com/bulk-sales.

Any source code or other supplementary material referenced by the author in this book is available to readers on GitHub via the book's product page, located at www.apress.com/978-1-4842-2810-4. For more detailed information, please visit http://www.apress.com/source-code.

Printed on acid-free paper

To all my true friends who supported and encouraged me in diffcult times.

Contents at a Glance

Contents

About the Author

Chaminda Chandrasekara is Microsoft Most Valuable Professional (MVP) for Visual Studio ALM and is also a Scrum Alliance Certified ScrumMaster®. He focuses on and believes in the continuous improvement of the software development lifecycle. He works as the ALM/DevOps Architect for Navantis IT (Pvt) Ltd, a fully owned subsidiary of Toronto, Canada–based Navantis, Inc.

Chaminda is an active Microsoft Community Contributor (MCC) who is well recognized for his contributions in Microsoft forums, TechNet galleries, and Wikis, and who contributes extensions to Visual Studio Team Services/TFS in the Microsoft Visual Studio marketplace. He also contributes to other open source projects in GitHub. His technical blog, found at http://chamindac.blogspot.com/, is popular among ALM practitioners around the world for its quick and descriptive tech guidance.

About the Technical Reviewer

Mittal Mehta has total 14 years of IT experience. Currently, he is working as a configuration manager and is Microsoft certified professional in TFS 2012. He also has experience working in build-release, configuration and automation area since last 8 years in Microsoft Technologies.

Acknowledgments

I would like to express my gratitude to Sanjaya Yapa, Project Manger at Navantis, who saw me through this book. He provided support, talked things over, read early drafts, and offered comments, supported reading proofs, all of which allowed me to write and design this book.

In addition, I must say thanks to Chaminda Bandara Somathilake, Software Archtect at Navantis, for providing support in defining the topics for the book.

I must mention Jeremy Garner-Howe and Indaka Raigama, who were my top managers some time back. The knowledge I gained while working with you was enormous, and the opportunities given by you for my growth really helped me to become who I am today.

Last and not least: I really value the support given by all those who have been with me over the course of the years and whose names I have failed to mention.

CHAPTER 1

■ ■ ■

Understanding the Concepts

By reading through this chapter, you will understand the concept of continuous delivery and how it helps a software organization to achieve DevOps. Further, you will learn what various tools, Microsoft VS Team Services, and Team Foundation Server have to offer when implementing release pipelines. This chapter will set the stage for you to get started with the walkthrough lessons, which start from Chapter 2. Furthermore, this chapter also provides you with recommendations for overcoming practical implementation roadblocks and building a robust deployment pipeline.

DevOps

DevOps is the buzz word that you hear in the industry today. It defines the culture and the practice of an organization. The aim of DevOps is to establish an environment where building, testing, and releasing software happens rapidly, frequently, and with a high degree of reliability, compared to the traditional waterfall type of development life cycle and manual deployment and testing. This requires an organization to automate the software delivery cycle and perform a significant amount of infrastructure changes or upgrades to support the new practices. In a DevOps (software **dev**elopment and information technology **ops**erations) culture, developers and IT pros are encouraged to collaborate and communicate with one another often, which emphasizes the concept of teamwork (see Figure 1-1).

© Chaminda Chandrasekara 2017
C. Chandrasekara, *Beginning Build and Release Management with TFS 2017 and VSTS*,
DOI 10.1007/978-1-4842-2811-1_1

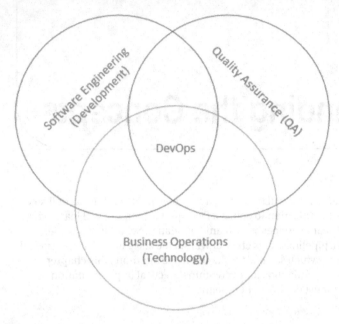

Figure 1-1. *DevOps at a glance*

Continuous Integration (CI)

Continuous integration (CI) is the process that ensures the stability of all the available developer source code. All working copies of source code are merged into the trunk/main line (instead of a main branch, this can be a code branch for a given iteration/sprint) and integrated with each other. The primary objective of maintaining a stable code base is achieved through automated builds of each code submitted and the execution of the unit tests (see Figure 1-2). This is done so that defects can be found and addressed quickly. This feature is especially powerful when combined with continuous delivery.

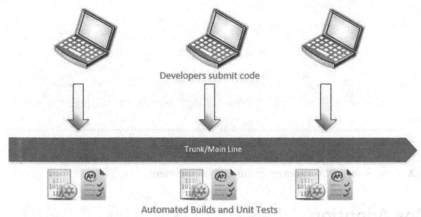

Figure 1-2. Continuous integration

Continuous Delivery (CD)

Development teams produce software in short cycles using modern-day software development approaches. One of the biggest challenges is ensuring the reliability of any software releases to the target environments at any given time. A straightforward and reusable deployment process is essential in order to reduce the cost, time, and risk of delivering software changes. These could be incremental updates to the application in production. In a nutshell, CD delivers software changes more frequently and reliably, compared to manual deployment and testing and DevOps can be considered a product of continuous delivery.

Continuous Deployment

Continuous delivery ensures every change can be deployed to production while having the option to hold the production deployment until a manual approval is given. On the other hand, continuous deployment lets every change to be automatically deployed to production. To implement continuous deployment, one must have continuous delivery in place, since continuous deployment is created by automating the approval steps of continuous delivery (see Figure 1-3).

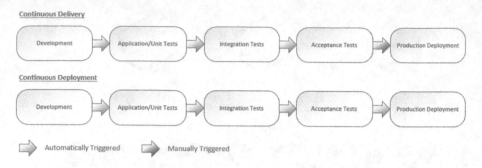

Figure 1-3. Continuous delivery versus continuous deployment

DevOps Adoption

An organization must go through many cultural and practical changes in order to implement DevOps. This might take a long time, and it requires continuous focus and a commitment to improving the way of work.

The following are key factors that are required for DevOps adoption:

- Use of process/methodology such as Agile/Scrum/XP, etc.

- Demand for frequent production releases

- Extensive availability of virtual infrastructure

- Deployment automation and configuration management

- A focus on test automation and continuous integration

- Significant amount of publicly available best practices

- Incremental adoption with systematic thinking, amplified feedback loops, and continual experiment and learning

---

■ **Note** A detailed discussion of DevOps is out of the scope of this book. You can find useful information on DevOps at the following links:

https://theagileadmin.com/what-is-devops/

https://en.wikipedia.org/wiki/DevOps

Release/Deployment Pipeline

The release pipeline delineates the sequence of actions involved in deployment, from retrieving the completed work from source control to delivering software to the end user. The software retrieved from version control has to be built, tested, and deployed in several stages before reaching the production environment via a release pipeline.

The process involves many individuals, teams, tools, and components, which vary based on the software development practice being used. A successful deployment pipeline should provide the visibility, control, and flexibility of the deployment flow to the teams/individuals using it (see Figure 1-4).

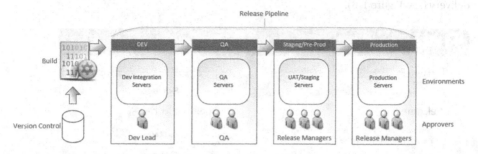

***Figure 1-4.** Release/deployment pipeline*

A rule of thumb is to deploy the same binaries/packages, which were built only once, across the pipeline. Configuration should be applied appropriately to the components deployed because each environment has its own configuration values. Therefore, each deployment stage definition on the release flow should contain the configuration values specific to that stage. These values are applied to the package being deployed while the deployment process is in the current stage.

TFS/VS Team Services Build & Release Management

Team Foundation Server and Visual Studio Team Services (online version of TFS) offer an impressive set of tools to implement continuous delivery. The new web-based extendable build system (the XAML-based build system is now deprecated) provides the necessary flexibility and capability to build almost any type of source code, including source code available in outside repositories such as GitHub.

Release management is now part of TFS and is capable of deploying to Windows, Linux, and OSX. (The previously used Client Server release management model is not discussed in this book.) See Figure 1-5 for a representation of a release workflow.

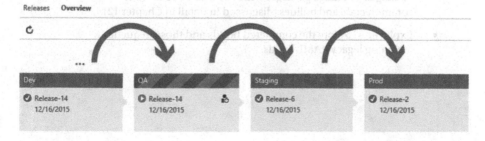

***Figure 1-5.** A release workflow*

Build & Release Tab

A team project (https://www.visualstudio.com/en-us/docs/setup-admin/create-team-project) contains a Build & Release tab that allows you to implement continuous delivery (see Figure 1-6).

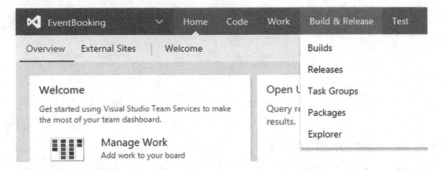

Figure 1-6. *Build & Release tab*

Let's look at the options available on the tab:

- **Builds** – Manage build definitions (to define steps for packaging source code into deployable packages) and builds (executed build definitions are the builds).

- **Releases** – Manage release definitions (defines the steps for deploying in each target environment) and deployments (executed release definitions are the deployments).

- **Task Groups** – Group a set of tasks that can be reusable in builds and releases.

- **Packages** – Manage packages with TFS and VSTS to share common code and utilities (discussed in detail in Chapter 12).

- **Explorer** – Explore the completed builds and those in queues, including legacy XAML builds.

Build & Release Agents and Pipelines

A concurrent pipeline in on-premise s TFS, allows you to run a single release at a given time. But you can run any number of concurrent builds with no limitation. Single, free concurrent p ipeline is available for each collection in a TFS instance. Every Visual Studio Enterprise subscriber contributes an additional concurrent pipeline to TFS. You can buy additional private pipelines from the Visual Studio Marketplace. For more information visit https://www.visualstudio.com/en-us/docs/build/concepts/licensing/concurrent-pipelines-tfs. You are required to configure at least one agent in order to build and deploy with Team Foundation Server, since it is a prerequisite for running a build or deployment in a given machine. Agents for TFS require no license, and a TFS license covers implementing any number of agents for on-premises TFS.

For VS Team Services, three hosted agents (two Windows and one Linux) are available with a free 240 minutes of build/deploy time altogether, while a single job is limited to 30 minutes. This is provided with one concurrent pipeline available free for VSTS, allowing you to run a single build or a release at a given time. With the purchase of first hosted concurrent pipeline 240 minutes total limit and 30 minutes job limit is removed. For more information on VSTS pipelines and to identify required number of pipelines for your team size, visit https://www.visualstudio.com/en-us/docs/build/concepts/licensing/concurrent-pipelines-ts. You can purchase hosted or private pipelines for VSTS as required by your teams. For private pipelines visit https://marketplace.visualstudio.com/items?itemName=ms.build-release-private-pipelines and for hosted pipelines visit https://marketplace.visualstudio.com/items?itemName=ms.build-release-hosted-pipelines. Any number of on-premises agents can be added free of charge, to VS Team Services. Visit https://www.visualstudio.com/en-us/products/visual-studio-team-services-pricing-vs.aspx and view the Additional Services tab for pipeline pricing.

Agent of TFS/VSTS is often referred to as a build agent (actually a build/deployment agent), due to build automation was introduced well before release managment. Agent is capable of building source code, executing unit test, executing deployments, configuring the target computers, and installing other software required to run your application.

Agent Pool

The agent pool specifies the security context and runtime environment for agents (see Figure 1-7). By default, four agent pools are available for VS Team Services, and one pool is available for on-premises TFS. Agent pools are scoped to the TFS Application Tier or VS Team Services Account. You can create agent pools on your own. Below are the four agent pools available in VSTS:

- **Hosted Pool** – Available with one free hosted agent on Windows for VS Team Services. When you buy each hosted pipeline, additional hosted agent get added to the VS Team Services Account.

- **Hosted VS2017 Pool** – Available with one free hosted agent on Windows with Visual Studio 2017 for VS Team Services. When you buy each hosted pipeline, additional hosted agent get added to the VS Team Services Account.

- **Hosted Linux Pool** – Available with one free agent on Linux for VS Team Services. When you buy each hosted pipeline, additional hosted agent get added to the VS Team Services Account.

- **Default Pool** – Available in both VS Team Services and on-premises TFS for setting up your own agents. This pool can be used to register private on-premises agents. You can add more agent pools similar to this pool, in both VSTS and TFS. You will learn more details about agent pools in Chapter 2.

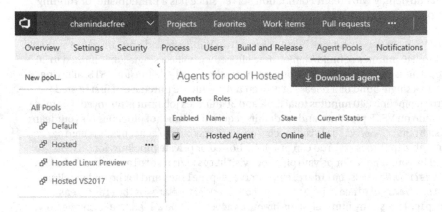

Figure 1-7. *Agent pools in VSTS*

Agent Queue

An agent queue provides access to a given agent pool containing one or more build/release agents. This allows more than one operation to be queued for execution, using an agent available in the pool. Agent queues are scoped to a team's project collection, so they can be used with build/release definitions in multiple team projects (see Figure 1-8).

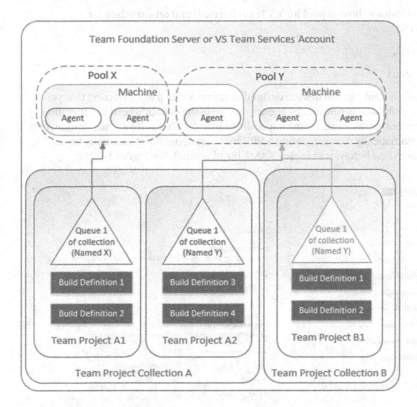

Figure 1-8. *Agent queues overview*

Agent

An agent runs inside an agent pool. An agent carries out operations sequentially assigned to an agent queue. Agents are capable of building solutions, delivering artifacts to target environments, installing applications, and configuring target environments. An agent can run on the following platforms:

- Windows (hosted pool for VS Team Services and on-premises for TFS)

- OSX

- Linux

An agent's system capabilities are defined as name–value pairs, ensuring that your build/release definition is run only by agents that meet the capability criteria specified by you. Environment variables and some capabilities like installed software and frameworks are added automatically. You can define additional user capabilities manually for an agent (similar to tags behavior in legacy XAML build agents). See Figure 1-9.

Figure 1-9. *Agent system and user capabilities*

Agent should have "line of sight" (capability to receive and transmit data from agent to target machines) to target environment so as to perform deployment or configuration action on the target. By default, VS Team Services' hosted agents have connectivity to Windows Azure websites and Windows servers running in Azure. To perform deployment actions targeting on-premises servers, you have to register at least one on-premises agent in an agent pool of VS Team Services. This agent should have "line of sight" to the target on-premises machines in order to perform deployments in them. See Figure 1-10.

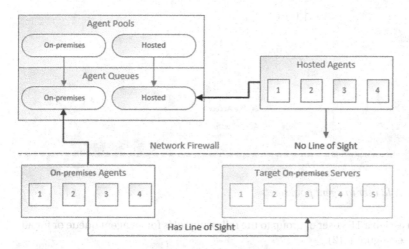

Figure 1-10. Hosted agents and on-premises agents' "line of sight"

Security—Agent Pool—Agent Queue

You can assign a TFS user or group to the following roles for an agent pool or for all the pools (see Figure 1-11):

- **Reader** - Can only view the agent pools

- **Service Account** - May view agents, create sessions, and listen for jobs from the agent pool

- **Administrator** - Can administer, manage, view, and use agent pools

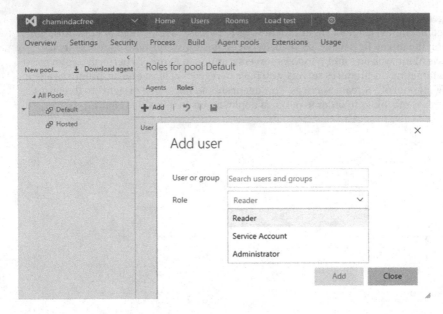

Figure 1-11. *Add user to agent pool roles*

You can assign a TFS user or group to the following roles for an agent queue or for all the queues (see Figure 1-12):

- **Reader** – Can only view the agent queues

- **User** – Can view and use agent queues, but cannot manage or create agent queues

- **Creator** – Can create and view agent queues, but cannot manage or use agent queues (all queues only)

- **Administrator** – Can administer, manage, view, and use agent queues

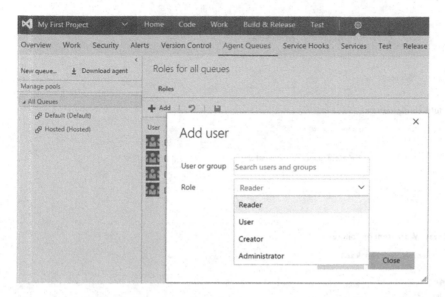

Figure 1-12. *Add user to agent queue roles*

Refer lessons in Chapter 2 to learn how to set up agent pools, queues, and agents.

Build Definition

A build definition is a template for your build in which you will set up the required steps for packaging your solution into deployable artifacts and the steps for executing unit tests.

A build definition has few tabs. Each tab serves a different purpose. (How to create a build definition is covered in Chapter 3.) See Figure 1-13.

Figure 1-13. *Build definition tabs*

The **Options** tab lets you build for multiple configurations, create a work item on build failure, and so forth. (How to build multi-configurations is explained in Chapter 3.) See Figure 1-14.

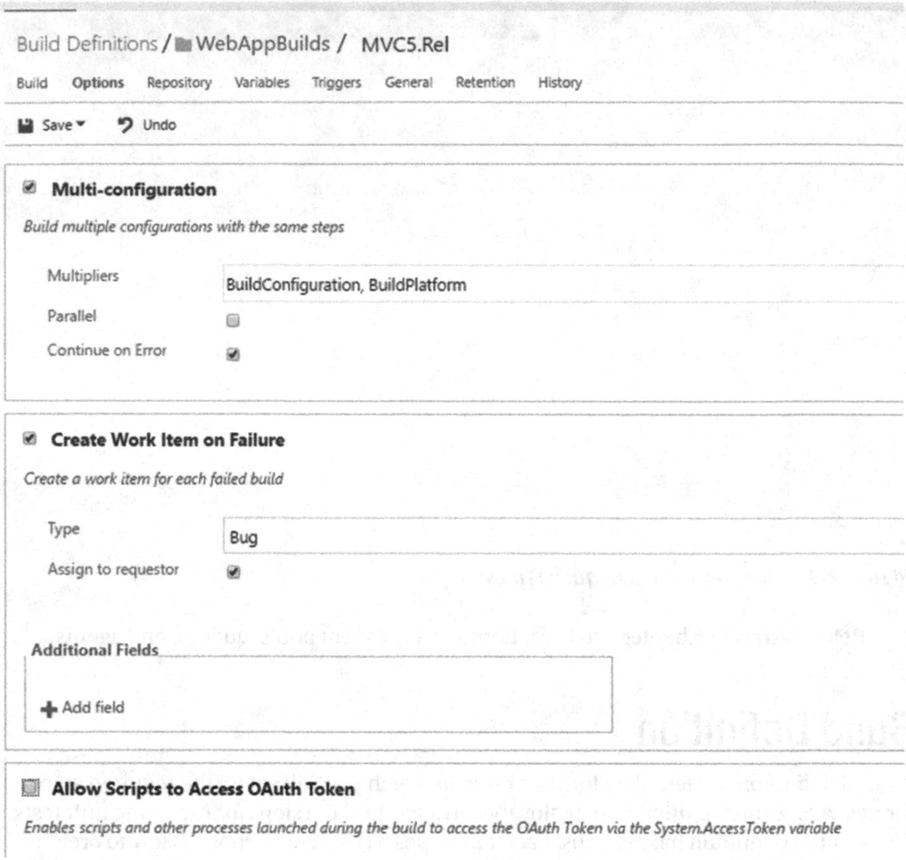

Build Definitions / ■ WebAppBuilds / MVC5.Rel

Build **Options** Repository Variables Triggers General Retention History

💾 Save ▾   🔄 Undo

☑ **Multi-configuration**

Build multiple configurations with the same steps

Multipliers	BuildConfiguration, BuildPlatform
Parallel	☐
Continue on Error	☑

☑ **Create Work Item on Failure**

Create a work item for each failed build

Type	Bug
Assign to requestor	☑

Additional Fields

➕ Add field

▨ **Allow Scripts to Access OAuth Token**

Enables scripts and other processes launched during the build to access the OAuth Token via the System.AccessToken variable

Figure 1-14. *Options tab*

The **Repository** tab is where you define the repository to use for the build. See Figure 1-15.

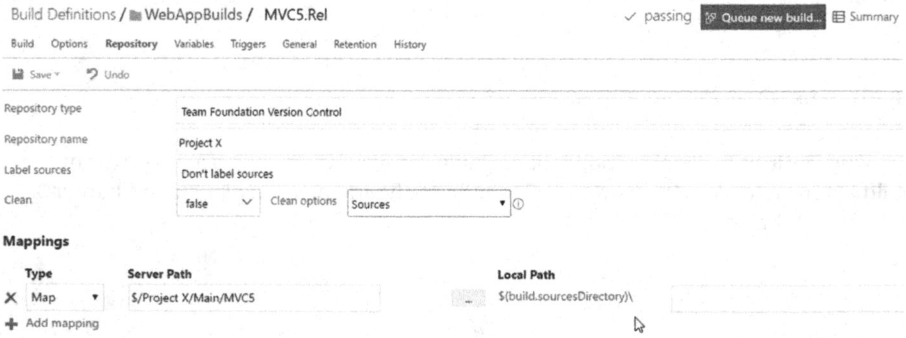

Build Definitions / ■ WebAppBuilds / MVC5.Rel   ✓ passing ⚙ Queue new build... ⊞ Summary

Build Options **Repository** Variables Triggers General Retention History

💾 Save ▾   🔄 Undo

Repository type	Team Foundation Version Control
Repository name	Project X
Label sources	Don't label sources
Clean	false ⌄ Clean options Sources ▾ ⓘ

Mappings

Type	Server Path	Local Path
✕ Map ▾	$/Project X/Main/MVC5	$(build.sourcesDirectory)\

➕ Add mapping

Figure 1-15. *Repository tab*

The **Variables** tab lets you define the custom variables to be used in the build steps. In build steps, you can use variables in $(variablename) format. Predefined build variables are explained at https://www.visualstudio.com/en-us/docs/build/define/variables. The "Allow at Queue Time" option lets you decide if a given build variable can be altered by the person who is queuing the build (for CI builds, the specified value is used by default since no human is involved in the queuing). See Figure 1-16.

Figure 1-16. *Variables tab*

The **Triggers** tab is where you define how the build should be triggered. It could be continuous integration, scheduled, or manual if the option is not predefined. See Figure 1-17.

Builds   Releases   Packages   Library   Task Groups   Explorer

Build Definitions / ■ WebAppBuilds / MVC5.Rel   ✓ passing

Build   Options   Repository   Variables   Triggers   General   Retention   History

■ Save ▼   ⤴ Undo

☑ **Continuous integration (CI)**

Build each check-in.

☑ Batch changes

Path filters

✗ Include   ▼ $/Project X   ⋯   ⓘ
➕ Add new filter

☑ **Scheduled**

Build at these times.

➕ Add new time...

24h time: 03 ▼ : 00 ▼   (UTC+05:30) Sri Jayawardenepura   ▼
☐ Su   ☑ M   ☑ Tu   ☑ W   ☑ Th   ☑ F   ☐ Sa

▣ **Gated Check-in**

Accept check-ins only if the submitted changes merge and build successfully

Figure 1-17. *Triggers tab*

The **General** tab lets you define the build's number format, timeouts, agent queue to use, and demands for agent capabilities. See Figure 1-18.

Figure 1-18. *General tab*

The **Retention** tab is where you can define for how long to keep the builds. See Figure 1-19.

Build Definitions / WebAppBuilds / MVC5.Rel	✓ passing

The retention rules are evaluated in order, with the first rule that matches a build applied. The maximum rule at the bottom matches all builds.

Days to keep:	10	Delete build record:	true
Minimum to keep:	1	Delete source label:	false
		Delete file share:	true
		Delete symbols:	true
		Delete test results:	true

Days to keep:	30	Delete build record:	true
Minimum to keep:	10	Delete source label:	false
		Delete file share:	true
		Delete symbols:	true
		Delete test results:	true

Figure 1-19. *Retention tab*

The **History** tab lets you view the definition update history and allows you to compare definition json files. You have the option to roll back changes to the definition. See Figure 1-20.

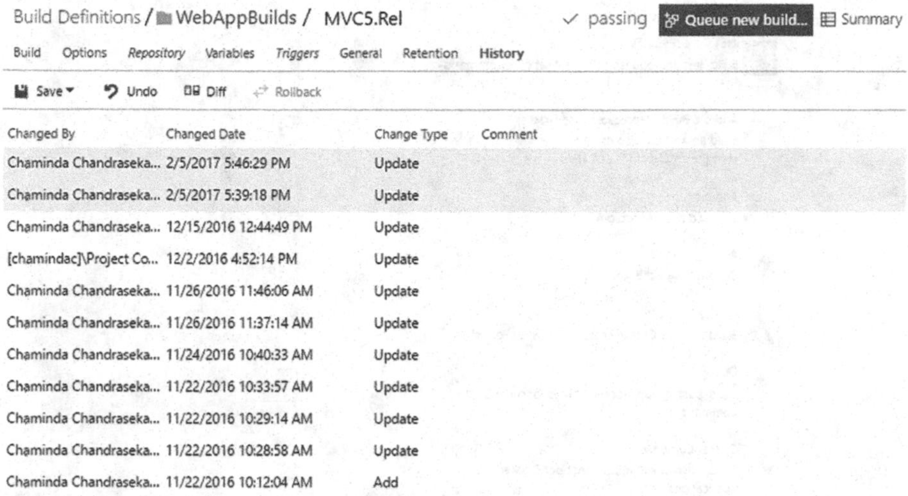

Figure 1-20. *History tab*

The **Build** tab is where you define build steps. You can add steps from the Task catalog by clicking **Add build step**. You have the ability to reorder/change build steps. To remove a build step, you can click on the red X next to the selected step, as shown in Figure 1-21.

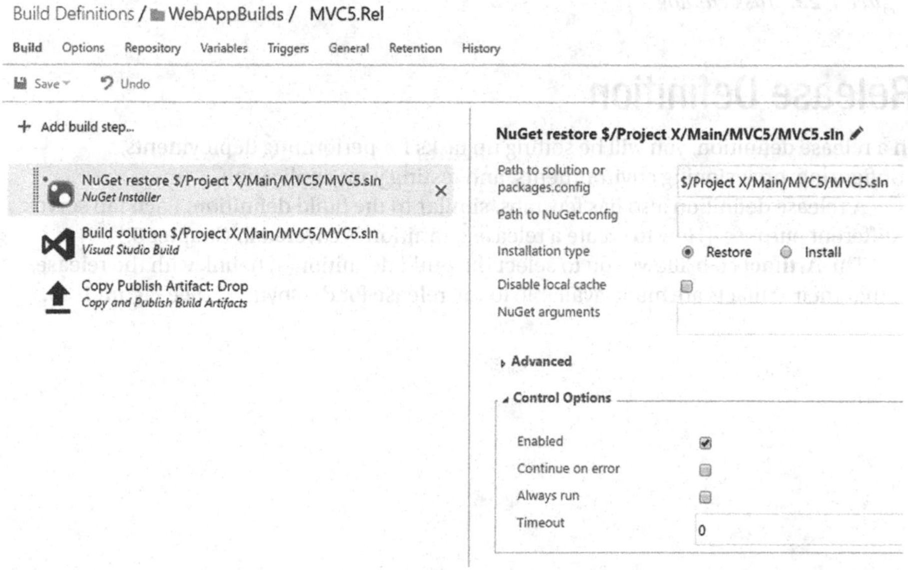

Figure 1-21. *Build tab*

17

The task catalog pops out when you click on **Add build step** (see Figure 1-22).

Figure 1-22. *Task catalog*

Release Definition

In a release definition, you will be setting up tasks for performing deployments, configuring, provisioning environments, and testing your application.

A release definition also has few tabs, similar to the build definition. Each tab serves a different purpose. (How to create a release definition is covered in Chapter 3.)

The **Artifacts** tab allows you to select the build definition(s) to link with the release, so that their artifacts are made available to the release for deployment. See Figure 1-23.

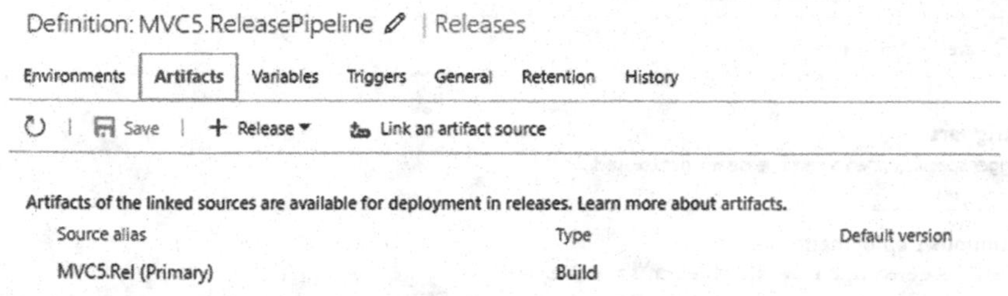

Definition: MVC5.ReleasePipeline ✎ | Releases

Environments | **Artifacts** | Variables | Triggers | General | Retention | History

↻ | 🖫 Save | **+** Release ▾   🔗 Link an artifact source

Artifacts of the linked sources are available for deployment in releases. Learn more about artifacts.

Source alias	Type	Default version
MVC5.Rel (Primary)	Build	

Figure 1-23. *Artifacts tab*

The **Variables** tab lets you define the variables common to all release environments (global variables). Predefined release variables are explained at `https://www.visual studio.com/en-us/docs/release/author-release-definition/understanding-tasks#predefvariables`. See Figure 1-24.

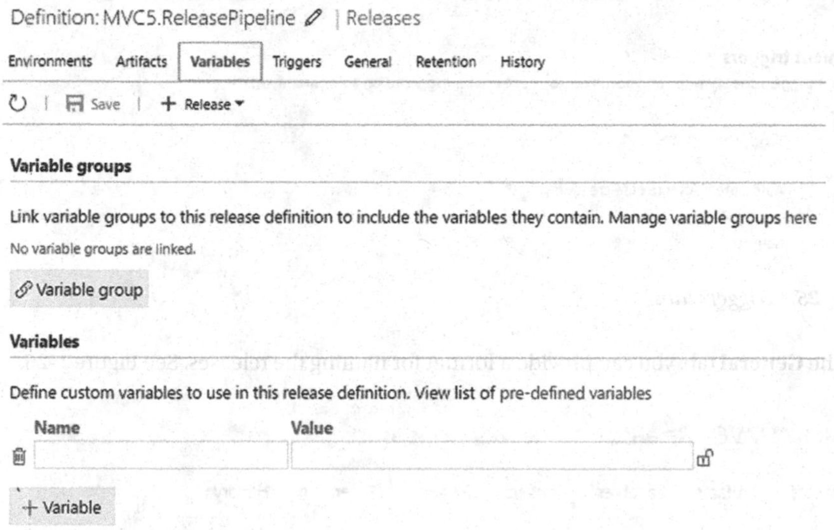

Definition: MVC5.ReleasePipeline ✎ | Releases

Environments | Artifacts | **Variables** | Triggers | General | Retention | History

↻ | 🖫 Save | **+** Release ▾

Variable groups

Link variable groups to this release definition to include the variables they contain. Manage variable groups here
No variable groups are linked.

🔗 Variable group

Variables

Define custom variables to use in this release definition. View list of pre-defined variables

Name	Value
🗑 | | | 🔓

+ Variable

Figure 1-24. *Variables tab*

The **Triggers** tab lets you define release triggers based on artifacts or schedules. See Figure 1-25.

Environments   Artifacts   Variables   *Triggers*   General   Retention   History

○ | 🖫 Save | ＋ Release ▾

Release triggers
Release trigger specifies when a new release will get created.

☑ **Continuous Deployment**
  Creates release every time a new artifact version is available.

＋ Add new trigger

Set trigger on artifact source | MVC5.Rel   ▼ | with tags ⓘ   Add...

☐ **Scheduled**
  Create a new release at a specified time.

Environment triggers
Environment triggers specify when and how a deployment will be triggered on an environment.

Environment	Trigger
QA	Automated: After release creation ✎
UAT	Manual ✎

Figure 1-25. *Triggers tabs*

In the **General** tab, you can provide a format for naming the releases. See Figure 1-26.

Definition*: MVC5.ReleasePipeline ✎ | Releases

Environments   Artifacts   Variables   *Triggers* | General | Retention   History

○ | 🖫 Save | ＋ Release ▾

Release name format | Release-$(rev:r) | ⓘ

Figure 1-26. *General tab*

The **Retention** tab allows you to define the period of time for which a completed release should be retained. See Figure 1-27.

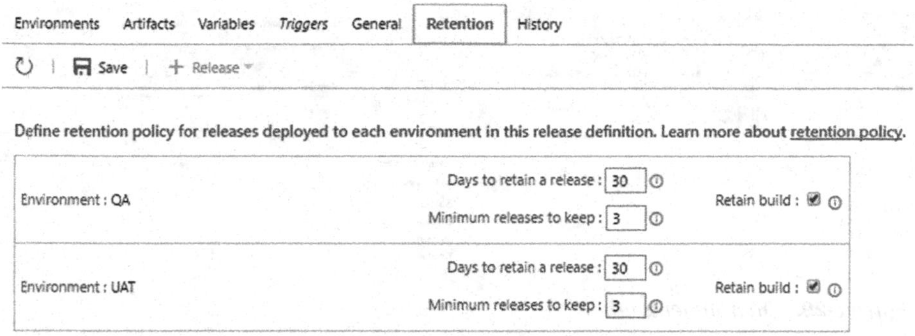

Environments	Artifacts	Variables	*Triggers*	General	Retention	History

↻ | 🖫 Save | + Release ▾

Define retention policy for releases deployed to each environment in this release definition. Learn more about retention policy.

Environment : QA	Days to retain a release : [30] ⓘ	Retain build : ☑ ⓘ
	Minimum releases to keep : [3] ⓘ	
Environment : UAT	Days to retain a release : [30] ⓘ	Retain build : ☑ ⓘ
	Minimum releases to keep : [3] ⓘ	

Figure 1-27. *Retention tab*

The **History** tab allows you to view and compare the release definition change history. However, there is no rollback feature available like in builds. See Figure 1-28.

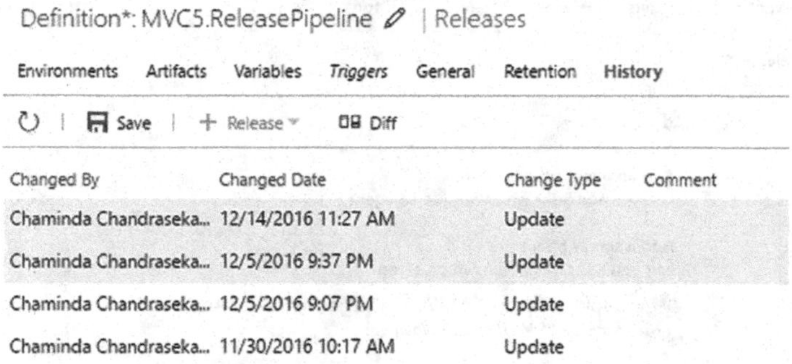

Definition*: MVC5.ReleasePipeline ✎ | Releases

Environments	Artifacts	Variables	*Triggers*	General	Retention	History

↻ | 🖫 Save | + Release ▾ | ▢▢ Diff

Changed By	Changed Date	Change Type	Comment
Chaminda Chandraseka...	12/14/2016 11:27 AM	Update	
Chaminda Chandraseka...	12/5/2016 9:37 PM	Update	
Chaminda Chandraseka...	12/5/2016 9:07 PM	Update	
Chaminda Chandraseka...	11/30/2016 10:17 AM	Update	

Figure 1-28. *History tab*

In the **Environments** tab, you can define multiple environments for the release pipeline. See Figure 1-29.

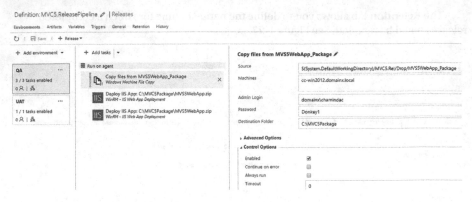

Figure 1-29. *Environments tab*

You can also add multiple agent phases and server phases to a release environment in this tab (see Figure 1-30).

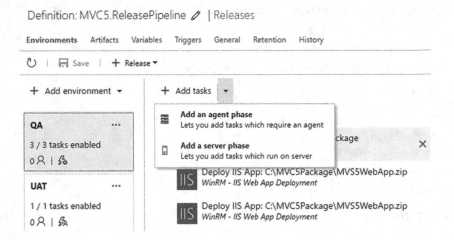

Figure 1-30. *Add agent or server phase to an environment*

A server phase can only contain Manual Intervention tasks at the moment. An agent phase can contain multiple tasks (the same task catalog as in build definition will be opened when **Add tasks** is clicked). You can set demands for an agent, and if required, a release environment can run on multiple agents in parallel. You can also define a timeout for an agent and skip artifacts' downloading if it is not required for that given agent. See Figure 1-31.

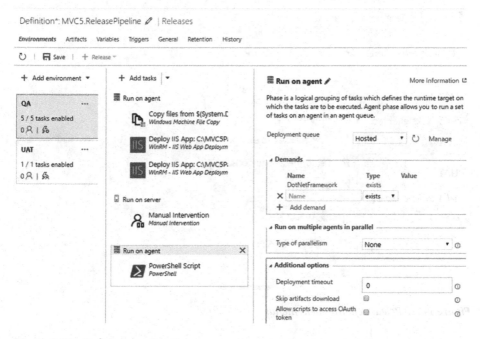

Figure 1-31. *Defining agent options*

Each environment has a menu allowing cloning, the creation of environment-specific variables, and more. See Figure 1-32.

Figure 1-32. *Release environment menus*

The environment configuration **Approvals** tab allows you to define pre-/post-approvers for deployment with a few options. See Figure 1-33.

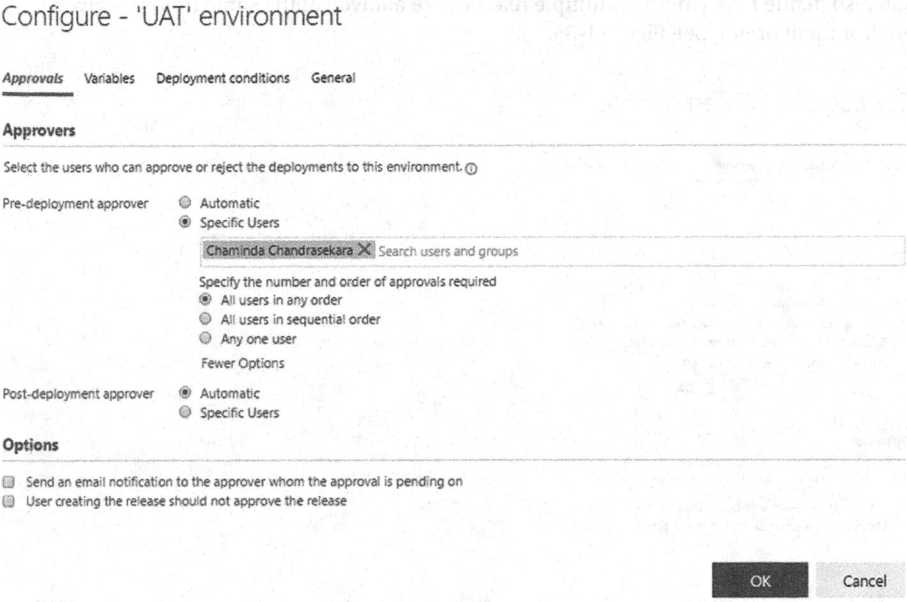

Configure - 'UAT' environment

Approvals   Variables   Deployment conditions   General

Approvers

Select the users who can approve or reject the deployments to this environment. ⓘ

Pre-deployment approver   ◯ Automatic
   ◉ Specific Users

       Chaminda Chandrasekara ✕ Search users and groups

       Specify the number and order of approvals required
       ◉ All users in any order
       ◯ All users in sequential order
       ◯ Any one user
       Fewer Options

Post-deployment approver   ◉ Automatic
   ◯ Specific Users

Options

☐ Send an email notification to the approver whom the approval is pending on
☐ User creating the release should not approve the release

OK   Cancel

Figure 1-33. *Approvals tab*

The environment configuration **Variables** tab allows you to define variables for a given environment. See Figure 1-34.

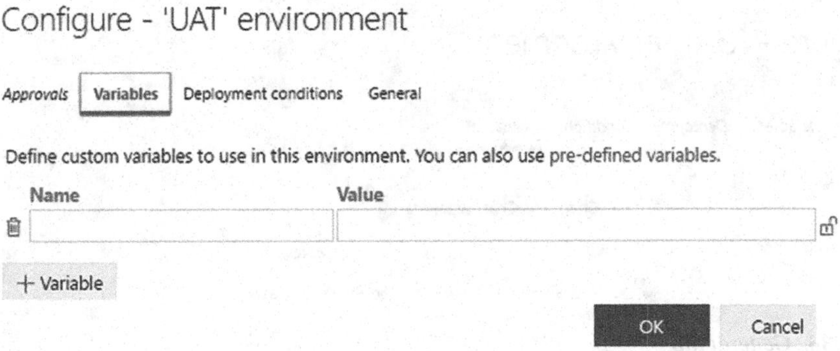

Configure - 'UAT' environment

Approvals | Variables | Deployment conditions   General

Define custom variables to use in this environment. You can also use pre-defined variables.

Name   **Value**

🗑   🔓

+ Variable

OK   Cancel

Figure 1-34. *Variables tab*

The environment configuration **Deployment conditions** tab lets you define how the deployment is triggered. It can be based on a previous successful/partially successful environment(s) or on a schedule, or can be done manually or after release creation. You can also define here whether multiple releases are allowed at the same time in a given environment or not. See Figure 1-35.

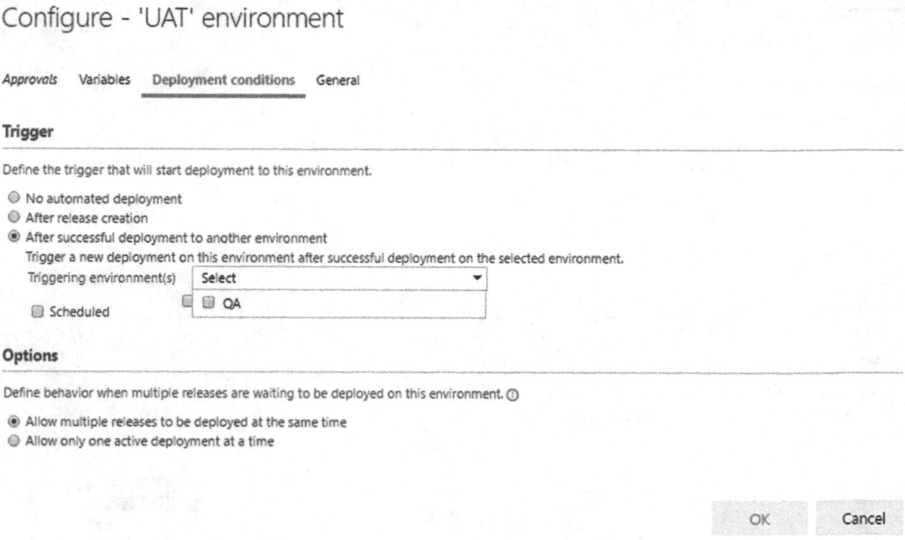

Configure - 'UAT' environment

Approvals   Variables   Deployment conditions   General

Trigger

Define the trigger that will start deployment to this environment.

○ No automated deployment
○ After release creation
◉ After successful deployment to another environment
   Trigger a new deployment on this environment after successful deployment on the selected environment.
   Triggering environment(s)   Select   ▼
   ☐ Scheduled   ☐ ☐ QA

Options

Define behavior when multiple releases are waiting to be deployed on this environment. ⓘ

◉ Allow multiple releases to be deployed at the same time
○ Allow only one active deployment at a time

OK   Cancel

Figure 1-35. *Deployment conditions tab*

In the environment configuration **General** tab you can specify an environment owner and how they should be notified. See Figure 1-36.

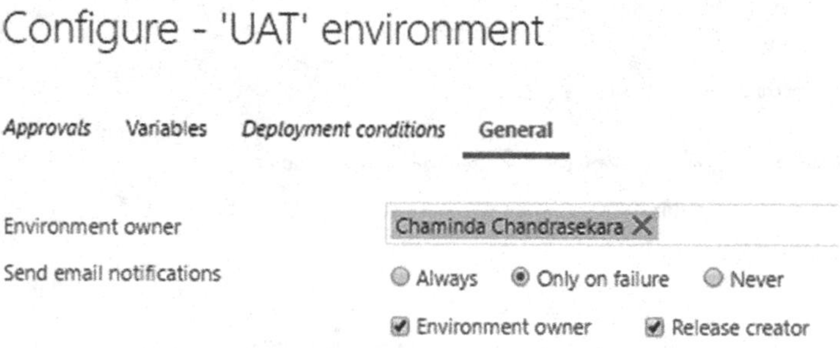

Configure - 'UAT' environment

Approvals   Variables   *Deployment conditions*   General

Environment owner   Chaminda Chandrasekara ✕

Send email notifications   ○ Always ◉ Only on failure ○ Never
                      ☑ Environment owner   ☑ Release creator

Figure 1-36. *General tab*

You will learn to use build and release definitions in Chapter 3.

Security for Build & Release Definitions

You can define who should have permission to edit build and release definitions, manage builds, and so on by using the security setting for builds and release management. The security settings allow you to prevent unauthorized modification of your build and release pipelines. The build/deployment configuration may cause disaster during execution in your production or other environments if incorrectly configured. Having proper access control in place for build and release definitions is mandatory to ensure the safety of your production and other environments.

All build definition permissions can be accessed by clicking on Security in the Builds tab (see Figure 1-37).

Figure 1-37. *Accessing project-level security for builds*

You can set up group and individual user permissions for all project-level build definitions. See Figure 1-38.

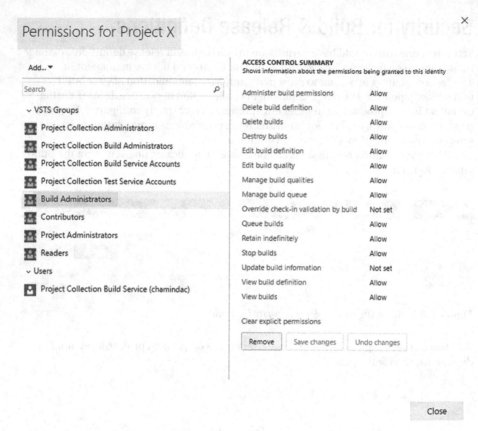

Figure 1-38. *Setting project-level security for builds*

An individual build permission can be set by clicking on Build Definitions ➤ Security. See Figure 1-39.

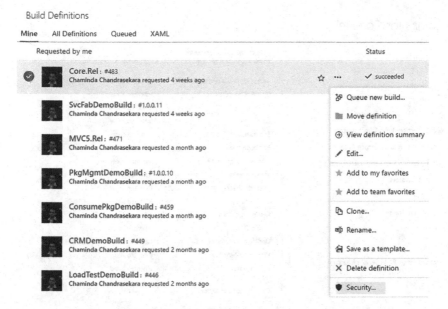

Figure 1-39. *Accessing individual build permissions from build definition menu*

Or, in edit (click Edit in build definition menu shown in Figure 1-39 open it in edit mode) mode of the build definition, you can click the Security button. See Figure 1-40.

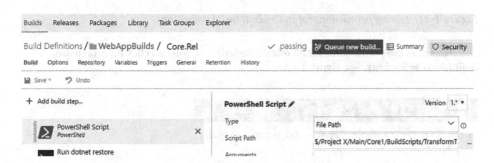

Figure 1-40. *Accessing individual build permissions from edit mode*

In the opened build definition security popup window, permissions can be set for TFS groups or individual users by adding the user or group and selecting the relevant permissions. See Figure 1-41.

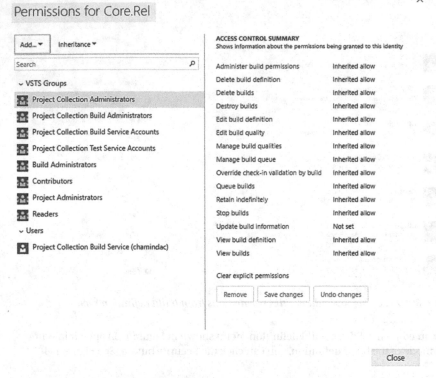

Figure 1-41. Setting permissions for individual build definitions

To access the permissions for all release definitions, you can click on All release definitions ➤ Security. See Figure 1-42.

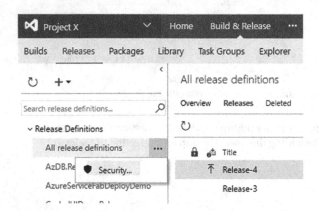

Figure 1-42. Accessing all release definitions security for a team project

For all release definitions in the team project, permissions can be set for an individual user or TFS groups by adding the user or group to the permissions popup window. See Figure 1-43.

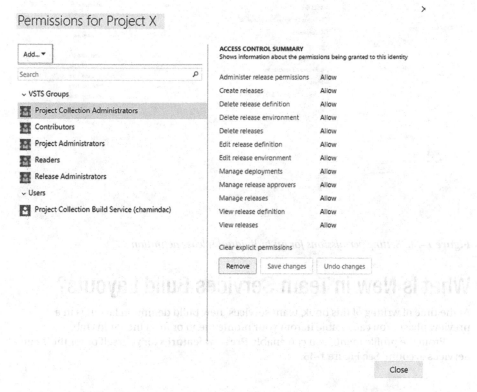

Figure 1-43. Setting permissions for all release definitions in a team project

To set permissions for an individual release definition, click on its menu ➤ Security. Then, set permissions for the release definition for individual users or TFS groups. See Figure 1-44.

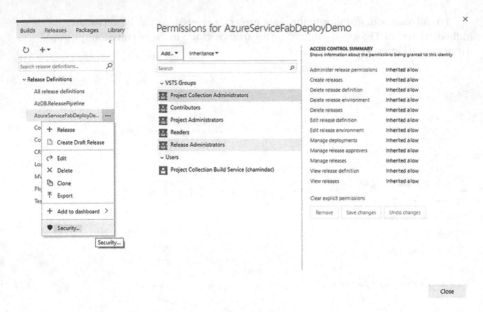

Figure 1-44. *Setting permissions for an individual release definition*

What Is New in Team Services Build Layouts?

At the time of writing of this book, team services' new build definition layout is in a preview phase. You can enable it from your profile menu or from the Builds tab.

From the profile menu, you can enable **Preview features** for yourself or for the Team Services account. See Figure 1-45.

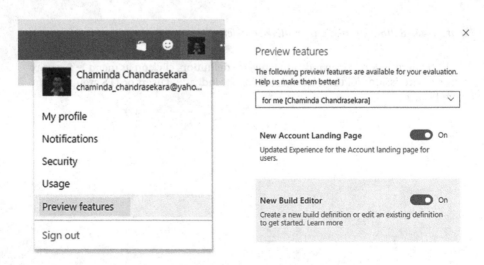

Figure 1-45. *Enabling a new build editor using the profile menu link*

Or, under the Builds tab, enable New Build Editor. Once enabled, it appears for new build definitions and for existing definitions when you edit them. See Figure 1-46.

Figure 1-46. *Enabling new build editor in Build & Release tab*

When creating a New Build Definition, it would appear as you see it in Figure 1-47. You can select a template or go with an empty template (process).

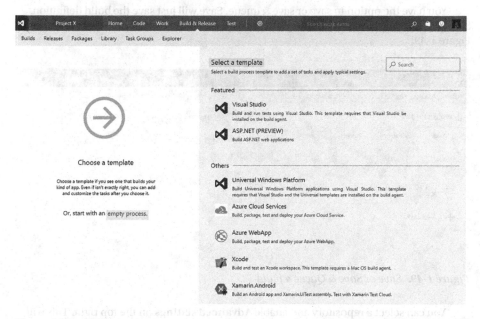

Figure 1-47. *Using an empty process or selecting a template to create a build definition*

The build definition name can be edited as shown in Figure 1-48.

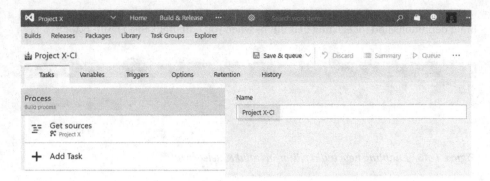

Figure 1-48. *Editing the build definition name*

You have the option to save or save & queue. Save will just save the build definition. Save & queue will save the definition and queue a new build using the definition. See Figure 1-49.

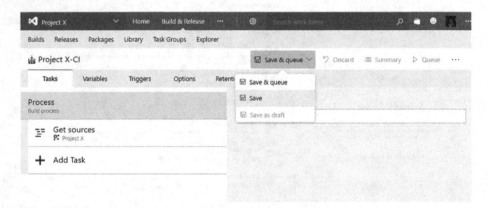

Figure 1-49. *Save or Save & Queue a build*

You can select a repository and enable **Advanced settings** on the top right. This will allow you to define additional options such as Tag source code for successful builds or Always clean local repository before getting source code. See Figure 1-50.

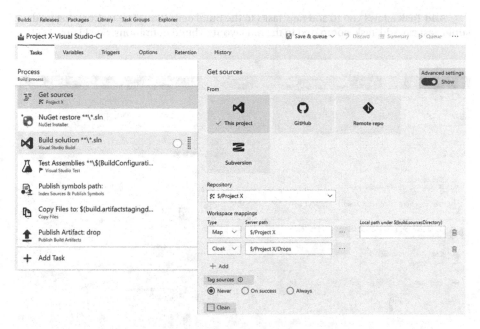

Figure 1-50. Setting advanced options in Get sources window

The **Remove** task option is available at the top right side of the page. You can select a task you want to remove (NuGet restore is selected in Figure 1-51) and click on Remove to remove it from the definition.

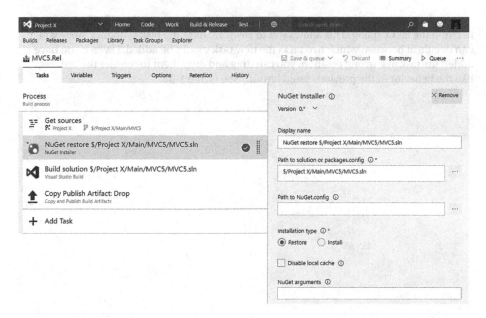

Figure 1-51. Removing task from build definition

Add Task allows you to add new tasks to the build definition. The task catalog loads super-fast via Add Task, compared to the old layout of build definitions. See Figure 1-52.

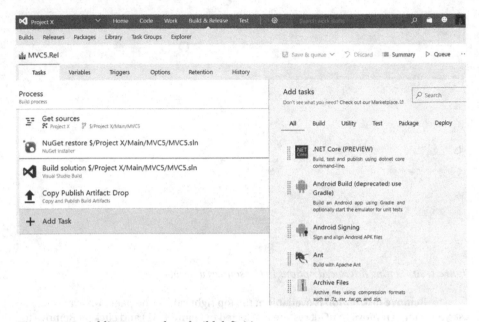

Figure 1-52. *Adding new tasks to build definition*

You can drag and drop tasks to the required position in the build definition tasks list from the task catalog. This allows you to easily manage the task sequence since you can decide in between which two tasks the new task should be added. (Even if you have added the task to a wrong position, you can drag and drop them to reorder the task list, like the behavior in the previous build layout.) See Figure 1-53.

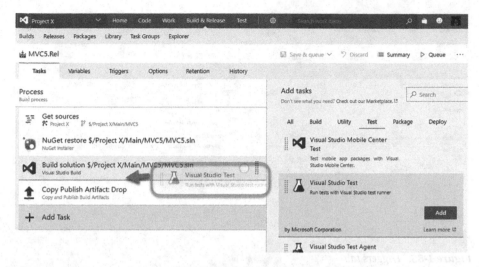

Figure 1-53. *Drag and drop tasks to build definition from the task catalog*

The **Variables** tab is not much changed other than the fresh look in the new layout. However, it shows signs of giving different categorizations to variables, as current variables are grouped as **Process variables**. See Figure 1-54.

Figure 1-54. *Variables tab*

The **Triggers** tab has a new look and feel, and you can use it to define the triggers for the build, such as continuous integration or scheduled. See Figure 1-55.

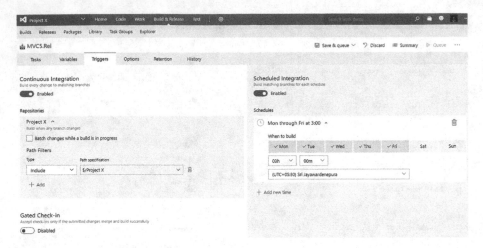

Figure 1-55. *Triggers tab*

The **Options** tab now includes **Agents** details, where you can select an agent pool to be used to locate an agent for the build. In addition to the agent pool you can define other general properties of a build definition, like build number format and so forth. The Demands section allows you to define the capabilities required in the agent in order to execute the build. These will be further discussed in Chapter 3. See Figure 1-56.

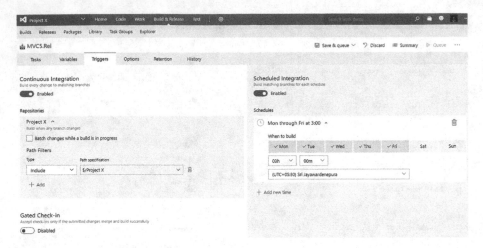

Figure 1-56. *Options tab*

The **Retention** tab that allow you to define how long a completed build should be retained, has a new look compared to previous layout. See Figure 1-57.

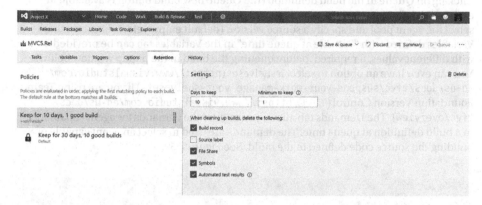

Figure 1-57. *Retention tab*

The **History** tab has the update history of the build definition. It allows the comparison of edits and the rollback of changes made to a build definition. See Figure 1-58.

Builds Releases Packages Library Task Groups Explorer			
🏛 **Core.Rel**		🖫 Save & queue ∨ ↻ Discard ☰ Summary ▷ Queue	
Tasks Variables Triggers Options Retention **History**			
✓ Changed By	Change Type	Changed Date	Comment
Chaminda Chandrasekara	Update	12/15/2016 12:44:08 PM	
✓ [chamindac]\Project Collection Service Accounts	Update	12/2/2016 4:52:14 PM	
•••			
Chaminda Chandrasekara	🖳 Compare Difference	11/29/2016 1:03:50 PM	
Chaminda Chandrasekara	↩ Revert Build	11/27/2016 5:21:44 PM	
Chaminda Chandrasekara	Update	11/27/2016 5:15:42 PM	
Chaminda Chandrasekara	Update	11/27/2016 5:08:11 PM	
Chaminda Chandrasekara	Update	11/27/2016 5:01:00 PM	
Chaminda Chandrasekara	Update	11/27/2016 4:47:06 PM	
Chaminda Chandrasekara	Add	11/27/2016 4:43:58 PM	

Figure 1-58. *History tab*

All the tabs in the build definition have the option of discarding unsaved changes. All tabs also have a link to view a summary page for the build and a **Queue** link to queue a new build.

Queuing a Build

Clicking on **Queue** in the build definition (the Queue new build button is available in each build definition menu item as well) will pop up a "Queue build" window. You can select the agent pool and specify a source version (default empty selects latest version). Variables defined with "Settable at queue time" in the Variables tab can be provided with different values, if required, before queuing the build in the popup window below. You can even have an option to select a shelveset (https://www.visualstudio.com/en-us/docs/tfvc/suspend-your-work-manage-your-shelvesets) if you are using Team Foundation Version Control (TFVC: https://www.visualstudio.com/en-us/docs/tfvc/overview). The Demands tab allows you to alter the demands for agent capabilities in a build definition at queue time. The demands are used to select an agent capable of building the source code defined in the build. See Figure 1-59.

Figure 1-59. *Queuing a build*

Build/Release REST API

Team Services and TFS support REST API for build and release. You can obtain build/release definition data and build/release data with these APIs. You can also trigger builds/releases and many other actions with these APIs. Refer to the following articles to learn more after completing the lessons in this book. (You will be able to understand more about these APIs when you know how to work with build and release management.)

https://www.visualstudio.com/en-us/docs/integrate/api/build/builds
https://www.visualstudio.com/en-us/docs/integrate/api/rm/overview

Recommendations

- Build once and then use the same binaries and/or packages across the deployment pipeline until it reaches production or is stopped due to not getting acceptance to move to the next stage.

- TFS/VSTS Build is solely to perform build tasks. Do not use deployment tasks in build definitions.

- Limit the artifact download to required sub-items for improved performance (extension can be used: `https://marketplace.visualstudio.com/items?itemName=chamindac.chamindac-vsts-release-task-download-artifacts`). Chapter 2 discusses how to install and manage extensions.

- Have a separate continuous integration build without generating artifacts in order to maintain a stable code base, and have a dedicated release build with artifacts for deployment purposes.

- Apply proper build versioning and apply build version number to deployed packages.

- Make sure to restore any pre-production (QA, UAT/Staging) environment to the same version as production before deploying to ensure stable deployment and stable application functionality on production.

These recommendations will be explained in practical terms in the lessons in the next chapters.

Summary

In this chapter, we have looked at the DevOps concepts briefly and identified continuous integration, continuous delivery, and deployment. These help an organization to establish DevOps. To become a DevOps-enabled organization, a company must improve its way of work as well by enacting required cultural and process improvements. The Team Foundation Server's tools and concepts, such as build pools, agents, build & release definitions, and overview, are given to prepare you for taking the lessons, which start from Chapter 2.

The next chapter focuses on getting the required pools, queues, and agents set up in different platforms to enable you to follow the rest of the chapters/lessons on builds and deployments.

CHAPTER 2

Configuring TFS2017/VSTS Build/Release Agents & Marketplace Extensions

By following the guidelines discussed in this chapter, you will acquire knowledge on how to set up new agent pools for TFS and VSTS, configure TFS agents for different scenarios, and use extensions from Visual Studio Marketplace to enhance features of TFS/VSTS.

Lesson 2.01 – Set Up Agent Pools and Queues

The aim of this lesson is to provide a step-by-step guide to creating new agent pools and queues in TFS/VSTS. Also, this lesson contains instructions for setting required permissions for agent pools and queues.

Prerequisites: You should have a VS Team Services account, created by following the instructions found at https://www.visualstudio.com/en-us/docs/setup-admin/team-services/sign-up-for-visual-studio-team-service, or have a TFS2017 server. Ensure you have been granted **Manage** permission for all pools. For more information on agent pool permissions, see Chapter 1.

Create a new team project called "Project X" by following the instructions at https://www.visualstudio.com/en-us/docs/setup-admin/create-team-project. We will use this project in the lessons in this chapter.

2.01.1 Set Up Agent Pool

The agent pool specifies the security context and runtime environment for agents. An agent pool can be defined to group agents to be used for the same purpose (for example, all agents doing builds can be assigned to an agent pool called "BuildAgentPool") or to group agents based on projects that they are used for.

1. In Team Foundation Home, click on **Settings**, then select **Agentpools** and then **New pool**. This creates the new pool. See Figure 2-1.

© Chaminda Chandrasekara 2017
C. Chandrasekara, *Beginning Build and Release Management with TFS 2017 and VSTS*,
DOI 10.1007/978-1-4842-2811-1_2

Figure 2-1. *New agent pool*

2. Provide a name ("ProjectX Release Pool") for the agent pool in the popup window. You can uncheck "Auto-Provision Queues in all Projects" to prevent provisioning a queue for each existing project. If you choose not to select this option, you can still create a queue for an existing pool in any team project at a later time. See Figure 2-2.

Figure 2-2. *Creating an agent pool*

3. If you see the error message shown in Figure 2-3, that means you do not have the Administrator role (this role provides Manage permissions) for All Pools.

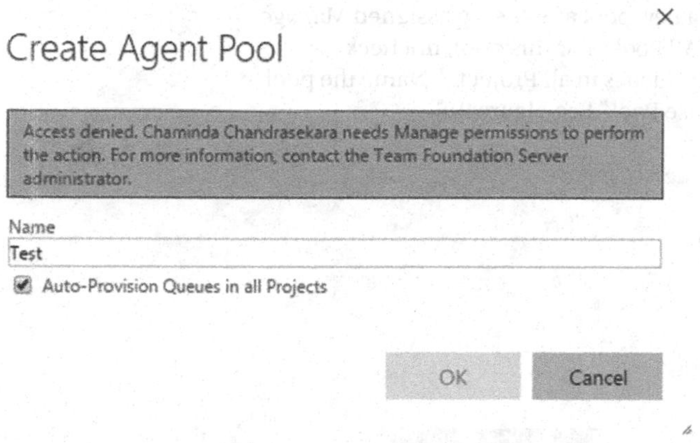

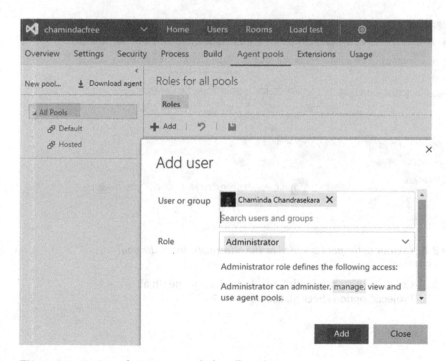

Figure 2-3. *Agent pool Manage permission error*

Ask your TFS administrator/VSTS Account Owner to promote you to an Administrator to All Pools to continue with the lesson. (Or you could use your own VSTS account to continue with the lesson.) See Figure 2-4.

Figure 2-4. *Assign administrator role for all pools*

4. You can create a new pool after being assigned Manage permission for All Pools. For this pool, uncheck "Auto-Provision Queues in all Projects." Name the pool "Project X Release Pool." See Figure 2-5.

Figure 2-5. *Creating a pool without provisioning queues*

You will be assigned to the Administrator role of the pool automatically once it is created. See Figure 2-6.

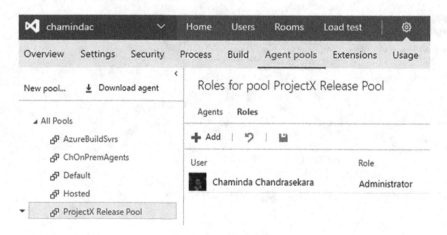

Figure 2-6. *Creator of the pool is added as the administrator to the pool*

5. Create another pool with "Auto-Provision Queues in all Projects" option checked. See Figure 2-7.

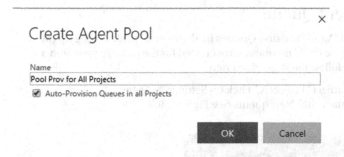

Figure 2-7. Creating a pool with provisioning queues

6. You will be able to see the queue in each project for the pool created with "Auto-Provision Queues in all Projects" checked, but not for the pool created without "Auto-Provision Queues in all Projects" checked. See Figure 2-8.

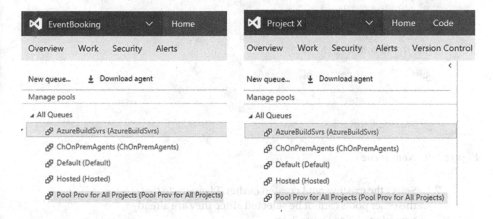

Figure 2-8. All team projects provisioned with a queue

In the preceding steps, we created two agent pools. One pool is provisioned with a queue in each team project. The other pool is not provisioned with a queue for any team projects.

2.01.2 Set Up Agent Queue

Since we have unchecked "Auto-Provision Queues in all Projects" while setting up the agent pool "ProjectX Release Pool," no queues are created for the pool. To provision a queue for a team project, follow the steps given here.

1. In the team project "Project X," click on Settings ➤ Agent Queues and then click New queue. See Figure 2-9.

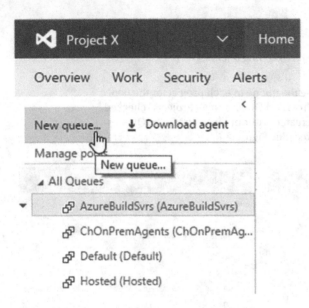

Figure 2-9. *New queue*

2. Select the existing pool created earlier. Please note that the other pools cannot be selected since they are already provisioned. See Figure 2-10.

Figure 2-10. *Creating a queue with an existing pool*

3. You will be assigned with the Administrator role for the created queue. The project administrators and build administrators also have the administrator role for the queue. See Figure 2-11.

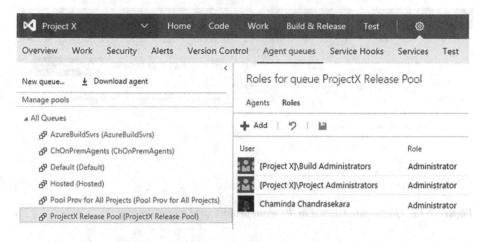

Figure 2-11. *Creator assigned to administrator role in queue*

4. You can create a new queue directly from the team project with a new pool. If you do this, "Auto-Provision Queues in all Projects" is not applied to that pool, and other team projects will not be provisioned with the queue. To understand that scenario, follow the steps given next.

In a team project, go to Settings ➤ Select Agent Queues, then click New queue. See Figure 2-12.

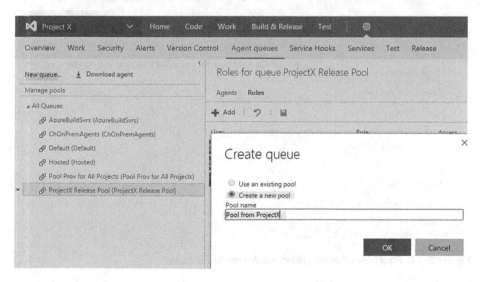

Figure 2-12. *Creating a new pool while creating a queue*

49

5. This will create a pool and then provision the queue in the team project. See Figure 2-13.

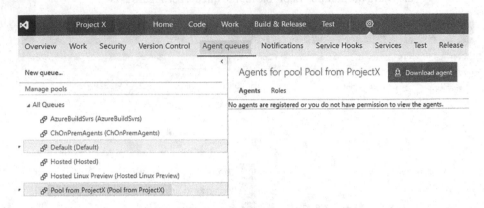

Figure 2-13. *Queue provisioned in the team project, and a pool created*

6. Go to Account Setting ➤ Agent Pools. Click on the pool that was created while creating the queue in the preceding steps. You will notice that the pool does not have "Auto-Provision Queues" checked. See Figure 2-14.

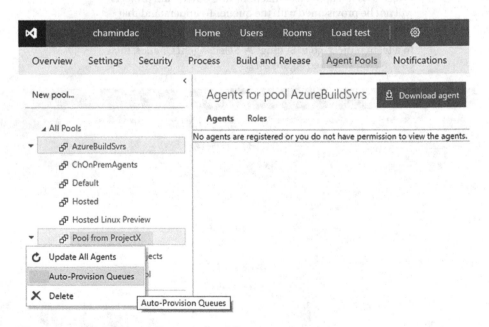

Figure 2-14. *Pool created from project while creating a queue*

We have looked at steps to provision an agent queue using an existing pool as well as at creating a new agent pool while provisioning the queue.

2.01.3 Auto-Provision Queues for Existing Pools

Even if you select "Auto-Provision Queues" from the popup menu of the pool, it will not affect any existing team projects. You will have to provision the queue for each team project manually, if required. Follow these steps to understand how it works:

1. Click on the popup menu for "Pool from ProjectX" in the Agent Pools tab of the account settings. Then, select "Auto-Provision Queues." See Figure 2-15.

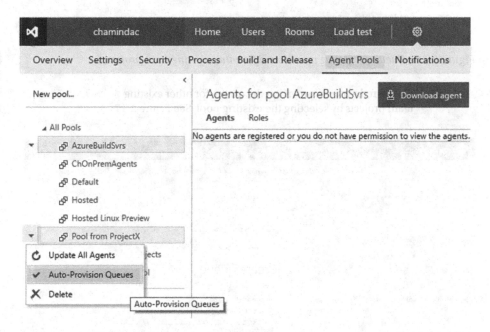

Figure 2-15. *Selecting auto-provision in an existing pool*

2. Open another team project and navigate to Settings, **Agent Queue** tab. You can see that the preceding step did not provision the queue for the pool in other team projects. In Figure 2-16, you can see that Project X (the team project you used to create the new queue while creating a new pool) is provisioned with a queue, while other team projects are not provisioned with the queue (one other team project, EventBooking, is shown in the figure).

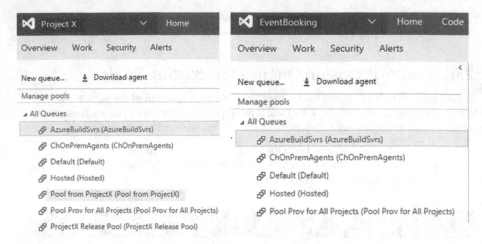

Figure 2-16. *Queue not getting provisioned for other existing team projects*

3. If required, you can provision the queue for other existing team projects by selecting the existing pool. See Figure 2-17.

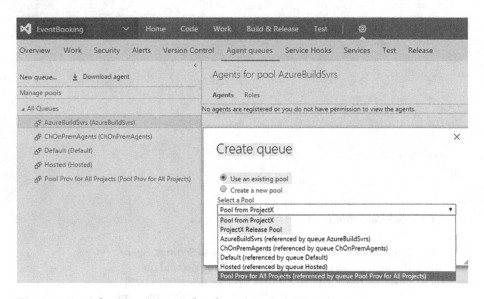

Figure 2-17. *Selecting existing pool and provisioning a queue*

4. If you create a new team project, all pools marked with "Auto-Provision Queues" will be provisioned for that new team project. Right now, all pools except ProjectX Release Pool are checked with "Auto-Provision Queues." See Figure 2-18.

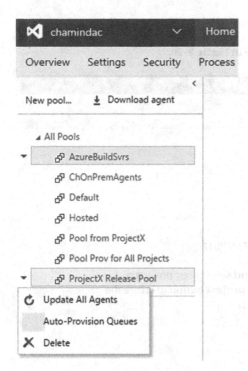

Figure 2-18. *ProjectX Release Pool not set for auto-provision*

5. Create a new team project called "ProjectY" to verify what we just discussed. Do so by going through the following steps. (You need to have Team Project Collection administrator permission to create a new team project.) Go to the Project Collection administration page and click on New Team Project. See Figure 2-19.

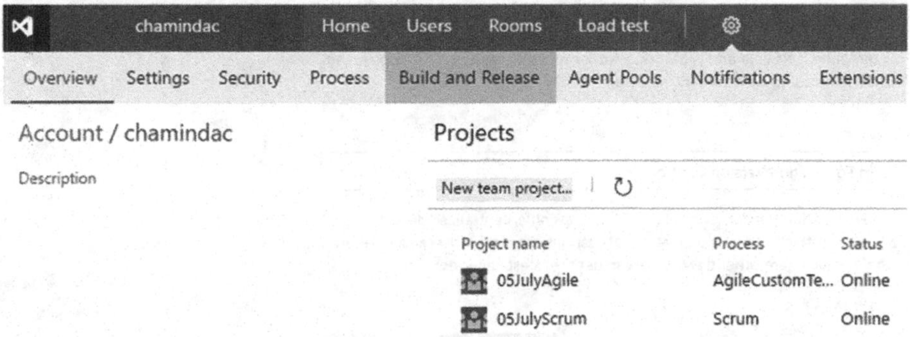

Figure 2-19. *Creating new team project VSTS*

You can see in the figure a VSTS account projects overview page. On-premises TFS collection administration pages will look something like what you see in Figure 2-20.

Demo
Home
Rooms
Overview
Users
Security
Build and Release
Agent pools
Extensions
Not all collection level administration is exposed in the web experience. For all administration operations at the collection level please use the Administration Console on your Team Foundation Server.
Collection / Demo
Description
New work item form
Enabled
Configure the opt-in model
Disable the new work item form
Projects
New team project...
Project name
Status
Description
DemoDummy
Online
ProjectX
Online

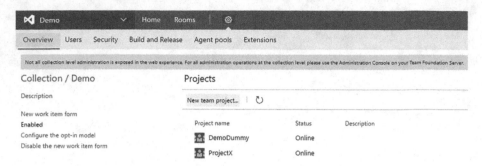

Figure 2-20. *Creating a new team project in TFS 2017*

6. Provide the team project name and select your preferred version control. Click the **Create project** button to create the new team project. See Figure 2-21.

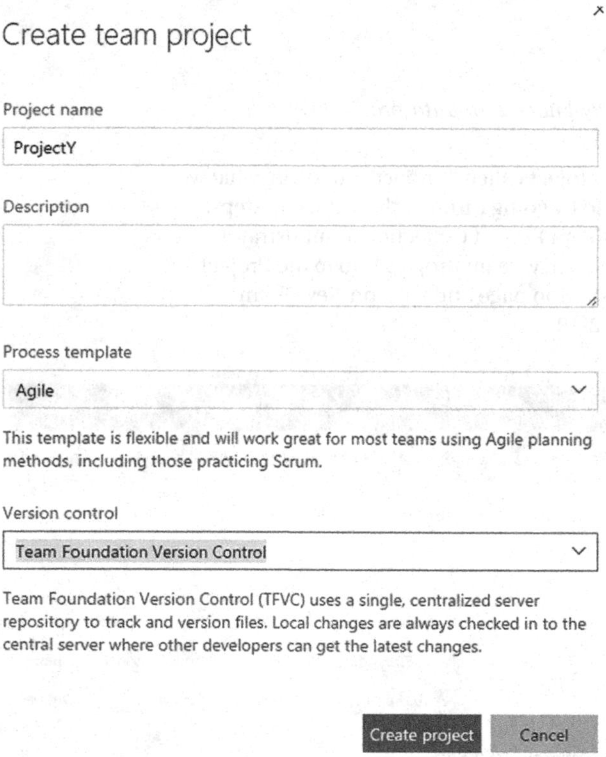

Create team project
Project name
ProjectY
Description
Process template
Agile
This template is flexible and will work great for most teams using Agile planning methods, including those practicing Scrum.
Version control
Team Foundation Version Control
Team Foundation Version Control (TFVC) uses a single, centralized server repository to track and version files. Local changes are always checked in to the central server where other developers can get the latest changes.
Create project
Cancel

Figure 2-21. *New team project*

7. In ProjectY, created in the previous step, queues are provisioned for all pools except for the Project X Release Pool, which does not have "Auto-Provision Queues" selected. See Figure 2-22.

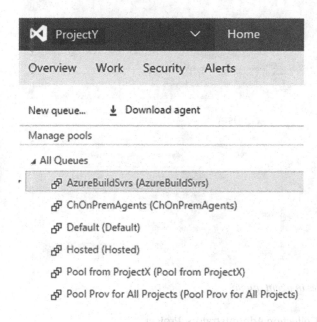

Figure 2-22. *Queues provisioned for pools specified with auto-provision*

In this lesson, you have discovered the ways to provision queues for existing team projects, as well as how the "Auto-Provision Queues" option in an agent pool behaves, both when selected and when unselected.

2.01.4 Assign Permissions for Agent Pools and Queues

There are a few different roles in agent pools and queues, which were explained in Chapter 1. You can assign individuals or a group of users to each of these roles.

1. Select the pool or queue and click **Roles**, then add the relevant user or group to the preferred role. See Figure 2-23.

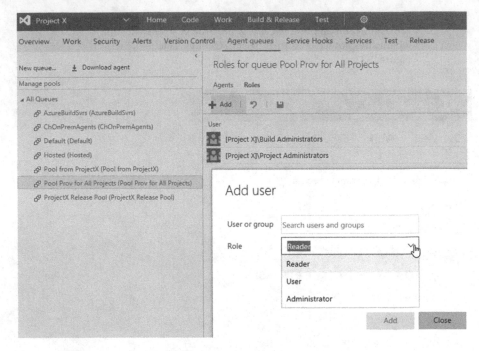

Figure 2-23. *Adding user to roles in agent queue*

2. By default, Project Collection Administrators, Project Administrators, and Build Administrators are granted the Administrator role for a queue in TFS2017. See Figure 2-24.

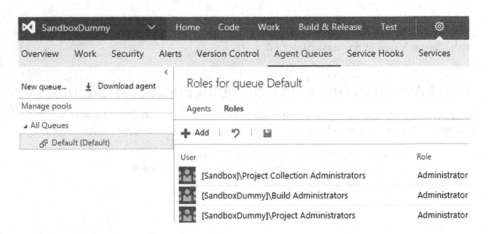

Figure 2-24. *Agent queue default permissions*

Permissions in agent pools and queues can be specified as
describe in above steps. To learn more details on agent pool
and queue roles refer to Chapter 1.

2.01.5 Create Agent Pool for Build Farm

Let's create a new agent pool called "BuildFarm" to be used in the lessons to follow in this
chapter.

1. Create an agent pool in TFS called "BuildFarm" by selecting
    Agent pools from the main page and then clicking **New pool**
    (let's use it as build server pool), with the option checked to
    auto-provision agent for all projects. See Figure 2-25.

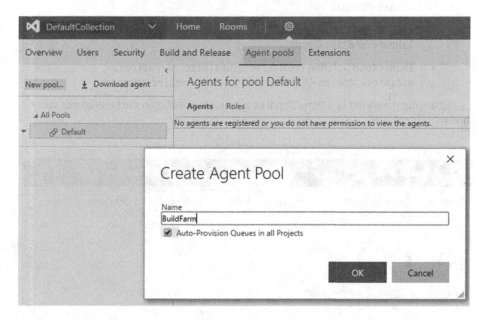

Figure 2-25. *Creating a pool as build farm*

When you create a pool in one project collection, it is available to other project
collections in the TFS, and all projects are provisioned with a queue.

In this lesson, you created agent pools and queues in a few different ways. You
allowed some agent pools to be accessible to all team projects and some agent pools to
only be accessible to a given project. Limiting access to a pool for a given team project
will be required when setting up deployment agents to be used with release management
for a given project. Such agents could even reside in the client's production environment
and be assigned specific permissions for users who are using roles available for agent
pools and queues.

Link VS Team Services Account to Azure Subscription for Billing Purposes

You can link the VS Team Services Account to an Azure subscription in order to purchase build/release pipelines in addition to the provided free pipeline. It is not mandatory to link VSTS to an Azure subscription to complete the lessons to follow, since they can be performed with the available free pipeline. Chapter 1 contains more information on agents, pipelines and the difference of them in on-premises TFS and VSTS.

To link a Team Services account to an Azure subscription, you need a VS Team Services account for which you are the account owner. You should have an Azure subscription with at least co-administrator permissions, and the subscription should not be one of the following:

- Azure Free Trial (`https://azure.microsoft.com/en-us/offers/ms-azr-0044p/`)

- Free Azure AD Subscription (`https://technet.microsoft.com/library/dn832618.aspx`)

- From Cloud Solution Provider Program (`https://partner.microsoft.com/en-US/Solutions/cloud-reseller-overview`)

Changing the owner of a Team Services account is possible in the Settings tab, as shown in Figure 2-26.

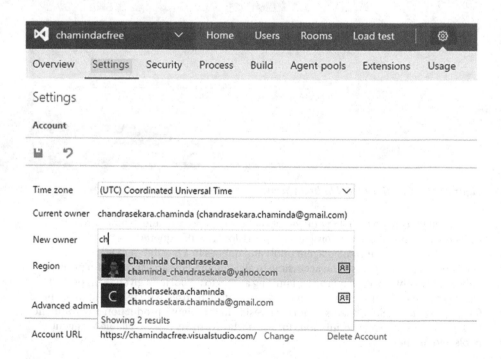

Figure 2-26. *Changing VSTS account owner*

You need to remove the spending limit of the Azure subscription indefinitely and link your credit card, even for Azure subscriptions that come with your VS subscription. VS subscription–granted free credits cannot be used as payment for Team Services features or users.

You can link your VS Team Services account in the Azure portal. Detailed instructions can be found here: https://www.visualstudio.com/en-us/docs/setup-admin/team-services/set-up-billing-for-your-account-vs.

Once the billing for VSTS is set up as per the instructions, you can purchase more hosted/private pipelines via Azure portal, which will take you to relevant VS Marketplace purchase pipeline page. See Figure 2-27.

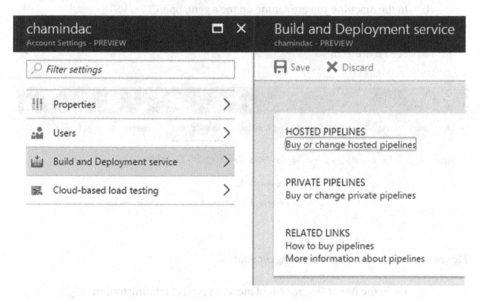

Figure 2-27. *Purchasing pipelines via Azure portal for VSTS*

To calculate the pricing for agents and other VS Team Services users, use the pricing calculator available here: https://azure.microsoft.com/en-us/pricing/calculator/?service=visual-studio-team-services.

Lesson 2.02 – Set Up Build/Release Agent

In this lesson, you will learn how to set up a build/release agent in the same domain as TFS. This will give you the knowledge required to set up your own build farm in your domain, set up agents for your QA environment deployments, and so on.

Prerequisites: You should have Manage permission for the pool that you are setting up the agent for, or you should have followed Lesson 2.01.5 and created a pool with name BuildFarm. You need to have PowerShell 3.0 or later available in the agent machine in which you are going to set up a build/release agent for TFS.

There are no known prerequisites for agents set up with Windows 10. Windows 7, 8.1, and Server 2012 R2 require the C Runtime update (`https://support.microsoft.com/en-us/kb/2999226`).

2.02.1 Set Up Build/Release Agent for On-Premises TFS-Interactive Mode

Running a build agent in interactive mode is required if you want to run UI tests with your builds (test automation is discussed in Chapter 9).

1. In the machine you are setting up the a gent, open TFS/VSTS web portal in a browser. Go to **Agent pools** tab of the project collection administration page and click **Download agent**. See Figure 2-28.

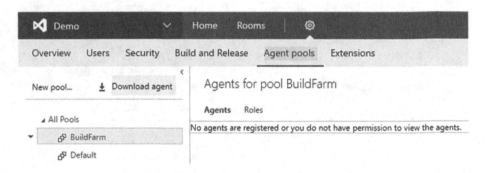

Figure 2-28. *Download agent from Agent pools tab*

Or, in the Agent Queues tab of the team project administration page, click Download agent. See Figure 2-29.

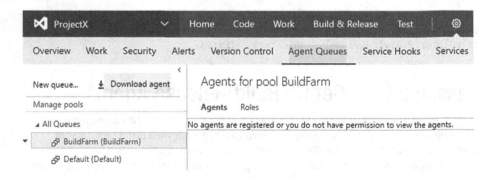

Figure 2-29. *Download agent from Agent Queues tab*

2. Download the Windows agent by clicking the **Download** option on the popup page. See Figure 2-30.

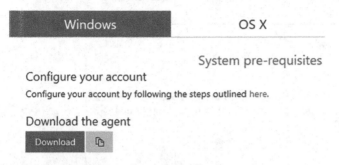

Figure 2-30. *Downloading Windows agent*

3. Extract the downloaded .zip file to a directory on your hard drive. See Figure 2-31.

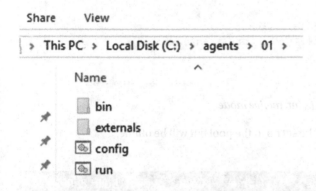

Figure 2-31. *Extracted agent files*

4. Using the command prompt, run config.cmd and provide a team foundation server URL, such as `http://youttfsserver:8080/tfs`.

5. For authentication, use default type **Integrated**. This will use your current, logged-in user to make the connection to TFS when configuring the agent. The user needs to have Manage permission to the agent pool. More information on authentication types is provided at the end of this lesson.

6. Provide the agent pool name and a name for the agent. Use default values for the working folder. Select **N** by pressing Enter to say **No** for the "run as service" question, since we want to run the agent in interactive mode. See Figure 2-32.

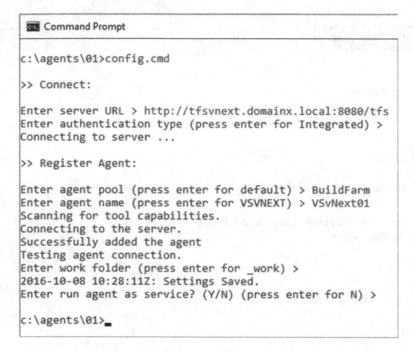

```
c:\agents\01>config.cmd

>> Connect:

Enter server URL > http://tfsvnext.domainx.local:8080/tfs
Enter authentication type (press enter for Integrated) >
Connecting to server ...

>> Register Agent:

Enter agent pool (press enter for default) > BuildFarm
Enter agent name (press enter for VSVNEXT) > VSvNext01
Scanning for tool capabilities.
Connecting to the server.
Successfully added the agent
Testing agent connection.
Enter work folder (press enter for _work) >
2016-10-08 10:28:11Z: Settings Saved.
Enter run agent as service? (Y/N) (press enter for N) >

c:\agents\01>_
```

Figure 2-32. *Configuring agent in interactive mode*

7. With this, agent will be set up in the pool but will be offline. See Figure 2-33.

Figure 2-33. *Agent configured but offline*

8. To bring the agent online, execute run.cmd. See Figure 2-34.

```
Select Command Prompt - run.cmd
c:\agents\01>run.cmd
Scanning for tool capabilities.
Connecting to the server.
2016-10-08 11:15:25Z: Listening for Jobs
```

Figure 2-34. Bringing agent online

This will start to run the agent in interactive mode, with the current logged-on user being used for the agent machine. The agent will be shown as online if you view it in the Agent Queues tab or Agent Pools tab. See Figure 3-35.

Figure 2-35. Agent is online

Running an agent in interactive mode is not as stable as running an agent as a Windows service. If the agent is stopped because of an issue, it must be started again manually. Getting an interactive mode agent to start automatically is described at http://donovanbrown.com/post/auto-start-build-agent-in-interactive-mode.

We can use an online agent to perform build or deployment tasks. If you want to remove an agent because it is no longer in use, you can do so by taking it offline before removing. The removal of an agent from a pool is described in the next lesson.

2.02.2 Remove Windows Build/Release Agent

You can remove an agent from a pool if it is no longer in use. The following steps describe how to remove an agent.

1. Open command prompt and change directory to the agent folder.

2. Run config.cmd with the **remove** argument. See Figure 2-36.

Agents for pool BuildFarm

Agents   Roles

No agents are registered or you do not have permission to view the agents.

```
Command Prompt
Microsoft Windows [Version 10.0.14393]
(c) 2016 Microsoft Corporation. All rights reserved.

C:\Users\tfsadmin>cd c:\agents\01

c:\agents\01>config.cmd remove
Removing service
Removing agent from the server
Enter authentication type (press enter for Integrated) >
Succeeded: Removing agent from the server
Removing .credentials
Succeeded: Removing .credentials
Removing .agent
Succeeded: Removing .agent

c:\agents\01>_
```

Figure 2-36. Removing an agent

When an agent is removed, it will be fully unconfigured and will no longer be visible in the agent pool.

2.02.3 Set Up Build/Release Agent for On-Premises TFS and Run as Windows Service

Let's configure an agent to run as a Windows service. This allows the agent to be stable and recover automatically in a failure, like other Windows services.

1. Open command prompt with Administrator privileges. Running the command prompt as an administrator is required in order to configure the agent as a service.

2. Run config.cmd and provide the TFS URL.

3. This time, use **Negotiate** as the authentication type. This will prompt for a username and password in order to connect to the server to configure the agent. Provide the user credentials that have Manage permission for the agent pool.

4. Provide the agent pool name and agent name.

5. Provide the work folder path or use default _work folder.

6. Choose to run agent as a service.

Provide your domain or local user credentials to run the agent. See Figure 2-37.

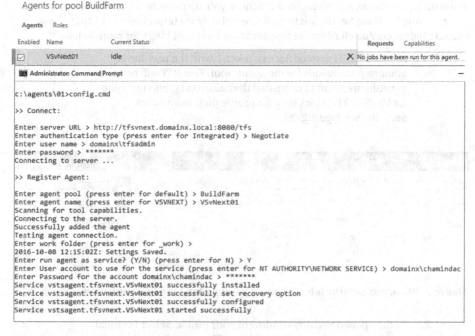

Figure 2-37. Configure agent as a service

7. After the Agent is configured and online, as shown in Figure 2-37, you can see a windows service is running in the services window of the agent machine. See Figure 2-38.

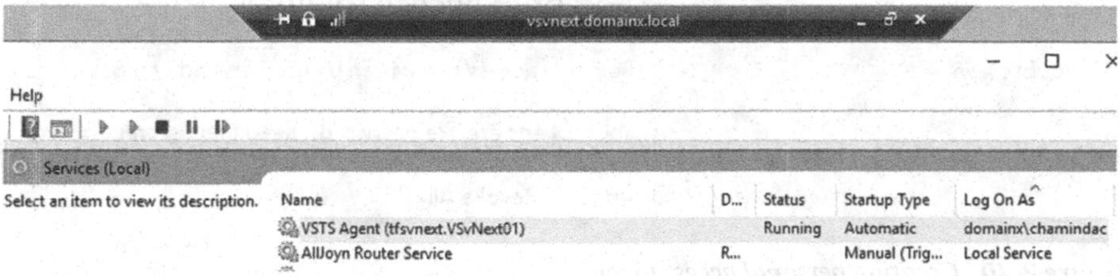

Figure 2-38. Agent running as a Windows service

The preceding steps guided you in setting up an agent as a service. An agent that is set up as a Windows service is sufficient to perform most of the code-building and deployment tasks in the Windows platform.

2.02.4 Set Up Build/Release Agent in an Untrusted Domain for VS Team Services or On-Premises TFS

Prerequisites: If you are using on-premises TFS, it should be available securely and publicly in order to set up agents in untrusted domains. In other words, your TFS server should have a public URL set up with SSL and should be accessible publicly via https to the untrusted domain or workgroup machine you are using to set up the agent. If you are using VS Team Services, it is available publicly via https. Refer to https://www.visualstudio.com/da-dk/docs/setup-admin/websitesettings for more details.

1. Create a PAT (Personal Access Token), with the user having Manage permissions for the agent pool. This PAT will be used to configure agent in untrusted domain/workgroup machine for VSTS or TFS. Click on your profile picture and click Security. See Figure 2-39.

Figure 2-39. *Access Security tab with a user having Manage pool permissions*

2. In the opened Security window of your profile, select Personal access tokens tab and click Add. See Figure 2-40.

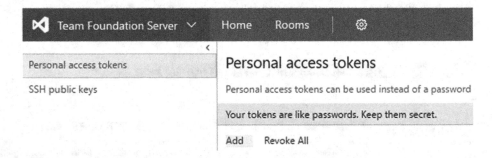

Figure 2-40. *Creating personal access token*

3. Then, select **Agent Pools (read, manage)** scope and, finally, hit the **Create Token** button on the bottom left corner of the screen. See Figure 2-41.

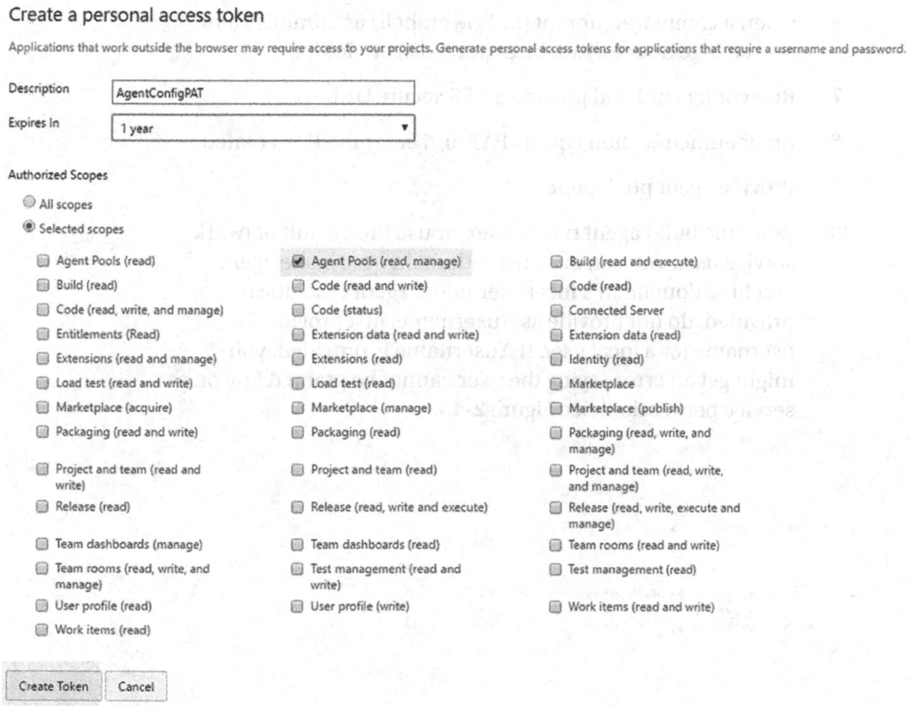

Create a personal access token

Applications that work outside the browser may require access to your projects. Generate personal access tokens for applications that require a username and password.

Description | AgentConfigPAT

Expires In | 1 year ▼

Authorized Scopes

○ All scopes
◉ Selected scopes

☐ Agent Pools (read)	☑ Agent Pools (read, manage)	☐ Build (read and execute)
☐ Build (read)	☐ Code (read and write)	☐ Code (read)
☐ Code (read, write, and manage)	☐ Code (status)	☐ Connected Server
☐ Entitlements (Read)	☐ Extension data (read and write)	☐ Extension data (read)
☐ Extensions (read and manage)	☐ Extensions (read)	☐ Identity (read)
☐ Load test (read and write)	☐ Load test (read)	☐ Marketplace
☐ Marketplace (acquire)	☐ Marketplace (manage)	☐ Marketplace (publish)
☐ Packaging (read and write)	☐ Packaging (read)	☐ Packaging (read, write, and manage)
☐ Project and team (read and write)	☐ Project and team (read)	☐ Project and team (read, write, and manage)
☐ Release (read)	☐ Release (read, write and execute)	☐ Release (read, write, execute and manage)
☐ Team dashboards (manage)	☐ Team dashboards (read)	☐ Team rooms (read and write)
☐ Team rooms (read, write, and manage)	☐ Test management (read and write)	☐ Test management (read)
☐ User profile (read)	☐ User profile (write)	☐ Work items (read and write)
☐ Work items (read)		

[Create Token] Cancel

Figure 2-41. Define scope and create token

4. Once the PAT is created, it will be displayed only once for you to copy. Copy it and keep it in a secure location. See Figure 2-42.

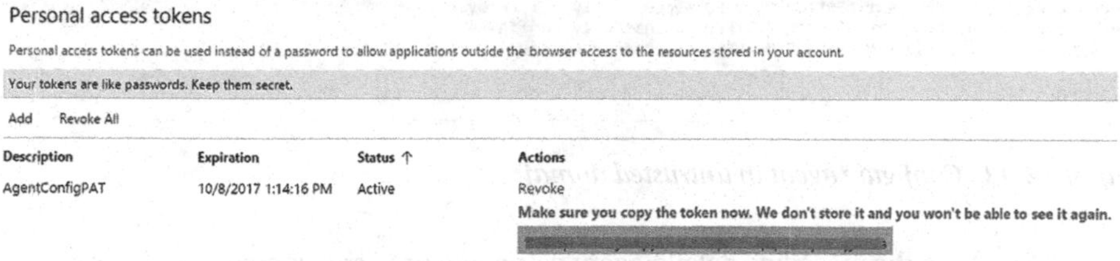

Personal access tokens

Personal access tokens can be used instead of a password to allow applications outside the browser access to the resources stored in your account.

Your tokens are like passwords. Keep them secret.

Add   Revoke All

Description	Expiration	Status ↑	Actions
AgentConfigPAT	10/8/2017 1:14:16 PM	Active	Revoke

Make sure you copy the token now. We don't store it and you won't be able to see it again.

Figure 2-42. Generated PAT only available once

5. Download the VS Team Services or on-premises TFS Windows build/release agent.zip file from the Agent Pools tab or Agent Queues tab. Extract the zip file content to a directory on the agent machine. (Refer to 2.02.1, steps 1, 2, and 3.)

6. Open a command prompt (or PowerShell) as administrator and change directory to the extracted agent folder.

7. Run config.cmd and provide a TFS secure URL.

8. Enter authentication type as PAT and enter the PAT created.

9. Provide agent pool name.

10. Enter the build agent run as user, or use the default network service user. You can even use a domain user in the agent machine domain. If a local user in the agent machine is provided, do not provide as .\username; just provide the username for a local user. If .\username is provided, you might get an error saying the user cannot be granted Log on as service permission. See Figure 2-43.

Figure 2-43. *Configure agent in untrusted domain*

11. With the preceding details, agent gets configured and comes online. See Figure 2-44.

Figure 2-44. *Untrusted domain agent running online*

You can follow the preceding steps to set up an agent in a different domain than your TFS server domain or in a workgroup. The same steps can be used to create an on-premises agent for VS Team Services. If your TFS is available via Internet (making TFS on-premises available via Internet is described at https://www.visualstudio.com/en-us/docs/setup-admin/tfs/admin/setup-secure-sockets-layer), you can set up a deployment agent in any machine that has an Internet connection, which allows you to access your TFS URL via internet.

2.02.5 Set Up Build/Release Agent in Ubuntu Linux

Prerequisites: You have an Ubuntu16.04LTS available to you, and you should have admin access on the machine. Based on the instructions from the previous lesson, you have created a PAT in your TFS or VS Team Services. You have the option of using credentials, instead of PAT, to configure an agent by using **Negotiate**, if you are using on-premises TFS.

   1. Download the Linux agent for Ubuntu 16.04 from agent download popup. See Figure 2-45.

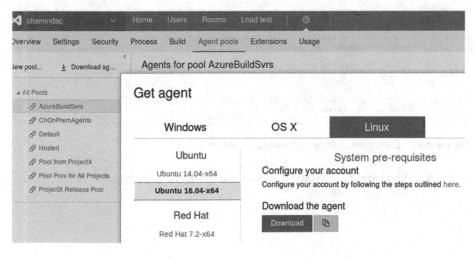

Figure 2-45. *Download agent for Ubuntu Linux*

69

2. Run Ubuntu terminal and execute the following commands to create a directory and extract the downloaded file to it. See Figure 2-46.

```
mkdirmyagent&& cd myagent
tar zxvf ~/Downloads/downloadedAgentFileName.tar.gz
```

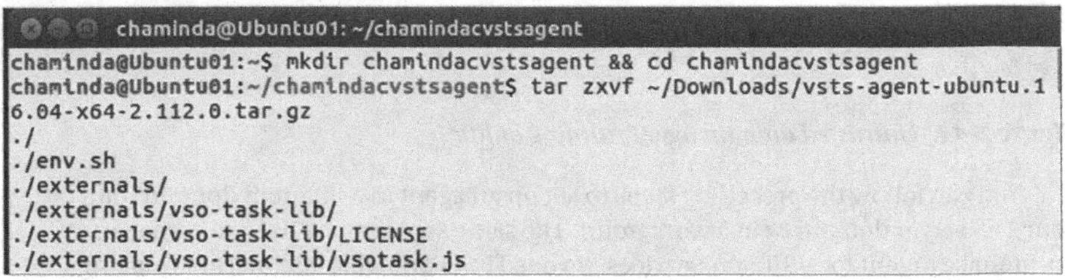

```
chaminda@Ubuntu01: ~/chamindacvstsagent
chaminda@Ubuntu01:~$ mkdir chamindacvstsagent && cd chamindacvstsagent
chaminda@Ubuntu01:~/chamindacvstsagent$ tar zxvf ~/Downloads/vsts-agent-ubuntu.1
6.04-x64-2.112.0.tar.gz
./
./env.sh
./externals/
./externals/vso-task-lib/
./externals/vso-task-lib/LICENSE
./externals/vso-task-lib/vsotask.js
```

Figure 2-46. *Extracting downloaded agent*

Execute ./config.sh to configure the agent. Provide the Team Services or TFS URL and provide PAT. (Negotiate credentials for on-premises TFS can be used instead of PAT. Read more details on credentials at the end of this lesson.) See Figure 2-47.

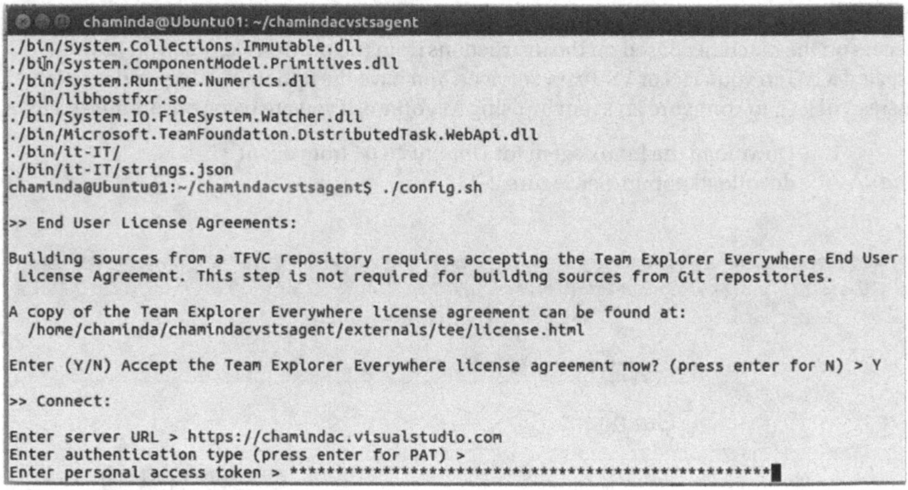

```
chaminda@Ubuntu01: ~/chamindacvstsagent
./bin/System.Collections.Immutable.dll
./bin/System.ComponentModel.Primitives.dll
./bin/System.Runtime.Numerics.dll
./bin/libhostfxr.so
./bin/System.IO.FileSystem.Watcher.dll
./bin/Microsoft.TeamFoundation.DistributedTask.WebApi.dll
./bin/it-IT/
./bin/it-IT/strings.json
chaminda@Ubuntu01:~/chamindacvstsagent$ ./config.sh

>> End User License Agreements:

Building sources from a TFVC repository requires accepting the Team Explorer Everywhere End User
 License Agreement. This step is not required for building sources from Git repositories.

A copy of the Team Explorer Everywhere license agreement can be found at:
  /home/chaminda/chamindacvstsagent/externals/tee/license.html

Enter (Y/N) Accept the Team Explorer Everywhere license agreement now? (press enter for N) > Y

>> Connect:

Enter server URL > https://chamindac.visualstudio.com
Enter authentication type (press enter for PAT) >
Enter personal access token > ************************************************█
```

Figure 2-47. *Executing ./config.sh to configure agent*

3. Enter agent pool to add the agent and specify an agent name. See Figure 2-48.

```
Enter server URL > https://chamindac.visualstudio.com
Enter authentication type (press enter for PAT) >
Enter personal access token > *************************************************
Connecting to server ...

>> Register Agent:

Enter agent pool (press enter for default) > ChOnPremAgents
Enter agent name (press enter for Ubuntu01) > UbuntuDemoAgnt01
Scanning for tool capabilities.
Connecting to the server.
Successfully added the agent
Testing agent connection.
Enter work folder (press enter for _work) >
2017-03-09 13:50:28Z: Settings Saved.
chaminda@Ubuntu01:~/chamindacvstsagent$ █
```

Figure 2-48. *Configuring agent for provided agent pool*

4. Agent is configured but will be offline. See Figure 2-49.

Figure 2-49. *Agent on Ubuntu is configured and offline*

5. Once the agent is configured, execute ./run.sh to bring the agent online. See Figure 2-50.

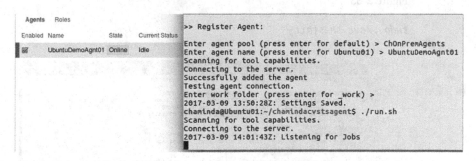

Figure 2-50. *Executing ./run.sh brings the agent online*

6. But if you close the terminal or press Ctrl+C, the agent will go offline. See Figure 2-51.

Figure 2-51. *Agent goes offline if terminal is closed or Ctrl+C is pressed*

7. To install the agent as a service in Linux, execute the following command from the agent folder. See Figure 2-52.

```
sudo ./svc.sh install
```

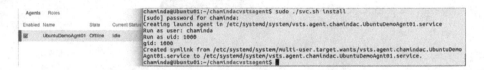

Figure 2-52. *Install the agent as a service in Ubuntu. Agent is still offline.*

8. To run the agent as a service, execute the following command. After executing the command, the agent will come online. You can press Ctrl+C or close the terminal. The agent will remain running since it has been configured as a service. See Figure 2-53.

```
sudo ./svc.sh start
```

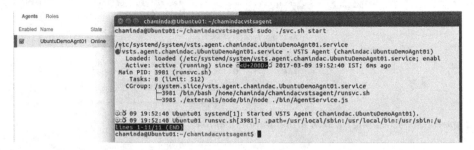

Figure 2-53. *Agent online as a service in Ubuntu*

9. In a new terminal, you can test the service status by executing the following command. See Figure 2-54.

```
sudo ./svc.sh status
```

Figure 2-54. *Check agent service status*

10. To stop service, execute the following:

```
sudo ./svc.sh stop
```

11. To uninstall, first stop the service and then execute the following:

```
sudo ./svc.sh uninstall
```

In this lesson, you have learned how to set up a Windows build/release agent in the same domain as TFS and for untrusted domains. Setting up agents in an untrusted domain helps to set up the required agents for production deployment scenarios. PAT (Personal Access Token) helps to set up agents in untrusted domains for on-premises TFS as well as set up private agents for VS Team Services. There are three types of authentications for configuring agents, and it is expected that users involved with all three types will have agent pool Manage (Administrator) permission:

- Integrated – uses logged-on user to connect and configure agent

- Negotiate – allows user to enter user credentials

- PAT – uses personal access token

The preceding authentication is used only for registering the agent. Once configured, an OAuth token (for more information on OAuth tokens and TFS/VSTS visit https://www.visualstudio.com/en-us/docs/integrate/get-started/auth/oauth) is downloaded and will be used by the agent to listen to incoming jobs from TFS or VSTS. When a build is running, another OAuth token is used depending on the scope defined in the build definition. This will be further discussed in the build definition lessons in Chapter 3.

Lesson 2.03 – Install and Manage Extensions from Marketplace

In this lesson, you will learn how to install extensions from Visual Studio Marketplace (https://marketplace.visualstudio.com/vsts) to enhance the functionality of TFS and VS Team Services. Many of these extensions are free, and some are paid.

Prerequisites: You should have administrator permissions for the TFS project collection.

2.03.1 Install Extension from Marketplace

You can install extensions from Visual Studio Marketplace (https://marketplace.visualstudio.com/vsts) to Team Services or TFS to enhance the functionality.

1. Click on **Browse Marketplace** in the top-right corner of the TFS web portal and select the marketplace component you want to install. Click on it. See Figure 2-55.

Figure 2-55. *Browsing the marketplace*

2. In the marketplace component window, click on the Install button. This will take you to the installation page after downloading the extension to your team project collection. See Figure 2-56.

Figure 2-56. *Installing an extension*

3. Select the project collection and click **Confirm** to install. See
    Figure 2-57.

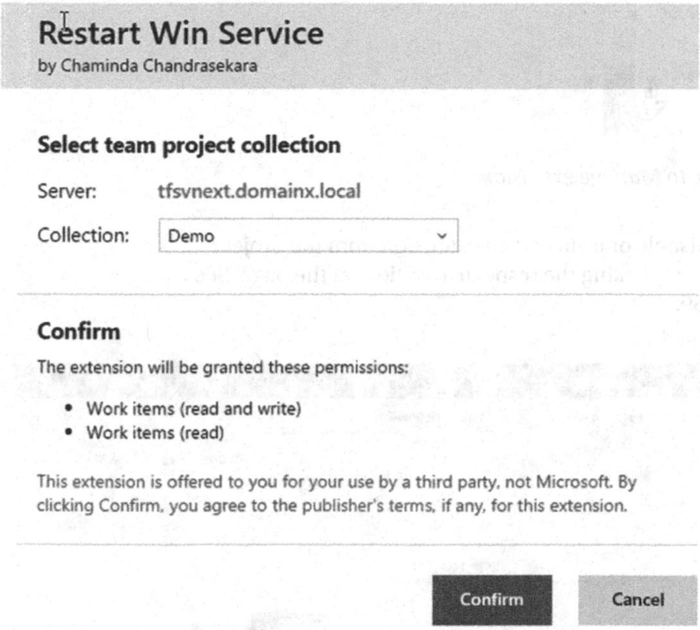

Restart Win Service
by Chaminda Chandrasekara

Select team project collection

Server: tfsvnext.domainx.local

Collection: Demo

Confirm

The extension will be granted these permissions:

- Work items (read and write)
- Work items (read)

This extension is offered to you for your use by a third party, not Microsoft. By
clicking Confirm, you agree to the publisher's terms, if any, for this extension.

Confirm   Cancel

Figure 2-57. Confirming the installation of extension

This will allow you use the installed extension. You will be doing this often while you
go through the rest of the chapters.

2.03.2 Manage Extension

The Manage Extensions page allows you to manage the extensions already installed from
Marketplace.

1. To manage extensions, click **Manage extensions** in the
    top-right corner of the TFS web portal while you are on a team
    project home page. See Figure 2-58.

Figure 2-58. *Navigate to Manage extensions*

2. You can disable or uninstall an extension from the project collection by clicking the respective option on the page. See Figure 2-59.

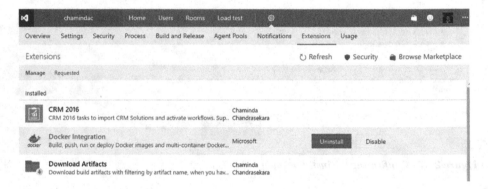

Figure 2-59. *Managing extensions*

Uninstalling or disabling an extension might affect the build/release definitions already using them. If it is an extension providing additional functionality to any other area of TFS/VSTS, that functionality will revert to the default behavior, once the extension is unintalled or disabled. Make sure to analyze the impact before you uninstall or disable an extension that is already in use.

2.03.3 Request an Extension

If you do not have Project Collection Administrator permissions as a TFS user, you can request an extension by following these steps:

1. Click on **Browse Marketplace** in the top-right corner of the TFS web portal and go to your preferred extension page, then click **Install**.

2. This will prompt you to provide a reason for requesting the extension and allow you to submit the request. See Figure 2-60.

Download Artifacts
by Chaminda Chandrasekara

Select team project collection

Server: tfsvnext.domainx.local

Collection: Demo   ⌄

Request Install

Only the team project collection administrator can install this extension in collection: Demo. Learn more

Provide reason for requesting the installation:

I need to download build artifacts partially to deployment servers. This extension allows to do that.

Your request will be sent to the administrators of this team project collection.

Confirm   Cancel

Figure 2-60. *Requesting extension*

3. Once the request is confirmed, your team project collection administrators will be notified via email about the request for the extension. The TFS project collection administrator is then able to install the requested extension by clicking **Manage Extension** and navigating to the Requested tab. Your team project collection administrator can either approve and install the extension or decline it. See Figure 2-61.

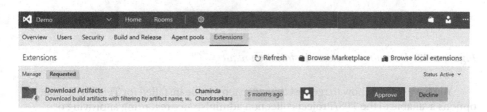

Figure 2-61. *Approving extension installation request*

4. Clicking the "5 months ago" link will show the reason for the request. See Figure 2-62.

Figure 2-62. View reason for the request of extension

5. If declining the extension, the administrator should provide a reason and reject the request for extension install. See Figure 2-63.

Figure 2-63. Declining extension installation request

You have learned how to request that an extension be installed for TFS/VSTS. The options available to the TFS/Project collection administrator regarding approving or declining the request, are also described.

2.03.4 Download Extensions for Installation

You have learned in previous lessons how to install an extension directly to TFS/VSTS by browsing Marketplace via the TFS/VSTS web portal. If you want to download an extension to install it in offline mode, follow these instructions:

1. You have the option of downloading the extension by directly browsing to https://marketplace.visualstudio.com/vsts. Click on the extension you prefer and click download (use a private/incognito browsing window if you do not see the download button on the component page). See Figure 2-64.

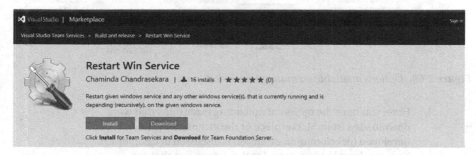

Figure 2-64. *Downloading an extension*

Uploading a downloaded extension is described in the next lesson.

2.03.5 Browse and Manage Local Extensions– On-Premises TFS

On-premises TFS allows you to manage any extensions installed in TFS on the Browse local extensions page.

1. Click **Manage Extensions** at the top-right corner of the TFS web portal.

2. On the Manage Extensions page, click on **Browse local extensions**. This is not available for VS Team Services. See Figure 2-65.

Figure 2-65. *Browse local extensions*

3. You can view the installed extensions and, by clicking on them, you will be allowed to install them to any other team project collection as well. At the bottom of the page, you can find the **Manage extensions** button. Click on it to go to the team foundation server's installed extension gallery. See Figure 2-66.

Figure 2-66. *Options available on manage extensions page*

4. Here, you have the option of uploading extensions that were downloaded from Marketplace or the extensions you have developed (developing an extension is discussed in Chapter 13). You can download updates for the extensions that are already installed. To install an extension to another team project collection, you can click on **Install**. See Figure 2-67.

Manage Extensions				Upload new extension
Name		Version	Updated	
Code Search Code Search provides fast, flexible and accurate searc...		0.0.100.1	a week ago	
Download Artifacts Download build artifacts with filtering by artifact name...		1.1.15	2 hours ago	Install
View details Update... Remove... Certificate	Management nage, secure, and share your team's software...	15.105.9...	a week ago	
	Tokens place tokens in files.	1.4.1	2 hours ago	

Figure 2-67. *Upload new extensions or manage existing local extensions*

In this short lesson, you learned how to install and manage TFS extensions form Marketplace. Extensions will be useful in achieving various build and release tasks. There are extensions that will enhance the other functionalities of TFS and VSTS as well. Creating your own build release extensions is described in Chapter 13.

Summary

Looking back at what you have learned throughout this chapter, you now know how to set up build and release agent pools, agent queues, and agents, and how to install extensions from Marketplace. This will allow you to set up build server farms and connect release environments to TFS or VSTS so as to automate deployments. Installing the TFS agent is not sufficient for a server/machine to work as a build server. The machine working as a build server should have Visual Studio versions and any other software that is required to build your application.

In the next chapter, we will take a closer look at builds and deployments of web applications to Azure platform and IIS.

CHAPTER 3

■ ■ ■

ASP.Net Web Application Deployment to Azure and IIS

The objective of this chapter and the lessons it encompasses is to guide you step by step in building and deploying ASP.NET MVC and ASP.NET Core web applications to Azure and IIS using TFS/Team Services build and release management.

Lesson 3.01 – Create ASP.Net Applications & Build with Team Foundation Builds

This lesson will guide you in creating web applications and testing them in Visual Studio 2017. Also, it provides guidance for building ASP.NET MVC web applications and .NET Core web applications with Team Foundation builds and tokenizing configurations with builds.

Prerequisites: You have VS Team Services or TFS 2017, and you have set up a team project with Team Foundation version control in it (https://www.visualstudio.com/en-us/docs/setup-admin/create-team-project). You have installed Visual Studio 2017 with ASP.NET and web development on your computer. .NET Core tools are included in VS 2017 (https://www.microsoft.com/net/core#windowsvs2017). See Figure 3-1.

Web & Cloud (5)

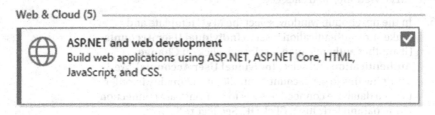

ASP.NET and web development
Build web applications using ASP.NET, ASP.NET Core, HTML, JavaScript, and CSS.

Figure 3-1. ASP.NET and web development

3.01.1 Create ASP.Net MVC App in VS 2017

Let's create an MVC web application using the available template.

1. In VS 2017, connect to the team project in Team Explorer. Then, open Source Control Explorer from Team Explorer home. In Source Control Explorer, expand your Team Project and create a folder called **Main**. See Figure 3-2.

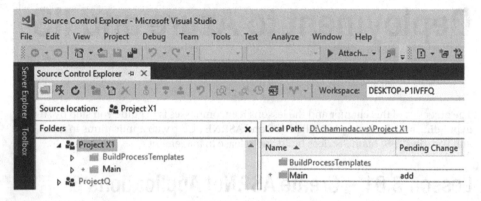

Figure 3-2. *Main folder in team project*

2. Create a new solution called "MVC5" using a blank solution template; put it in the Main folder. Make sure to check the "Add to Source Control" option to allow it to be added to TFVC repository.

3. Right click on the MVC solution in the Solution Explorer and select Add ➤ New Project.

4. In the popup dialog, select C# Web ➤ ASP.NET Web Application (.Net Framework) project, name the project "MVCWebApp," and click OK.

5. In the next popup window, select the MVC template and make sure authentication is set to **Individual User Accounts** (if another authentication is selected, click on **Change Authentication** and select **Individual User Accounts**). We are doing this to get account-controller functionality in order to get a database connection so as to demonstrate connection string parameterization. Click **OK**. See Figure 3-3.

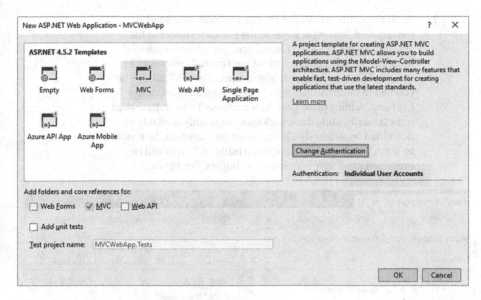

Figure 3-3. Creating the MVC project

6. This will add a new MVC web application project to the solution. See Figure 3-4.

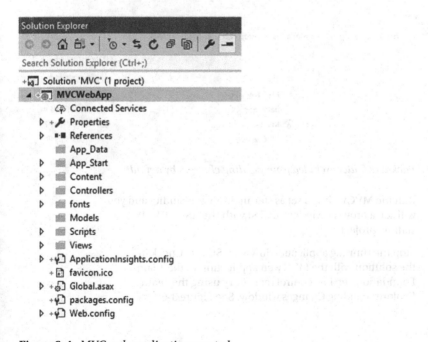

Figure 3-4. MVC web application created

7. Build the solution in Visual Studio. This will download the required NuGet packages to the Packages folder in the Solution folder. In VS 2017, this Packages folder is excluded from the "pending changes to source control" repository by default. This is a really great improvement over VS 2015, where you had to undo the Packages folder in the Source Control Explorer (Adding packages folder increase TFS database sizes unnecessarily while those packages are readily available to download on demand). These NuGet packages can be restored in Team Foundation builds using a build task. This will be explained in a future lesson in this chapter. See Figure 3-5.

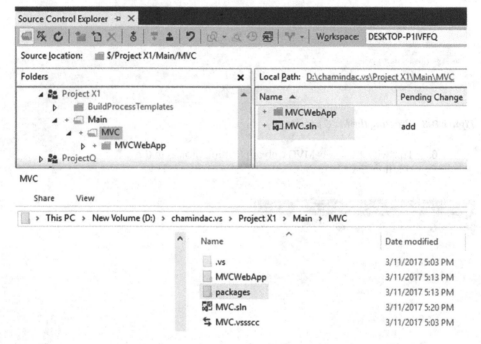

Figure 3-5. *Packages folder excluded from pending changes by default*

8. Run the MVCWebApp set as startup in Visual Studio, and you will see a browser window loaded with the ASP.NET MVC sample project.

9. Stop the running application in Visual Studio. Check in the solution with the MVC web application to the Team Foundation version-control repository using the Team Explorer Pending Changes window. See Figure 3-6.

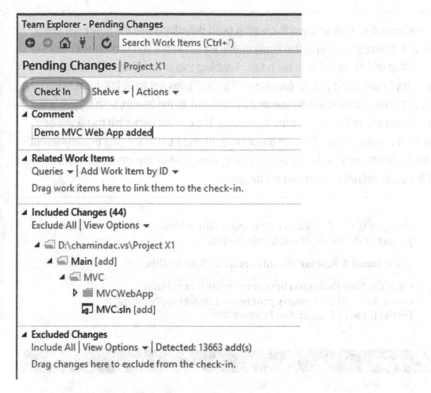

Figure 3-6. *Check the solution in to source control*

In this lesson, you have created an MVC web application project and checked it in to the source control repository. You will be using this solution in the next lesson to create a build in the Team Foundation Server team project.

3.01.2 Build ASP.Net MVC App in TFS/VSTS

Let's create a build definition in the team project for the MVC web application solution that you created in the previous lesson.

■ **Note**   The screen layouts involved in creating build definitions use the new build editor (in preview at the time of writing of this book) in this lesson to get you familiar with the new changes that will be available in the future. Enabling this preview layout is explained in Chapter 1. If you are using TFS on-premises (TFS 2017 does not have this build editor), the layouts of the build definition tabs are slightly different. In the lesson, both layouts will be shown in cases where the changes are significant. The current layout tab name will be mentioned for the same fields if they are shown in a different tab in the new preview layout. You can identify the correct tab to use by comparing new preview layouts and current layouts of the build definition described in Chapter 1.

1.   Navigate to the TFS/VSTS web portal of the relevant team project and click the Build & Release tab.

2.   In the **Build & Release** tab submenu, click on **Builds**.

3.   Click the New Definition button to create a new build definition, and click **empty process** to use an empty template for the build definition. See Figure 3-7.

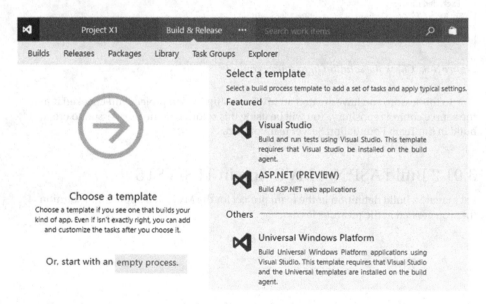

Figure 3-7. *Creating an empty process template build definition–new preview layout*

If you are using TFS on-premises (which does not have the new preview build layouts at the time of writing of this book) or not using the preview build layouts in VSTS, you will see a popup window from which to select a build template. Select Empty and click on Next. See Figure 3-8.

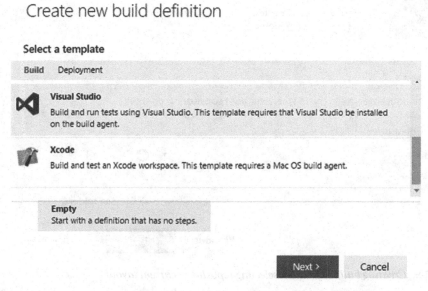

Figure 3-8. Creating empty process template build definition–current layout

In the current build layout, you will be presented with another window from which to select the repository to use for the build. You have to select the agent pool to be used. The agent pool should have an agent capable of building the project. Agents, agent pools, and queues are described in Chapter 2. Click **Create** to create the build definition. See Figure 3-9.

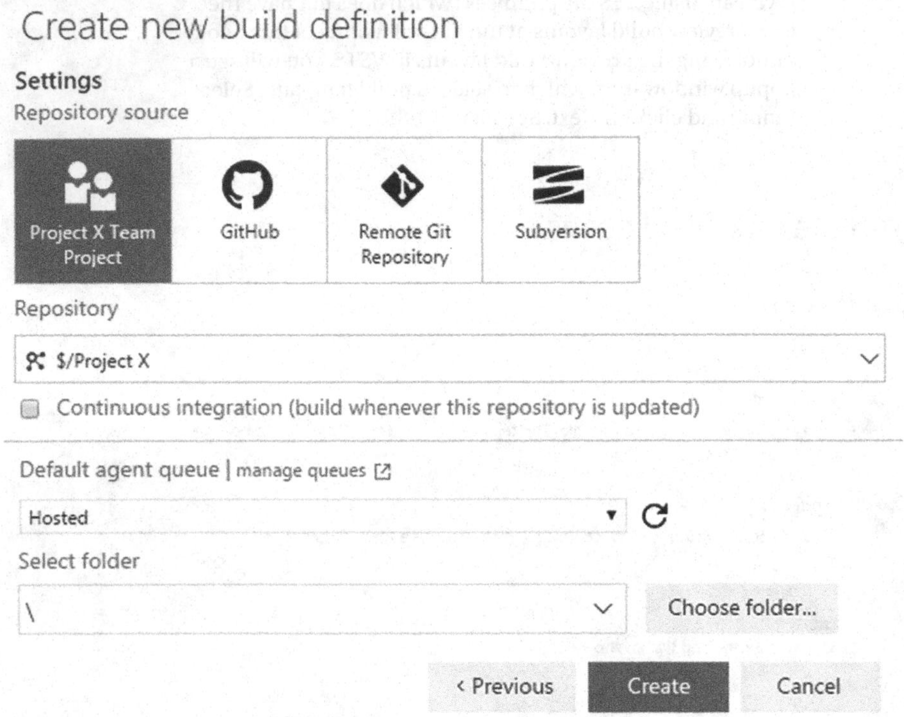

Create new build definition
Settings
Repository source
Project X Team Project
GitHub
Remote Git Repository
Subversion
Repository
$/Project X
Continuous integration (build whenever this repository is updated)
Default agent queue | manage queues
Hosted
Select folder
\
Choose folder...
‹ Previous
Create
Cancel

***Figure 3-9.** Creating build definition: selecting repository–current layout*

4. If you are using the current layout, you will see build tabs similar to those in Figure 3-10 after Step 3 of this lesson.

Project X
Home
Code
Work
Build & Release
Test
Build Definitions / *
Build
Options
Repository
Variables
Triggers
General
Retention
History
Save
Add build step...

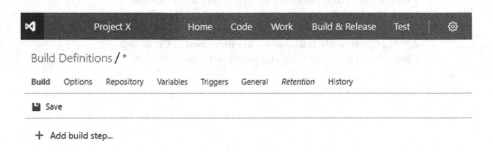

***Figure 3-10.** Created build definition–current layout*

In the new preview layout (you will be in this window after step 3), name the build definition "MVC.CI" (CI stands for continuous integration build; details are explained in a later step of the lesson) by clicking Process in the Tasks tab of the build definition (see Figure 3-11). In the current layout, you have to click the Save button (see Figure 3-10) to provide a name for the build definition.

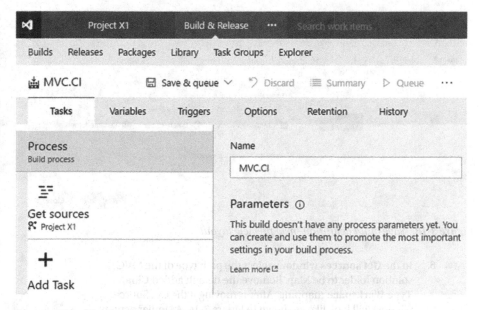

Figure 3-11. *Naming the build definition–new preview layout*

5. Click on Save to save the build definition (see Figure 3-12; for current layout click Save. Refer to Figure 3-10).

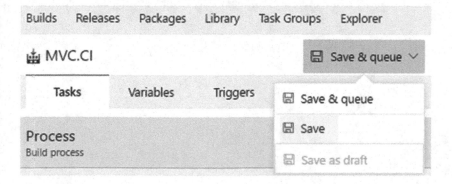

Figure 3-12. *Save build definition–new preview layout*

In the popup window, you can click on **Choose Folders** and then create folders to organize the build definitions in a team project (there is a similar window in the current layout with a field to provide the build definition name). Create a folder named "WebAppBuilds" and select it, click **OK**, and then click **Save** to save the new build definition. See Figure 3-13.

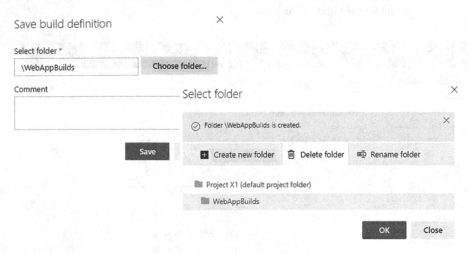

Figure 3-13. *Save build definition–new preview layout*

6.   In the **Get sources** window, select the path type of the MVC solution folder to be Map. Remove the default added **Cloak Type Workspace** mapping. After removing it the Get Sources window will look like as shown in Figure 3-14. A similar activity can be performed in the **Repository** tab of the current layout.

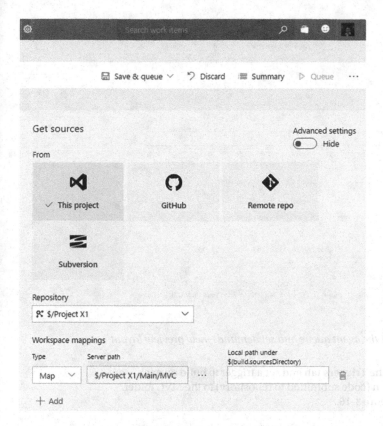

Figure 3-14. Save build definition–new preview layout

7. In the **Options** tab (General tab of the current layout) select
the agent queue. The selected agent queue must have an
agent and must have Visual Studio 2017 installed in order to
build the web application project. You can add demands for
the agent in the Options tab (General tab in current layout).
For more details, refer to Chapter 1's agent capabilities topic.
Authorization scope is set to current project since the build
is building code from only the current team project. See
Figure 3-15.

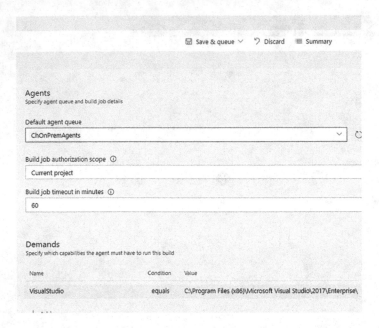

Figure 3-15. Select the agent queue and set demands–new preview layout

8. Go to the **Triggers** tab and set a trigger to build on each check-in (code submitted to repository) to the MVC folder. See Figure 3-16.

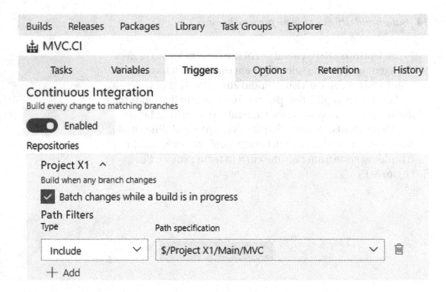

Figure 3-16. Build for each check-in–new preview layout

9. Go to the **Variables** tab and define variables for BuildConfiguration and BuildPlatform to use release and any cpu, so that the solution will be built for release configuration on any cpu platform, enabling the app to run o n x86 or x64 machines. These will be created automatically if you create a build definition with the Visual Studio build template. The "Settable at queue time" option allows the value to be changed when queuing a build. See Figure 3-17.

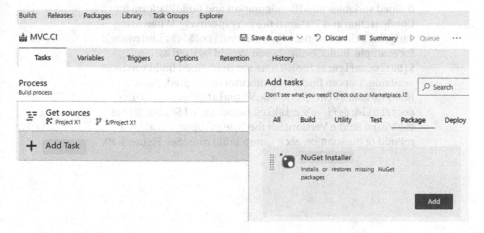

Builds	Releases	Packages	Task Groups	Explorer

⛏ MVC.CI				🖫 Save & queue ∨	≣ Summary	▷ Queue

Tasks	**Variables**	Options	Retention	History

Process variables	Name	Value		Settable at queue time
	system.collectionId	cdbf67ea-c6ac-4257-aad7-c3a2d7ac62c9	🔒	☐
	system.teamProject	Project X1		
	system.definitionId	80		
	system.debug	false		☑
	BuildConfiguration	release		
	BuildPlatform	any cpu		
	＋ Add			

Figure 3-17. Variables for configuration and platform–new preview layout

10. Click on Add Task in **Tasks** tab (or on Add Build Step in Builds tab of current layout) of the build definition. From the Task Catalog's **Package** tab, Add the NuGet Installer task to the build definition. See Figure 3-18.

Builds	Releases	Packages	Library	Task Groups	Explorer

⛏ MVC.CI				🖫 Save & queue ∨	⟲ Discard	≣ Summary	▷ Queue	⋯

Tasks	Variables	Triggers	Options	Retention	History

Process
Build process

Add tasks
Don't see what you need? Check out our Marketplace.🔗   🔍 Search

☷ Get sources	All	Build	Utility	Test	**Package**	Deploy
𝒳 Project X1 𝒫 $/Project X1						

＋ Add Task

⬤ NuGet Installer
Installs or restores missing NuGet packages

Add

Figure 3-18. Add NuGet Installer–new preview layout

95

11. In the NuGet Installer task added, select the MVC solution and set it to restore packages. This will enable the restoring of required NuGet packages before building the solution. See Figure 3-19.

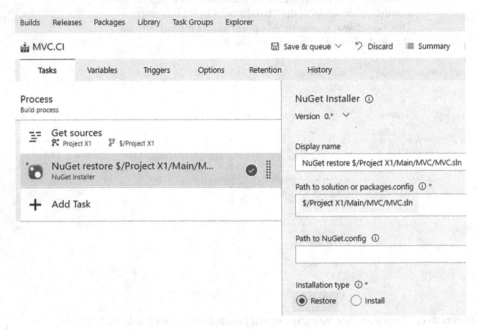

Figure 3-19. *Variables for configuration and platform–new preview layout*

12. Add a Visual Studio build task from the Task Catalog to the Tasks tab (Build tab in current layout), then provide the MVC solution path as the solution to build. Use the defined variables BuildConfiguration and BuildPlatform for Configuration and Platform fields, respectively. When using variables in build steps, follow the syntax of $(variablename); for example, BuildConfiguration should be used as $(buildConfiguration). There are predefined build variables available. You can find more information on predefined build variables at https://www.visualstudio.com/en-us/docs/build/define/variables. Select Visual Studio 2017 as the Visual Studio Version. Set the "Clean" option to allow a rebuild of the solution each time a build runs. See Figure 3-20.

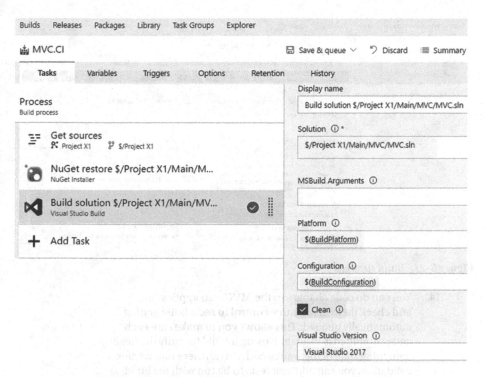

Figure 3-20. Visual Studio build step–new preview layout

13. Save the definition and then queue a build. This will pop up the Build Queue window explained in Chapter 1. Click the Queue button on the popup window. You will see a build begin running. The Build should be successful; its status is shown in the build summary. This build does not publish any output. It just compiles the solution. See Figure 3-21.

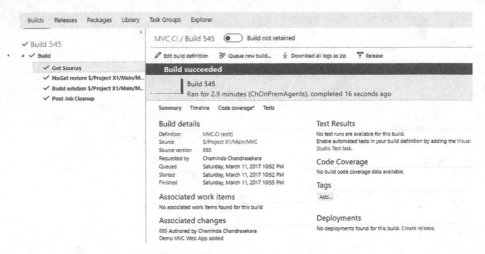

Figure 3-21. *Build succeeds*

14. You can do code changes in the MVC web application and check them in to source control to see a build getting automatically queued. This allows you to make sure each code submitted is validated, using a build to verify the healthy compiling state of the source code. To further enhance this validation, you can add unit tests to be run with the build, which will be described in Chapter 9 on test automation. You can set up notifications in VSTS/TFS to send you/the team an email alert upon build failure and so forth. To set up notifications, go to Settings ➤ Notifications and click **New**. Then, select **Build** in the Category column and **A build fails** in the Template column. Click **Next** to configure build failure notification email. See Figure 3-22.

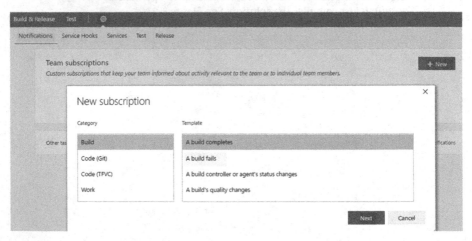

Figure 3-22. *Build notifications*

15. You can set up a few options for notifications, such as sending emails to all team members or specific team members, or to a set of given email addresses, etc. Further, you can set up notifications for different filter criteria, such as sending a notification if a given named build definition fails. After setting criteria and other parameters, click Finish to set up the notification. After notification setup, you have the option to enable or disable it in the Notifications tab. Do experiments with notification criteria by failing (you can submit code with compilation errors to fail a build) and making builds successful. See Figure 3-23.

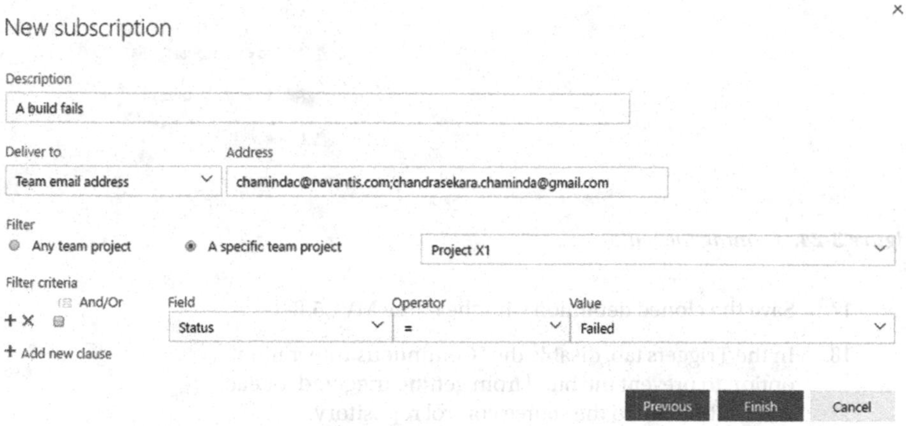

Figure 3-23. Build notifications settings

16. To generate deployable output for the MVC web application, let's clone this build and create a release build definition. To clone the build, go to Build & Release ➤ All Definitions, click on the link menu (...) of the definition, and then click **Clone**. See Figure 3-24.

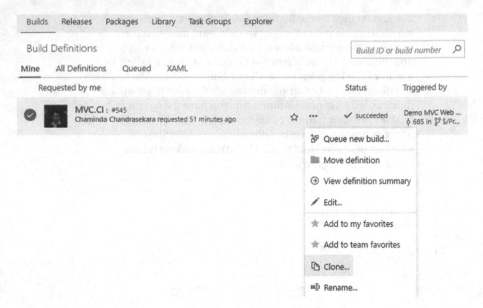

Figure 3-24. *Cloning the build*

17. Save the cloned definition with the name MVC5.Rel.

18. In the Triggers tab, disable the "Continuous Integration" option to prevent the build from getting triggered for each code submitted to the source control repository.

19. In the Visual Studio Build task, add the following MSBuild arguments:

```
/p:DeployOnBuild=true /p:WebPublishMethod=Package
/p:PackageAsSingleFile=true /p:OutDir="$(build.stagingDirectory)"
```

These arguments will publish the website for XCopy mode deployments, and a deployment package will be created, which can be deployed with msdeploy. See Figure 3-25.

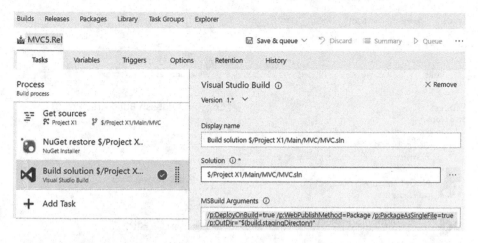

Figure 3-25. Build arguments

20. Add the Copy and Publish step/task from the Task Catalog to the build definition, to enable publishing the artifacts after the build completed. The provided copy root is $(build.stagingDirectory), which is used as OutDir in the Visual Studio Build step. Set contents to copy as _PublishedWebsites*** and provide a name for Artifact Name field. Set Artifact Type to Server. See Figure 3-26.

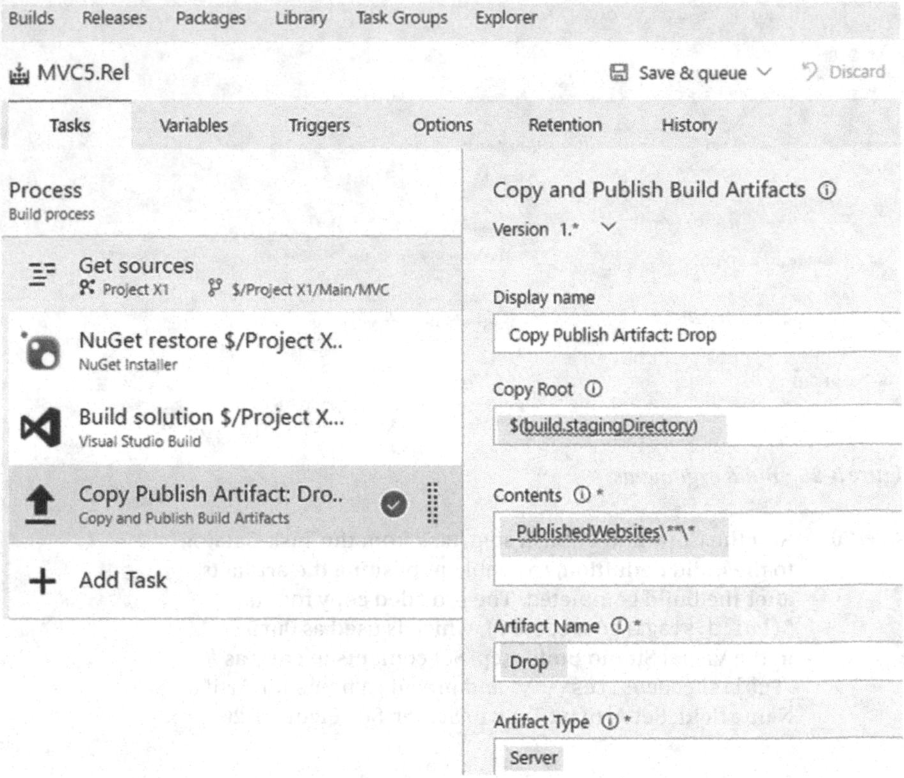

Figure 3-26. *Copy and Publish Artifacts task*

21. Leave the Options tab of the definition, as it was already set up when the MVC.CI build was created.

■ **Note** Build multi-configuration allows you to build for multiple configurations. You can specify variables such as BuildConfiguration in the Variables tab and use it to build multiple configurations, as shown in Figure 3-27, which uses the current layout of build definitions. Skip this step (21) and go to step 22, if you do not want to try out multiple configurations now.

Build Definitions / ■ WebAppBuilds / MVC5.Rel

Build   Options   Repository   **Variables**   Triggers   General   Retention   History

💾 Save ▾   ⤴ Undo

List of predefined variables

Name	Value
system.collectionId	cdbf67ea-c6ac-4257-aad7-c3a2d7ac62c9
system.definitionId	48
✕ system.debug	false
✕ BuildConfiguration	release, debug
✕ BuildPlatform	any cpu
✚ Add variable	

Figure 3-27. Multiple build configurations

> Then, use the variables in the Multi-configuration Multipliers
> field, in the Options tab to build multiple configurations.
> See Figure 3-28.

Build Definitions / ■ WebAppBuilds / MVC5.Rel

Build   **Options**   Repository   Variables   Triggers   General   Retention

💾 Save ▾   ⤴ Undo

☑ **Multi-configuration**

Build multiple configurations with the same steps

Multipliers	BuildConfiguration, BuildPlatform
Parallel	☐
Continue on Error	☑

Figure 3-28. Configure multi-configuration build

This allows you to build multiple configurations in a single build. You can see in
Figure 3-29 that the build is building for both debug and release configurations. After
trying out the multiple configurations, reverse the actions performed in this step (21)
before proceeding to next step (22).

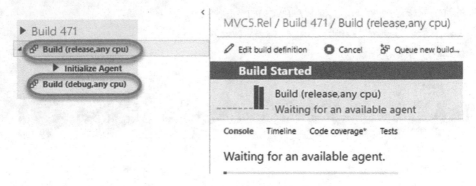

Figure 3-29. Build executes for multiple configurations

22. The **"Create work item on failure"** option allows you to create a work item and assign it to the build requestor if a build fails. See Figure 3-30.

Build Definitions / ■ WebAppBuilds / MVC5.Rel

Build **Options** Repository Variables Triggers General

💾 Save ▾   🔁 Undo

☑ **Create Work Item on Failure**
Create a work item for each failed build

Type

    Bug

Assign to requestor   ☑

Figure 3-30. Creating work item on build failure

23. In the Build definition, the **Retention** tab allows you to define rules for retaining builds after completion of build execution. See Figure 3-31.

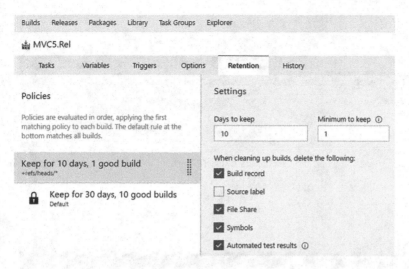

Figure 3-31. Retaining completed builds

24. Queue a build, and once the build is completed, you can view and download the artifacts to deploy them manually, if required. Or, you can explore and view the artifacts. From the Explorer view, if necessary, you can partially download the artifacts. The MVCWebApp folder contains the site-published files for xcopy deployments. MVCWebApp_Package contains a web-deployment package that can be deployed using msdeploy. See Figure 3-32.

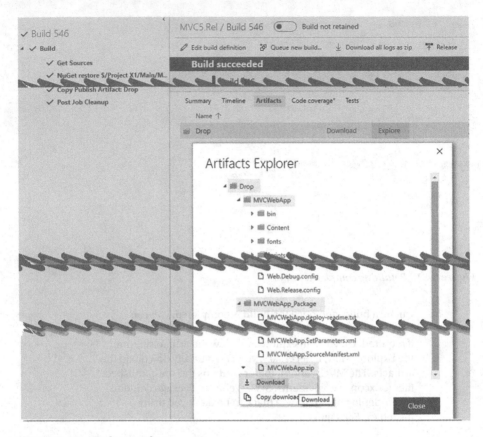

Figure 3-32. *Explore artifacts*

In this lesson, you have built an MVC web application with Team Foundation builds and generated deployable artifacts, which you can download using the Artifacts explorer of the completed build summary page. Artifacts explorer lets you download individual build artifact items so that you can filter only required components for your target server. For example a target DB server may need only database componets to be installed as web server only requires web application componets to be deployed.

3.01.3 Tokenize ASP.Net MVC 5 App Configurations with Build

The connection strings, application settings, and so on can be tokenized by the build to allow them to be updated at the time of deployment.

1. Open the web.config file and add a new app setting called "ClientId" and provide a value for it. See Figure 3-33.

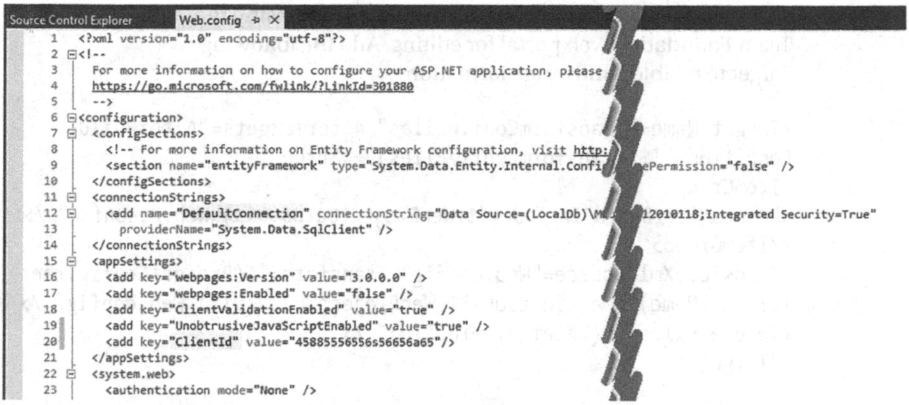

```
Source Control Explorer        Web.config  ◆ ✕
   1    <?xml version="1.0" encoding="utf-8"?>
   2  ⊟<!--
   3      For more information on how to configure your ASP.NET application, please
   4      https://go.microsoft.com/fwlink/?LinkId=301880
   5      -->
   6  ⊟<configuration>
   7  ⊟   <configSections>
   8        <!-- For more information on Entity Framework configuration, visit http:
   9        <section name="entityFramework" type="System.Data.Entity.Internal.Confi     Permission="false" />
  10      </configSections>
  11  ⊟   <connectionStrings>
  12  ⊟     <add name="DefaultConnection" connectionString="Data Source=(LocalDb)\M    12010118;Integrated Security=True"
  13          providerName="System.Data.SqlClient" />
  14      </connectionStrings>
  15  ⊟   <appSettings>
  16        <add key="webpages:Version" value="3.0.0.0" />
  17        <add key="webpages:Enabled" value="false" />
  18        <add key="ClientValidationEnabled" value="true" />
  19        <add key="UnobtrusiveJavaScriptEnabled" value="true" />
  20        <add key="ClientId" value="45885556556s56656a65"/>
  21      </appSettings>
  22  ⊟   <system.web>
  23        <authentication mode="None" />
```

Figure 3-33. App settings and connection strings

2. In web.release.config (configuration used in the TFS build), set the transformations as follows (see Figure 3-34):

```
<connectionStrings>
<add name="DefaultConnection" connectionString="__defaultDBConnection__"
providerName="System.Data.SqlClient" xdt:Transform="SetAttributes"
xdt:Locator="Match(name)"/>
</connectionStrings>
<appSettings>
<add key="ClientId" value="__ClientId__"
xdt:Transform="SetAttributes" xdt:Locator="Match(key)"/>
</appSettings>
```

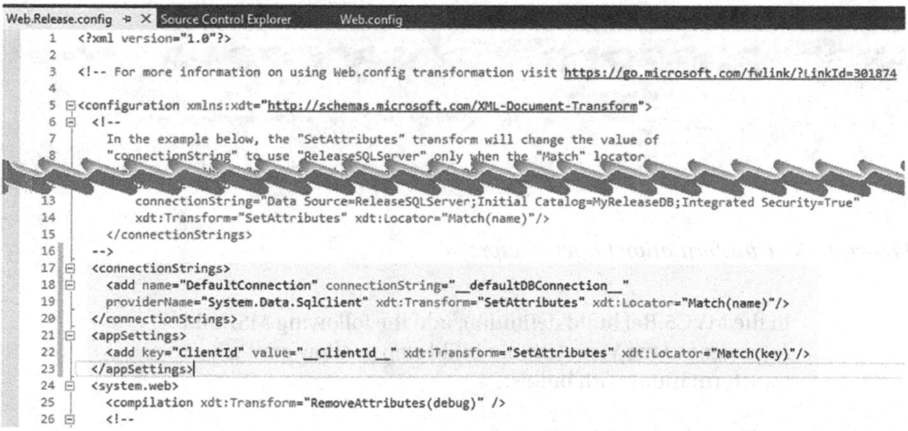

```
Web.Release.config  ◆ ✕ Source Control Explorer        Web.config
   1    <?xml version="1.0"?>
   2
   3    <!-- For more information on using Web.config transformation visit https://go.microsoft.com/fwlink/?LinkId=301874
   4
   5  ⊟<configuration xmlns:xdt="http://schemas.microsoft.com/XML-Document-Transform">
   6  ⊟   <!--
   7      In the example below, the "SetAttributes" transform will change the value of
   8      "connectionString" to use "ReleaseSQLServer" only when the "Match" locator
  13          connectionString="Data Source=ReleaseSQLServer;Initial Catalog=MyReleaseDB;Integrated Security=True"
  14          xdt:Transform="SetAttributes" xdt:Locator="Match(name)"/>
  15      </connectionStrings>
  16      -->
  17  ⊟   <connectionStrings>
  18  ⊟     <add name="DefaultConnection" connectionString="__defaultDBConnection__"
  19          providerName="System.Data.SqlClient" xdt:Transform="SetAttributes" xdt:Locator="Match(name)"/>
  20      </connectionStrings>
  21  ⊟   <appSettings>
  22        <add key="ClientId" value="__ClientId__" xdt:Transform="SetAttributes" xdt:Locator="Match(key)"/>
  23      </appSettings>
  24  ⊟   <system.web>
  25        <compilation xdt:Transform="RemoveAttributes(debug)" />
  26  ⊟     <!--
```

Figure 3-34. Transformations in web.release.config

3. Open the MVCWebApp.csproj file in a notepad or using the Team Foundation web portal for editing. Add the following Target to enable config transformations:

```
<Target Name="TransformConfigFiles" AfterTargets="AfterBuild"
Condition="'$(TransformConfigFiles)'=='true'">
<ItemGroup>
<DeleteAfterBuild Include="$(WebProjectOutputDir)\Web.*.config" />
</ItemGroup>
<TransformXml Source="Web.config" Transform="$(ProjectConfigTrans
formFileName)" Destination="$(WebProjectOutputDir)\Web.config" />
<Delete Files="@(DeleteAfterBuild)" />
</Target>
```

This transformation target will process transformations in web.release.config and update the web.config file with tokens. It will then remove the web.debug.config and web.release. config files from the built artifacts. This will allow a clean build output with just one web.config. See Figure 3-35.

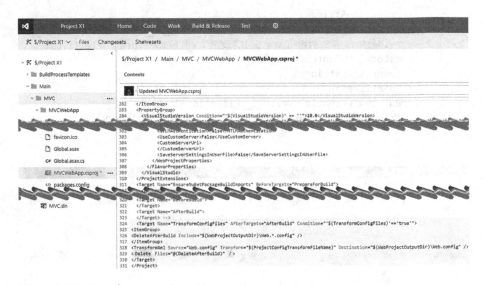

Figure 3-35. *Transformation target in .csproj*

4. In the MVC5.Rel build definition, add the following MSBuild Argument to the Visual Studio Build step to allow config transformations with builds:

```
/p:TransformConfigFiles=true
```

5. Queue a new build and download the web config from the artifacts explorer of the completed build, to verify the configuration tokens have been applied. See Figure 3-36.

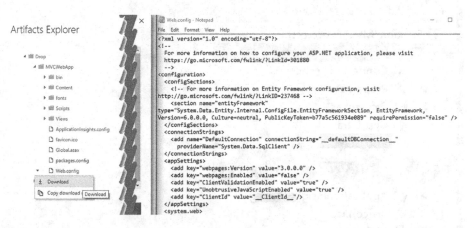

Figure 3-36. Transformation applied in web.config

6. However, if you download the .SetParameters.xml file from the MVC5WebApp_Package, it only has the connection string parameter and deployment target. See Figure 3-37.

Figure 3-37. SetParameters file only has connection string.

7. To get the app settings in web.config to the .SetParameters. xml file, add a Parameters.xml file to the MVC5WebApp project. See Figure 3-38.

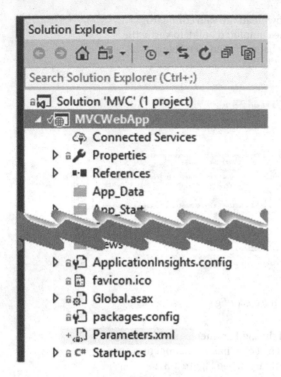

Figure 3-38. Adding Parameters.xml file

8. Add the following content to the Parameters.xml file
   (see Figure 3-39):

```
<parameters>
<parameter name="ClientIdParam" defaultValue="__ClientId__">
<parameterEntry kind="XmlFile" scope="\\web.config$"
match="/configuration/appSettings/add[@key='ClientId']/@value" />
</parameter>
</parameters>
```

$/Project X / Main / MVC5 / MVS5WebApp / **Parameters.xml**

ⓘ Checked in changeset ◊ 590: Updated Parameters.xml

Contents   History   Compare

🖉 Edit   ⬇ Download

```
1  <?xml version="1.0" encoding="utf-8" ?>
2  <parameters>
3    <parameter name="ClientIdParam" defaultValue="__ClientId__">
4      <parameterEntry kind="XmlFile" scope="\\web.config$" match="/configuration/appSettings/add[@key='ClientId']/@value" />
5    </parameter>
6  </parameters>
7
```

Figure 3-39. Parameters.xml

110

9. With this, when the build generates .SetParameters.xml it will include the tokenized parameter for the app settings as well. See Figure 3-40.

```
MVS5WebApp.SetParameters.xml - Notepad                                          -
File  Edit  Format  View  Help
<?xml version="1.0" encoding="utf-8"?>
<parameters>
  <setParameter name="IIS Web Application Name" value="Default Web Site/MVS5WebApp_deploy" />
  <setParameter name="ClientIDParam" value="__ClientId__" />
  <setParameter name="DefaultConnection-Web.config Connection String" value="__defaultDBConnection__" />
</parameters>
```

Figure 3-40. *.SetParameters.xml file with tokenized app settings*

10. As a next step, we need to get the "IIS Web Application Name" value tokenized. To do this, we create a publish profile by right clicking on the web project and then clicking **Publish**.

11. In the opened window in VS 2017, click on the **Publish** screen, select **IIS, FTP, etc.**, and click the **Publish** button. See Figure 3-41.

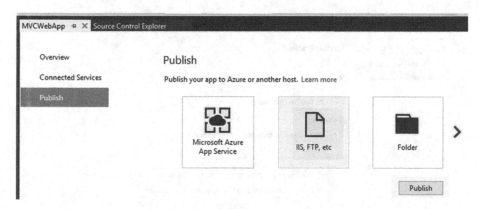

Figure 3-41. *IIS, FTP publish*

12. Set Publish method on the **Connection** screen to be Web Deploy Package. For Package location and Site name, provide token values __MVC5WebAppZip__ and __MVC5SiteName__ respectively. The package location provided here is not important, as it will be overridden by the TFS build. See Figure 3-42.

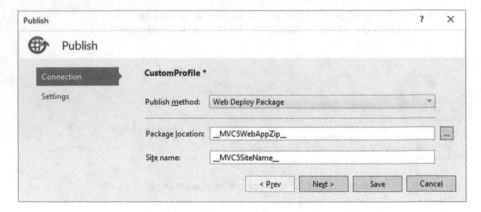

Figure 3-42. *Web deploy package publish profile*

In the next screen, i.e., **Settings**, set Configuration field to
Release and click the **Save** button. See Figure 3-43.

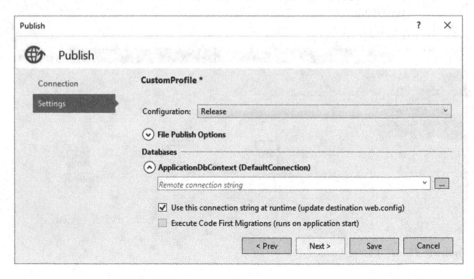

Figure 3-43. *Save publish profile*

13. This will generate a Cutom.pubxml file in Properties ➤
PublishProfiles in the web application project. Rename the file
to TFSPublish.pubxml. See Figure 3-44.

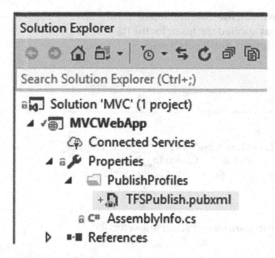

Figure 3-44. Save publish profile

14. Check in/submit the TFSPublish.pubxml file to the source control repository.

15. In the build definition, modify the MSBuild Arguments in the Visual Studio Build screen to use the publish profile. See Figure 3-45.

```
/p:DeployOnBuild=true should be changed to
/p:DeployOnBuild=true;PublishProfile="TFSPublish"
```

Visual Studio Build ⓘ   ✕ Remove

Version 1.* ∨

Display name

Build solution $/Project X1/Main/MVC/MVC.sln

Solution ⓘ *

$/Project X1/Main/MVC/MVC.sln	···

MSBuild Arguments ⓘ

```
/p:DeployOnBuild=true;PublishProfile="TFSPublish"
/p:WebPublishMethod=Package /p:PackageAsSingleFile=true
/p:OutDir="$(build.stagingDirectory)" /p:TransformConfigFiles=true
```

Figure 3-45. Change build arguments to use publish profile

113

16. Queue a new build and download the .SetParameters.xml file from the build artifacts. It has applied the token for the IIS Web Application Name parameter. See Figure 3-46.

MVCWebApp.SetParameters.xml - Notepad

File   Edit   Format   View   Help

```
<?xml version="1.0" encoding="utf-8"?>
<parameters>
  <setParameter name="IIS Web Application Name" value="__MVC5SiteName__" />
  <setParameter name="ClientIdParam" value="__ClientId__" />
  <setParameter name="DefaultConnection-Web.config Connection String"
value="__defaultDBConnection__" />
</parameters>
```

Figure 3-46. *IIS Web Application Name as parameter in .SetParameters file*

In this lesson, you have enabled web configuration transformation and other parameterization to enable the tokenizing of configurations and other parameters so as to allow them to be changed at deployment time. This enables you to use the same binary package to deploy into multiple targets (QA, UAT, etc.).

■ **Note**   We have used preview build layouts in the previous lessons to get you familiar with the upcoming changes to Build Editor in TFS/VSTS. From the next lesson onward, we will be using the current layouts of build definitions since preview layouts are not available to TFS 2017 on-premises at the time of writing this book. This will enable you to understand the complexities in the build definitions in future lessons without getting confused by the layout differences.

3.01.4 Create ASP.Net Core Web App in VS 2017

Let's create a Core web application in Visual Studio 2017 so we can also build it with Team Foundation builds in a later lesson.

1. Create a new solution named "Core1" in the Main folder. Make sure to check the "Add to Source Control" box.

2. Right click on the solution and select **Add ➤ New Project**

3. In the popup dialog, select C# .NET Core ➤ ASP.NET Core Web Application (.NET Core).

4. Name the project "CoreWebApp" and click **OK**. See Figure 3-47.

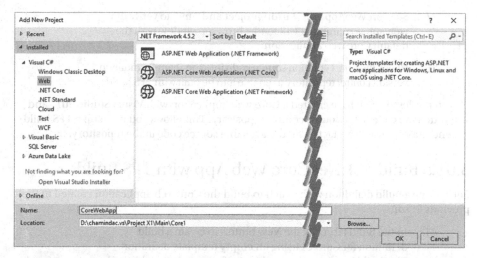

Figure 3-47. Creating core web application project

5. Select Web Application template from the Core 1.0 templates in the popup window. Make sure authentication is set to **Individual User Accounts** (we are doing this to get account controller functionality in order to get a database connection so as to demonstrate connection string parameterization) and click **OK**. See Figure 3-48.

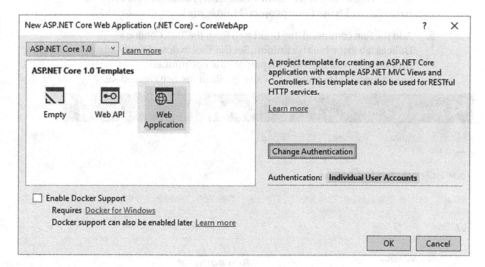

Figure 3-48. Selecting Core web application template

6. This will add a new ASP.NET Core Web Application Project to the solution.

115

7. Set CoreWebApp as a startup project and run it to verify the web app is running. It will load a browser window with the default Core web application.

8. Check the Core1 solution source code into the Team Foundation version control repository to enable it to be built with TFS builds.

In this lesson, you have created a Core web application with Visual Studio 2017 and submitted the code to the source control repository. This allows you to set up a TFS build to generate deployable artifacts with the available source code in the repository.

3.01.5 Build ASP.Net Core Web App with TFS Build

Let's create a build definition with which to build the Core web application created in the previous lesson.

1. In the Build tab, click the **New** button to create a build definition for Core.CI using an empty template definition. This build is going to be used to verify the code is stable in the .NET core web application added to the repository.

2. Add BuildConfiguration and BuildPlatform variables in the Variables tab with values of release and any cpu, respectively.

3. Map the source control path $/**yourteamproject**/Main/Core1 in the Repository tab.

4. In the Triggers tab, select Continuous Integration and set the path filter to $/**yourteamproject**/Main/Core1.

5. Add the Run command line build step from the Task Catalog's Utilities tab to the build definition. Set the Tool to dotnet and Arguments to restore. This will prepare the environment (agent machine) to build .NET Core applications. See Figure 3-49.

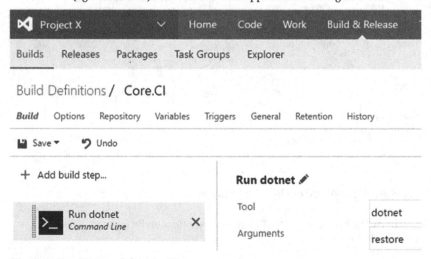

Figure 3-49. *Restore dotnet build step*

6. Add a Visual Studio build step and set the solution path to the Core1 solution. Type the Build Platform and Build Configuration variables, defined in the Variables tab, into the Platform and Configuration fields, respectively. This will build the solution in both **release** and **any cpu** configurations. See Figure 3-50.

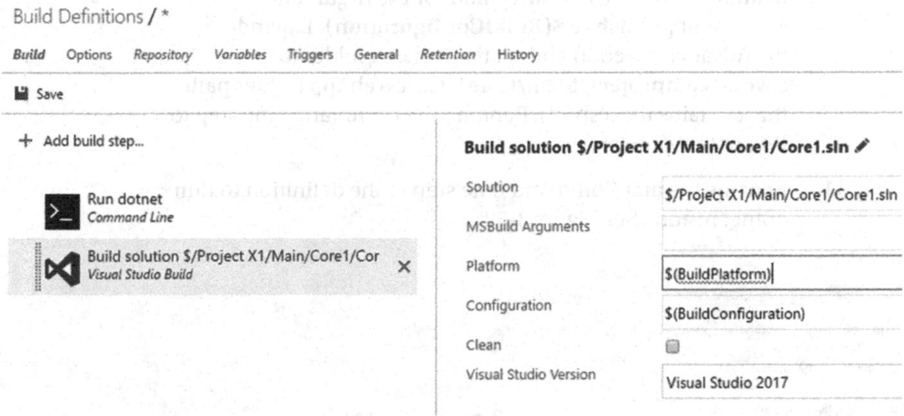

Figure 3-50. Build step to build the Core web application

7. In the General tab of the build definition, select an agent queue that has an agent with Visual Studio 2017 available in it. Set a demand for Visual Studio 2017 in the Demands section, as shown in Figure 3-51.

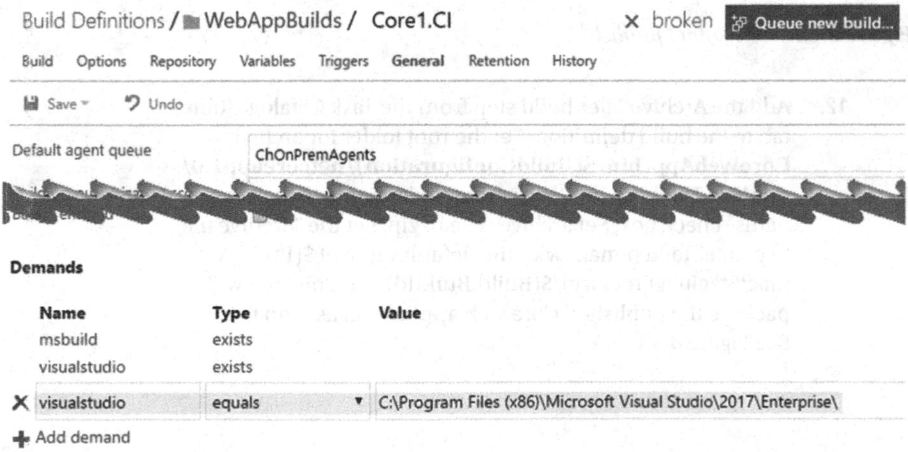

Figure 3-51. Demand for Visual Studio 2017

8. Queue a new build and verify the build status in the Build Summary tab. The build should succeed in compiling the solution.

9. Clone the build definition and create a Core1.Rel build definition.

10. Add a new Command Line build step to the Core1.Rel definition. Set Tool to **dotnet**, and for the Arguments field, input **publish -c $(BuildConfiguration)**. Expand the Advanced section and set the working folder to **$/yourteamproject**/Main/Core1/CoreWebApp (folder path that contains the .csproj). Rename the Command Line step to Run dotnet publish.

11. Rename the first Command Line step in the definition to Run dotnet restore. See Figure 3-52.

Figure 3-52. *Run dotnet publish*

12. Add the Archive Files build step from the Task Catalog Utility tab to the build definition. Set the root folder for archiving to **CoreWebApp/bin/$(BuildConfiguration)/netcoreapp1.0/ publish**. Uncheck the "Prefix root folder name to archive paths" check box. Set archive type to zip. Let the "Archive file to create" feild remain with the default value of $(Build.Ar tifactStagingDirectory)/$(Build.BuildId).zip. This step will package the published Core web application as a zip file. See Figure 3-53.

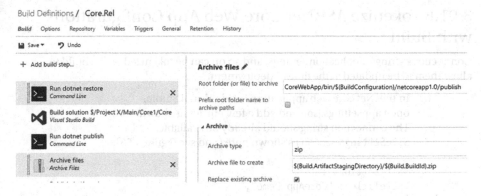

Figure 3-53. Add archive file step

13. Add the Publish Build Artifacts build step from Task Catalog's Utility tab to the build definition. Set Path to Publish field to $(Build.ArtifactStagingDirectory), Artifact Name field to Drop, and Artifact Type to Server. See Figure 3-54.

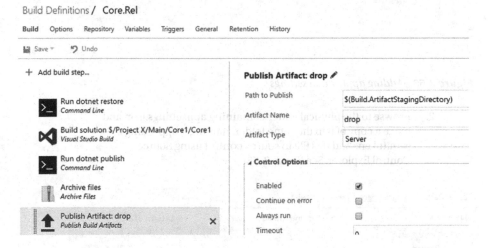

Figure 3-54. Publish Build Artifacts build task

14. Queue a build and download the artifacts. You will see that a zip file named by build number is created and available to download.

You have created a build definition with which to package Core web applications as zip files, which can be used with release management to deploy the application to target platforms, such as IIS and Azure App Service Apps.

119

3.01.6 Tokenize ASP.Net Core Web App Configurations with Build

Connections strings, application settings, and so on can be tokenized by the build to allow them to be updated at the time of deployment.

1. In the .Net core web application inside Visual Studio, open appsettings.json and add a few entries as shown. The connection string should already be available. Add a SiteSettings section as shown here (and see Figure 3-55):

```
"SiteSettings": {
"SiteTitle": "CoreApp Demo",
"ClientId": "4545445664656"
  },
```

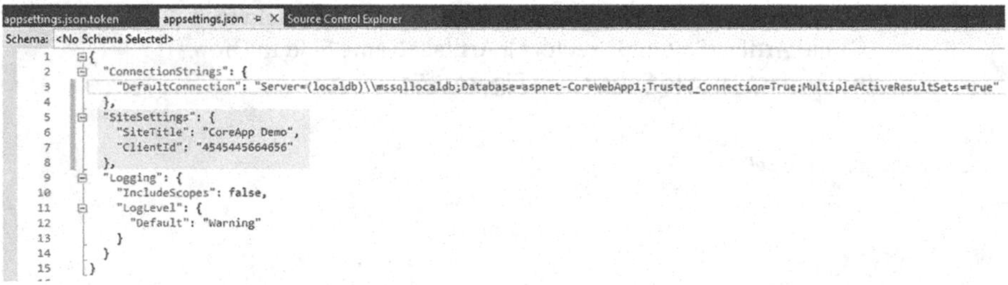

Figure 3-55. Adding application settings

2. Browse to the physical folder containing appsettings.json and make a copy of it in the same folder, naming it appsettings. json.token. Add this file to source control using Source Control Explorer. See Figure 3-56.

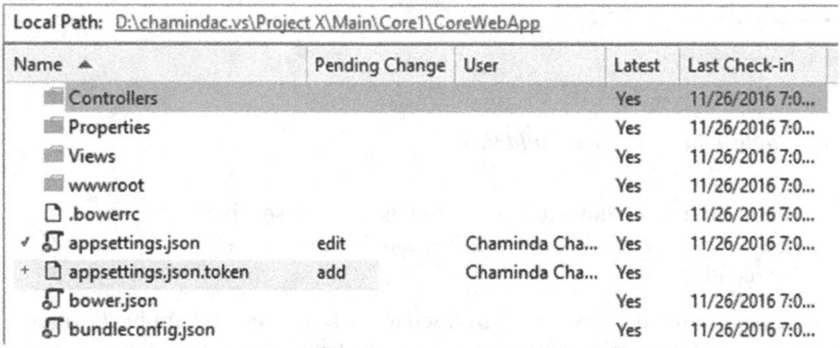

Local Path: D:\chamindac.vs\Project X\Main\Core1\CoreWebApp

Name ▲	Pending Change	User	Latest	Last Check-in
Controllers			Yes	11/26/2016 7:0...
Properties			Yes	11/26/2016 7:0...
Views			Yes	11/26/2016 7:0...
wwwroot			Yes	11/26/2016 7:0...
.bowerrc			Yes	11/26/2016 7:0...
✓ appsettings.json	edit	Chaminda Cha...	Yes	11/26/2016 7:0...
+ appsettings.json.token	add	Chaminda Cha...	Yes	
bower.json			Yes	11/26/2016 7:0...
bundleconfig.json			Yes	11/26/2016 7:0...

Figure 3-56. Copy of appsettings.json as token file

3. Open appsettings.json.token and edit the values to be tokens by adding prefixes and suffixes of __ (double underscore). These tokens can be replaced at the deployment time to values required for the target environment. See Figure 3-57.

```
appsettings.json.token  ⊸ ×  appsettings.json        Source Control Explorer
Schema: <No Schema Selected>
    1    ⊟{
    2    ⊟    "ConnectionStrings": {
    3             "DefaultConnection": "__DefaultConnection__"
    4         },
    5    ⊟    "SiteSettings": {
    6             "SiteTitle": "__SiteTitle__",
    7             "ClientId": "__ClientId__"
    8         },
    9    ⊟    "Logging": {
   10             "IncludeScopes": false,
   11    ⊟        "LogLevel": {
   12                 "Default": "Warning"
   13             }
   14         }
   15    }
```

Figure 3-57. Tokenizing settings

4. In Source Control Explorer, create a folder called BuildScripts in the Core1 solution folder and add a new PowerShell script file named TransformTokens.ps1. Add the following content to the script file:

```
$TokenFiles = gci $Env:BUILD_SOURCESDIRECTORY -recurse
-include "*.token"

foreach ($TokenFile in $TokenFiles)
{
    $OrginalFile = $TokenFile -replace ".token", ""
    Write-Host $TokenFile
    Write-Host $OrginalFile

    if ([IO.File]::Exists($OrginalFile))
    {
        Remove-Item $OrginalFile -Force
        Rename-Item -Path $TokenFile -NewName $OrginalFile
    }
}
```

5. The preceding script will remove the appsettings.json with the build and rename appsettings.json.token to appsettings.json. This method keeps the tokenized parameters in the .token file for each setting in appsettings.json.

6. Check in to source control the appsettings.json and appsettings.json.token files and the build script TransformTokens.ps1.

7. Edit the Core.Rel build definition and add a PowerShell build step (PowerShell Script task). Set the script TransformTokens. ps1 as the script to execute. See Figure 3-58.

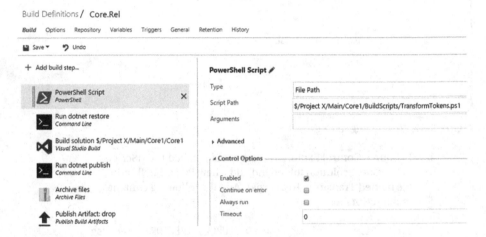

Figure 3-58. *Transform tokens build step*

8. Queue a build and download the build artifact zip file. Extract it and check appsetting.json to verify that it contains the tokens for the values in question. See Figure 3-59.

Figure 3-59. *Build transforming app settings*

In this lesson, you have enabled application settings transformations using a .token file and a PowerShell script–based build task.

You have created two ASP.NET web applications, MVC and Core, in the previous few lessons. Also, you have enabled configuration transformations for both of the web applications and set up builds to generate deployable artifacts. In the next few lessons, let's get these applications deployed to IIS using Team Services release management.

Lesson 3.02 – Deploy ASP.NET Web Applications to IIS

This lesson will provide a step-by-step guide to deploying ASP.NET MVC5 and .NET Core 1 web applications to IIS using the release management features of TFS and Team Services.

3.02.1 Deploy MVC5 Web Application to IIS

Prerequisites: Install IIS deployment extension to TFS/VSTS from Marketplace https://marketplace.visualstudio.com/items?itemName=ms-vscs-rm.iiswebapp (for instructions on installing Marketplace extensions, refer to Chapter 2). Set up build/release agent on a machine that has line of sight to the machine with IIS. On

the IIS machine, configure WinRM (https://msdn.microsoft.com/en-us/library/
aa384372(v=vs.85).aspx) and the Win RM IIS extension (http://www.dell.com/support/
Article/lk/en/lkbsdt1/SLN293852/EN). Allow file and printer sharing on the IIS machine
so that you can ping it from the agent machine. Make sure Web Deploy is installed on
the IIS machine (https://www.iis.net/learn/install/installing-publishing-
technologies/installing-and-configuring-web-deploy-on-iis-80-or-later).

1. Go to the IIS machine and set up a new website, MVC5Demo.
    Right click on the site and select **Deploy ➤ Configure Web
    Deploy Publishing**. See Figure 3-60.

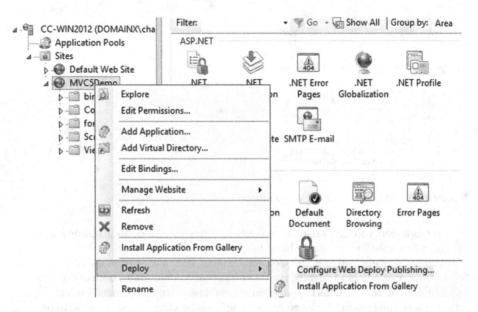

Figure 3-60. *Create site in IIS and configure Web Deploy*

2. Configure web deployment for the site by clicking on the
    Setup button. See Figure 3-61.

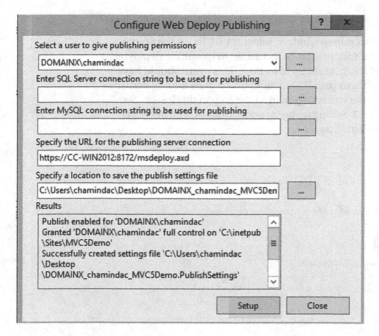

Figure 3-61. Setting up Web Deploy

3. In the **Build & Release** tab of the TFS/VSTS web portal, choose the **Releases** tab and click on the **New Definition** button. See Figure 3-62.

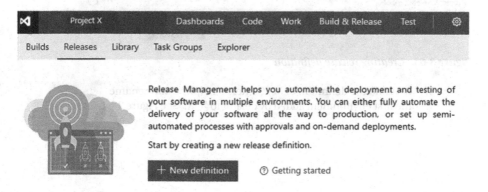

Figure 3-62. Create New Release

4. In the popup window, select Empty definition and click **Next**.

5. In the next popup window, select MVC5.Rel in the Source (build definition) field. Select an agent queue for deployment that has an agent set up in its pool. This agent should have line of sight to your IIS machine. You will be adding demands to select the correct agent in a later step in this lesson. See Figure 3-63. Setting up agent pools, queues, and agents is explained in Chapter 2.

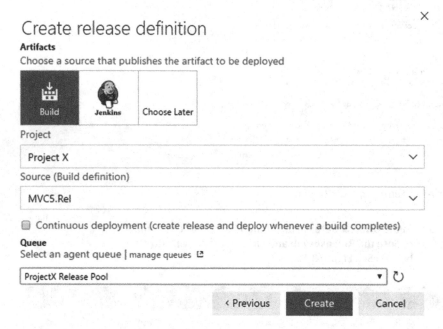

Figure 3-63. *Creating release definition*

6. Rename the definition to MVC5.ReleasePipline and rename the first environment added by default to "QA." See Figure 3-64.

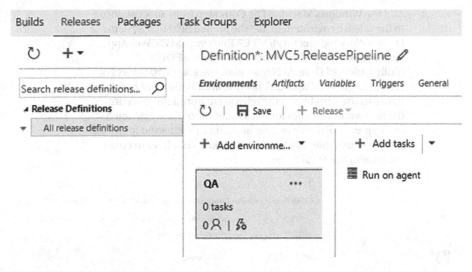

Figure 3-64. Renaming environment to QA

7. Click on **Run on agent** and set the demands to locate the correct agent (set the agent.name demand) for deployment. See Figure 3-65.

Figure 3-65. Setting agent demand with agent name

8. Add the Windows Machine File Copy step from Task catalogue to the release environment. Set the Source field to $(System. DefaultWorkingDirectory)/MVC5.Rel/Drop/MVS5WebApp_ Package. For the Machines field, provide the FQDN (Fully Qualified Domain Name) of the target IIS machine. For Admin Login and Password, provide admin user and password (you can use variables in the release environment to secure the password; variables for release definitions are explained in Chapter 1) of the target machine. Set a destination folder on the target machine as a local path. (You do not have to create the folder.) See Figure 3-66.

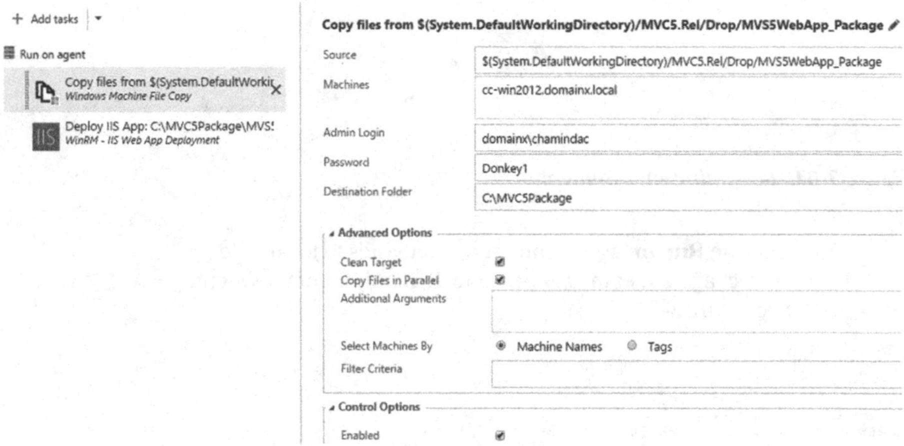

Figure 3-66. *Copy file command to copy deployment package to target*

9. Add the Win RM IIS Web App Deployment task from the Task Catalog to the release environment to Run on agent phase. For the Machines field, provide target IIS machine FQDN. Provide admin login information for the target IIS machine. In the Deployment section, provide the Web Deploy Package location (this is copied by previous task to local folder of the IIS machine). Web Deploy Parameter File should be .SetParameters.xml. Provide override values for .Setparameters.xml in Override Parameters field. Each entry should be in a separate line. See Figure 3-67.

```
name="IIS Web Application Name",value="MVC5Demo"
name="ClientIdParam",value="222223333344"
name="DefaultConnection-Web.config Connection String",
value="Server=localhost;Database=MVC5DemoDB;"
```

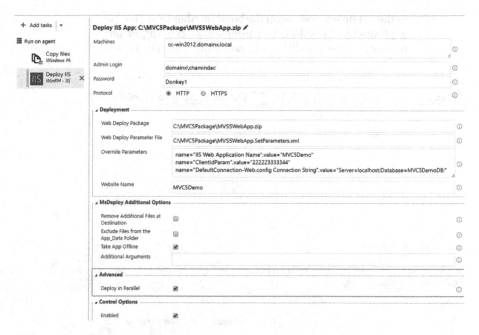

Figure 3-67. *WinRM IIS app deployment*

Check the "Take App Offline" option to allow taking the web application offline while deploying.

10. Save the release definition and create a new release by clicking the Release menu arrow and then selecting **Create Release**. See Figure 3-68.

Figure 3-68. *Creating a new release*

11. In the popup window, select the build number to use for the deployment. Check the QA environment is set to trigger after release creation and click the **Create** button. See Figure 3-69.

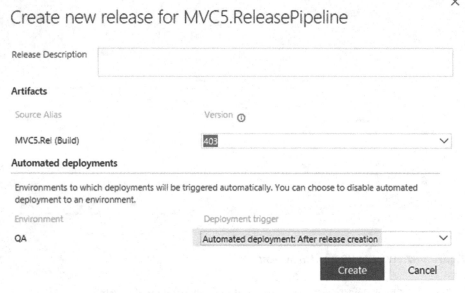

Figure 3-69. *Creating new release*

12. You can view the release progress by clicking on the release name link, that appears aft er creating the release, on top of the release definition and viewing the release log. See Figure 3-70.

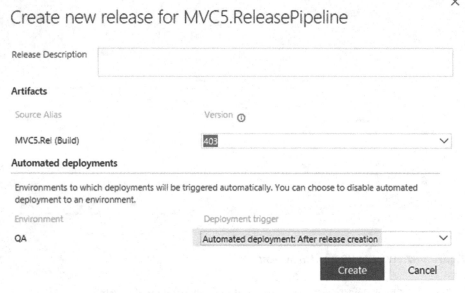

Figure 3-70. *Release in progress*

13. Once the deployment is completed, verify the IIS target machine. The site should be up and running, and web.config should have been applied with the values from the release definition step. See Figure 3-71.

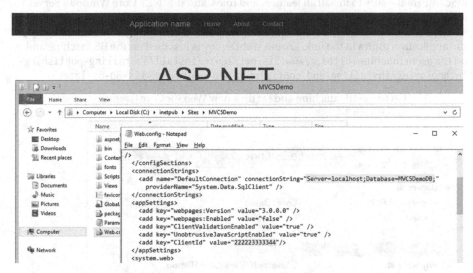

Figure 3-71. *Site deployed and web.config applied with values from release definition*

You have successfully deployed the MVC web application to IIS via TFS release management. You learned how to replace tokenized parameters in the .SetParameters file with the environment-specific values via the IIS Win RM deployment component. The lesson used target environment values directly in IIS WIN RM. Instead, you can create variables in the environment by clicking on Environment menu ➤ Configure variables. These variables then can be used in the IIS Win RM component. For example, instead of the following line

```
name="ClientIdParam",value="222223333344"
you can use
name="ClientIdParam",value="$(System.ClientID)"
```

to replace the ClientId parameter, if a variable named System.ClientId is defined. Follow what you see in Figure 3-72:

Configure - 'QA' environment

Approvals · *Variables* · Deployment conditions · General

Define custom variables to use in this environment. You can also use pre-defined variables.

	Name	Value	
🗑	System.ClientId	222223333344	🔓

+ Variable

OK   Cancel

Figure 3-72. *Variables for configuration parameters*

131

3.02.2 Deploy .NET Core Web Application to IIS

Prerequisites: In addition to the prerequisites for Lesson 3.02.1, follow the instructions in https://docs.microsoft.com/en-us/aspnet/core/publishing/iis and set up the IIS machine (make sure to install all features and roles, and the .NET Core Windows Server Hosting bundle found at https://aka.ms/dotnetcore_windowshosting_1_1_0) with the prerequisites of the .NET Core. However, skip the application configuration and deploy the application topics in the link. Ensure WebDeploy is installed on the IIS machine and on the agent machine (https://www.iis.net/learn/install/installing-publishing-technologies/installing-and-configuring-web-deploy-on-iis-80-or-later).

1. Go to the IIS machine and set up a new WebSiteCore1Demo. See Figure 3-73.

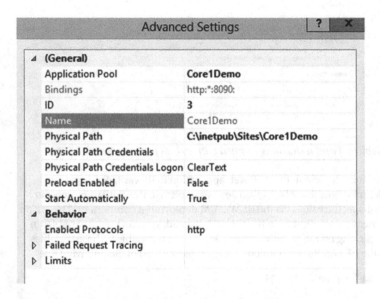

Figure 3-73. *Site settings for hosting core web application*

2. Configure Web Deploy publishing for the site, copy the URL, and add FQDN to make it accessible via network. Keep it for use in a later step (https://CC-WIN2012.domainx. local:8172/msdeploy.axd). See Figure 3-74.

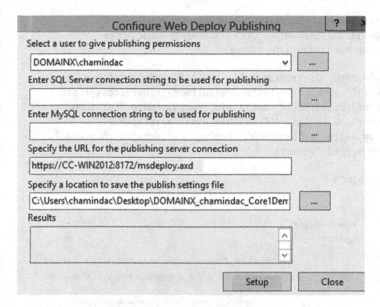

Figure 3-74. Configure Web Deploy publishing

3. Create a new release definition with an empty template to deploy the .NET Core web application to IIS. Use the same build as Core.Rel and set the agent pool to the team project release agent pool. Name the definition "Core1.ReleasePipeline."

4. Change the name of the environment to "QA" and set demands to locate the agent set up with web deploys (does not have to be the IIS machine. Using the IIS machine and setting up the agent there is also OK).

5. Add PowerShell tasks to the release environment and set it to run the following inline PowerShell script:

```
param($MSDeployPath, $package, $websiteName, $computerName,
$deployUser, $deployUserPwd)

. "$MSDeployPath\msdeploy" -verb:sync -source:package=$package
-dest:contentPath="$websiteName",computerName=$computerName,
username=$deployUser,password=$deployUserPwd,AuthType="Basic"
-enablelink:contentlibextension -enableRule:AppOffline
-enableRule:DoNotDeleteRule -allowUntrusted

Write-Host "##vso[task.complete result=Succeeded;]DONE"
```

6.   Pass the arguments seen in the following example to the script
     (change the computer name FQDN and website name values
     as per your machine and site names):

```
-MSDeployPath "C:\Program Files (x86)\IIS\Microsoft Web
Deploy V3" -package "$(System.DefaultWorkingDirectory)/Core.
Rel/drop/$(Build.BuildNumber).zip" -websiteName "Core1Demo"
-computerName "https://CC-WIN2012.domainx.local:8172/
msdeploy.axd?site=Core1Demo" -deployUser "domainx\chamindac"
-deployUserPwd "Donkey1"
```

See Figure 3-75.

Figure 3-75.   *Using PowerShell task to execute MSDeploy*

7.   Save and queue a new release, and the Core web application
     gets deployed to IIS. See Figure 3-76.

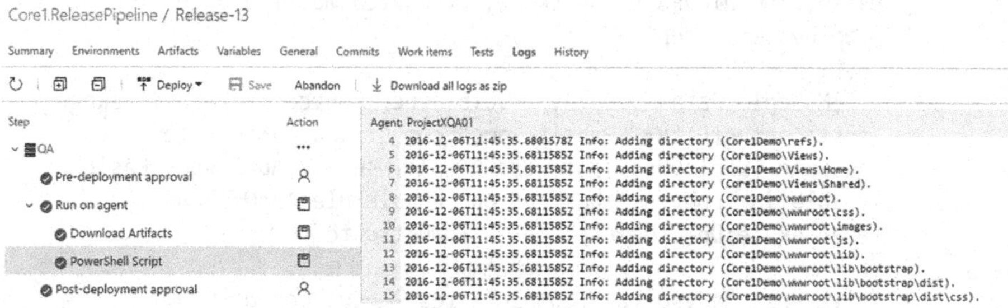

Figure 3-76.   *Deploying Core web application to IIS*

In this lesson, you have learned how to deploy the Core web app with release management using PowerShell. You can do further experiments and even create your own component for deploying Core web applications to IIS once you have completed this book. How to create your own build/release tasks is covered in Chapter 13.

Lesson 3.03 – Deploy ASP.NET Web Application to Azure App

The objective of this lesson is to provide a step-by-step guide to deploying ASP.NET MVC5 and .NET Core 1 web applications to the Azure App Service using the release management features of TFS and Team Services.

Prerequisites: You must have an Azure subscription, and you should be familiar with creating Azure App Service web apps. You should also have required access permissions (https://docs.microsoft.com/en-us/azure/azure-resource-manager/resource-group-create-service-principal-portal) to Azure.

3.03.1 Link Azure Subscription to TFS/VSTS Team Project

In this lesson, we will be enabling the connectivity between TFS/VS Team Services, Team Project, and your Azure account to enable deployments. We have two options for enabling the link between Azure and TFS/VSTS: classic and Resource Manager (RM). For this lesson, we will be using Azure RM.

1. In Team Project, click on Settings and then the **Services** tab, and then go to Endpoints ➤ Azure Resource Manager. See Figure 3-77.

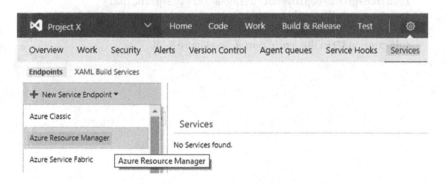

Figure 3-77. *Creating Azure Resource Manager endpoint*

2. In the popup window, click on the link to view the full details form. See Figure 3-78.

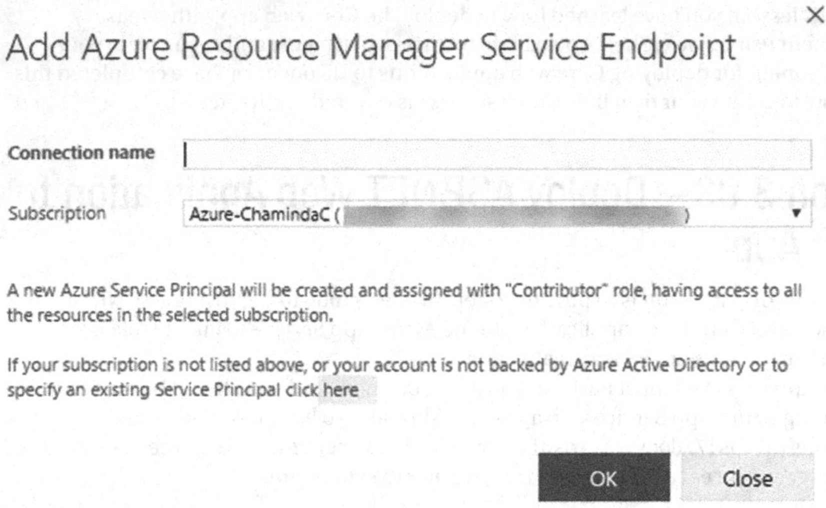

×

Add Azure Resource Manager Service Endpoint

Connection name | |

Subscription | Azure-ChamindaC (⬛⬛⬛⬛⬛⬛⬛⬛⬛⬛⬛⬛⬛) ▼ |

A new Azure Service Principal will be created and assigned with "Contributor" role, having access to all the resources in the selected subscription.

If your subscription is not listed above, or your account is not backed by Azure Active Directory or to specify an existing Service Principal click here

| OK | Close |

Figure 3-78. Azure subscription service endpoint

3. Leave that popup windows open. Open another browser window and download the PowerShell found at https:// github.com/Microsoft/vsts-rm-documentation/blob/ master/Azure/SPNCreation.ps1. Right click and get the properties of the downloaded script and unblock it. Then, run it to create a Service Principal (the blog post here has detailed steps: https://blogs.msdn.microsoft. com/visualstudioalm/2015/10/04/automating-azure- resource-group-deployment-using-a-service-principal- in-visual-studio-online-buildrelease-management/). You can find the Azure subscription name and the subscription ID in the Azure portal. See Figure 3-79.

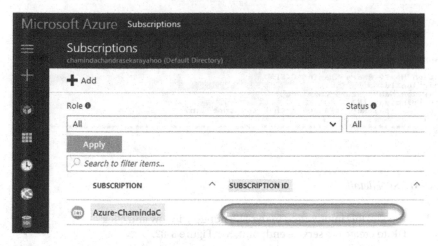

Figure 3-79. Azure subscription name and ID

4. Running SPNCreation.ps1 will prompt you for the Azure
    subscription name. Provide that as well as a password for
    the prompt. This password is used to set up for SPN (service
    principal name), and it should not be the subscription owner
    password. See Figure 3-80.

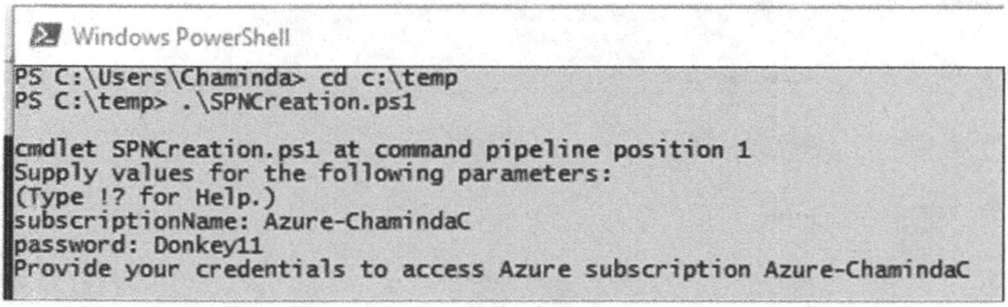

```
PS C:\Users\Chaminda> cd c:\temp
PS C:\temp> .\SPNCreation.ps1

cmdlet SPNCreation.ps1 at command pipeline position 1
Supply values for the following parameters:
(Type !? for Help.)
subscriptionName: Azure-ChamindaC
password: Donkey11
Provide your credentials to access Azure subscription Azure-ChamindaC
```

Figure 3-80. Running SPNCreation.ps1

With this information, a window will pop up in which to
provide your Azure subscription login details. Once you are
logged in, the script will create the Service Principal, and you
will get the ID and key information. See Figure 3-81.

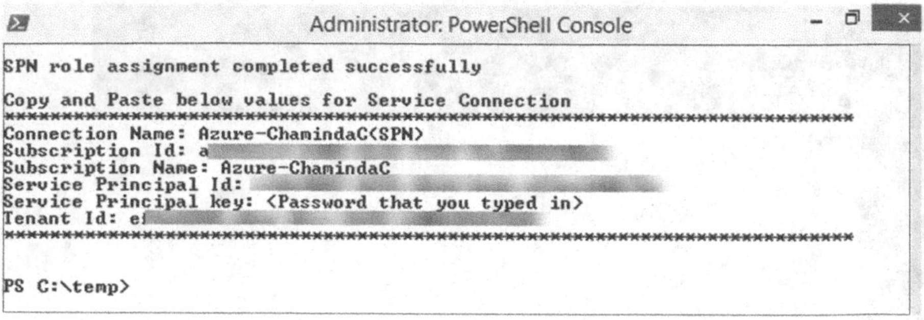

Figure 3-81. SPN details

5. Provide this information in the TFS popup window and click **OK** to create the service endpoint. See Figure 3-82.

Figure 3-82. Creating service end point in team project

You have created a service endpoint with which to link your Azure subscription to a team project. This is useful when you are not using the same Microsoft account for the deployment target Azure subscription and for your Team Services account (in a production scenario, the target Azure subscription owner is not the Team Services account owner). But, if you are using the same Microsoft account for both your Azure subscription and the Team Services account, the Azure subscription will be listed to select when you try to create a service end point in step 2 of this lesson. Once selected, it will be linked to the team project automatically after you authorize when prompted.

3.03.2 Deploy ASP .NET MVC5 Web App to Azure App Service

Prerequisites: You need a TFS agent set up with Azure PowerShell v1.3.0 (https://github.com/Azure/azure-powershell/releases/tag/v1.3.0-March2016) and WebDeploy 3.5 or higher installed with bundled SQL support. This can be installed with Microsoft Web Platform Installer (https://www.microsoft.com/web/gallery/install.aspx?appid=wdeploynosmo).

1. Open the MVC5.ReleasePipeline release definition created in Lesson 3.02.1 and add a new environment by setting it to run upon successful completion of the QA environment added earlier. Name the new environment "UAT." See Figure 3-83.

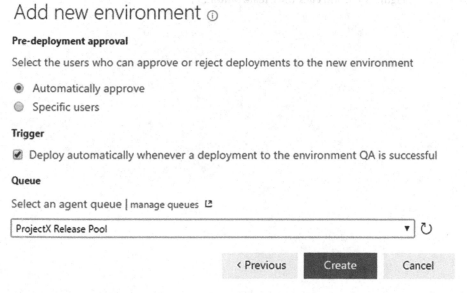

Figure 3-83. *Add new environment to release definition*

2. Set it to run on the agent set up with the specified prerequisites.

3. Add the Azure App Service Deploy step to the environment from the Deploy tab in the Task Catalog. Select the Azure RM endpoint created in Lesson 3.03.1. See Figure 3-84.

Figure 3-84. *Azure App Service Deploy step*

4. In Azure portal, under App Services, click **Add**, then select Web App. In the Web App window, click Create to create a new app service, Web App. Fill in the details as shown in Figure 3-85, and click the Create button.

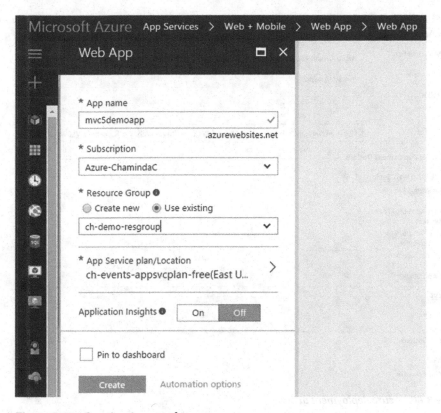

Figure 3-85. *Creating Azure web app*

5. Select the app service's name after using the Refresh button near the dropdown menu. Select the package to deploy and set it to use WebDeploy. Take the application offline while deploying. See Figure 3-86.

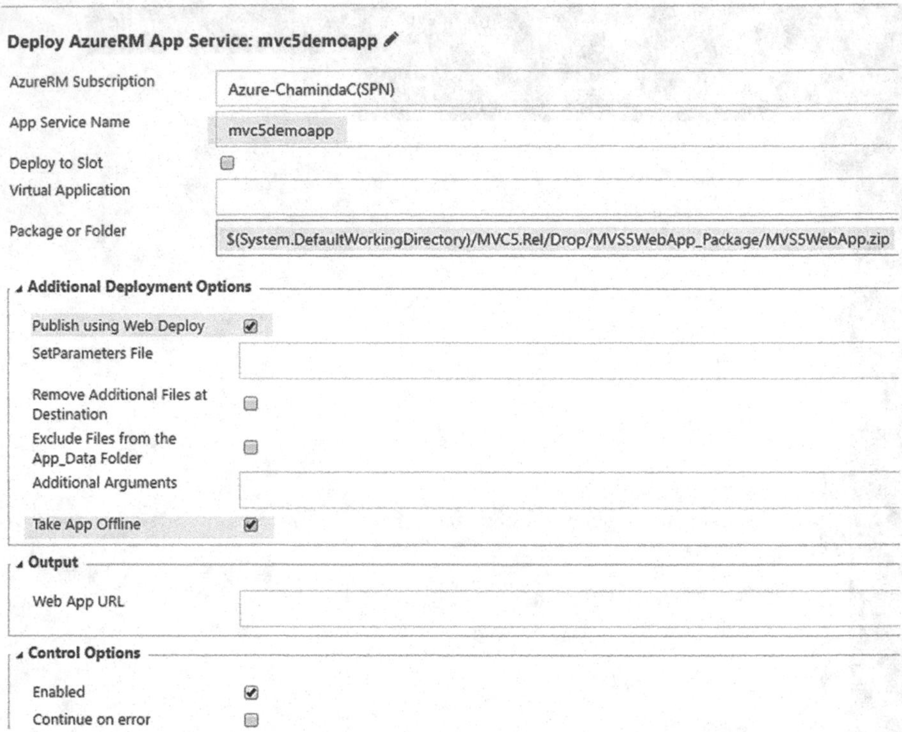

Deploy AzureRM App Service: mvc5demoapp ✎

AzureRM Subscription	Azure-ChamindaC(SPN)
App Service Name	mvc5demoapp
Deploy to Slot	☐
Virtual Application	
Package or Folder	$(System.DefaultWorkingDirectory)/MVC5.Rel/Drop/MVS5WebApp_Package/MVS5WebApp.zip

⊿ Additional Deployment Options

Publish using Web Deploy	☑
SetParameters File	
Remove Additional Files at Destination	☐
Exclude Files from the App_Data Folder	☐
Additional Arguments	
Take App Offline	☑

⊿ Output

Web App URL	

⊿ Control Options

Enabled	☑
Continue on error	☐

Figure 3-86. *Azure deployment task*

6. Trigger a release. You can see MVC5 web app get deployed to the first environment and, upon success, get deployed to Azure App Service. You can browse to the Azure App Service's site URL (available on the Azure Portal Web App overview page) and verify that the MVC application is deployed and running. See Figure 3-87.

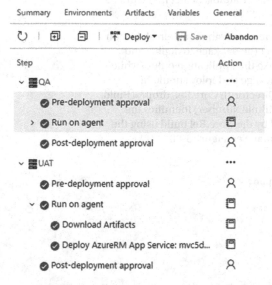

Figure 3-87. MVC web application deploying to Azure

In this lesson, you have learned how to deploy an MVC web application to Azure App Service using Team Services release management. Learn about Azure App Services (https://docs.microsoft.com/en-us/azure/app-service-web/web-sites-configure) and experiment with deployments by changing the configuration of deployment tasks in release management.

3.03.3 Deploy ASP .NET Core Web App to Azure App Service

Prerequisites: You need a TFS agent set up with Azure PowerShell v1.3.0 (https://github.com/Azure/azure-powershell/releases/tag/v1.3.0-March2016) and WebDeploy 3.5 or higher installed with bundled SQL support. This can be installed with Microsoft Web Platform Installer (https://www.microsoft.com/web/gallery/install.aspx?appid=wdeploynosmo).

1. Open the Core1.ReleasePipeline release definition created in Lesson 3.02.2 and add a new environment by setting it to run upon successful completion of the QA environment added earlier. Name new environment "UAT."

2. Set it to run on the agent set up with the prerequisites specified.

3. In the Azure portal, create a new app service called "Web App."

4. Add the Azure App Service Deploy step to the environment from the Deploy tab in the Task Catalog. Select the Azure RM endpoint created in Lesson 3.03.1.

5. Select the app service's name after using the Refresh button near dropdown menu. Select the package to deploy and set it to use Web Deploy. Take the application offline while deploying. Note that the package to deploy should be $(System.DefaultWorkingDirectory)/Core.Rel/drop/$(Build.BuildNumber).zip. $(Build.BuildNumber) identifies the name of the zip file created by the Core.Rel build using the buildnumber.zip name format. See Figure 3-88.

Deploy AzureRM App Service: CoreDemoAppAz ✏   Version 2.*

Azure Subscription	Azure-ChamindaC(SPN) ∨ ↻
App Service name	CoreDemoAppAz ∨ ↻
Deploy to slot	☐ ⓘ
Virtual Application	ⓘ
Package or Folder	$(System.DefaultWorkingDirectory)/Core.Rel/drop/$(Build.BuildNumber).zip ⋯

▲ **Additional Deployment Options**

Publish using Web Deploy	☑
SetParameters File	
Remove Additional Files at Destination	☐
Exclude Files from the App_Data Folder	☐
Additional Arguments	
Take App Offline	☑

▲ **Output**

App Service URL	

▲ **Control Options**

Enabled	☑

Figure 3-88. *Core web application deployment task*

6. Trigger a release, and you can see the ASP .NET Core web app get deployed to the first environment (IIS) and, upon success, get deployed to Azure App Service. See Figure 3-89.

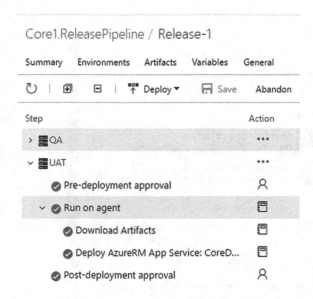

Figure 3-89. *Core web application deploying to Azure*

You have deployed an ASP.NET Core web application to Azure App Service using Team Foundation release management.

Summary

You have learned the basics of TFS/VSTS release management in this chapter. You are now capable of creating release environments and adding deployment actions to them. To further enhance your knowledge, carry out the following experiments.

1. Use approvers in pre- and post-deployment. You can set approvers for each environment and at execution time override these approvals. Experiment and learn. To get environment approvers, click on the menu in each environment (explained in Chapter 1). See Figure 3-90.

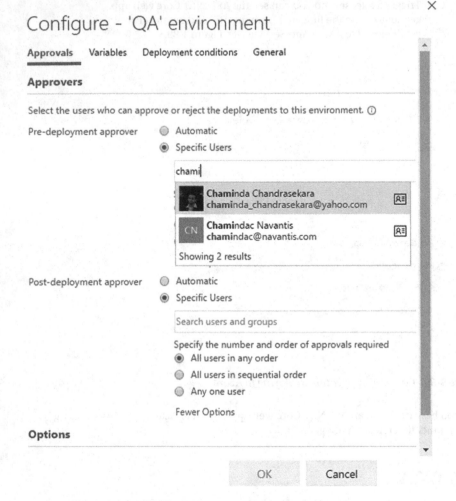

Figure 3-90. Approvers in deployment environments

2. Try different deployment conditions. You can trigger deployment after one or more environments are done, on a schedule, or right after release created with the definition. See Figure 3-91.

×

Configure - 'QA' environment

Approvals   Variables   *Deployment conditions*   General

Trigger

Define the trigger that will start deployment to this environment.

○ No automated deployment
○ After release creation
◉ After successful deployment to another environment
   Trigger a new deployment on this environment after successful deployment on the selected environment.
   Triggering environment(s) | Select   ▼ |

             ☐ Also trigger for partially succeeded deployment(s)
   ☑ Scheduled
   Trigger a new deployment to this environment at a specified time.
   24h time: | 03 ▼ | : | 00 ▼ | | (UTC+05:30) Sri Jayawardenepura   ▼ |
   Su☐ M☑ Tu☑ W☑ Th☑ F☑ Sa☐

Options

Define behavior when multiple releases are waiting to be deployed on this environment. ⓘ

◉ Allow multiple releases to be deployed at the same time
○ Allow only one active deployment at a time

| OK | | Cancel |

Figure 3-91. *Deployment conditions for environments*

Trigger on Partially succeeded environments allow you to continue an environment deployment tasks even if the previous environment had errors in tasks set to continue on error (deployment step failed is not considered a failure of the deployment to environment if you select "Continue on error" check box in Control Options section of the task). See Figure 3-92.

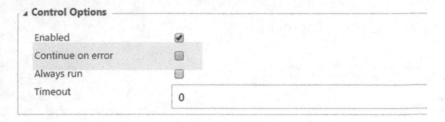

Figure 3-92. *Continue to next task on error in the current task*

3. Try the Manual Intervention server space task from Task Catalog. See Figure 3-93.

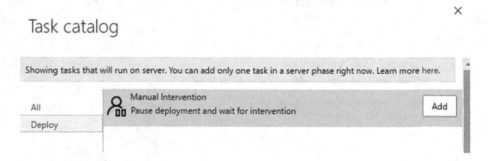

Figure 3-93. *Manual intervention*

4. Try deployment timeouts and skip artifacts for non-deployment actions on environments. See Figure 3-94.

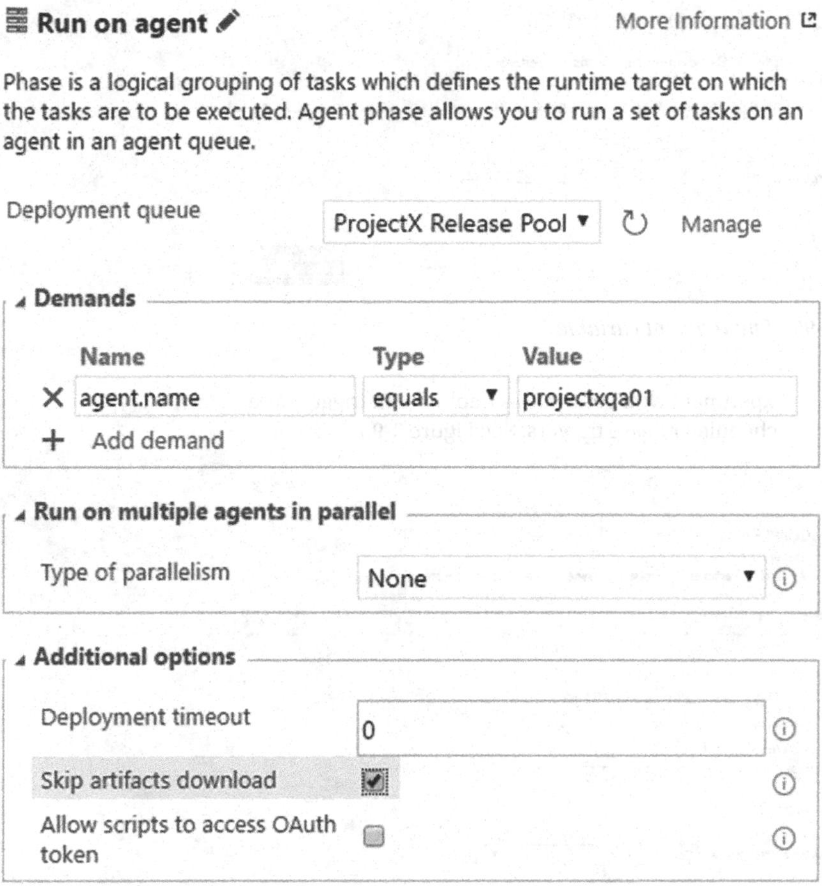

▤ Run on agent ✏

More Information ↗

Phase is a logical grouping of tasks which defines the runtime target on which the tasks are to be executed. Agent phase allows you to run a set of tasks on an agent in an agent queue.

Deployment queue ProjectX Release Pool ▼ ↻ Manage

◢ Demands

Name	Type	Value
✕ agent.name	equals ▼	projectxqa01
✛ Add demand		

◢ Run on multiple agents in parallel

Type of parallelism None ▼ ⓘ

◢ Additional options

Deployment timeout 0 ⓘ

Skip artifacts download ☑ ⓘ

Allow scripts to access OAuth token ☐ ⓘ

Figure 3-94. Run on agent additional options

5. Use variables with release definitions. Access them in deployment or build steps using the syntax $(variablename). You can define variables at the release definition level and at each environment level. Predefined variables (https://www. visualstudio.com/en-us/docs/release/author-release-definition/understanding-tasks#predefvariables) are available to use for any release definition. If you have defined variables with names releasedefvar01 and releaseenvvar01, you can use them in any text field of a deployment/build step using $(releasedefvar01) and $(releaseenvvar01). See Figure 3-95.

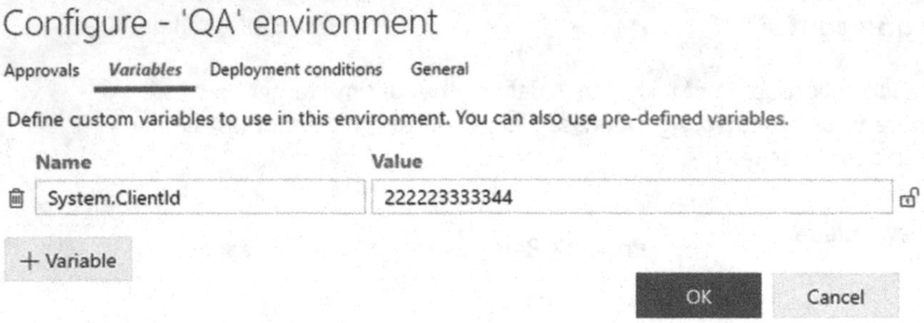

Configure - 'QA' environment

Approvals   *Variables*   Deployment conditions   General

Define custom variables to use in this environment. You can also use pre-defined variables.

Name	Value	
🗑 System.ClientId	222223333344	🔓

+ Variable

OK   Cancel

Figure 3-95. *Environment variables*

6. Experiment with continuous deployment triggers and scheduled release triggers. See Figure 3-96.

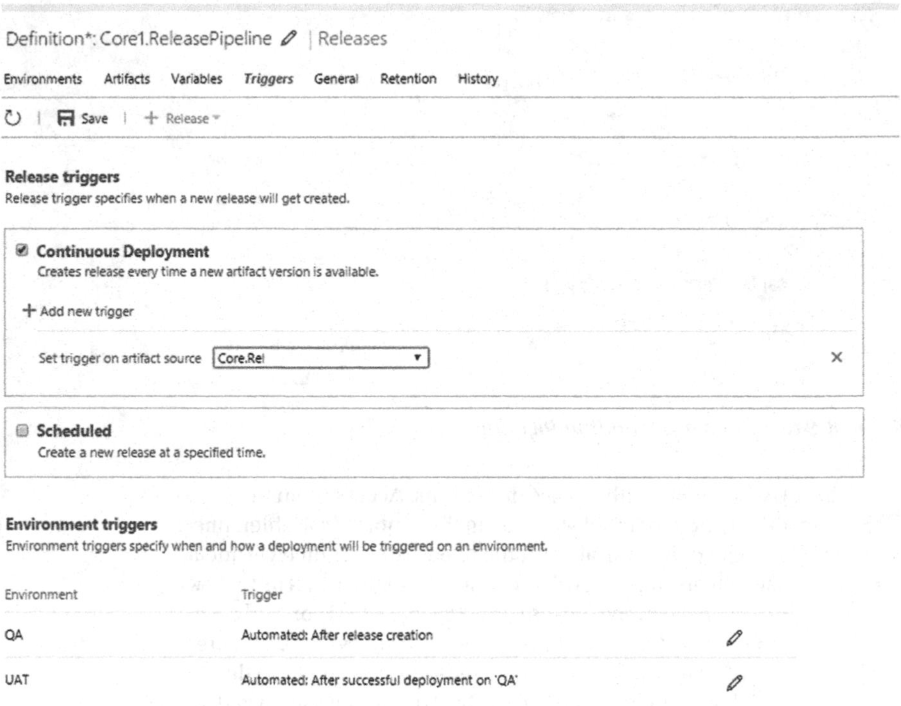

Definition*: Core1.ReleasePipeline ✎ | Releases

Environments   Artifacts   Variables   *Triggers*   General   Retention   History

↻ | 🖫 Save | + Release ▾

Release triggers
Release trigger specifies when a new release will get created.

☑ **Continuous Deployment**
   Creates release every time a new artifact version is available.

 + Add new trigger

   Set trigger on artifact source | Core.Rel   ▼ | ✕

☐ **Scheduled**
   Create a new release at a specified time.

Environment triggers
Environment triggers specify when and how a deployment will be triggered on an environment.

Environment	Trigger	
QA	Automated: After release creation	✎
UAT	Automated: After successful deployment on 'QA'	✎

Figure 3-96. *Continuous deployment*

7. Further experiment with Azure slot deployments, swap
   deployment slots, and usage of slot settings. Read below
   articles and experiment.

   https://docs.microsoft.com/en-us/azure/app-service-web/web-sites-staged-publishing
   http://chamindac.blogspot.com/2016/08/azure-website-swap-slotwith-vsts.html

In the next chapter, you will learn about building Docker-enabled web applications and deploying to Azure App Services on Linux using Team Services release management.

CHAPTER 4

■ ■ ■

Build as Docker and Deploy to Azure

This chapter will take you through the steps required to build ASP.Net Core as a Docker container and upload the image to the Azure container registry (to learn more visit https://docs.microsoft.com/en-us/azure/container-registry/) using a Team Services build. You will also learn how to use the Docker container image in the Azure container registry to host an application in Azure App Service on Linux (more information available at https://docs.microsoft.com/en-us/azure/app-service-web/app-service-linux-intro).

■ **Note** The Docker tools for Team Services are still evolving. As of writing of this book, the Team Services tasks for Docker are in their early stages. The chapter summary describes a few more upcoming options regarding Azure's capabilities to handle Docker containers and VSTS Release Management's capabilities when combined with Visual Studio 2017.

Prerequisites: Ensure you have a 64-bit Windows 10 Pro, Enterprise, or Education (1511 November update, Build 10586 or later) machine installed with Visual Studio 2017 RC3 or later. You need a Team Services account and the extension for Docker (https://marketplace.visualstudio.com/items?itemName=ms-vscs-rm.docker) installed for that account. You are familiar working with Azure portal to create web apps etc.

Set Up the Environment to Develop Docker-enabled Application

The following steps will guide you in setting up VS 2017 and Docker for Windows, enabling you to create Docker-enabled .NET Core applications.

1. Make sure you have installed Visual Studio 2017 RC3 or later with ASP.NET and web development to enable web application development. See Figure 4-1.

© Chaminda Chandrasekara 2017
C. Chandrasekara, *Beginning Build and Release Management with TFS 2017 and VSTS*,
DOI 10.1007/978-1-4842-2811-1_4

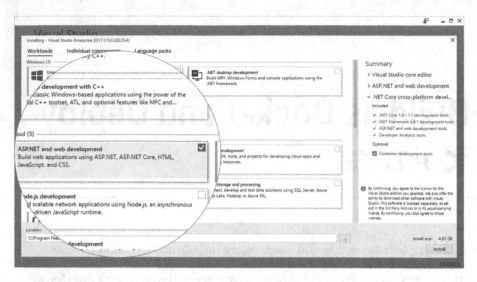

Figure 4-1. *Install VS 2017 ASP.NET and web development*

2. Install .NET Core cross-platform development, including container development tools. Container development tools allow you to create Docker-enabled ASP.NET core applications. See Figure 4-2.

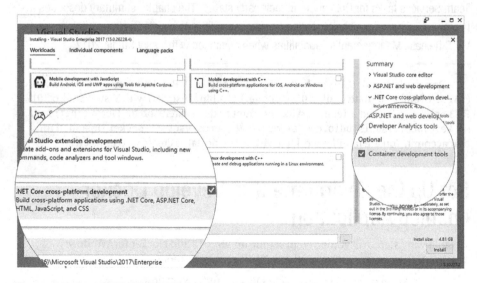

Figure 4-2. *Install VS 2017 .NET Core cross-platform development*

3. Download Docker for Windows from `https://docs.docker.com/docker-for-windows/install/#download-docker-for-windows`. Docker for windows allow you to develop Docker enabled applications in a Windows PC. For more information visit `https://www.docker.com/docker-windows`. Once completed, run downloaded MSI and click **Install**; follow the installation wizard steps. See Figure 4-3.

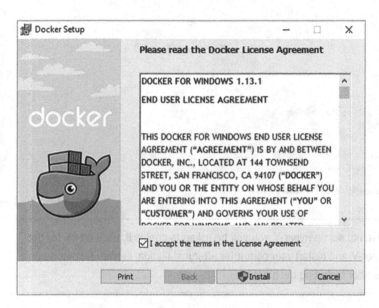

Figure 4-3. *Installing Docker for Windows*

4. Once the installation has completed, you will see an option available to "**Launch Docker.**" Select it and click on **Finish**. See Figure 4-4.

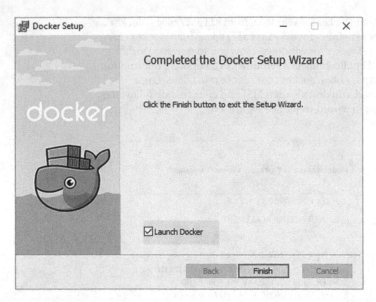

Figure 4-4. Select Launch Docker and Finish

■ **Note** If you have not set up Hyper-V, you will be asked to enable it. Click on OK for the message, install Hyper-V, and restart your computer after installation. Launch Docker again from the Start menu after restarting the machine.

---

5. Docker is shown as starting in the system tray. Once it has completed setting things up, you will be notified, as shown in Figure 4-5.

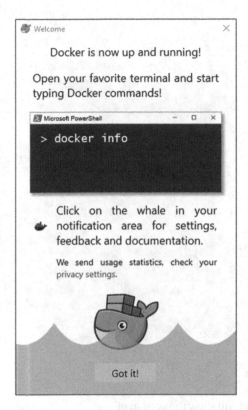

Figure 4-5. Docker is up and running

6. Open PowerShell and run a few Docker commands to confirm that Docker is running as expected on your machine.

docker info – This command will show the information about Docker for Windows. See Figure 4-6.

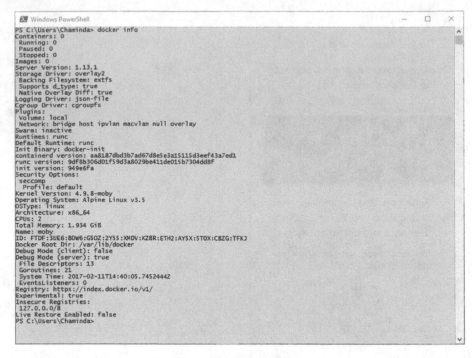

Figure 4-6. *Docker for Windows information*

docker version – This command will show the version of
Docker for Windows. See Figure 4-7.

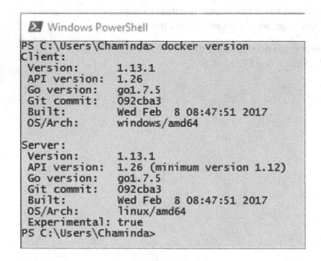

Figure 4-7. *Docker for Windows version*

7. In your computer's system tray, right click on Docker and select **Settings**. See Figure 4-8.

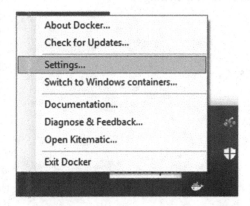

Figure 4-8. Launch Docker settings

8. Share the hard disk drives to Docker in the **Shared Drives** tab of the Docker Settings popup window. The system drive and the drive on which you plan to have your source code must be shared with Docker. Click **Apply** after selecting the desired drives to save the settings. See Figure 4-9.

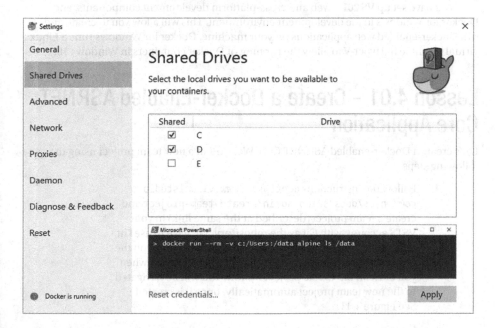

Figure 4-9. Sharing drives with Docker

9. Clicking **Apply** in the Shared Drives tab will open a popup window asking for authentication. Provide the credentials of the user you are logged on as to enable file sharing. See Figure 4-10.

Figure 4-10. *Authorizing shared drives access for Docker*

You have set up VS 2017, web and cross-platform development components, and Docker for Windows in the development environment. This will allow you to create and run Docker-enabled web applications on your machine. Docker for Windows runs a Linux virtual machine in Hyper-V to allow the running of Docker containers in Windows 10.

Lesson 4.01 – Create a Docker-Enabled ASP.NET Core Application

Let's create a Docker-enabled ASP.NET Core Web API in a new team project using the following steps.

1. Follow the instructions at https://www.visualstudio. com/en-us/docs/setup-admin/create-team-project and create a team project (described at the same link) in your VSTS account, with Git as the repository. We have to use Git repository since we are going to build the application on the Linux platform. The new team project will be created when you click on the Create project button. You will be navigated to the new team project automatically, once it is created. See Figure 4-11.

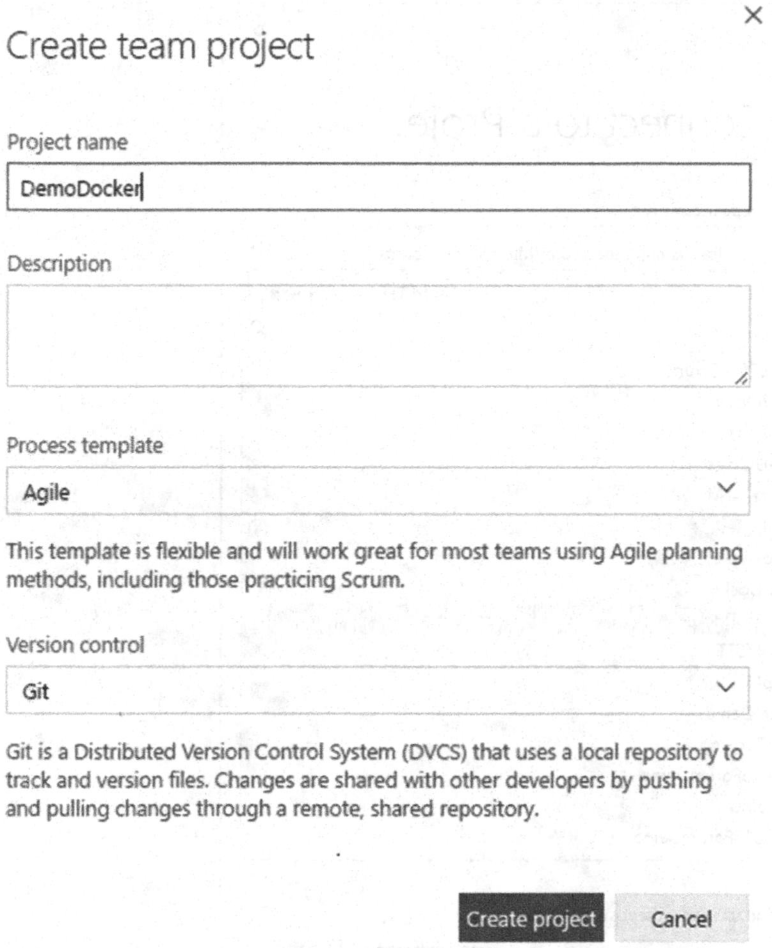

×

Create team project

Project name

DemoDocker|

Description

Process template

Agile ⌄

This template is flexible and will work great for most teams using Agile planning methods, including those practicing Scrum.

Version control

Git ⌄

Git is a Distributed Version Control System (DVCS) that uses a local repository to track and version files. Changes are shared with other developers by pushing and pulling changes through a remote, shared repository.

Create project   Cancel

Figure 4-11. Creating the team project

2. Open Visual Studio 2017 and, in Team Explorer, click on
    Manage Connections ➤ Connect to Project. In the resulting
    popup window, select your Microsoft account. If you are
    not signed in to your Microsoft account in VS 2017, sign in
    or add your Microsoft account using the **Showing hosted
    repositories for** dropdown. Select the Git repository of the
    team project created in Step 1 of this lesson, provide a **Path**
    for the local repository, and click the **Clone** button to clone
    the repository to your machine. See Figure 4-12.

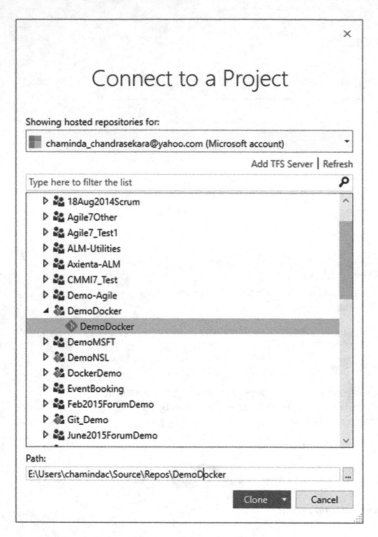

Figure 4-12. *Cloning the Git repository*

3. Create a new VS solution by clicking **New** under the **Solutions** tab in the Team Explorer window. See Figure 4-13.

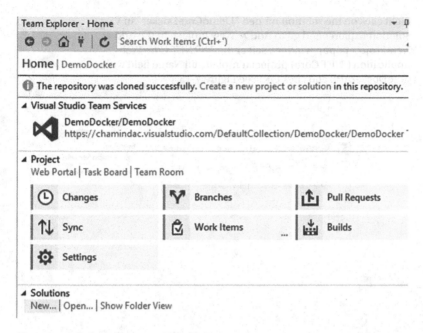

Figure 4-13. Creating a new VS solution

4. Select the Blank Solution template to create a new empty VS solution and name it "DemoCoreDocker." See Figure 4-14.

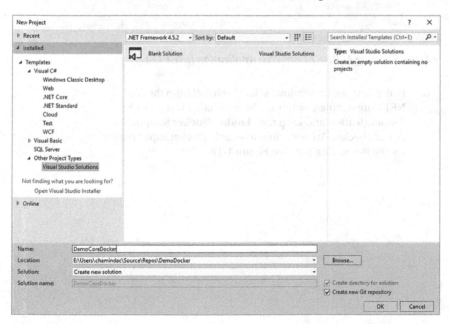

Figure 4-14. Creating an empty solution in Visual Studio

5. Right click on the solution named "DemoCoreDocker" in VS Solution Explorer and go to Add ➤ New Project. In the Add New Project popup window, select the ASP.NET Core Web Application (.NET Core) project template, fill Name field with CoreDockerAPI, and click OK. See Figure 4-15.

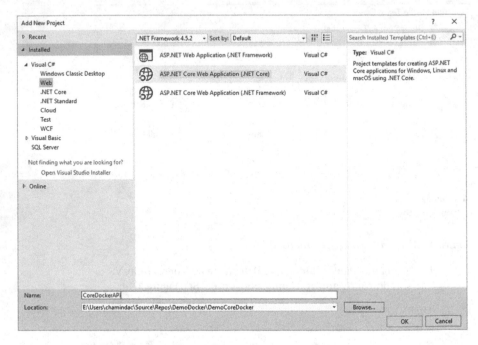

Figure 4-15. *Selecting ASP.NET Core Web Application (.NET Core)*

6. In the next popup window, select Web API from the ASP. NET Core template options. Check whether it is set as **No Authentication** and keep the **"Enable Docker Support"** box unchecked. We are going to enable Docker support after testing the application. See Figure 4-16.

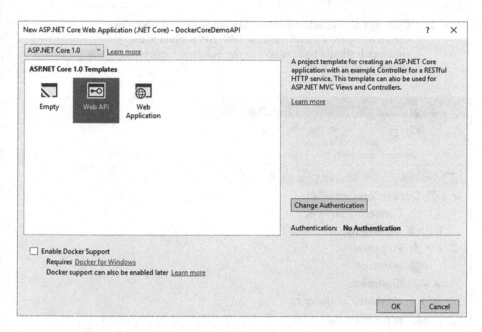

Figure 4-16. Creating ASP.NET Core Web API

If any other Authentication option is shown, click **Change Authentication** and set it to **No Authentication**. Click OK. See Figure 4-17.

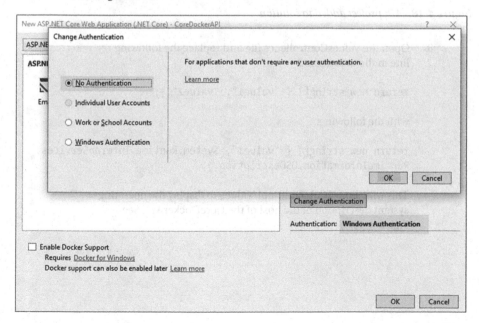

Figure 4-17. No authentication required

7. Clicking OK after selecting Web API template in the window shown in Figure 4-16 will add the Web API project to the solution. It should be available in the Solution Explorer, as shown in Figure 4-18.

Figure 4-18. *API project added to solution*

8. Open the ValuesController.cs file and replace the following line in the Get method

```
return new string[] { "value1", "value2" };
```

with the following:

```
return new string[] { "value1", System.Runtime.InteropServices.
RuntimeInformation.OSDescription };
```

This will allow the default /api/values to display the operating system description of the host of the CoreDockerAPI. See Figure 4-19.

```
ValuesController.cs ⇄ ✕
DockerCoreDemoAPI                    ▾ ᵃₜ DockerCoreDemoAPI.Controllers.ValuesControlle ▾ ⊕ Get(int id)            ▾
  1    ⊟using System;
  2     using System.Collections.Generic;
  3     using System.Linq;
  4     using System.Threading.Tasks;
  5     using Microsoft.AspNetCore.Mvc;
  6
  7    ⊟namespace DockerCoreDemoAPI.Controllers
  8     {
  9         [Route("api/[controller]")]
         0 references | 0 changes | 0 authors, 0 changes
 10    ⊟    public class ValuesController : Controller
 11         {
 12             // GET api/values
 13             [HttpGet]
         0 references | 0 changes | 0 authors, 0 changes
 14    ⊟        public IEnumerable<string> Get()
 15             {
 16                 return new string[] { "value1", System.Runtime.InteropServices.RuntimeInformation.OSDescription };
 17             }
 18
```

```
Solution Explorer
○ ○ ⌂ ⌖ ▾  ○ ▾ ↰ ∅
Search Solution Explorer (Ctrl+;)
  Solution 'DemoDocker'
  ▲  DockerCoreDemoAPI
       ⅁ Connected Services
    ▷ ■ Dependencies
    ▷ ᴶ Properties
    ⊟ wwwroot
    ▲  Controllers
       ▷ c# ValuesController.cs
    ▷ ⚙ appsettings.json
    ▷ c# Program.cs
    ▷ c# Startup.cs
```

Figure 4-19. *Allow web API to show host OS description*

9. Run the application by hitting F5 or use IIS Express, as shown in Figure 4-20.

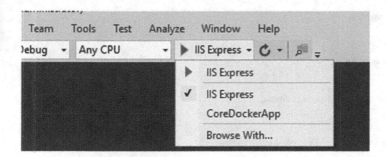

Figure 4-20. *Running the web API*

A browser window will launch, and you will see that the API is returning the current OS description as "Microsoft Windows" with the version number. This confirms the web API you have created is not yet enabled with Docker and is still running on the Windows platform. See Figure 4-21.

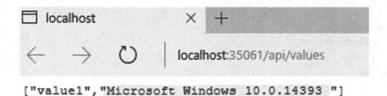

Figure 4-21. *Web API running on Windows OS*

10. Since we have a working web API project, before making any additional changes we should commit it to the repository. For this, click on **Changes** in the Team Explorer **Home** and commit the solution to the local Git repository. Then, you can push the changes to the Git repository of the team project by clicking on Push. We must push to the repository, since this is the first set of code that is committed. To learn more about working with Team Foundation Git with Visual Studio, refer to the article at https://www.visualstudio.com/en-us/docs/git/gitquickstart. See Figure 4-22.

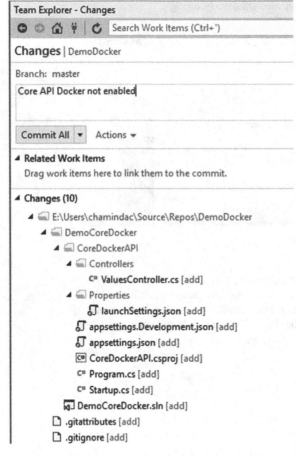

Figure 4-22. *Committing the solution to Git repository*

11. Let's add Docker support to the web API to enable it to be deployed as a Docker container. Right click on DockerCoreDemoApp in the Solution Explorer page and go to Add ➤ Docker Support. See Figure 4-23.

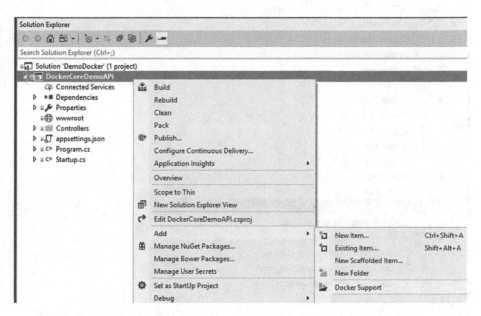

Figure 4-23. Adding Docker support to web API

12. New docker-compose.dcproj (it is the project highlighted in blue in Figure 4-24) and .yml files are added at the solution level. A Dockerfile is added to the CoreDockerAPI project, along with a .dockerignore file. Dockerfiles and .yml files contain the information required to compose a Docker container, while the .dockerignore file has the information on which content to ignore when packaging. You do not have to change anything for this lesson. You can get more information about these files in the following articles:

https://docs.docker.com/compose/compose-file/
https://docs.docker.com/engine/reference/builder/

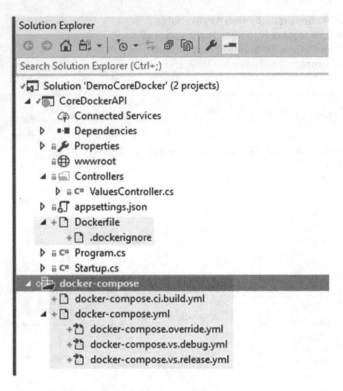

Figure 4-24. *Docker-enabled web API*

13.   docker-compose should be set as the startup project to enable
       running it with Visual Studio. If not available, right click on
       docker-compose and choose Set as Startup Project. Then,
       hit F5 or click on Docker, as shown in Figure 4-25, to run
       the web API in Docker. This will take few minutes to run, as
       it is building a Docker image and deploying it to a Docker
       container (Docker on Windows is enabled by running a Linux
       Docker container in Hyper-V).

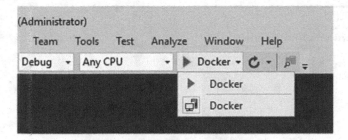

Figure 4-25. *Running web API with Docker*

A browser window will be launched, and you can see the running OS description shown as Linux. This confirms the web API is running in a Docker container on Linux. See Figure 4-26.

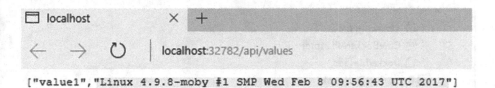

```
["value1","Linux 4.9.8-moby #1 SMP Wed Feb 8 09:56:43 UTC 2017"]
```

Figure 4-26. *Web API running on Linux Docker container*

14. Commit the new files to the local Git repository and sync changes with the team project Git repository to enable them to be built with a Team Services build in a future lesson in this chapter (https://www.visualstudio.com/en-us/docs/git/gitquickstart). See Figure 4-27.

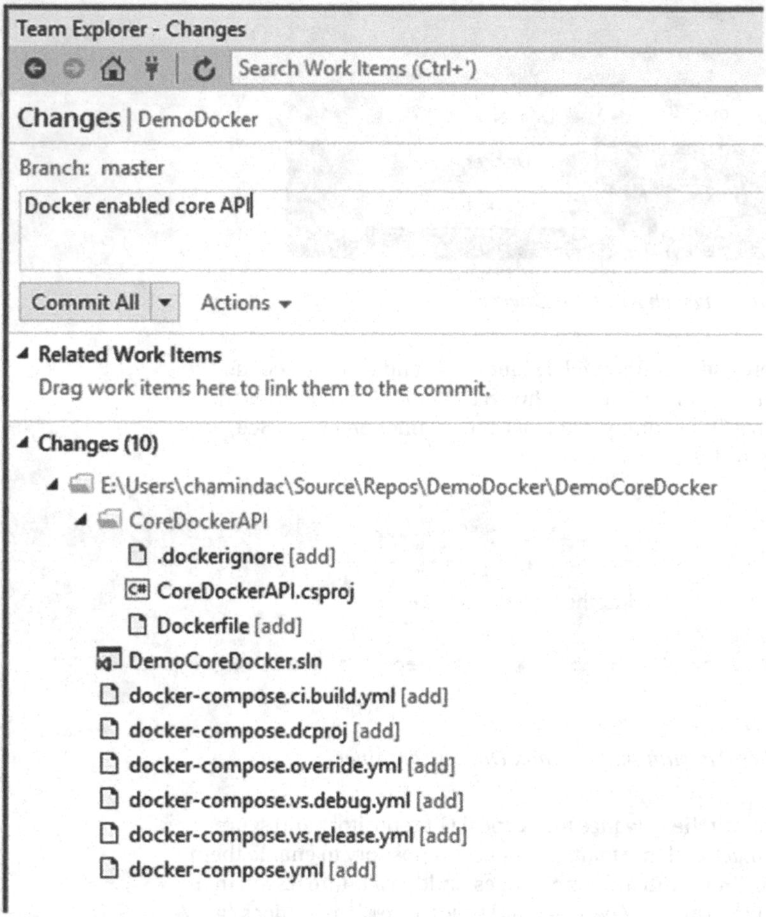

Team Explorer - Changes

⊙ ⊙ ⌂ ⅄ | ↻   Search Work Items (Ctrl+')

Changes | DemoDocker

Branch: master

Docker enabled core API|

Commit All ▼   Actions ▼

◢ **Related Work Items**
   Drag work items here to link them to the commit.

◢ **Changes (10)**

◢ 🖳 E:\Users\chamindac\Source\Repos\DemoDocker\DemoCoreDocker

   ◢ 🖿 CoreDockerAPI

     🗋 .dockerignore [add]

     [C#] CoreDockerAPI.csproj

     🗋 Dockerfile [add]

   🗗 DemoCoreDocker.sln

   🗋 docker-compose.ci.build.yml [add]

   🗋 docker-compose.dcproj [add]

   🗋 docker-compose.override.yml [add]

   🗋 docker-compose.vs.debug.yml [add]

   🗋 docker-compose.vs.release.yml [add]

   🗋 docker-compose.yml [add]

Figure 4-27. Committing Docker-enabled web API to Git repository

In this lesson, you have created a new team project with the team foundation Git as the source control repository and added a Docker-enabled web API to it. You managed to test the API locally and confirmed it can build a Docker image, which can be run on a Docker container on Linux.

Lesson 4.02 – Create Azure Container Registry

An Azure container registry lets you store images of containers, such as Docker Swarm, DC/OS, and Kubernetes, and of Azure services like Service Fabric, App Services, and so forth. It is a private Docker registry and provides you with local, network-close storage of your container images within your subscription. Learn more from `https://docs.microsoft.com/en-us/azure/container-registry/container-registry-intro`.

1. Go to the Azure portal and click the green + sign to add a new item. Type "Azure Container" in the search field and select Azure Container Registry from the list. See Figure 4-28.

Figure 4-28. Searching for Azure rontainer registry

In the search results, select Azure Container Registry by Microsoft. See Figure 4-29.

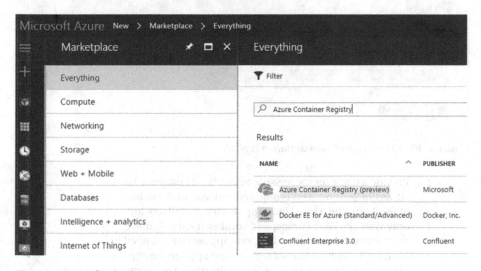

Figure 4-29. Selecting Azure Container Registry

2. Click on Create in the window that opens. See Figure 4-30.

Figure 4-30. *Creating the Azure container registry*

3. Provide a name for the registry. Select West Europe or West US as the location. This is required, since as of the writing of this book, the Azure Linux app service is available for only West US, West Europe, and Southeast Asia. To make the container available to the Linux app service, we need to have both, Azure container registry and app service app on Linux, set to the same region. Select the option to create a new resource group and provide a name. Enable Admin User, as we are going to use this user's username and password (both auto-generated) to connect the group to the app service app on Linux and so forth. Click on Create after providing all the information, as shown in Figure 4-31.

Figure 4-31. Filling in required information to create the container registry in Azure

4. The new resource group gets created with the name provided
in the previous step. You can click on Resource Groups in the
Azure portal to view the new resource group. See Figure 4-32.

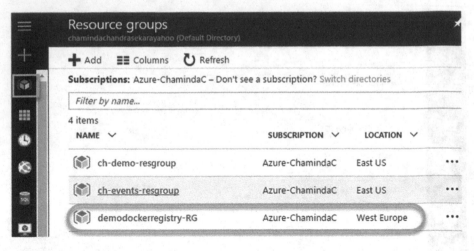

Figure 4-32. *New resource group*

5. Click on the new resource group name. You can see in the resource group that an Azure container registry gets created. See Figure 4-33.

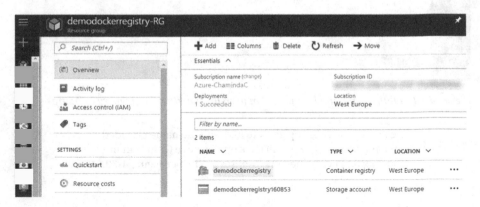

Figure 4-33. *New Azure container registry created*

You have created an Azure container registry using the Azure portal in this lesson. You will be using it in a future lesson in this chapter to deploy with the Docker-enabled ASP.NET Core web API, which we created in a previous lesson in this chapter.

Lesson 4.03 – Create Azure App Service on Linux App

The Azure app service on Linux can host web apps on Linux. The **app service app on Linux** you will create in this lesson will be used to host the Docker-enabled web API you created in a previous lesson in this chapter. Learn more at https://docs.microsoft.com/en-us/azure/app-service-web/app-service-linux-intro.

1. In the Azure portal, click on Resource Groups and click **Add**. You are going to use this new resource group to create an Azure app service app on Linux. See Figure 4-34.

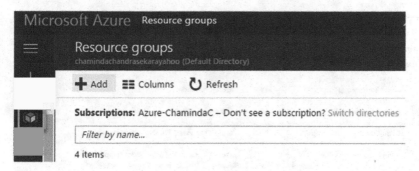

Figure 4-34. Adding a new resource group

2. Provide a name for the resource group and select the location as West Europe (region should be same region as that for the Azure container registry in the previous lesson). Click on Create. See Figure 4-35.

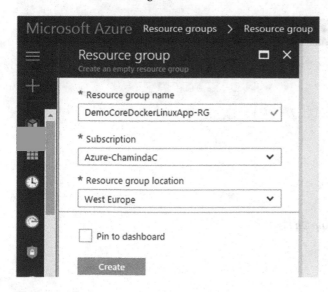

Figure 4-35. Creating new resource group

177

3. Now, we have both an Azure container registry resource group (created in the previous lesson) and a resource group for App Service App on Linux in the same region, West Europe. See Figure 4-36.

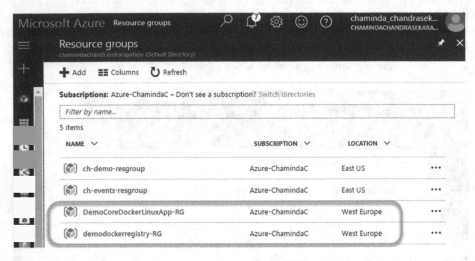

Figure 4-36. Both resource groups set to same region

4. In the Azure portal, click on the green + to add a new item and search for "app on linux." Select **Web App On Linux**. See Figure 4-37.

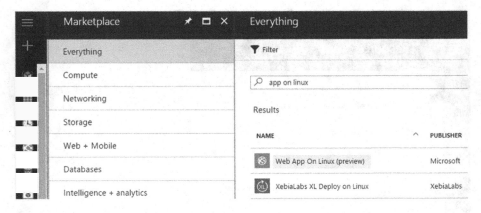

Figure 4-37. Selecting Web App On Linux

5.   Click **Create** on the preview page to create a web app on
      Linux. See Figure 4-38.

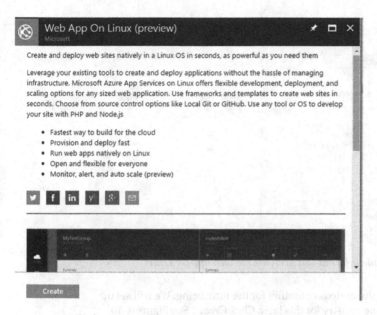

Figure 4-38. *Creating web app on Linux*

6.   Provide a name for the app. Select the **"Use Existing"**
      Resource Group option and select the resource group created
      in this lesson. You will see that a new **service plan** is created
      in the West Europe region (region should be the same region
      that you used for the Azure container registry in the previous
      lesson). Click on **Configure container** to configure the
      container option before creating the app. See Figure 4-39.

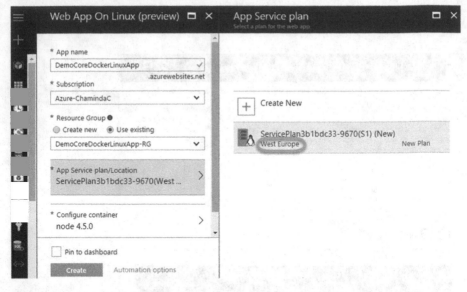

Figure 4-39. *Provide information to create the web app on Linux*

7. Leave the node.js container for the time being. We will set up a private registry for this later. Click Create. See Figure 4-40.

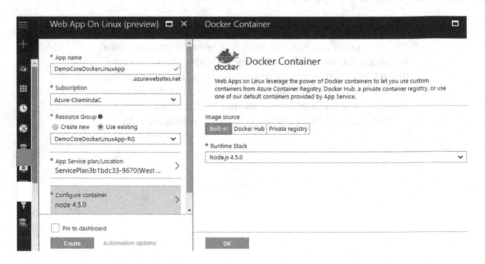

Figure 4-40. *Configure container*

8. A new app service app gets created. Click on its name. See Figure 4-41.

Figure 4-41. *App service app on Linux is created*

9. In the app overview, click on the available URL. See Figure 4-42.

Figure 4-42. *URL of the new web app*

10. The new web app should load in a new tab in the browser. See Figure 4-43.

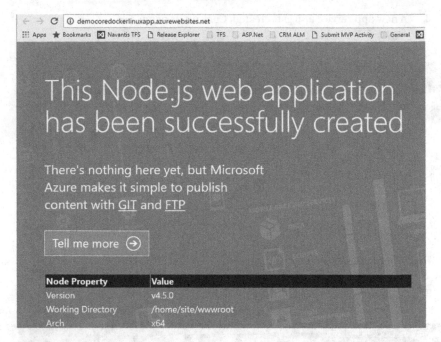

Figure 4-43. *Web app on Linux is ready*

In this lesson, you have created a new Azure app service app on Linux in the same region where we created the Azure container registry in the previous lesson. You will be using this app to host the Docker-enabled ASP.NET Core web API, which was created in a previous lesson.

Lesson 4.04 – Create a Build to Push Container Image to Azure Container Registry

Prerequisites: You need to install the Team Services extension called "Docker Integration" from `https://marketplace.visualstudio.com/items?itemName=ms-vscs-rm.docker` to your Team Services account. Installation of marketplace extensions is explained in Chapter 2.

1. First, link the Azure container registry to the team project. Go to **Services** tab of the settings in the team project and click **New Service Endpoint**, and then select **Docker Registry**. This will open a popup window for **Add new Docker Registry Connection**. See Figure 4-44.

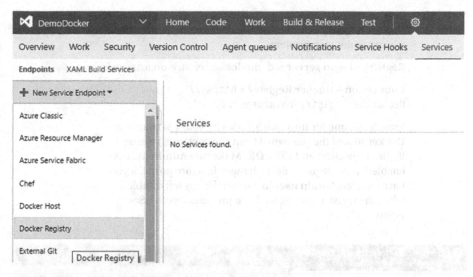

Figure 4-44. *Linking Docker registry to Team Services*

2. In another browser window, open the Access Key section of the container registry in the Azure portal. See Figure 4-45.

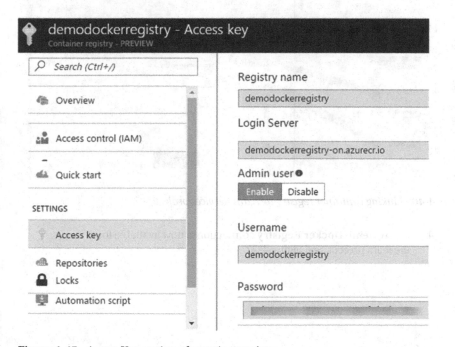

Figure 4-45. *Access Key section of container registry*

3. Provide the registry connection information in the **Add new Docker Registry Connection** window to connect Docker registry to the team project.

   Registry - Login server = demodockerregistry-on.azurecr.io

   Connection – Docker Registry = https:// demodockerregistry-on.azurecr.io

   Provide a name for the connection. Use your **username** as **Docker Id** and the **password** from the container registry in the connection and Click **OK**. Make sure **Admin user** is enabled in the registry. Save changes in Azure portal, if you have enabled **Admin user** just now (if it was left disabled when the registry was created in a previous lesson). See Figure 4-46.

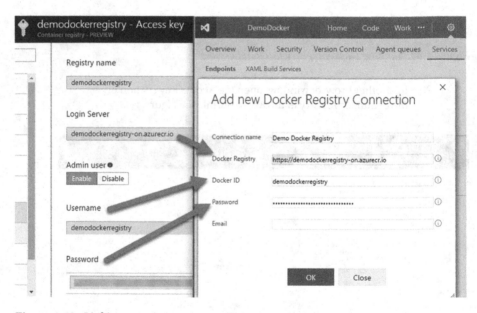

Figure 4-46. *Linking container registry to Team Services project*

4. A new **Demo Docker Registry** connection is now available for the team project. See Figure 4-47.

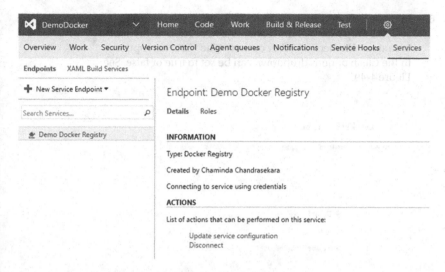

Figure 4-47. Docker registry is connected to team project

5. Create a new empty build definition named "DockerDemoBuild" in the Build & Release tab of the team project. Select agent queue Hosted Linux (Preview) in the General tab of the build definition. Provide a build number format, such as *$(date:yyyyMMdd)$(rev:.r)*. See Figure 3-48.

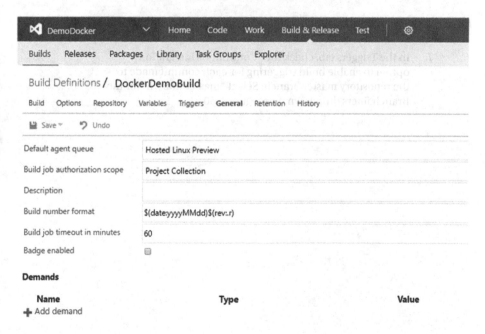

Figure 4-48. Build definition using hosted Linux agent pool

6. In the Repository tab of the build definition, select Git and select the repository of the team project. Set default branch to **master**. Uncheck all other options. The "Sources" option in the Clean options dropdown can be set to true or false. See Figure 4-49.

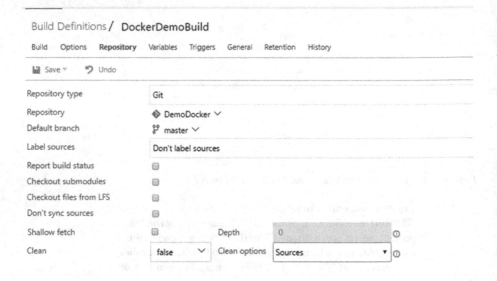

Figure 4-49. *Repository selected for the build definition*

7. In the Triggers tab, check the "Continuous integration" option to enable build triggering for each commit made to the repository master branch. Select "master branch" for the Branch filters dropdown. See Figure 4-50.

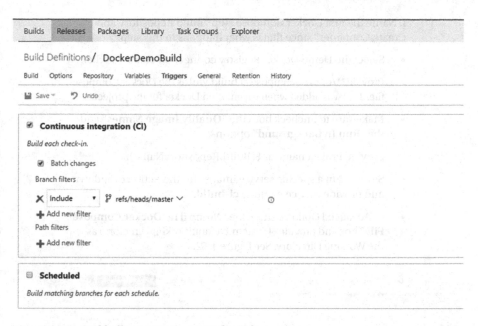

Figure 4-50. Build all commits to master branch

8. Leave Variables tab as it is.

9. For Options and Retention tabs, do not make any changes.

10. In the Build tab, add three build steps using the Docker Compose task that comes with the Docker Integration extension (https://marketplace.visualstudio.com/items?itemName=ms-vscs-rm.docker). See Figure 4-51.

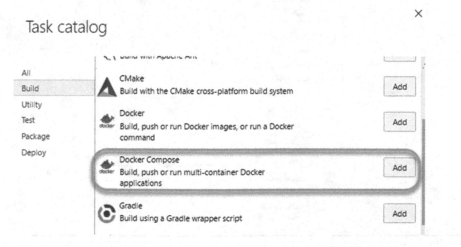

Figure 4-51. Add Docker Compose tasks to build definition

11.   **i.** Name the first Docker Compose step "Build Repository and Create Container" since that is what happens in this step.

- Select the Demo Docker Registry connection created earlier.

- Provide **/docker-compose.ci.build.yml as the Docker Compose file. This was added when we enabled Docker for the project.

- Make sure to uncheck both the **"Qualify Image Names"** and the **"Run In Background"** options.

- Provide Project name as $(Build.RepositoryName).

- Select "Run a specific service image" for the Action dropdown and provide service name as **ci-build**.

- In Advanced Options, check the **"No-op if no Docker Compose File"** box and provide $(System.DefaultWorkingDirectory) as the Working Directory. See Figure 4-52.

Figure 4-52. *Build repository and create container*

ii. Name the second Docker Compose step "Build Services Image." The container generated in the previous step will be packaged as an image in this step.

- Select the Demo Docker Registry and provide **/docker-compose.yml as the Docker Compose file.

- For Additional Docker compose file, provide docker-compose.ci.yml.

- Set Environment Variable to DOCKER_BUILD_SOURCE=. This will set its value to empty while running the task.

- For Project Name, type in $(Build.Repository.Name) and check the "Qualify Image Names" box.

- Select "Build service images" from the Action dropdown.

- Type "RTM" in Additional Image Tags field.

- Check options for "Include Source Tags" and "Include Latest Tag." These tags are useful when referring to a container image. You can see the RTM tag being used when the wiring up of the Azure Container Registry with the Azure app service app on Linux is done. See Figure 4-53.

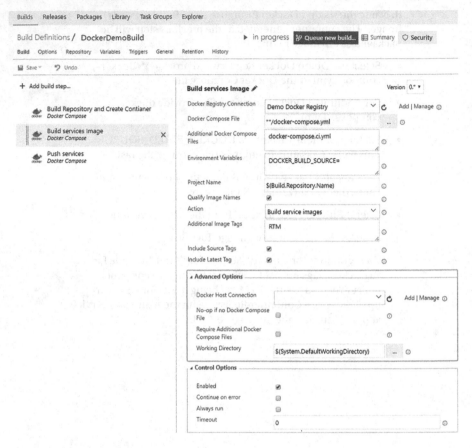

Figure 4-53. *Build container service image*

iii. In the third Docker Compose task, we are pushing the container image to the Azure Container Registry.

- Provide all options similar to previous task, except the Action. Action should be set to "Push service images."

- Follow the screenshot in Figure 4-54 to set the parameters properly.

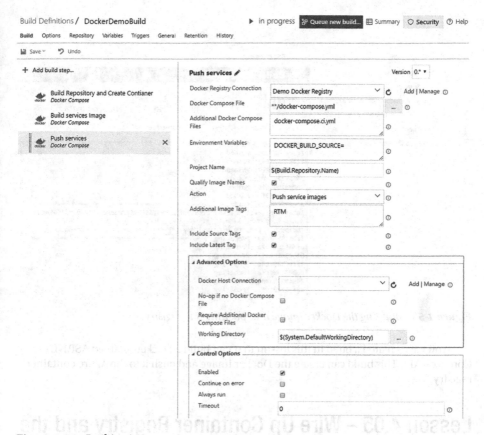

Figure 4-54. Pushing image to Azure container registry

12.   Save the build definition and queue a new build. You can see
        the build is pushing a container image with the application's
        API name and using the RTM tag specified. See Figure 4-55.

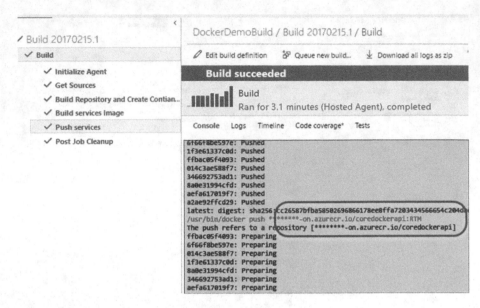

Figure 4-55. *Building the Docker image and pushing it to registry*

You have created a build in this lesson that can build a Docker-enabled ASP.NET Core web API. This build can create the Docker image and push it to the Azure container registry.

Lesson 4.05 – Wire Up Container Registry and the App Service App on Linux

The next step is to wire this Azure app service app on Linux with the Azure container registry that was pushed with a Docker container image in the previous lesson.

1. Open the app service app on Linux and the Azure container registry in two browser windows. Navigate to the Azure container registry's Access key and make sure to enable Admin user. See Figure 4-56.

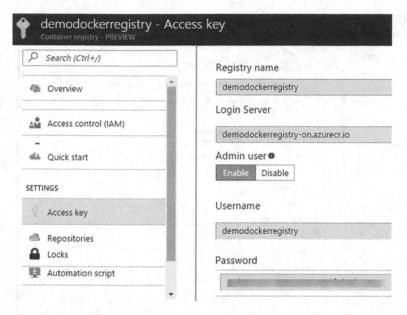

Figure 4-56. Make sure admin user enabled in access key of registry

2. In a third browser window, navigate to Web App on Linux and go to Docker Containers section. Select Private registry. See Figure 4-57.

Figure 4-57. *Private registry for Docker container in Linux app*

3. Set up private registry information as follows.

The Login Server name in the registry should be used to create the Image Source and Server URL, as shown here:

Registry - Login server = demodockerregistry-on.azurecr.io

App - Image and Tag = demodockerregistry-on.azurecr.io/ap pnameinsourcecode:imagetag

demodockerregistry-on.azurecr.io/coredockerapi:RTM

(RTM tag was used in the build definition and the image was pushed with the tag. We are setting the container to use that image by providing the tag.)

App – Server URL = `http://demodockerregistry-on.azurecr.io`

For username and password, copy from the registry form, and save. See Figure 4-58.

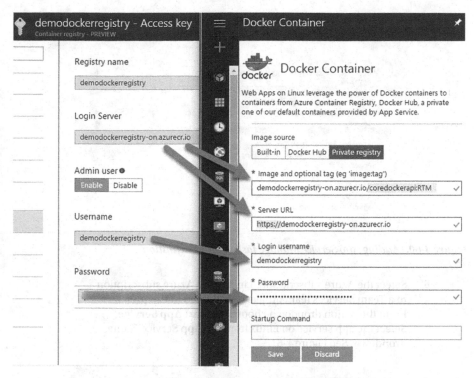

Figure 4-58. *Configure private registry as Docker container on Linux app*

4. You can now browse the app using the URL of the app service app on Linux plus api/values. See the app running in the Docker container and showing as running on Ubuntu in the browser. See Figure 4-59.

Figure 4-59. *ASP.NET Core app running on Ubuntu as Linux app service*

5. Let's carry out some changes to the code and get them deployed to the app service app on Linux. To do this, add an additional step to the build definition created previously. Add the Azure App Service Manage task to the build definition. See Figure 4-60.

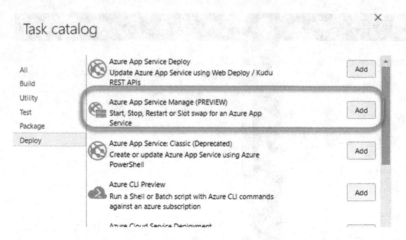

Figure 4-60. *Adding App Service Manage task to build definition*

6. Select the Azure subscription. Linking the Azure subscription to a Team Services team project is explained in Chapter 3. From the Action dropdown choose "**Restart App Service.**" Select the app service on Linux from the App Service Name dropdown. See Figure 4-61.

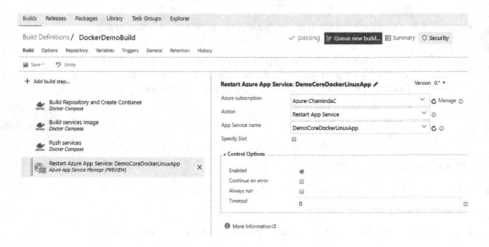

Figure 4-61. *Restart Linux app on Azure task*

7. In the ValuesController.cs file's Get method, change following line"

```
return new string[] { "value1", System.Runtime.InteropServices.
RuntimeInformation.OSDescription };
```

to

```
return new string[] { "Hello World", System.Runtime.
InteropServices.RuntimeInformation.OSDescription };
```

and commit and sync the code changes to the team project Git repository using the team explorer **Changes** tab. See Figure 4-62.

Figure 4-62. *Making a code change*

8. The build gets kicked in once the code syncs to the Git repository, since we have enabled continuous integration. Refresh the URL of the Azure app service on Linux, and the change will be available. See Figure 4-63.

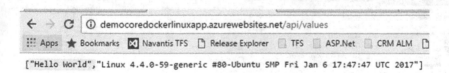

Figure 4-63. *Code change available in the Linux app on Azure*

You have learned how to deploy a Docker-enabled ASP.NET Core web API to the Azure app service app on Linux using a private container registry in this lesson.

Summary

In this chapter, you have learned how to build a Docker container with a Team Services build and push it to the Azure container registry. Using the Azure app service on Linux, you were able to host the container as a private registry. This is not an ideal production-ready scenario, since we have omitted usage of release managment steps here. Deploying the containers to Azure container service (`https://docs.microsoft.com/enus/azure/container-service/container-service-intro`) would be the robust way of hosting Docker containers in Azure. But for learning purposes, this was sufficient. Instead of the Azure container registry, you could use a Docker hub registry with the Team Services builds that use Docker integration extensions.

Azure Container Services and Team Services

You can explore the capabilities of Azure container services to host production systems. Azure container services allow you to deploy and manage containers. For more information, visit the following:

```
https://azure.microsoft.com/en-us/services/container-service/
https://docs.microsoft.com/en-us/azure/container-service/container-service-intro
https://docs.microsoft.com/en-us/azure/container-service/
```

Visual Studio 2017 + Visual Studio Team Services offer a great capability to generate build and release pipelines automatically when using the extension `https://marketplace.visualstudio.com/items?itemName=VSIDEDevOpsMSFT`. `ContinuousDeliveryToolsforVisualStudio` with Visual Studio 2017. You can add extensions directly via Visual Studio 2017 Extensions and Updates. See Figure 4-64.

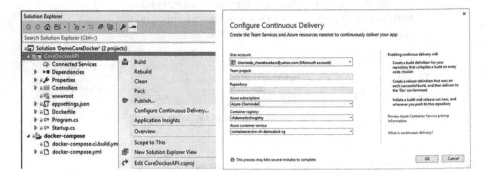

Figure 4-64. *Configuring continuous delivery for Azure container services*

The build and release definitions will be generated by linking to required Azure resources as well. See Figure 4-65.

Figure 4-65. *Visual Studio 2017 generates the build and release definitions*

Build definitions are capable of building Docker containers and pushing them to the Azure container registry. See Figure 4-66.

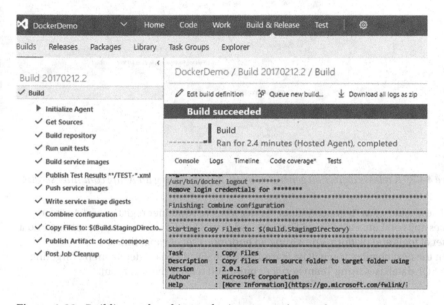

Figure 4-66. *Building and pushing to the Azure container registry*

A release definition capable of deploying to Azure container services is created as DC/OS (Data Centre OS - allows deploying and scaling clustered workloads while abstracting underlying hardware - for more information visit https://docs.microsoft.com/en-us/azure/container-service/container-service-mesos-marathon-ui and https://docs.microsoft.com/en-us/azure/container-service/container-service-intro#deploying-anapplication). The capabilities found in the Docker Deploy component (the Docker Integration Marketplace extension adds this release task to Team Services) will be enhanced to support many other types of deployments soon. See Figure 4-67.

199

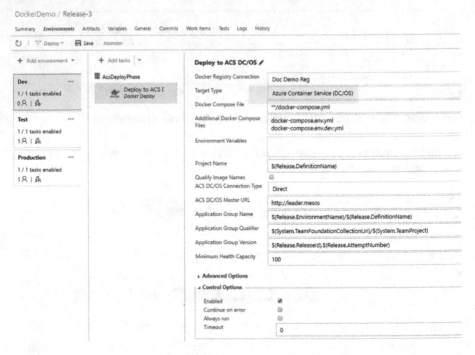

DockerDemo / Release-3

Summary *Environments* Artifacts Variables General Commits Work Items Tests Logs History

↻ | ⊤ Deploy ˅ ⊟ Save Abandon

+ Add environment ▾	+ Add tasks	▾	**Deploy to ACS DC/OS** ✎	
	▤ AcsDeployPhase	Docker Registry Connection	Doc Demo Reg
Dev ⋯	🐳 Deploy to ACS [	Target Type	Azure Container Service (DC/OS)
1 / 1 tasks enabled	Docker Deploy	Docker Compose File	**/docker-compose.yml
0 🔏	🕸		Additional Docker Compose Files	docker-compose.env.yml
Test ⋯			docker-compose.env.dev.yml
1 / 1 tasks enabled		Environment Variables	
1 🔏	🖧			
Production ⋯		Project Name	$(Release.DefinitionName)
1 / 1 tasks enabled		Qualify Image Names	☐
1 🔏	🖧		ACS DC/OS Connection Type	Direct
		ACS DC/OS Master URL	http://leader.mesos
		Application Group Name	$(Release.EnvironmentName)/$(Release.DefinitionName)
		Application Group Qualifier	$(System.TeamFoundationCollectionUri)/$(System.TeamProject)
		Application Group Version	$(Release.ReleaseId).$(Release.AttemptNumber)
		Minimum Health Capacity	100

▸ **Advanced Options**

▴ **Control Options**

Enabled	☑
Continue on error	☐
Always run	☐
Timeout	0

Figure 4-67. *A release definition generated by VS 2017 targeting an Azure container service*

These features in Azure container services, Azure container registry, and Azure app services apps on Linux with Team Services and Visual Studio show signs of evolving into a rich set of tools and platforms providing an enormous set of capabilities.

In the next chapter, you will be learning about SQL database deployment, targeting Azure SQL databases using Team Services build and release management.

▆▆▆

CHAPTER 5

Azure SQL and TFS/VSTS Build and Release

This chapter will include hands-on lessons on managing Azure SQL databases with TFS/VSTS release management tasks. By the end, you will be able to create database projects with Visual Studio, you will build them with TFS build and deploy via TFS release management to Azure.

Lesson 5.01 – Create SQL Project with Visual Studio

Let's create an SQL project to get the database schema development under source control.

1. Create a Visual Studio solution by clicking File ➤ New ➤ Project in Visual Studio.

2. Select Other Project Types ➤ Visual Studio Solutions and create a blank solution in your team project local path, say \ TeamProjectX\Main. Name the solution "DBDemo" and check the "**Add to Source Control**" option. This adds the solution as a pending change to source control. See Figure 5-1.

© Chaminda Chandrasekara 2017
C. Chandrasekara, *Beginning Build and Release Management with TFS 2017 and VSTS*,
DOI 10.1007/978-1-4842-2811-1_5

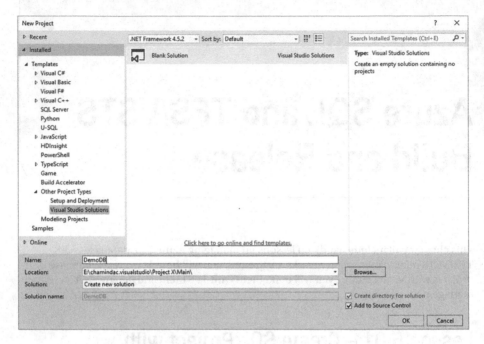

Figure 5-1. Creating a Visual Studio solution

3. In the solution DBDemo, right click and go to Add ➤ New Project and select SQL Server ➤ SQL Server Database Project. Name the project as "AzDB" and click OK. This will add an SQL database development project to the solution. See Figure 5-2.

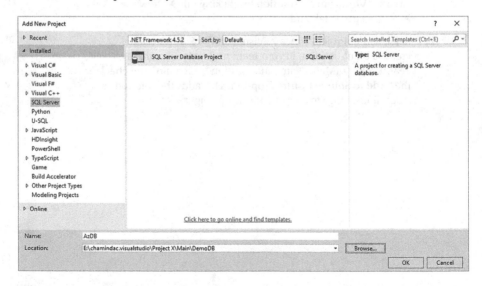

Figure 5-2. Adding an SQL Server database project

4. Right click on the AzDB project and choose Properties. In Project Settings, change the Target Platform to Microsoft Azure SQL Database V12 and save the project by clicking the Save button in Visual Studio. See Figure 5-3.

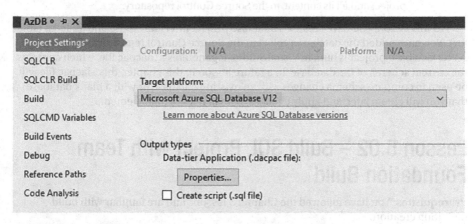

Figure 5-3. Setting DB to Azure SQL Database V12

5. Add folder named **dbo** to the **AzDB** project. In the dbo folder, add another folder named **Tables**. Then, right click on the Tables folder, click Add Table, and create a table called "Customer." Add ID and Name fields to the Customer table and save using Visual Studio. See Figure 5-4.

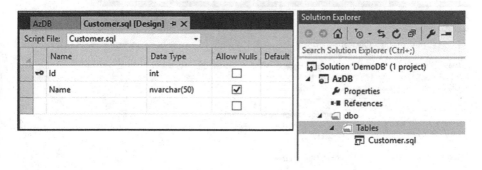

Figure 5-4. Creating a database table in database project in VS

6. Right click on the solution in Solution Explorer and click Rebuild to build the solution. This should build the database project successfully in Visual Studio. In the Pending Changes window of Team Explorer, check-in/submit the solution, including database project and all its content, to the Source Control repository.

In this lesson, you have created a database project in Visual Studio and added a table to it. You have added the database project to the Source Control repository. When an SQL server database project is built in Visual Studio, it generates a .dacpac file, which contains the current schema of the database. In a future lesson in this chapter, this .dacpac file will be used to compare schema changes with an existing database or with a blank database that you will create later, and apply changes to it via release management.

Lesson 5.02 – Build SQL Project with Team Foundation Build

Prerequisites: You have followed the Chapter 3 lessons and are familiar with build definition creation.

Let's create a build definition with which to build the database project created in the previous lesson.

1. Create a new build definition with the empty template and name it "DB.Rel."

2. In the Repository tab, set the server path to $/Project X/Main/DemoDB. See Figure 5-5.

Builds	Releases	Packages	Library	Task Groups	Explorer

Build Definitions / **DB.Rel**

Build	Options	**Repository**	Variables	Triggers	General	Retention	History

💾 Save ▾   ⤺ Undo

Repository type	Team Foundation Version Control
Repository name	Project X
Label sources	Don't label sources
Clean	false ∨ Clean options Sources ▼

Mappings

	Type	Server Path
✕	Map ▼	$/Project X/Main/DemoDB
✚	Add mapping	

Figure 5-5. Setting repository

3. Add a demand for SqlPackage in the General tab so as to enable .dacpac creation and building of the database project with the TFS build. VS 2015 availability on the build server will provide the necessary SSDT (SQL Server Data Tools). The latest versions of SSDT can be obtained for VS 2015 from `https://msdn.microsoft.com/en-us/mt186501.aspx`. If you are using VS 2017 you should install "Data Storage and Processing" workload to allow using SQL projects. Even workloads such as Azure, ASP.Net and Web Development, and .Net Core Cross Platform Development also enable SQL Projects for VS 2017. See Figure 5-6.

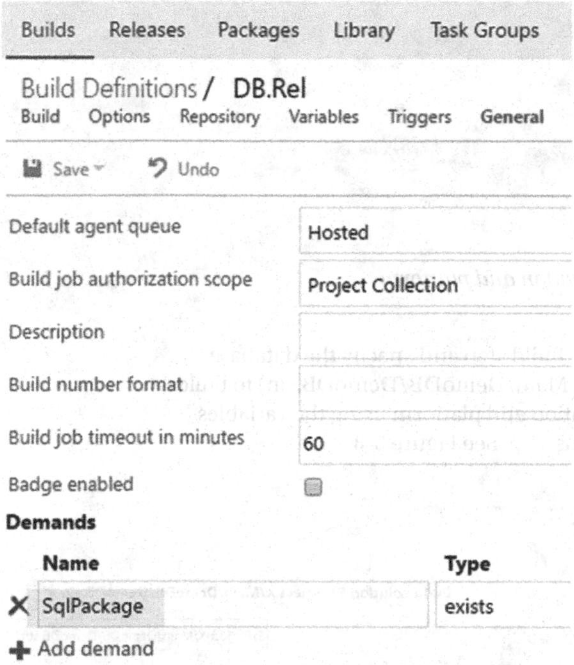

Builds	Releases	Packages	Library	Task Groups

Build Definitions / **DB.Rel**

Build	Options	Repository	Variables	Triggers	**General**

💾 Save ▾   🔁 Undo

Default agent queue	Hosted
Build job authorization scope	Project Collection
Description	
Build number format	
Build job timeout in minutes	60
Badge enabled	▣

Demands

Name	**Type**
✗ SqlPackage	exists

➕ Add demand

Figure 5-6. *Add demand for SqlPackage*

4. Define BuildConfiguration and BuildPlatform variables with values of release and any cpu, respectively. See Figure 5-7.

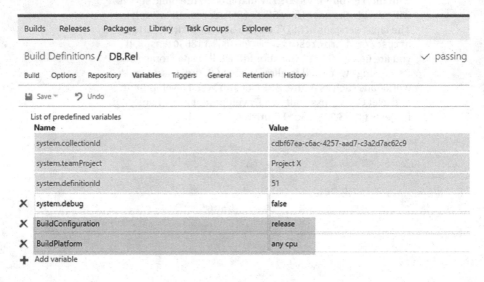

Figure 5-7. *Setting build configuration and platform*

5. Add the Visual Studio Build step and specify the database solution ($/Project X/Main/DemoDB/DemoDB.sln) to build. Provide the configuration and platform using the variables defined in the previous step. See Figure 5-8.

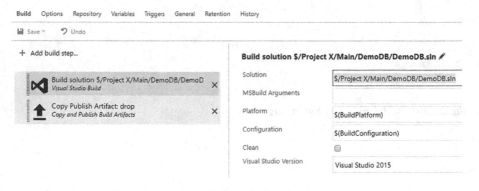

Figure 5-8. *Build the solution*

6. Add the Copy & Publish Artifacts build step and set the Contents field to ****/*.dacpac**. Set Artifact Name to **drop** and Artifact Type to **Server**. See Figure 5-9.

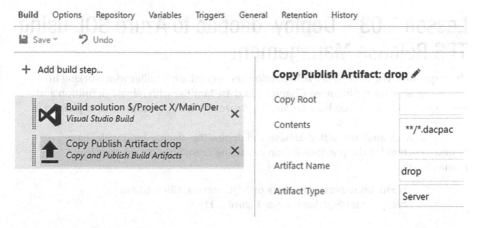

Figure 5-9. *Copy & publish .dacpac*

7. Queue a build and check the Artifacts explorer of the build to verify that .dacpac is available as build output. See Figure 5-10.

Figure 5-10. *.dacpac file available as build artifact*

You have created a build definition that can package an SQL database project into a .dacpac file. This .dacpac file can be used in release management to deploy database schema changes to a target Azure SQL database.

Lesson 5.03 – Deploy .dacpac to Azure SQL using TFS Release Management

Prerequisites: You have Azure subscription access and are familiar with working in Azure portal. You have followed Chapter 3 and are familiar with release definition and environment creation. You have created an Azure RM Service Endpoint as explained in Chapter 3.

Let's create an Azure SQL database and deploy the .dacpac built with Team Foundation build in the previous lesson to it using Team Foundation release management.

1. Go to Azure portal and click on SQL Servers. Click Add to create a new SQL Server. See Figure 5-11.

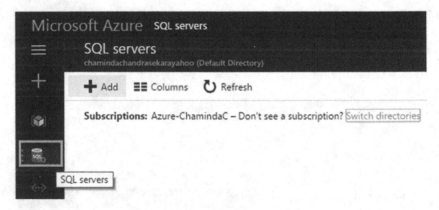

Figure 5-11. *Adding SQL Server in Azure*

2. In the tab that appears, provide a server name and credentials for Azure SQL Server. Select your subscription and select an existing resource group, or opt to create a new resource group (if new resource group, provide a name). Select Location and check the option to allow Azure services to access the server (this will allow the SQL server to be accessed from the Azure app service and so on. This is not mandatory, as we are not going to connect a web app with the databases in the server created in this chapter). See Figure 5-12.

Figure 5-12. *Creating SQL Server in Azure*

3. Go to SQL databases in Azure portal and click Add to create a new Azure SQL database. See Figure 5-13.

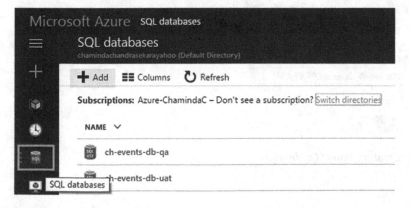

Figure 5-13. *Add Azure SQL database*

209

4.   In the tab that appears, provide a name for the database. Use the resource group of the SQL server created in the previous step as the resource group here. Select the created SQL server. Select "Blank database" from the Select source dropdown to create an empty database. Select "Basic pricing tier" if you want to reduce the cost. Fill in other information as shown in Figure 5-14 and click the Create button.

Figure 5-14. *Creating Azure SQL database*

5. Now you have an empty SQL database in Azure. Let's get it deployed with the database schema in the .dacpac that you built in the previous lesson. We will do so using Team Foundation release management. Create a release definition using the linked artifact from the DB.Rel build created in the previous lesson. Set the default added first environment agent, to demand for both sqlpackage and Azure PowerShell. Both of these demands are required in order to deploy .dacpac to the target Azure SQL database. See Figure 5-15.

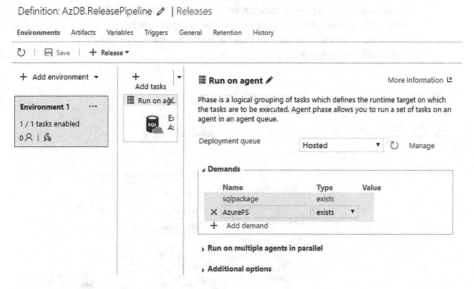

Figure 5-15. *Demands for sqlpackage and AzurePS*

6. Check the Artifacts tab to see if the DB.Rel build created in the previous lesson is linked to the release definition. If not, add it by clicking "Link an artifact source" and selecting the build definition in the popup window. Once added, it should appear as shown in Figure 5-16.

Definition: AzDB.ReleasePipeline ✎ | Releases

| Environments | **Artifacts** | Variables | Triggers | General | Retention | History |

↻ | 🖫 Save | ✛ Release ▾   ⤓ Link an artifact source

Artifacts of the linked sources are available for deployment in releases. Learn more about artifacts.

Source alias	Type	Default version
DB.Rel (Primary)	Build	

Figure 5-16. *Verify the artifacts from DB.Rel build are linked*

7. Add the release task **Azure SQL Database Deployment** from the Task Catalog to Environment1 in the release definition. In the Azure Connection Type dropdown select the service endpoint created for the Azure RM subscription (linking Azure RM subscription as a service endpoint to a team project is described in Chapter 3). Provide the Azure SQL Server name and the database name. **Server Admin Login** is the login specified when the database server was created in Azure. Store this password in a variable in the release definition or environment, and use the variable in the task. For the Type field in the Deployment Package section, select "SQL DACPAC File." Then select the artifact path for the .dacpac. Set the Firewall settings to AutoDetect and remove the rule after the task ends. See Figure 5-17.

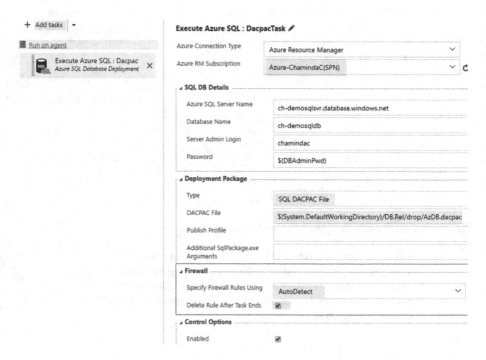

Figure 5-17. *Azure SQL database deployment task*

8. Create a release, and then you can verify successful database deployment to Azure as shown in Figure 5-18.

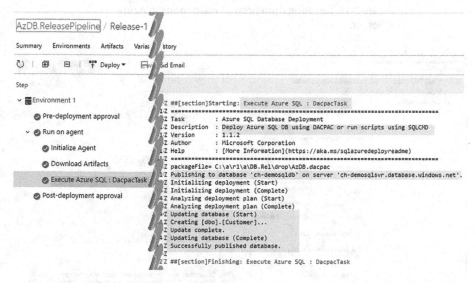

Figure 5-18. Deploying to Azure SQL database

9. Connect to the Azure SQL database in Visual Studio Server Explorer to check whether the database has been updated with the schema. You may encounter an issue here, as shown in Figure 5-19, resulting from firewall restrictions in Azure SQL Server.

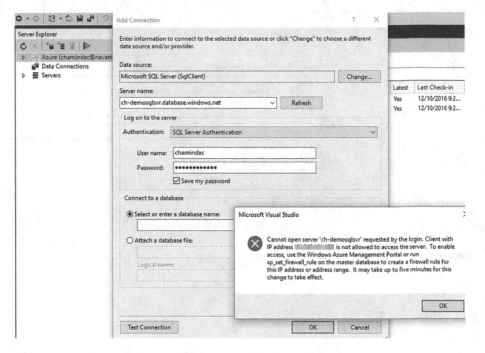

Figure 5-19. *Connecting Azure SQL is prevented by firewall*

If the Azure firewall prevents access to the server when trying to access the selected database, as shown in Figure 5-19, set the firewall rule for the Azure SQL database server for the IP address shown in the error message. Do this by clicking on Azure SQL Server in the Azure portal, then clicking on **Firewall**. You then can add the IP shown in the error message as **Start IP** and **End IP**, give it a **Rule Name,** and save. See Figure 5-20.

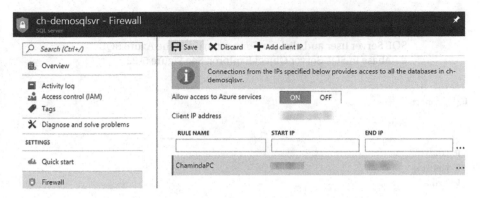

Figure 5-20. *Add firewall rule to Azure SQL server*

10. This connects your Azure SQL database as a data connection in Server Explorer, and you can view the schema changes applied with the deployment via VS Team Services/TFS release using .dacpac. To view the Azure SQL database in SQL Server Object Explorer in Visual Studio, right click on the database in Server Explorer and select **Open in SQL Server Object Explorer**. See Figure 5-21.

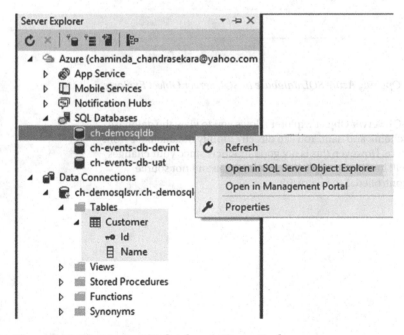

Figure 5-21. *View Azure SQL database in Server Explorer*

11. In the popup window, almost all of the information will be auto-filled. You must provide the password for the Azure SQL Server user and click on Connect to open the Azure SQL database in SQL Server Object Explorer. See Figure 5-22.

Figure 5-22. Opening Azure SQL database in SQL Server Object Explorer

12. SQL Server Object Explorer allows you to view the database schema and data. You can directly modify the database from here. However, this is not good practice, since your changes will be directly applied to the database and not source controlled. See Figure 5-23.

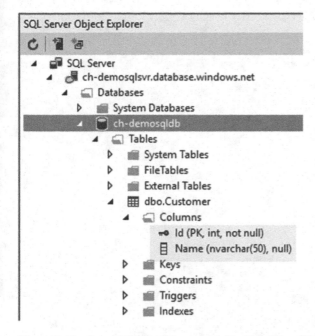

Figure 5-23. Azure SQL database opened in SQL Server Object Explorer

In this lesson, you created a release definition with which you successfully deployed a .dacpac file built with TFS build to a target Azure SQL server database.

Summary

You have learned how to use TFS builds to build an Azure SQL project that was created in Visual Studio, and to get the .dacpac file as output. Then, you used the Azure SQL Deployment task in TFS/VSTS release management to deploy the database schema to the target Azure database. As further experiments, you can make modifications to the database schema of the SQL project in Visual Studio and deploy the project to the target Azure SQL database using the build and release definitions created in this chapter.

In the next chapter, you will learn how to develop micro-services applications and build and deploy them to Azure Service Fabric using TFS/VSTS builds and release management.

CHAPTER 6

■■■

Team Services for Azure Service Fabric Deployments

This chapter offers hands-on lessons on creating ASP.NET Core applications for Azure Service Fabric and getting them built and deployed to Azure Service Fabric via Visual Studio Team Services release management. It will also give you a deeper understanding of implementation with Visual Studio and deployment with Team Services.

Azure Service Fabric

Azure Service Fabric provides you with a platform for managing scalable and reliable microservices in the cloud. To learn more about Azure Service Fabric, refer to https:// docs.microsoft.com/en-us/azure/service-fabric/service-fabric-overview. You can learn about microservices software architecture in more depth by referring to https://martinfowler.com/articles/microservices.html, https://smartbear.com/ learn/api-design/what-are-microservices/, and many other articles available online.

■ **Note**   Using Visual Studio 2015 is recommended for this chapter, since all code and screenshots in the lessons are based on it.

Lesson 6.01 – Set Up Azure Service Fabric SDK for Visual Studio

Prerequisites: You need Visual Studio 2015 update 2 or higher, or Visual Studio 2017. You must have Web Platform Installer 5.0 on your machine (https://www.microsoft.com/ web/downloads/platform.aspx).

Let's take a look at the steps required to set up the environment for developing an Azure Service Fabric application.

© Chaminda Chandrasekara 2017
C. Chandrasekara, *Beginning Build and Release Management with TFS 2017 and VSTS*,
DOI 10.1007/978-1-4842-2811-1_6

For Visual Studio 2015:

1. Download Azure Service Fabric SDK from http://www.
microsoft.com/web/handlers/webpi.ashx?command=getin
stallerredirect&appid=MicrosoftAzure-ServiceFabric-
VS2015 or search for Azure Service Fabric in Web Platform
Installer. Select the latest SDK and tools for VS 2015 to
allow developing microservices applications (https://
docs.microsoft.com/en-us/azure/service-fabric/
service-fabric-overview#applications-composed-of-
microservices) targeting Azure Service Fabric. See Figure 6-1.

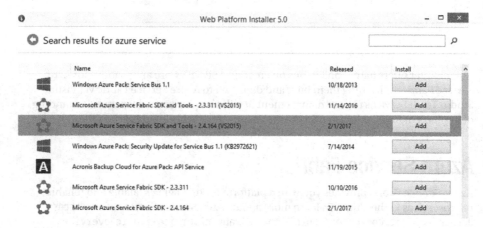

Figure 6-1. *Service Fabric SDK and tools for VS 2015*

2. Install it on your machine. Make sure Visual Studio 2015 is
closed while installing.

3. You can see the Service Fabric Application template in VS
2015 once installation has completed. See Figure 6-2.

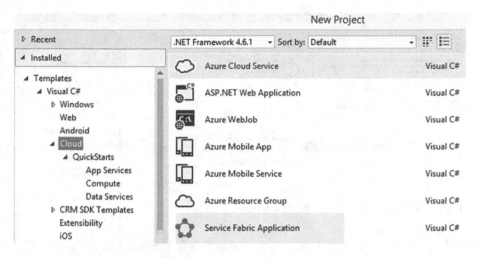

Figure 6-2. *Service Fabric Application project template in VS 2015*

For Visual Studio 2017:

1. Install ASP.NET and web development to get the ASP.NET Core development tools. See Figure 6-3.

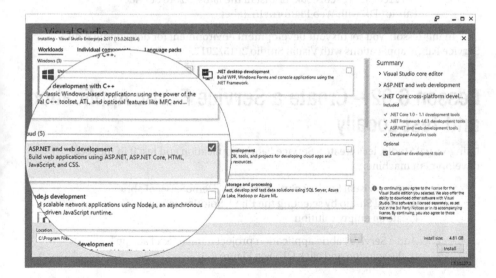

Figure 6-3. *Getting ASP.NET Core development tools for VS 2017*

2. Install Azure Development for Visual Studio 2017, which will install the Service Fabric tools as well. See Figure 6-4.

221

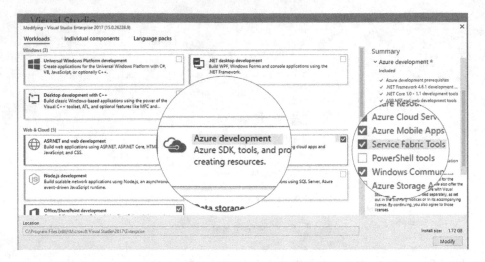

Figure 6-4. Azure Development for VS 2017

3. Download and install the latest Azure Service Fabric SDK
   from http://www.microsoft.com/web/handlers/webpi.ashx
   ?command=getinstallerredirect&appid=MicrosoftAzure-
   ServiceFabric-CoreSDK, or install the latest Azure Service
   Fabric SDK with Web Platform Installer.

In this lesson, you set up your development environment for developing Azure
Service Fabric applications with Visual Studio 2015/2017.

Lesson 6.02 – Create a Service Fabric Application and Test Locally

Using Visual Studio, let's create a Service Fabric application and test it in the local
development machine.

1. Create a Visual Studio solution named "DemoServiceFabric"
   in Visual Studio by selecting the Blank Solution template to
   create an empty solution.

2. Add a Service Fabric application project named "SvcFabApp"
   to the solution and click OK. See Figure 6-5.

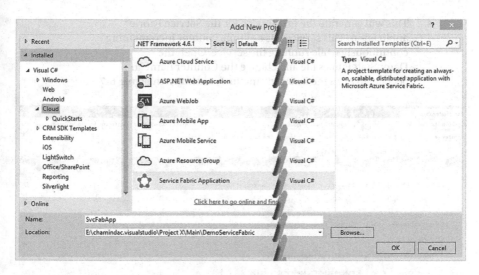

Figure 6-5. *Adding Service Fabric Application project*

3. You will be presented with several application templates.
    Select Stateful Service and provide DemoStateFull as Service
    Name. Stateful service lets you create a service with persistent
    state. We are choosing it here because it is the simplest type
    of service to understand the basics of micro-services. To learn
    more on different templates available here visit https://
    docs.microsoft.com/en-us/azure/service-fabric/
    service-fabric-choose-framework. Click OK. See Figure 6-6.

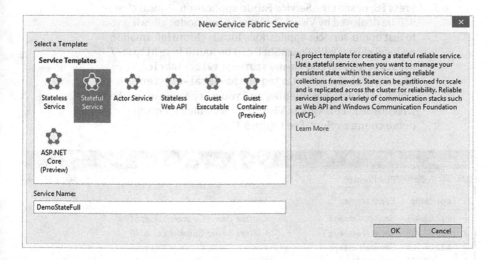

Figure 6-6. *Stateful Service template*

4. This will generate the first service for the Service Fabric application. This service has a simple counter incrementing continuously while running the service. Open the DemoStateFull.cs file and change the Counter name to DemoCounter in the RunAsync method, as shown in Figure 6-7.

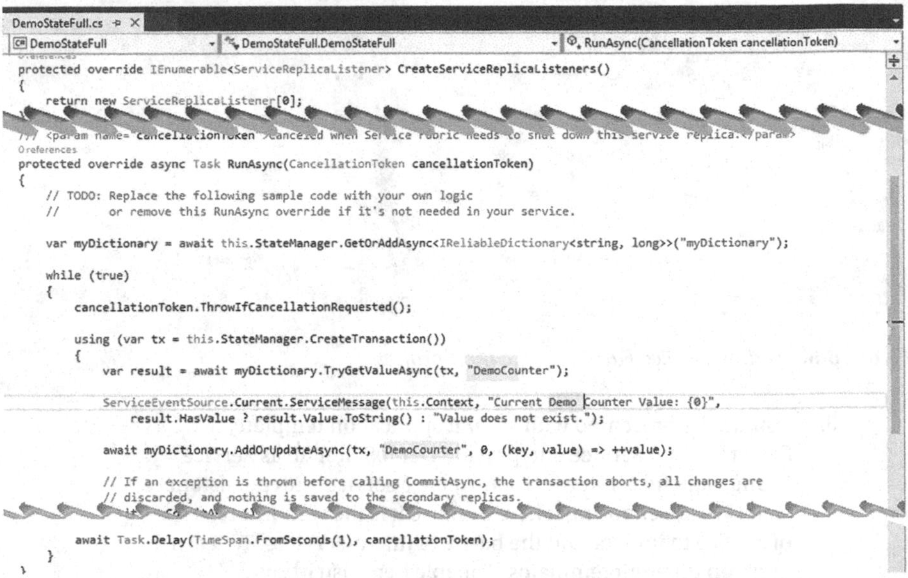

```
DemoStateFull.cs ⊅ ✕
DemoStateFull                    ▼ 🔩 DemoStateFull.DemoStateFull                    ▼ 🔧 RunAsync(CancellationToken cancellationToken)    ▼
protected override IEnumerable<ServiceReplicaListener> CreateServiceReplicaListeners()
{
    return new ServiceReplicaListener[0];
}

/// <param name="cancellationToken">Canceled when Service Fabric needs to shut down this service replica.</param>
0 references
protected override async Task RunAsync(CancellationToken cancellationToken)
{
    // TODO: Replace the following sample code with your own logic
    //       or remove this RunAsync override if it's not needed in your service.

    var myDictionary = await this.StateManager.GetOrAddAsync<IReliableDictionary<string, long>>("myDictionary");

    while (true)
    {
        cancellationToken.ThrowIfCancellationRequested();

        using (var tx = this.StateManager.CreateTransaction())
        {
            var result = await myDictionary.TryGetValueAsync(tx, "DemoCounter");

            ServiceEventSource.Current.ServiceMessage(this.Context, "Current Demo Counter Value: {0}",
                result.HasValue ? result.Value.ToString() : "Value does not exist.");

            await myDictionary.AddOrUpdateAsync(tx, "DemoCounter", 0, (key, value) => ++value);

            // If an exception is thrown before calling CommitAsync, the transaction aborts, all changes are
            // discarded, and nothing is saved to the secondary replicas.

        await Task.Delay(TimeSpan.FromSeconds(1), cancellationToken);
    }
}
```

Figure 6-7. *Changing the counter name*

5. Press F5, or start the Service Fabric application. A local cluster will be deployed by Visual Studio with five nodes allowing you to test micro-services applications locally (More information on local cluster with PowerShell can be found here https://docs.microsoft.com/en-us/azure/service-fabric/service-fabric-get-started-witha-local-cluster), which will take a few minutes, and you will be able to see the Diagnostic Events view in Visual Studio, which shows the demo counter values. See Figure 6-8.

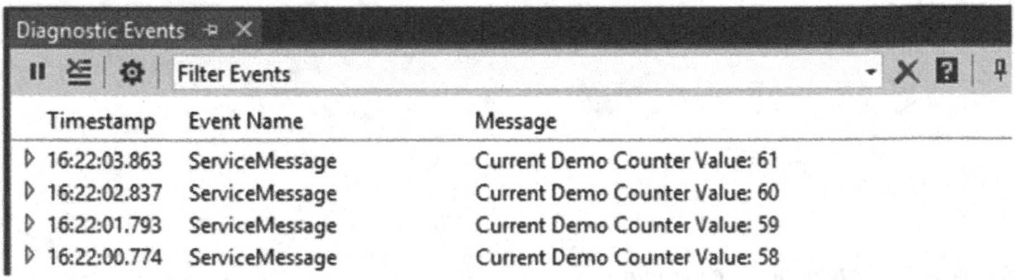

Diagnostic Events ⊅ ✕

	Filter Events	
Timestamp	**Event Name**	**Message**
▷ 16:22:03.863	ServiceMessage	Current Demo Counter Value: 61
▷ 16:22:02.837	ServiceMessage	Current Demo Counter Value: 60
▷ 16:22:01.793	ServiceMessage	Current Demo Counter Value: 59
▷ 16:22:00.774	ServiceMessage	Current Demo Counter Value: 58

Figure 6-8. *Counter shown in Diagnostic Events view*

6. You can pause the Diagnostic Events view and inspect
    the message. You can do more experiments by disabling
    the running node and so forth, as explained in the article
    mentioned in the following note.

■ **Note**   Detailed discussions on Azure Service Fabric applications are out of the scope of
the book. Stateful service is explained in more detail in the following article: https://docs.
microsoft.com/en-us/azure/service-fabric/service-fabric-create-your-first-
application-in-visual-studio. This Channel 9 video (https://channel9.msdn.com/
Blogs/Azure/Creating-your-first-Service-Fabric-application-in-Visual-Studio)
explains it more clearly. The preceding steps in the book are provided as prerequisites to
setting up builds and releases to deploy to Azure Service Fabric.

---

7. You can view/manage the local cluster using the Service
    Fabric Local Cluster Manager available in the system tray
    once you have deployed the application to the local cluster by
    running the "DemoServiceFabric" solution in Visual Studio.
    See Figure 6-9.

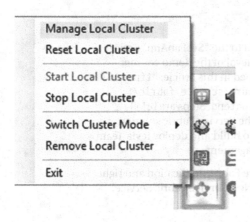

Figure 6-9. *Service Fabric menu*

8. The "Manage Local Cluster" option will launch Service
    Fabric Explorer and allow you to view/manage nodes and
    applications in the cluster (more information is available in
    the articles mentioned in the preceding note). See Figure 6-10.

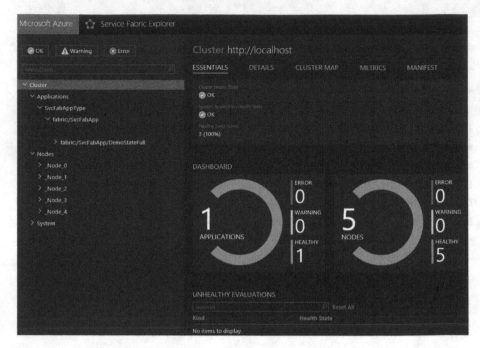

Figure 6-10. *Service Fabric Explorer*

9. Let's add a web service front end to the "SvcFabApp" Service Fabric solution to allow the retrieval of the demo counter value and exposing it, as explained in this article: `https://docs.microsoft.com/en-us/azure/service-fabric/service-fabric-add-a-web-frontend`. Steps are briefly described next for completing the Service Fabric solution ("SvcFabApp") so as to be able to build and deploy it via Team Services build and release management.

10. Expand the "SvcFabApp" Service Fabric application and right click on Services. Go to Add ➤ New Service Fabric Service. See Figure 6-11.

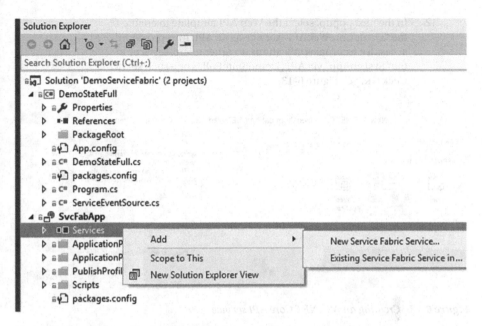

Figure 6-11. *Add new Service Fabric service*

11. Select ASP.NET Core for creating stateless reliable service and type "DemoCoreWebAPI" in the Service Name field. Click OK. See Figure 6-12.

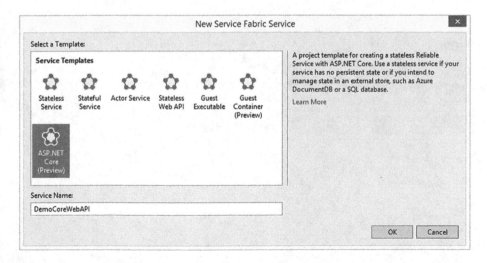

Figure 6-12. *Creating an ASP.NET Core reliable service*

12. In the next popup, select the Web API template to enable the "DemoCoreWebAPI" service as an API, thus providing access for external applications, to other micro-services in the "SvsFabApp", via API (DemoStateFull is one such service). Click OK. See Figure 6-13.

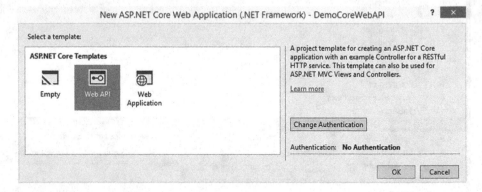

Figure 6-13. *Creating an ASP.NET Core API service*

13. This adds an ASP.NET Core Web API project to the Service Fabric solution along with additional files required to package it as a Service Fabric service. See Figure 6-14.

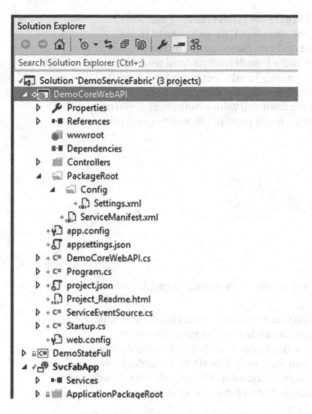

Figure 6-14. Web API created as a service for Service Fabric application

14. Press F5 in Visual Studio to inspect the added web API. Once it is deployed to the local Service Fabric cluster, it will open a browser window. A Visual Studio output window will show the application-launching status.

15. A browser window launched with URL, like http:// localhost:8295 (port number may vary), will show an error loading page message always. Instead of launching a browser window, if you get the message "The application URL is not set or is not an HTTP/HTTPS URL so the browser will not be opened to the application" in the output window of Visual Studio, follow the instructions here: http://stackoverflow.com/ questions/40997359/getting-error-in-service-fabric-the- application-url-is-not-set-or-is-not-an-htt.

16. Copy the URL (like http://localhost:8295/) and add api/values so that the complete URL looks like http://localhost:8295/api/values. Paste it in a Chrome browser, which will let you view the json default payload returned, which has ["value1", "value2"] as the default value returned by API (ASP.NET Core API template generated code has this default value returning from api/values controller). If you try on Internet Explorer 11, it will prompt you to download json. See Figure 6-15.

Figure 6-15. *Web API running as a service in the local service fabric cluster*

17. Stop the Visual Studio solution from running by clicking Stop in Visual Studio. Undo the added NuGet packages (these packages were automatically downloaded and added during the building of the solution inside Visual Studio) folder from Source Control Explorer, as shown in Figure 6-16. Then, check in the solution to source control before proceeding to the next step.

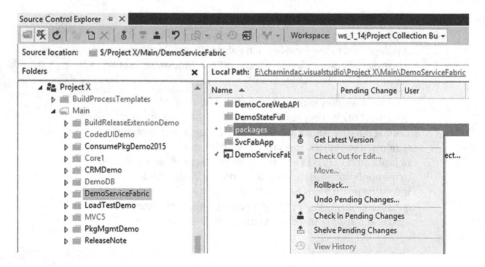

Figure 6-16. *Undo packages folder*

230

18. Now, we are going to expose the DemoCounter's actual
     values from the stateful service via a web API in the Service
     Fabric application. To communicate with the stateful service,
     we need to add an interface between the stateful service
     and its clients. For this, add a Class Library project named
     "DemoStateFull.Interface" to the solution and make sure to
     select .NET framework 4.5.2. See Figure 6-17.

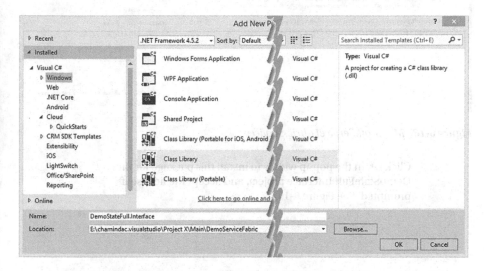

Figure 6-17. Creating interface for stateful service

19. Right click on the DemoStateFull.Interface project and then
     click Manage NuGet Packages.

20. Search for the Microsoft.ServiceFabric.Services package and
     click Install. Make sure to use version 2.4.164, as the code
     in this book uses that NuGet package version. If you use the
     latest versions, the code in this book may not be usable. See
     Figure 6-18.

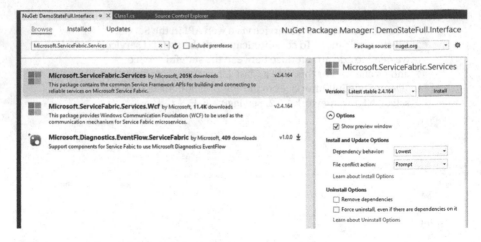

Figure 6-18. *Microsoft.ServiceFabric.Services*

21. Click OK in the popup widow to install this package for the DemoStateFull.Interface project, and accept the license if prompted. See Figure 6-19.

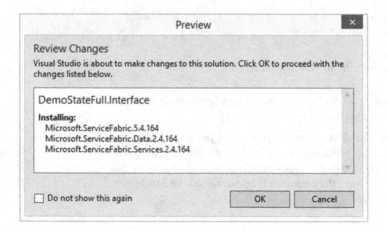

Figure 6-19. *Installing Microsoft.ServiceFabric.Services*

22. After the NuGet package is installed, rename the default added Class1.cs to "IDemoCounter.cs" so that it has a meaningful name for its purpose. See Figure 6-20.

Search Solution Explorer (Ctrl+;)

✓🔍 Solution 'DemoServiceFabric' (4 projects)
▷ 🔒🌐 DemoCoreWebAPI
▷ 🔒C# DemoStateFull
◢ +C# DemoStateFull.Interface
  ▷ +🔧 Properties
  ▷ ■-■ References
  ▷ ⊙C# IDemoCounter.cs
    +📄 packages.config
◢ 🔒📦 SvcFabApp
  ▷ ■-■ Services
  ▷ 🔒📁 ApplicationPackageRoot
  ▷ 🔒📁 ApplicationParameters
  ▷ 🔒📁 PublishProfiles
  ▷ 🔒📁 Scripts
    🔒📄 packages.config

Figure 6-20. Renaming as IDemoCounter.cs

23.   Open IDemoCounter.cs and add the following code to create
      an interface method named GetDemoCountAsync that allows
      you to get the demo counter values from the stateful service.

```
using System;
using System.Collections.Generic;
using System.Linq;
using System.Text;
using System.Threading.Tasks;
using Microsoft.ServiceFabric.Services.Remoting;

namespace DemoStateFull.Interface
{   public interface IDemoCounter : IService
    {
Task<long> GetDemoCountAsync();
    }
}
```

24.   Right click on the References of the **DemoStateFull**
      project and select Add Reference. In the popup window,
      select **DemoStateFull.Interface** and add it to the project
      so as to allow the implementation of interface method
      GetDemoCountAsync in the project. See Figure 6-21.

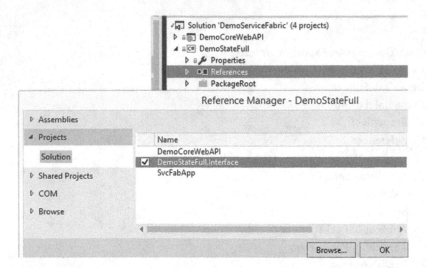

Figure 6-21. Adding a reference to DemoStateFull.Interface

25. Open DemoStateFull.cs in the DemoStateFull project and implement the IDemoCounter interface as shown in Figure 6-22.

```
DemoStateFull.cs ⊕ ✕  Source Control Explorer
C# DemoStateFull                                          ⦁ ⚙ DemoStateFull.DemoStateFull
     1      ⊟using System;
     2       using System.Collections.Generic;
     3       using System.Fabric;
     4       using System.Linq;
     5       using System.Threading;
     6       using System.Threading.Tasks;
     7       using Microsoft.ServiceFabric.Data.Collections;
     8       using Microsoft.ServiceFabric.Services.Communication.Runtime;
     9       using Microsoft.ServiceFabric.Services.Runtime;
    10       using DemoStateFull.Interface;
    11
    12      ⊟namespace DemoStateFull
    13       {
    14      ⊟    /// <summary>
    15           /// An instance of this class is created for each service replica by the Se
    16           /// </summary>
             3 references | Chaminda Chandrasekara, 1 day ago | 1 author, 1 change
    17      ⊟    internal sealed class DemoStateFull : StatefulService, IDemoCounter
    18           {
                 1 reference | Chaminda Chandrasekara, 1 day ago | 1 author, 1 change
    19      ⊟        public DemoStateFull(StatefulServiceContext context)
    20                   : base(context)
    21               { }
    22
                 1 reference | 0 changes | 0 authors, 0 changes
    23      ⊟        public Task<long> GetDemoCountAsync()
    24               {
    25                   throw new NotImplementedException();
    26               }
    27
    28      ⊟        /// <summary>
    29               /// Optional override to create listeners (e.g., HTTP, Service Remoting, lient
    30               /// </summary>
```

Figure 6-22. Implementing DemoStateFull.Interface

26. Replace the GetDemoCountAsync method code with the following code in the DemoStateFull.cs file. This code reads the value from the DemoCounter and returns it to the caller of the GetDemoCountAsync method. See Figure 6-23.

```
public async Task<long> GetDemoCountAsync()
    {
        var myDictionary =
            await this.StateManager.GetOrAddAsync<IReliable
            Dictionary<string, long>>("myDictionary");

        using (var tx = this.StateManager.CreateTransaction())
        {
            var result = await myDictionary.
            TryGetValueAsync(tx, "DemoCounter");
            return result.HasValue ? result.Value : 0;
        }
    }
```

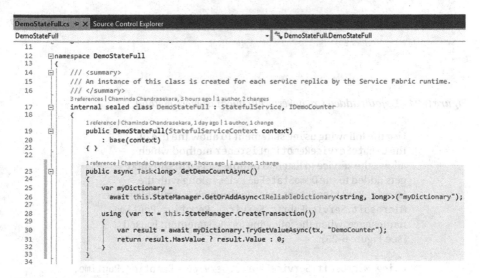

Figure 6-23. *Getting DemoCount value*

27. Replace the CreateServiceReplicaListeners method in the DemoStateFull.cs file with the following code to expose the stateful service using a service remoting listener. See Figure 6-24.

235

```
protected override IEnumerable<ServiceReplicaListener>
CreateServiceReplicaListeners()
    {
        return new List<ServiceReplicaListener>()
        {
            new ServiceReplicaListener(
                (context) =>
                    this.CreateServiceRemoting
                    Listener(context))
        };
    }
```

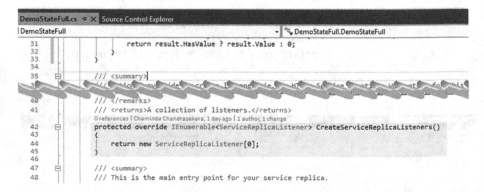

Figure 6-24. *Default added CreateServiceReplicaListeners method*

Use the following using statement to allow the use of
the CreateServiceRemotingListener method which
allows the service to listen to remote calls. This method
gets added to the DemoStateFull class along with the
ServiceRemotingExtensions class, which is available in the
Microsoft.ServiceFabric.Services.Remoting.Runtime
namespace, when the following using statement is used
(see Figure 6-25):

using Microsoft.ServiceFabric.Services.Remoting.Runtime;

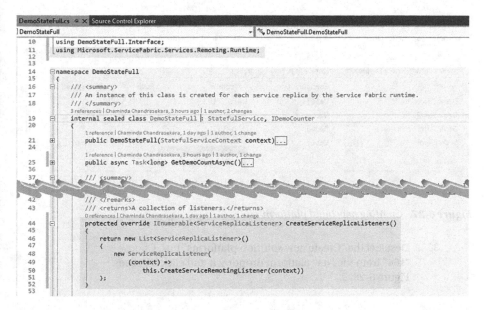

Figure 6-25. *Expose stateful service with CreateServiceReplicaListeners method*

28. Add a reference to DemoStateFull.Interface from DemoCoreWebAPI to allow the calling of the GetDemoCountAsync method using the interface. See Figure 6-26.

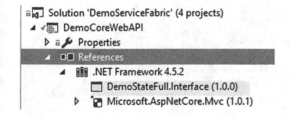

Figure 6-26. *Reference to interface from API*

29. Right click on the DemoServiceFabric solution in Solution Explorer and open Configuration Manager. You can see in Figure 6-27 that the DemoStateFull.Interface project is set to build platform Any CPU. You need to change it to x64 since Service Fabric application only supports x64 for services. Click on menu and click <New…>.

237

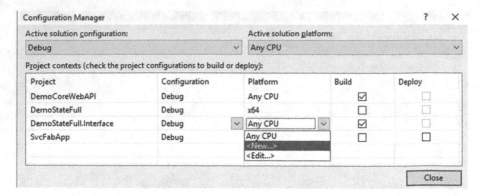

Figure 6-27. *Creating new build platform*

30. Deselect the "Create new solution platforms" box. Choose "x64" from the New platform dropdown and click OK. See Figure 6-28.

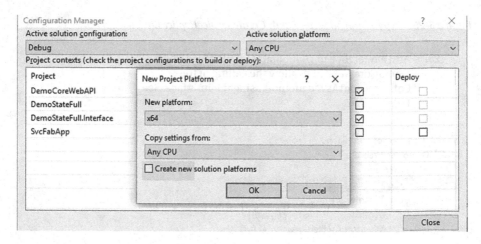

Figure 6-28. *Creating x64 build platform*

31. Make sure the release and debug build configuration looks like Figure 6-29.

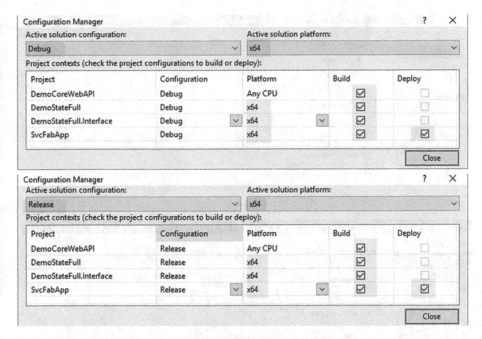

Figure 6-29. *Release and debug configuration with x64 build platform*

32. In the DemoStateFull.Interface properties window, go to the Build tab. Make sure the Output path fields are set as bin\Debug\ and bin\Release\ for the debug and release configurations, respectively, as shown in Figure 6-30.

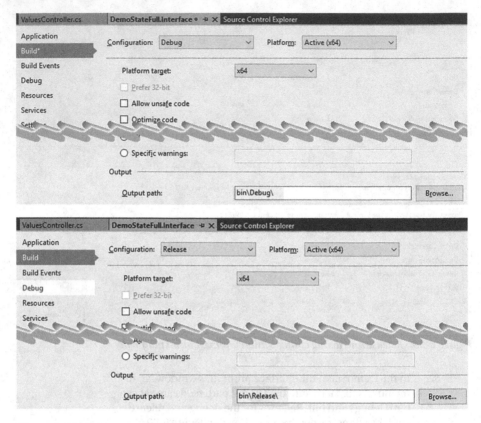

Figure 6-30. Release and debug output paths

33. Open the ValuesController.cs file in the DemoCoreWebAPI. Replace the default Get method (shown in Figure 6-31) with the following code so that it looks like what is shown in Figure 6-32. This code change to the Get method will allow you to get the value of the demo counter from the stateful service and return it as the return value of the API ValuesController's Get method.

```
public async Task<IEnumerable<string>> Get()
        {
            IDemoCounter demoCounter =
        ServiceProxy.Create<IDemoCounter>(new Uri("fabric:/
        SvcFabApp/DemoStateFull"), new ServicePartitionKey(0));

            long count = await demoCounter.GetDemoCountAsync();

            return new string[] { count.ToString() };
        }
```

```
ValuesController.cs  ⇄ X  Source Control Explorer
DemoCoreWebAPI..NET Framework 4.5.2              ▾  DemoCoreWebAPI.Controllers.ValuesController
  1 ⚡    using System;
  2       using System.Collections.Generic;
  3       using System.Linq;
  4       using System.Threading.Tasks;
  5       using Microsoft.AspNetCore.Mvc;
  6
  7       namespace DemoCoreWebAPI.Controllers
  8       {
  9           [Route("api/[controller]")]
            0 references | Chaminda Chandrasekara, 1 day ago | 1 author, 1 change
 10           public class ValuesController : Controller
 11           {
 12               // GET api/values
 13               [HttpGet]
                0 references | Chaminda Chandrasekara, 1 day ago | 1 author, 1 change
 14               public IEnumerable<string> Get()
 15               {
 16                   return new string[] { "value1", "value2" };
 17               }
 18
 19               // GET api/values/5
 20               [HttpGet("{id}")]
```

Figure 6-31. *Default available Get method*

```
ValuesController.cs  ⇄ X  Source Control Explorer
DemoCoreWebAPI..NET Framework 4.5.2              ▾  DemoCoreWebAPI.Controllers.ValuesController        ▾  Get(int id)
  1       using System;
  2       using System.Collections.Generic;
  3       using System.Linq;
  4       using System.Threading.Tasks;
  5       using Microsoft.AspNetCore.Mvc;
  6       using DemoStateFull.Interface;
  7       using Microsoft.ServiceFabric.Services.Remoting.Client;
  8       using Microsoft.ServiceFabric.Services.Client;
  9
 10       namespace DemoCoreWebAPI.Controllers
 11       {
 12           [Route("api/[controller]")]
            0 references | Chaminda Chandrasekara, 1 day ago | 1 author, 1 change
 13           public class ValuesController : Controller
 14           {
 15               // GET api/values
 16               [HttpGet]
                0 references | Chaminda Chandrasekara, 1 day ago | 1 author, 1 change
 17               public async Task<IEnumerable<string>> Get()
 18               {
 19                   IDemoCounter demoCounter =
 20                   ServiceProxy.Create<IDemoCounter>(new Uri("fabric:/SvcFabApp/DemoStateFull"), new ServicePartitionKey(0));
 21
 22                   long count = await demoCounter.GetDemoCountAsync();
 23
 24                   return new string[] { count.ToString() };
 25               }
 26
```

Figure 6-32. Get *method changed to retrieve value from demo stateful service*

Make sure to use the following using statements to enable
access to **DemoStateFull.Interface** and other required
services in Service Fabric:

```
using DemoStateFull.Interface;
using Microsoft.ServiceFabric.Services.Remoting.Client;
using Microsoft.ServiceFabric.Services.Client;
```

34. Press F5 in Visual Studio to run the application in the local cluster. You can add api/values to the end of the URL in the launched browser and keep on refreshing to retrieve updated counter values. See Figure 6-33.

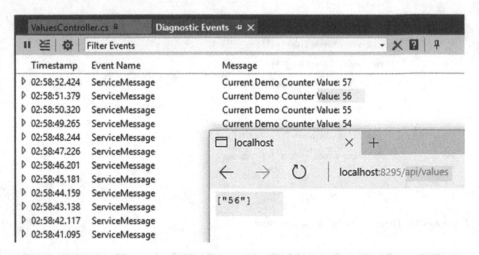

Figure 6-33. API returning demo counter value from stateful service

You have created a stateful service using Visual Studio that is running with Service Fabric. The stateful service has an incrementing counter named DemoCounter, and you have created an API running in Service Fabric to expose the value of the counter.

Lesson 6.03 – Create an Azure Service Fabric Cluster

Let's create an Azure Service Fabric cluster to host the stateful service and the web API in the SvcFabApp project created in the previous lesson.

1. In Azure portal, click on the green + to add new item, and then search for Service Fabric. Select the Service Fabric cluster. See Figure 6-34.

Figure 6-34. *Azure Service Fabric cluster*

2. In the screen that appears, click the Create button to start creating the cluster. See Figure 6-35.

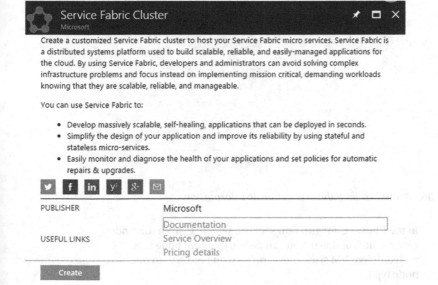

Figure 6-35. *Create Azure Service Fabric cluster*

3. On the Basics screen, provide a name for the cluster. Select Windows as the operating system. Set up credentials and select your Azure subscription. If you already have a resource group, you can select it or opt to create a new one in a preferred location. Click OK to proceed. See Figure 6-36.

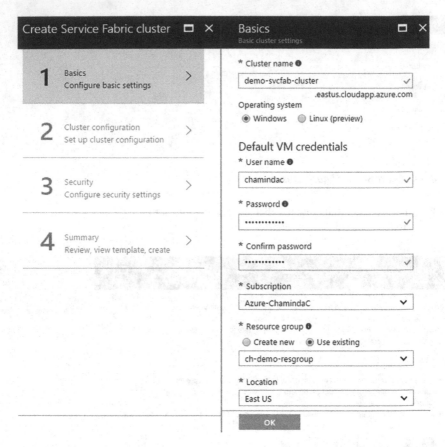

Figure 6-36. *Azure Service Fabric cluster basic information*

4. In the Cluster Configuration section, select "1" from the Node type count dropdown. You can define different node types with different VM sizes and so on by using more than one node type.

    In the Node Type Configuration section, give a name and select "Bronze" from both the Durability tier and Reliability tier dropdowns to go for cheaper options, as this is a demo. Select a VM size and set the VM scale capacity to 3. Ignore the warning shown saying this will be a test cluster (setting up as a test cluster is OK for learning purposes) and click OK in both sections, as shown in Figure 6-37.

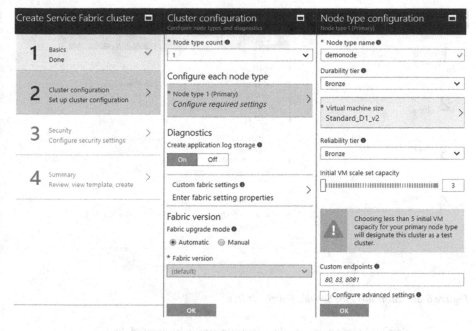

Figure 6-37. *Azure Service Fabric cluster configuration*

5. Security mode is set to Unsecure for this lesson. If you want to create a secure cluster, you need an SSL certificate from an authorized certificate provider. See Figure 6-38.

Figure 6-38. *Setting up as an unsecure cluster*

6. Review the summary and click the Create button. See Figure 6-39.

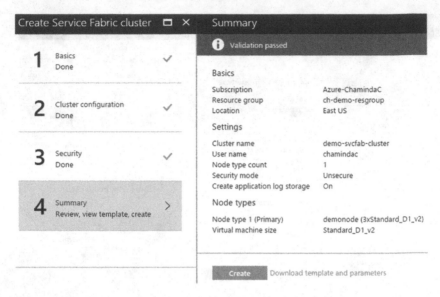

Figure 6-39. *Summary for Service Fabric cluster*

7. Service Fabric clusters take a few minutes to be created. You can view the created cluster by searching for Service Fabric in the **All resources** section of the Azure portal and clicking on Service Fabric Clusters. See Figure 6-40.

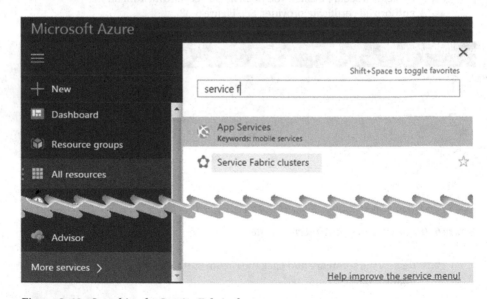

Figure 6-40. *Searching for Service Fabric cluster*

8. Click on the Service Fabric cluster name to view the details of the cluster. See Figure 6-41.

Figure 6-41. *New Service Fabric cluster*

9. In the overview, it shows the number of nodes running (three nodes, since we created with three nodes for the lesson) and the applications running (no applications deployed yet) in the cluster. To view the Service Fabric Explorer, click on the link highlighted in Figure 6-42.

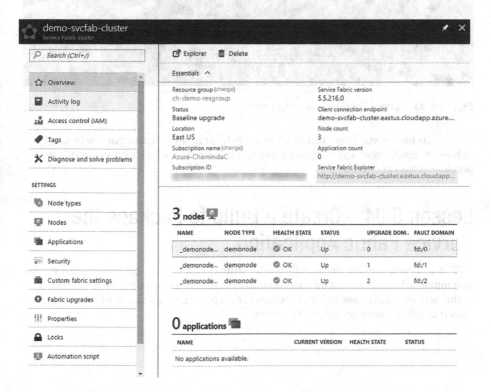

Figure 6-42. *Service Fabric cluster overview*

10.   Service Fabric Cluster Explorer shows information about the applications and nodes running and many other useful bits of information, like the Local Cluster Explorer you saw in a previous lesson. See Figure 6-43.

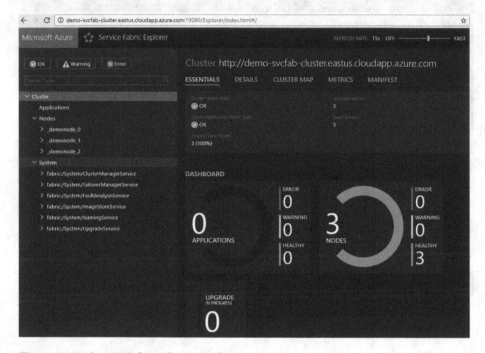

Figure 6-43. *Service Fabric Cluster Explorer*

In this lesson, you have created a Service Fabric cluster in Azure that can be used to host the application with a stateful service and a web API, which were created in a previous lesson of this chapter.

Lesson 6.04 – Create a Build to Package the Service Fabric Application

VSTS and TFS 2017 allow you to easily build Azure Service Fabric applications using built-in templates. If you are using a previous version of TFS, you can try the steps described in this article: http://www.colinsalmcorner.com/post/continuous-deployment-of-service-fabric-apps-using-vsts-or-tfs.

1. Before creating a build definition, you have to tokenize the cluster connection endpoint in the Service Fabric application you have developed and add application-upgrade capability. Open the Cloud.xml file in the PublishProfiles folder of the SvcFabApp to view the contents before performing the next steps. See Figure 6-44.

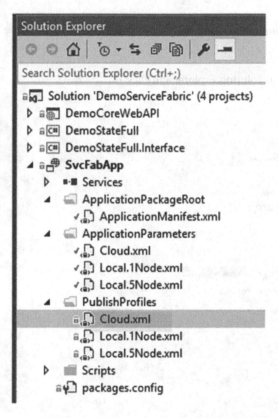

Figure 6-44. Open Cloud.xml in PublishProfiles folder of SvcFabApp

This file by default contains an empty cluster connection endpoint, as shown in Figure 6-45. Let's look at the file's contents after performing the following steps in order to see how the file is getting updated with those steps.

```
Cloud.xml ⁃⋊ X  Source Control Explorer
  1    <?xml version="1.0" encoding="utf-8"?>
  2  ⊟<PublishProfile xmlns="http://schemas.microsoft.com/2015/05/fabrictools">
 20                              AzureActiveDirectory="true"
 21                              ServerCertThumbprint="0123456789012345678901234567890123456789" />
 22       -->
 23       <ClusterConnectionParameters ConnectionEndpoint="" />
 24       <ApplicationParameterFile Path="..\ApplicationParameters\Cloud.xml" />
 25  </PublishProfile>
```

Figure 6-45. *Empty connection endpoint in the Cloud.xml file in PublishProfiles folder of SvcFabApp*

> 2. Right click on SvcFabApp in Solution Explorer and click Publish. See Figure 6-46.

Figure 6-46. *Publish Service Fabric application to add tokens*

> 3. In the Publish Service Fabric Application window, select the Microsoft account used for your Azure subscription. You can add your account if it has not already been added. Note that the Cloud.xml file is selected as the publish profile. See Figure 6-47.

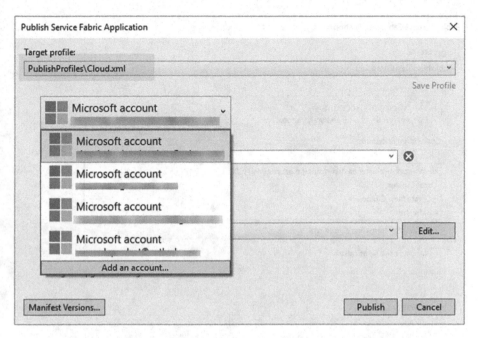

Figure 6-47. Selecting Microsoft account

4. Once the account has been connected, you can refresh to load the Azure Service Fabric connection endpoint URL. See Figure 6-48.

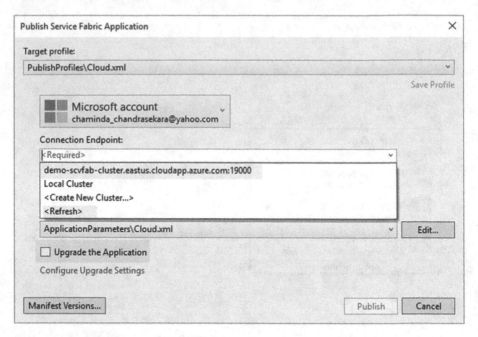

Figure 6-48. Selecting connection endpoint

5. Select the endpoint URL. You can see the connection is valid, as indicated by the green check mark (see Figure 6-49). Since our Azure Service Fabric cluster is not secure, if you clicked the Publish button (**do not click publish now**), it would publish the Service Fabric application to Azure directly from Visual Studio. But do not proceed as such, because we want to publish in a more systematic way, using Team Services build and release management. We are using this publish window just to tokenize the publish profile and save the profile as described in the next step.

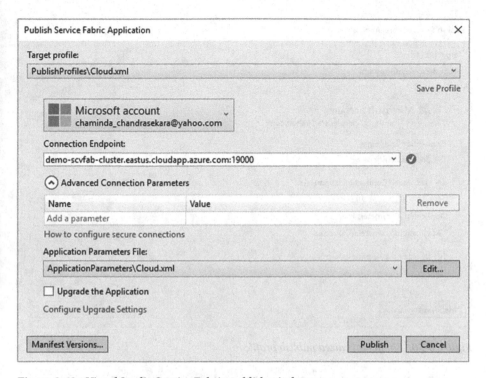

Figure 6-49. Visual Studio Service Fabric publish window

6. Type __ConnectionEndpoint__ (prefix and suffix with double underscore) in the Connection Endpoint field and select the "Upgrade the Application" check box. Click **Save Profile** and close the window. See Figure 6-50.

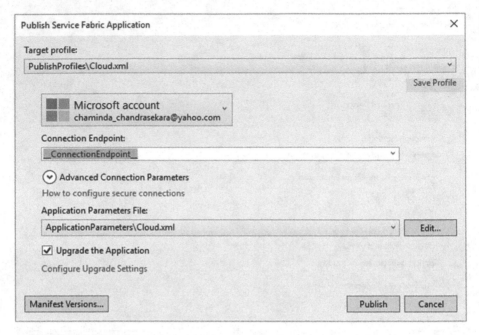

Figure 6-50. *Saving tokenized publish profile*

7. You can see that the Cloud.xml file in the PublishProfiles of
SvcFabApp get updated as shown in Figure 6-51. Since we
have tokenized the connection endpoint, we can use any
Azure Service Fabric cluster at deployment time.

```
Cloud.xml  ⊕ ✕  Source Control Explorer
 1    <?xml version="1.0" encoding="utf-8"?>
 2  ⊟<PublishProfile xmlns="http://schemas.microsoft.com/2015/05/fabrictools">
20                              AzureActiveDirectory="true"
21                              ServerCertThumbprint="01234567890123456789012345678901123456789" />
22    -->
23      <ClusterConnectionParameters ConnectionEndpoint="__ConnectionEndpoint__" />
24      <ApplicationParameterFile Path="..\ApplicationParameters\Cloud.xml" />
25  ⊟   <UpgradeDeployment Mode="Monitored" Enabled="true">
26        <Parameters FailureAction="Rollback" Force="True" />
27      </UpgradeDeployment>
28    </PublishProfile>
```

Figure 6-51. *Publish profile tokenized and upgrade enabled*

8. Open the Cloud.xml file from the ApplicationParameters
folder of the SvcFabApp. Make sure DemoCoreWebAPI_
InstanceCount is set to -1 to ensure that DemoCoreWebAPI
gets deployed to each machine in a multi-machine cluster (we
have set up a single-machine cluster, but this setting ensures
multi-machine cluster deployment capability). If you inspect

the local node application parameters (Local.1Node.xml), you will see this value is set to 1. Read more about this at https:// docs.microsoft.com/en-us/azure/service-fabric/ service-fabric-add-a-web-frontend#how-web-services-work-on-your-local-cluster. See Figure 6-52.

Figure 6-52. *Application parameters Cloud.xml*

9. Now that you have tokenized the publish profile and have the required application settings in place, let's create a build definition with which to build and package the Service Fabric application. In the Team Services Build tab of the TFS/VSTS web portal, create a new build definition using the Azure Service Fabric Application template, as shown in Figure 6-53.

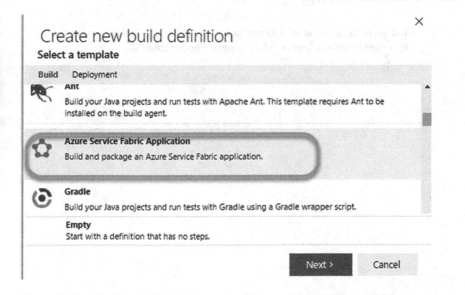

Figure 6-53. *Creating build definition to build Azure Service Fabric Application*

10. This creates a build definition with a few tasks, as shown in Figure 6-54. Name the definition "SvcFabDemoBuild."

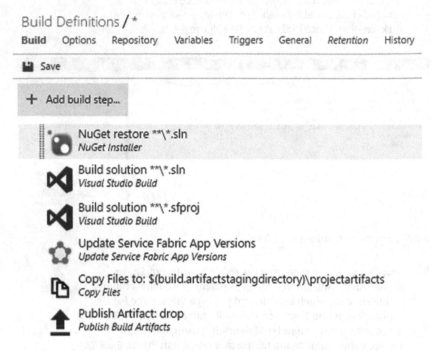

Figure 6-54. Build definition steps

11. First, go to the Repository tab and select the DemoServiceFabric solution folder path. See Figure 6-55.

Build Definitions / **SvcFabDemoBuild**

Build   Options   **Repository**   Variables   Triggers   General   Retention   History

💾 Save ▾   ⤺ Undo

Repository type	Team Foundation Version Control
Repository name	Project X
Label sources	Don't label sources
Clean	false ⌄ Clean options Sources ▾ ⓘ

Mappings

	Type	Server Path
✕	Map ▾	$/Project X/Main/DemoServiceFabric
➕	Add mapping	

Figure 6-55. Setting repository path

12. In the Variables tab, shown in Figure 6-56, you can see that the template has created build configuration and build platform variables, which have been set as release and x64, respectively, as required by the Service Fabric application.

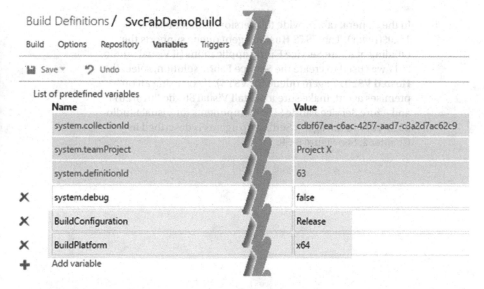

Build Definitions / **SvcFabDemoBuild**

Build   Options   Repository   **Variables**   Triggers

💾 Save ▾   ⤺ Undo

List of predefined variables

	Name	Value
	system.collectionId	cdbf67ea-c6ac-4257-aad7-c3a2d7ac62c9
	system.teamProject	Project X
	system.definitionId	63
✕	system.debug	false
✕	BuildConfiguration	Release
✕	BuildPlatform	x64
➕	Add variable	

Figure 6-56. Build Configuration and Platform variables

13. In the Triggers tab, in the Continuous Integration section, select the path of the DemoServiceFabric solution folder, as shown in Figure 6-57.

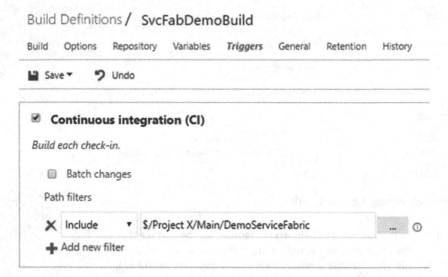

Figure 6-57. Continuous Integration settings

14. In the General tab, provide the version number format as 1.0.0$(rev:.r). The VSTS **Hosted** agent queue supports the building of Azure Service Fabric applications (if Visual Studio 2017 was used to create the Service Fabric solution, select the **Hosted VS2017** agent queue for VSTS). If you using an on-premises agent, make sure to install Visual Studio 2015/2017 and Azure Service Fabric SDK/components for Visual Studio 2015/2017 in the agent. Setting up agents is described in Chapter 2. See Figure 6-58.

Build Definitions / **SvcFabDemoBuild**

Build   Options   Repository   Variables   Triggers   **General**   Retention   History

💾 Save ▾   ⟲ Undo

Default agent queue	Hosted
Build job authorization scope	Project Collection
Description	
Build number format	1.0.0$(rev:.r)
Build job timeout in minutes	60
Badge enabled	☐

Demands

Name	Type
msbuild	exists
visualstudio	exists
➕ Add demand	

Figure 6-58. Build number format and agent

15.   Leave Options, Retention, and History tabs as they are.

16.   In the Build tab, select the NuGet Installer step and select the
DemoServiceFabric solution path for the **Path to solution**
field. Set the Installation type to Restore, as in Figure 6-59.
Expand the Advanced section and make sure to select 3.5.0
for the NuGet version. This allows the restoring of packages
required by the Core web API used in the solution. The
command-line step with the **dotnet restore** command
(as described in Chapter 3 on building ASP.NET Core
applications) cannot be used with this project structure. You
will run into the issue discussed at https://github.com/
dotnet/cli/issues/3199 since we are referring to the class
library .csproj from the Core web API.

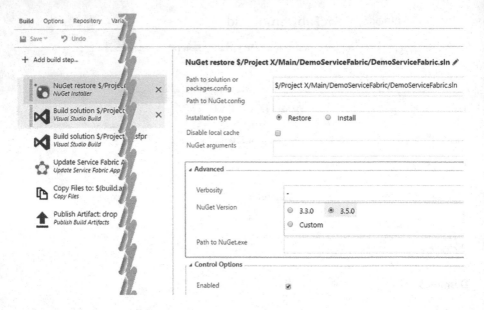

Figure 6-59. *NuGet restore step*

17. In the first Visual Studio Build step, select the DemoServiceFabric solution to build, as shown in Figure 6-60. Select Visual Studio 2015 or 2017, depending on the version you used. Make sure the build configuration and build platform variables are used in the relevant fields.

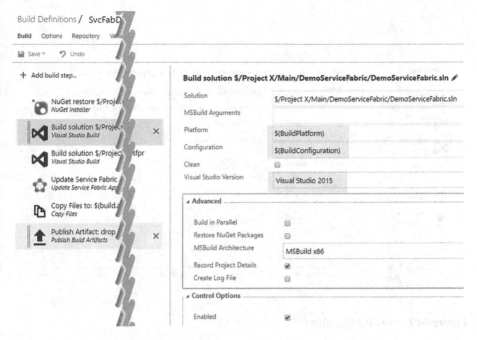

Figure 6-60. *Building the solution*

18. In the second Visual Studio Build task, select the SvcFabApp.
sfproj (Service Fabric project) to build. This will package the
Service Fabric application. Provide the following MS build
arguments.

```
/t:Package /p:PackageLocation=$(build.artifactstaging
directory)\applicationpackage
```

Select correct Visual Studio version (2015/2017 depending on
the version you have used) and make sure build platform and
build configuration variables are used. See Figure 6-61.

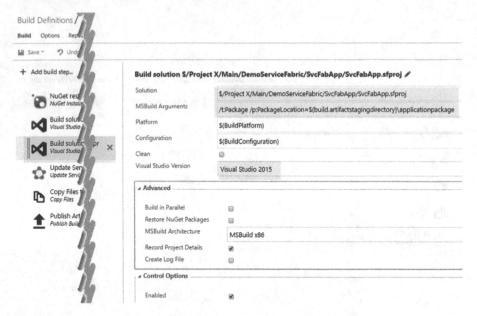

Figure 6-61. *Building the .sfproj*

19. In the Update Service Fabric App Versions task, provide the
Application Package path as $(build.artifactstagingdirectory)\
applicationpackage. Version value should be specified
as $(build.BuildNumber). (Note that in the default value
provided with the template, there is a " . " in front of $(build.
BuildNumber), so it reads as .$(build.BuildNumber). Remove
the prefixing " . " character, since we are going to replace the
version.) Choose "Replace" for the Version Behavior field.
Uncheck the **"Update only if changed"** option to allow the
updating of the version even if no changes from previous
builds have been made. This step properly updates the
Service Fabric application manifest and services manifest
versions. See Figure 6-62.

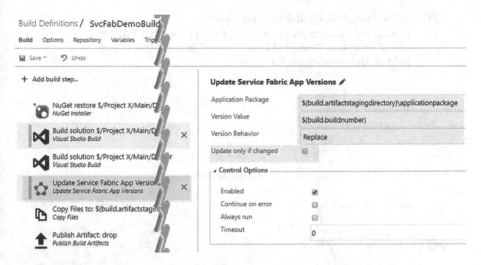

Figure 6-62. Updating Service Fabric app version

20. In the Copy Files task, provide $(build.sourcesdirectory) as the Source Folder. Specify the following values as content to copy from the publish profiles and application parameters folders:

```
**\PublishProfiles\*.xml
**\ApplicationParameters\*.xml
```

Set target folder as $(build.artifactstagingdirectory)\ projectartifacts. See Figure 6-63.

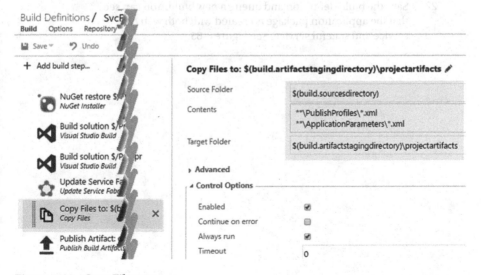

Figure 6-63. Copy Files step

21. In the Publish Build Artifacts step, specify $ (build.artifactstagingdirectory) as the path to publish. Provide "drop" in Artifact Name field and "Server" in the Artifact Type field, as shown in Figure 6-64.

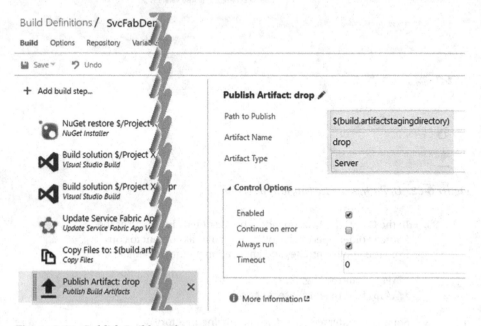

Figure 6-64. *Publish Build Artifacts step*

22. Save the build definition and queue a new build. You can see that the application package is created with both web API service and stateful service. See Figure 6-65.

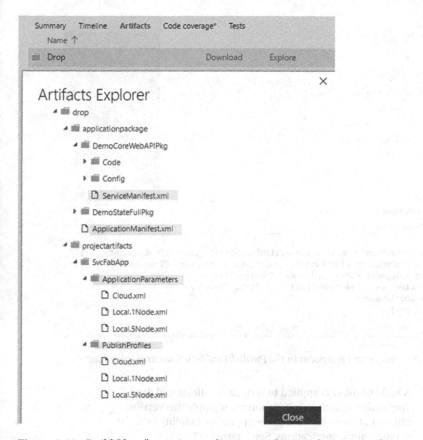

Figure 6-65. *Build "drop" contains application package and project artifacts*

23. If you download the publish profile Cloud.xml, you can see the __ConnectionEndpoint__ token, as in Figure 6-66.

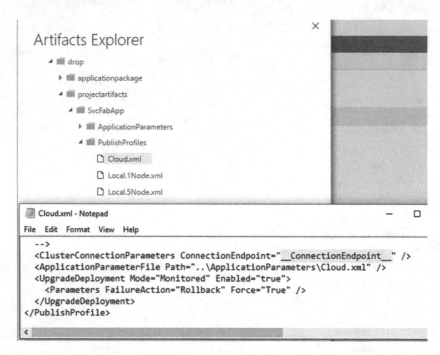

Figure 6-66. *Connection endpoint in the PublishProfiles\cloud.xml tokenized*

24. A build number is applied to service manifests and the application manifest. It is important to apply this version number in these files to enable upgrade capability in Azure Service Fabric applications. See Figure 6-67.

Figure 6-67. Build number applied to application and service manifests

You have created a build definition to package a Service Fabric application. The build was configured to output the required project artifacts (application parameters and publish profiles) for enabling deployment.

Lesson 6.05 – Deploy to Azure Service Fabric Cluster

You have built the Service Fabric application package using VSTS/TFS build and created a Service Fabric cluster in Azure. The next step is to get the built packages deployed to the cluster using Team Services/TFS release management.

1. Create a new release definition using the Azure Service Fabric Deployment template. After selecting the template, click Next. See Figure 6-68.

Create release definition
Select a template

Deployment

Deploy your Azure App Service.

Azure Cloud Service Deployment
Deploy an Azure Cloud Service

Azure Service Fabric Deployment
Deploy an Azure Service Fabric application

Empty
Start with an empty definition

Next >   Cancel

Figure 6-68. *Azure Service Fabric Deployment template*

2. In the next popup window, select SvcFabDemoBuild as the build source and select "Continuous deployment" to enable deployment when a new artifact from the build definition becomes available. Click Create to create a release definition. See Figure 6-69.

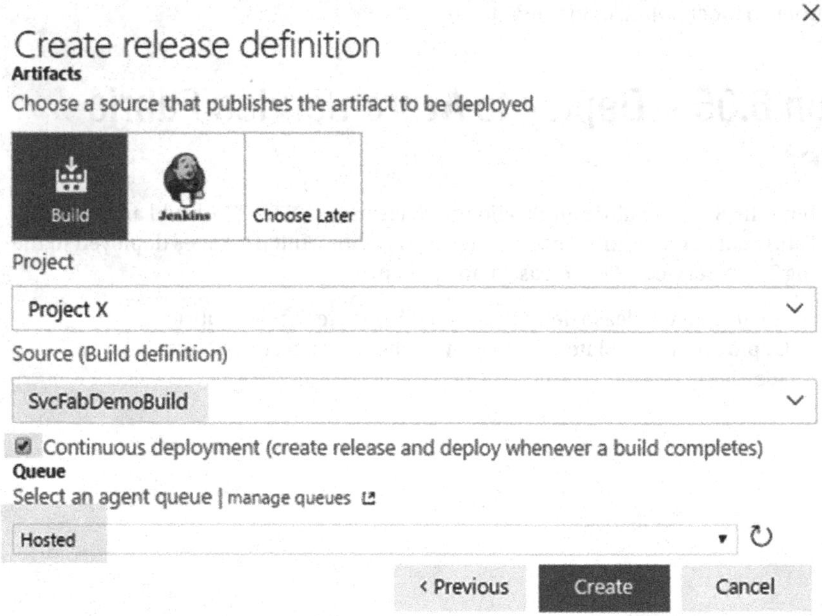

✕

Create release definition
Artifacts

Choose a source that publishes the artifact to be deployed

| Build | Jenkins | Choose Later |

Project

Project X   ⌄

Source (Build definition)

SvcFabDemoBuild   ⌄

☑ Continuous deployment (create release and deploy whenever a build completes)
Queue
Select an agent queue | manage queues ⌐

Hosted   ▾ ↻

< Previous   Create   Cancel

Figure 6-69. *Create release definition*

3. You can see a default environment, and that a Deploy Service Fabric Application task has been added to the definition. Let's leave this task as it is for the time being and come back to it later. See Figure 6-70.

Figure 6-70. Service Fabric Application Deployment task

4. Go to the Artifacts tab, and you can see SvcFabDemoBuild is selected (Figure 6-71).

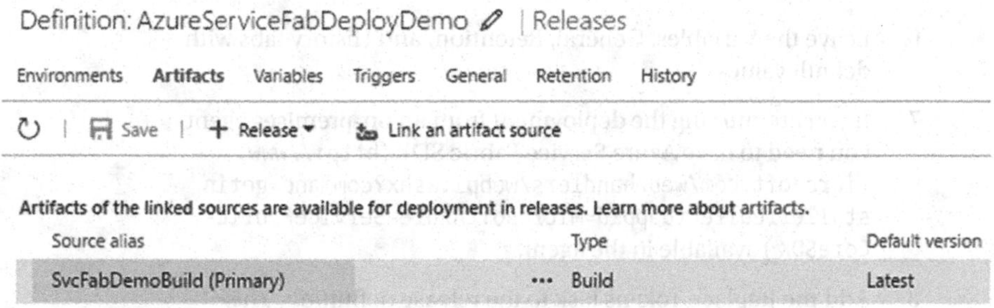

Figure 6-71. Linked artifacts

5. In the Triggers tab, you can see that continuous deployment is set up, as shown in Figure 6-72. This allows a change to be deployed to Azure Service Fabric once a new artifact becomes available with a new build.

Definition: AzureServiceFabDeployDemo ✎ | Releases

Environments   Artifacts   Variables   **Triggers**   General   Retention   History

↻ | 🖫 Save | ➕ Release ▾

Release triggers

Release trigger specifies when a new release will get created.

☑ **Continuous Deployment**

Creates release every time a new artifact version is available.

➕ Add new trigger

Set trigger on artifact source | SvcFabDemoBuild   ▾ | with tags ⓘ   Add...

☐ **Scheduled**

Create a new release at a specified time.

Environment triggers

Environment triggers specify when and how a deployment will be triggered on an environment.

Environment	Trigger
Environment 1	Automated: After release creation

Figure 6-72. Set up for continuous deployment

6. Leave the Variables, General, Retention, and History tabs with
    default values.

7. If you are running the deployment from an on-premises agent,
    you need to have Azure Service Fabric SDK (http://www.
    microsoft.com/web/handlers/webpi.ashx?command=getin
    stallerredirect&appid=MicrosoftAzure-ServiceFabric-
    CoreSDK) available in the agent.

8. Add the Replace Tokens task to the release definition. This
    extension can be downloaded from Marketplace at https://
    marketplace.visualstudio.com/items?itemName=qetza.
    replacetokens . Setting up extensions for build and release is
    described in Chapter 2.

    In the Replace Tokens task, select the publish profiles
    directory ($(System.DefaultWorkingDirectory)/
    SvcFabDemoBuild/drop/projectartifacts/SvcFabApp/
    PublishProfiles) as the root directory and cloud.xml as
    the target file. In the Advanced section, specify __ (double
    underscore) as both token prefix and token suffix, since
    we have specified __ConnectionEndpoint__ in the publish
    profile. See Figure 6-73.

Figure 6-73. *Replace Tokens task*

In the Environment menu, click on Configure variables. Add a new environment variable named **ConnectionEndpoint** (token value in Cloud.xml is **ConnectionEndpoint** prefixed and suffixed with __) with a value like that shown in Figure 6-74. This allows the **__ConnectionEndpoint__ to be replaced with a value like below.**

```
demo-scvfab-cluster.eastus.cloudapp.azure.com:19000
```

You can copy this value from the Azure Service Fabric Cluster Overview page.

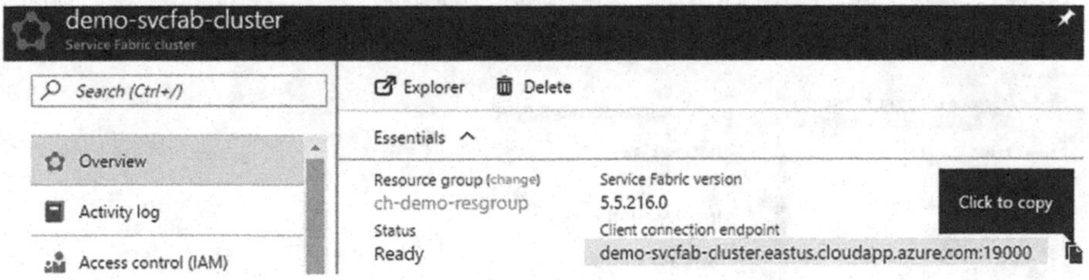

Figure 6-74. *Azure Service Fabric client connection endpoint*

9. In the Service Fabric Application Deployment task, click the Add link (highlighted in Figure 6-75), which appears next to the Cluster Connection field. In the popup window, specify the connection endpoint as follows, prefixing with http://:

```
http://demo-scvfab-cluster.eastus.cloudapp.azure.
com:19000
```

Provide a name for the connection and click OK.

271

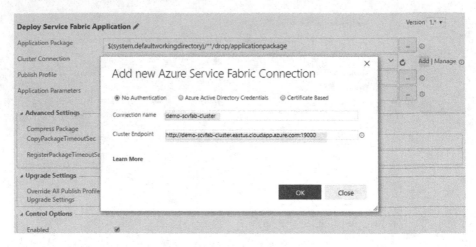

Figure 6-75. *Azure Service Fabric Connection*

You can click the Manage link next to the Cluster Connection field to go to the Services tab in Settings and add an Azure Service Fabric endpoint. It will show the same popup window as in Figure 6-75, and you can create the endpoint. We are using no authentication since we have created the Azure Service Fabric cluster as non-secure. You can use other options with a secure cluster. See Figure 6-76.

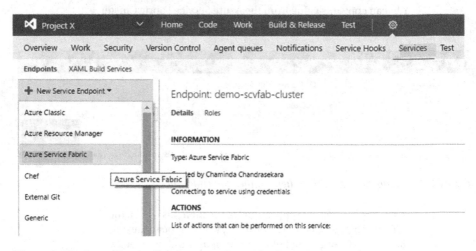

Figure 6-76. *Azure Service Fabric connection endpoint in Services tab*

10. Refresh the cluster connections and select the connection created. See Figure 6-77.

Deploy Service Fabric Application ✐

Application Package	$(system.defaultworkingdirectory)/**/drop/applicationpackage	...	ⓘ
Cluster Connection	demo-scvfab-cluster	⌄ C	Add
Publish Profile	$(system.defaultworkingdirectory)/**/drop/projectartifacts/**/PublishProfiles/Cloud.xml	...	ⓘ
Application Parameters		...	ⓘ

◢ **Advanced Settings**

Compress Package ▢
CopyPackageTimeoutSec
RegisterPackageTimeoutSec

◢ **Upgrade Settings**

Override All Publish Profile ▢
Upgrade Settings

◢ **Control Options**

Enabled ☑
Continue on error ▢

Figure 6-77. Selecting cluster connection

11. Save the release definition as AzureServiceFabDeployDemo.

12. Create a release by clicking **Create Release** in the release definition. It will deploy the Azure Service Fabric application. See Figure 6-78.

AzureServiceFabDeployDemo / **Release-3**

| Summary | Environments | Artifacts | Variables | General | Commits | Work items | Tests | Logs | History |

↻ | ⭱ Deploy ▾   🖫 Save   Abandon

Details

Release-3

Manually created by Chaminda Chandrasekara 12 hours ago

🏗 SvcFabDemoBuild / 1.0.0.10 (Build)   ⑂ $/Project X/Main/DemoServiceFabric

Environments

Environment	Actions	Deployment status	Triggered	Completed	Tests
Environment 1	•••	SUCCEEDED	12 hours ago	12 hours ago	No tests

Issues

No issues reported in this release.

Figure 6-78. Deployment to Azure Service Fabric completed

13. In the Azure Service Fabric cluster, the current application version is deployed (notice the version number in Figure 6-79).

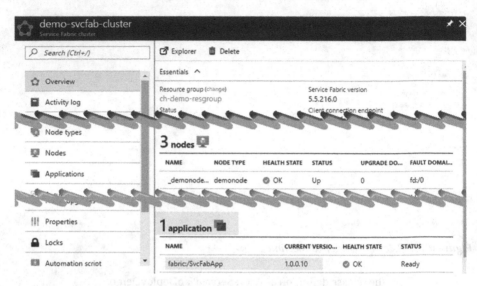

Figure 6-79. *Application deployed to Azure Service Fabric cluster*

14. We could test the web API locally using http://localhost:8295/api/values, since the service manifest of the web API specified the port as 8295. See Figure 6-80.

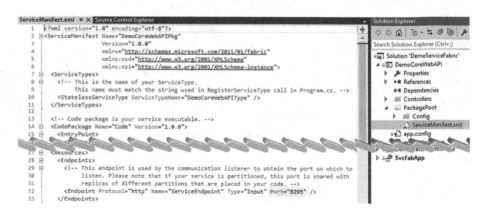

Figure 6-80. *Endpoint is set to use a given port*

But if we try to run the connection endpoint URL with port 8295 to get values from the web API, as seen here, nothing will be returned:

```
http://demo-scvfab-cluster.eastus.cloudapp.azure.
com:8292/api/values
```

See Figure 6-81.

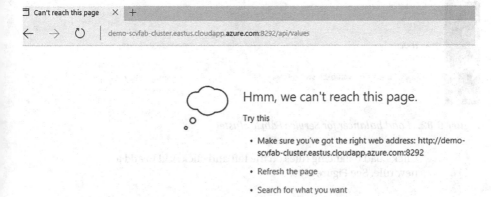

Figure 6-81. *Web API cannot be accessed from the Azure Service Fabric cluster*

This is because we have our web API behind a load balancer, and we need to map the backend port 8295 with a front port.

To map backend port 8295 (or port in your service manifest for web API) to load balancer front end port, search for load balancers in the More Services field in Azure portal. Click on the load balancers. Then, select the load balancer with your Service Fabric cluster name. See Figure 6-82.

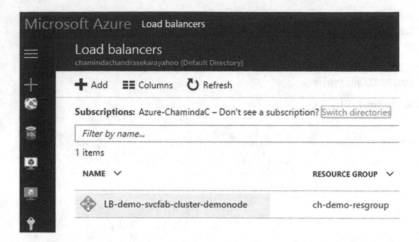

Figure 6-82. *Load balancer for Service Fabric cluster*

Click Load balancing rules on the left and click Add to add a new rule. See Figure 6-83.

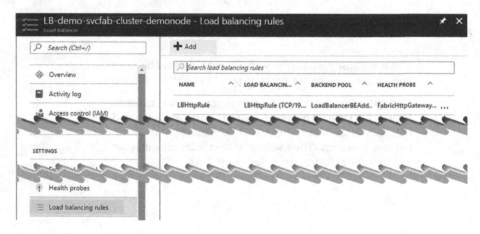

Figure 6-83. *Load balancing rules*

Create a new rule with port set as 85 (your preference port is OK) and backend port as 8295 (or port number in your web API service manifest). Save the rule by clicking OK. See Figure 6-84.

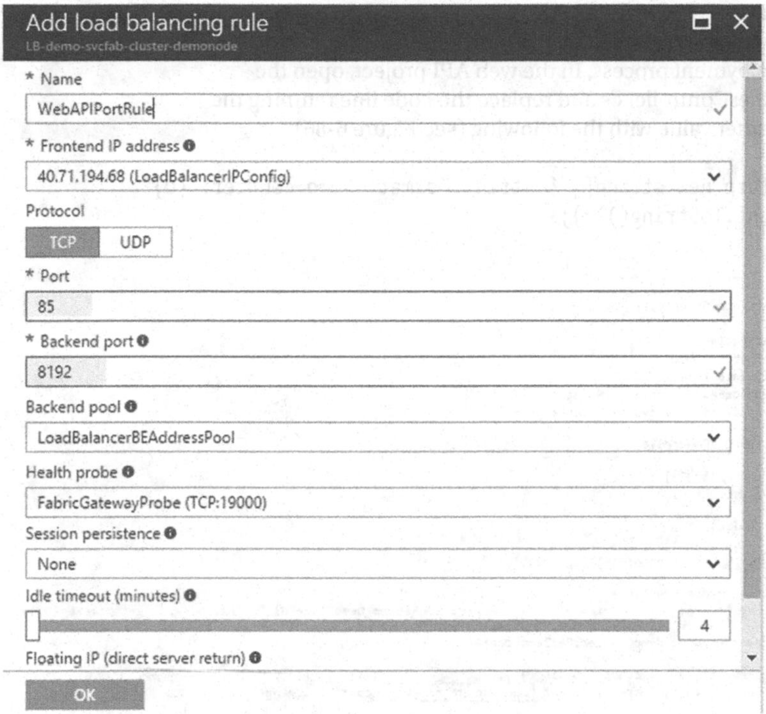

Add load balancing rule
LB-demo-svcfab-cluster-demonode

* Name

WebAPIPortRule

* Frontend IP address ❶

40.71.194.68 (LoadBalancerIPConfig)

Protocol

| TCP | UDP |

* Port

85

* Backend port ❶

8192

Backend pool ❶

LoadBalancerBEAddressPool

Health probe ❶

FabricGatewayProbe (TCP:19000)

Session persistence ❶

None

Idle timeout (minutes) ❶

4

Floating IP (direct server return) ❶

OK

Figure 6-84. *Load balancing rule for web API*

Now you can run the URL that follows and get the counter value from the deployed Service Fabric application in the Azure Service Fabric cluster. See Figure 6-85.

```
http://demo-scvfab-cluster.eastus.cloudapp.azure.
com:85/api/values
```

← → C ⓘ demo-scvfab-cluster.eastus.cloudapp.azure.com:85/api/values

["111160"]

Figure 6-85. *Web API in Azure Service Fabric cluster*

15. Let's open the DemoServiceFabric solution in Visual
     Studio and make a small code change to verify the upgrade
     deployment process. In the web API project, open the
     ValuesController.cs and replace the code line retuning the
     counter value with the following (see Figure 6-86):

```
return new string[] { string.Format("Demo counter: {0}",
count.ToString()) };
```

```
using System;
using System.Collections.Generic;
using System.Linq;
using System.Threading.Tasks;
using Microsoft.AspNetCore.Mvc;
using DemoStateFull.Interface;
using Microsoft.ServiceFabric.Services.Remoting.Client;
using Microsoft.ServiceFabric.Services.Client;

namespace DemoCoreWebAPI.Controllers
{
    [Route("api/[controller]")]
    public class ValuesController : Controller
    {
        // GET api/values
        [HttpGet]
        public async Task<IEnumerable<string>> Get()
        {
            IDemoCounter demoCounter =
            ServiceProxy.Create<IDemoCounter>(new Uri("fabric:/SvcFabApp/DemoStateFull"), new ServicePartitionKey(0));

            long count = await demoCounter.GetDemoCountAsync();

            return new string[] { count.ToString() };
            return new string[] { string.Format("Demo counter: {0}", count.ToString()) };
        }

        // GET api/values/5
        [HttpGet("{id}")]
        public string Get(int id)
        {
```

Figure 6-86. *Code change in web API*

16. Check in the changes to source control, providing a comment
     "Format counter value message", to trigger a build and a
     deplyment to deploy the changes to Azure Service Fabric. See
     Figure 6-87.

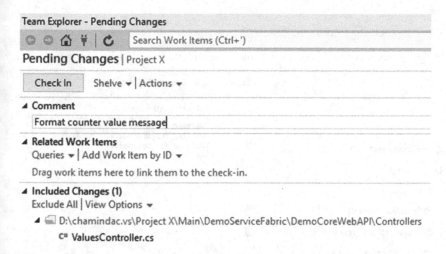

Figure 6-87. *Code change check-in to source control*

17. A build will automatically be triggered, and, once it completes, a deployment will be triggered. See Figure 6-88.

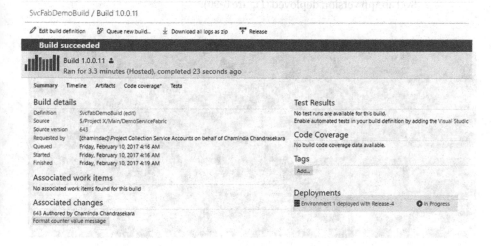

Figure 6-88. *Build completes and triggers deployment*

18. You can see the deployment in progress as it upgrades the Server Fabric application. See Figure 6-89.

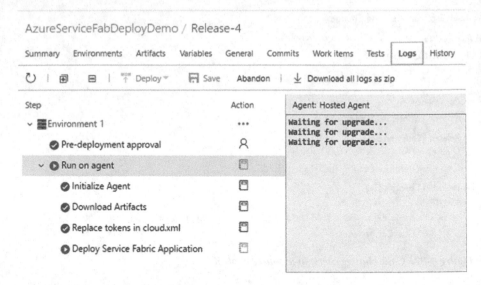

Figure 6-89. Service Fabric application upgrading

19. Once the upgrade is complete, you can see the new SvcFabApp version deployed (Figure 6-90).

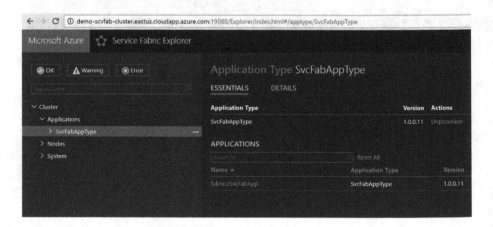

Figure 6-90. New Service Fabric application version deployed

20. When the web API is accessed, you can see that the changes are in effect. See Figure 6-91.

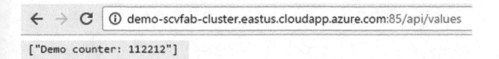

Figure 6-91. Changes to Web API are in effect

In this lesson, you created a release definition with which to deploy your Service Fabric application–which is created with Visual Studio and packaged with TFS build–to the Azure Service Fabric cluster.

Summary

In this chapter, you learned how to implement continuous delivery to Azure Service Fabric using Team Services/TFS. With this knowledge, you can learn more about building microservice applications without worrying about how to get them deployed.

In the next chapter, you will learn about task groups and build/release definition history usage.

■ ■ ■

CHAPTER 7

Task Groups, Folders, and Build/Release Definition History

In this chapter, you will learn what a task group is and how to create and use them. Using the history and the comments provided by updaters of the definitions, you will be able to identify changes made to the build or the release definitions. You will also get to learn about grouping build or release definitions using folders and the use of tags.

What Is a Task Group?

A sequence of tasks can be encapsulated into a reusable task in the Task Catalog using a task group. This allows a task group to be added to a build or release definition like a normal task. You have the option to abstract the task information while extracting the required parameters from the encapsulated tasks. Task groups are scoped at the team-project level and are not visible to other team projects.

Lesson 7.01 – Create a Task Group

Let's use a few PowerShell tasks to show what can be done with task groups. You can use any of the available tasks in a task group, but PowerShell tasks are used here to make the concept easy to understand.

© Chaminda Chandrasekara 2017
C. Chandrasekara, *Beginning Build and Release Management with TFS 2017 and VSTS*,
DOI 10.1007/978-1-4842-2811-1_7

1. Create a new build definition with an empty template.
   Add three PowerShell tasks from the Task Catalog and add the
   following PowerShell as an inline script to all three tasks
   (see Figure 7-1):

```
parame
$CommonParam,
$TaskParam1,
$TaskParam2
)
write-host "Task 1 CommonParam Value:" $CommonParam
write-host "Task 1 TaskParam1 Value:" $TaskParam1
write-host "Task 1 TaskParam2 Value:" $TaskParam2
```

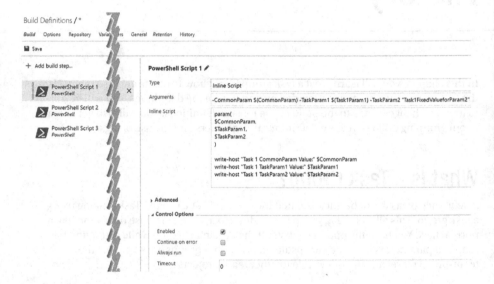

Figure 7-1. *Build definition with three PowerShell tasks*

2. For the first, second, and third tasks, provide the arguments as
   specified here (see Figure 7-2):

   First Task Arguments:

```
-CommonParam $(CommonParam) -TaskParam1
$(Task1Param1) -TaskParam2 "Task1FixedValueforParam2"
```

Second Task Arguments:

```
-CommonParam $(CommonParam) -TaskParam1
"Task2FixedValueforParam1" -TaskParam2
"Task2FixedValueforParam2"
```

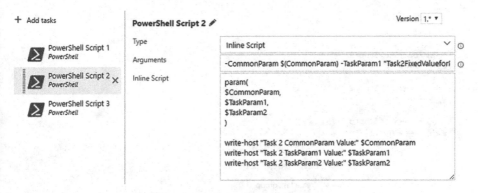

Figure 7-2. PowerShell task two

Third Task Arguments (see Figure 7-3):

```
-CommonParam $(CommonParam) -TaskParam1
"Task3FixedValueforParam1" -TaskParam2
$(Task3Param2)
```

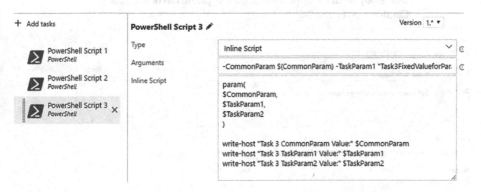

Figure 7-3. PowerShell task three

285

3. Select all three PowerShell tasks and right click; select "Create task group" from the dropdown. See Figure 7-4.

Figure 7-4. *Grouping tasks*

4. In the popup window, define the default values and descriptions (not mandatory) for parameters. Provide a description and select Utility for the Task Catalog category. You can select **Build, Deploy, Package, Utility,** or **Test** as the category of the task group so that it appears in the appropriate tab of the Task Catalog. See Figure 7-5.

Create task group

Name	Demo Task Group
Description	Demo Task Group with three PowerShell Tasks
Category	Utility

Parameters

The following parameters and values are from the configuration variables used in the underlying tasks.

Name	Value	Description
CommonParam		Common Param for all tasks
Task1Param1		Task One Param One
Task3Param2	Task3Param2DefaultParamValueforGroup	Task Three Param Three

Create   Cancel

Figure 7-5. *Creating a task group*

5. This will instantly convert the tasks in the build definition to the task group. You can see the default values specified appear, and the parameters defined are ready for values to be entered. The description entered can be viewed when the mouse hovers over the information icon. See Figure 7-6.

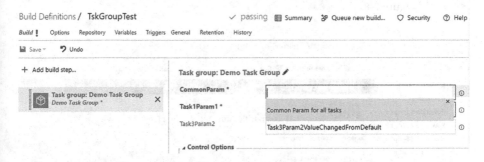

Figure 7-6. *Build definition tasks converted to task group*

6. Provide values for the parameters CommonParam and Task1Param1. Make sure to enable the task execution by selecting "Enabled" in the Control Options section. See Figure 7-7.

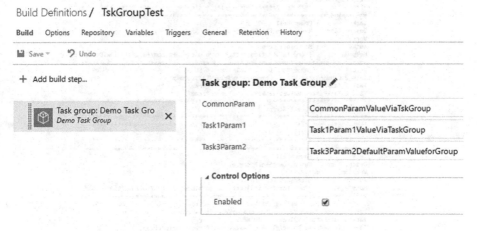

Figure 7-7. *Using task group in build definition*

7. Save the build definition, giving it the name "TskGroupTest,"
   and queue a new build. You will see all of the values (values
   specified in encapsulated tasks and values provided as
   parameters in the task group) appear in the log. This way you
   can expose required parameters from the task group while
   hiding any private values inside the task group you create. See
   Figure 7-8.

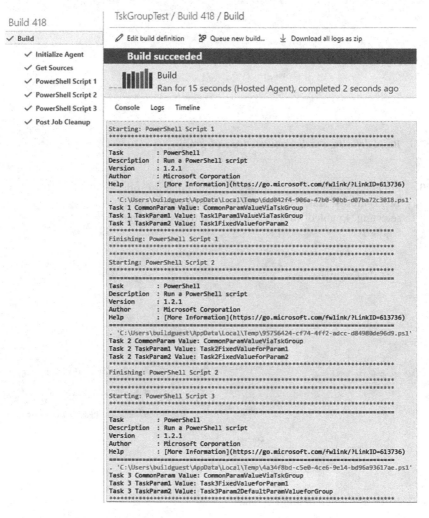

Figure 7-8. *Values in task group and parameters provided to task group shown in log*

8. Change a default value, and you will see the effects when a new build is queued. See Figure 7-9.

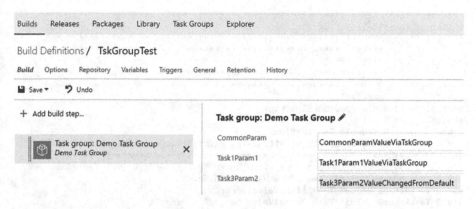

Figure 7-9. *Change Task3Param2*

9. When saving the build definition, make sure to provide a comment. This will be useful when the history of the build definition is inspected. See Figure 7-10.

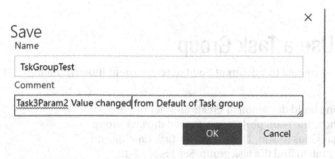

Figure 7-10. *Saving build definition*

10. Queue a new build, and it shows the changed value in PowerShell task three. See Figure 7-11.

```
****************************************************************************
Finishing: PowerShell Script 2
****************************************************************************
****************************************************************************
Starting: PowerShell Script 3
****************************************************************************
============================================================================
Task          : PowerShell
Description   : Run a PowerShell script
Version       : 1.2.1
Author        : Microsoft Corporation
Help          : [More Information](https://go.microsoft.com/fwlink/?LinkID=613736)
============================================================================
. 'C:\Users\buildguest\AppData\Local\Temp\9bffb089-2291-447e-ae9f-0772a5986569.ps
Task 3 CommonParam Value: CommonParamValueViaTskGroup
Task 3 TaskParam1 Value: Task3FixedValueforParam1
Task 3 TaskParam2 Value: Task3Param2ValueChangedFromDefault
****************************************************************************
```

Figure 7-11. *Task3Param2 shown when build is running*

In this lesson, you learned how to easily create a task group using existing tasks in a build definition. In the same way, you can create a task group using a set of tasks in a release definition.

Lesson 7.02 – Use a Task Group

You can use a task group you created in a different build or release definition within the team project.

1. Open an existing build definition or create another build definition in the same team project you created the task group in during the previous lesson. Then, open up Task Catalog and go to the Utility tab to find the task group. See Figure 7-12.

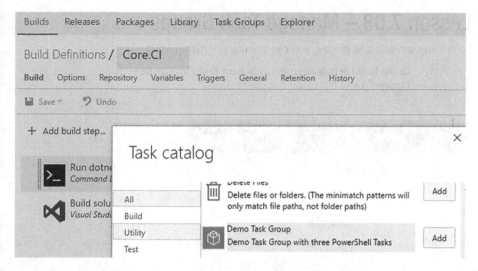

Figure 7-12. Task group available as a task in Task Catalog in a build definition

2. The same thing can be done with a release definition. See Figure 7-13.

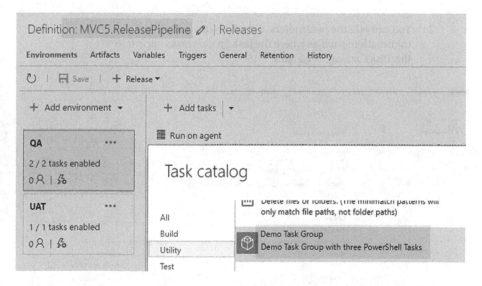

Figure 7-13. Task group available as a task in Task Catalog in a release definition

You can create your own task groups using the existing tasks in your build or release definition and reuse them in other build/release definitions you are creating in the same team project. This allows you to avoid duplication of the same set of tasks in different build/release definitions and increases the maintainability of the definitions.

Lesson 7.03 – Manage Task Groups

To manage existing task groups, you can use the Task Groups tab.

1. In the Build & Release menu, click on Task Groups. See Figure 7-14.

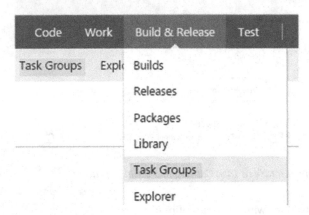

Figure 7-14. *Task groups*

2. You can edit the parameters' default values and other information, such as where the task group's tasks appear in the Task Catalog. See Figure 7-15.

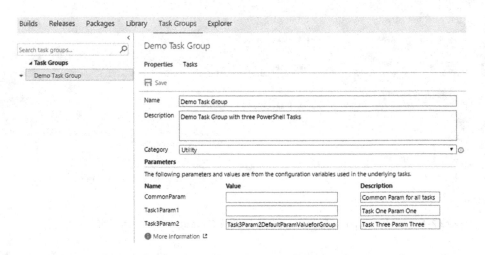

Figure 7-15. *Editing a task group*

3. Click on Tasks to view the steps in the task group. You can edit the individual tasks in a task group and add new tasks from the Task Catalog to the task group by clicking on Add tasks. See Figure 7-16.

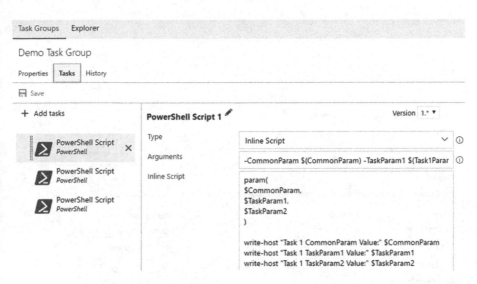

Figure 7-16. *Editing task group tasks*

4. Add another PowerShell task and use the same inline script. Pass arguments as given below (see Figure 7-17):

```
-CommonParam $(CommonParam) -TaskParam1
"Task3FixedValueforParam1" -TaskParam2
$(Task4Param2)
```

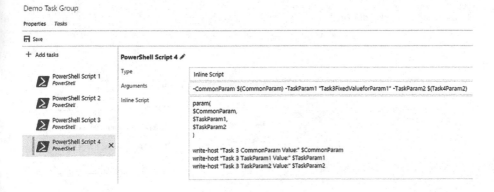

Figure 7-17. *Adding a new task to task group*

5. You can see a new parameter getting added to the task group since you specified $(Task4Param2) as a parameter for the fourth task, which was added in the previous step. Do not provide a default value for the new parameter. See Figure 7-18.

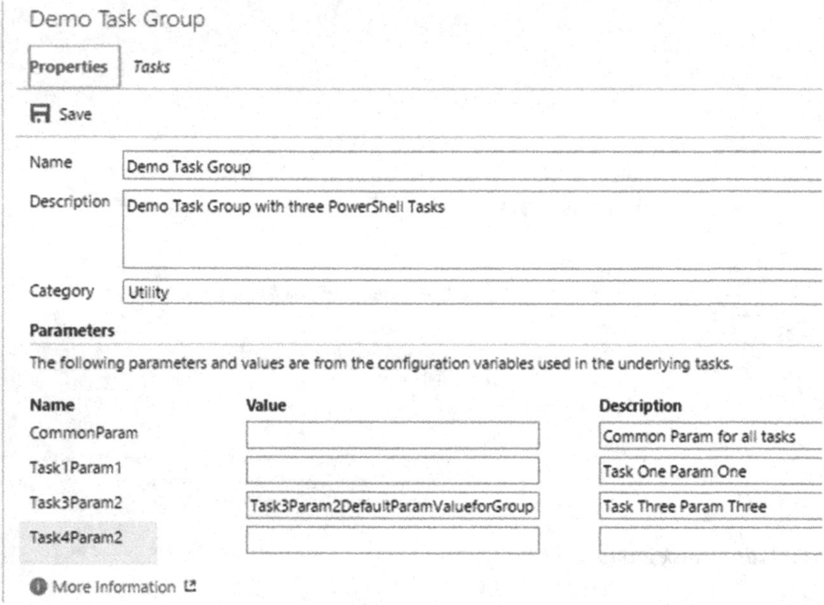

Demo Task Group

Properties	Tasks

🖫 Save

Name	Demo Task Group
Description	Demo Task Group with three PowerShell Tasks
Category	Utility

Parameters

The following parameters and values are from the configuration variables used in the underlying tasks.

Name	Value	Description
CommonParam		Common Param for all tasks
Task1Param1		Task One Param One
Task3Param2	Task3Param2DefaultParamValueforGroup	Task Three Param Three
Task4Param2		

ⓘ More Information ↳

Figure 7-18. New parameter in task group

6. Save the task group and open the build definition that is using the task group so the definition can be edited. The build definition now has another mandatory parameter for the task (task group task from catalog). See Figure 7-19.

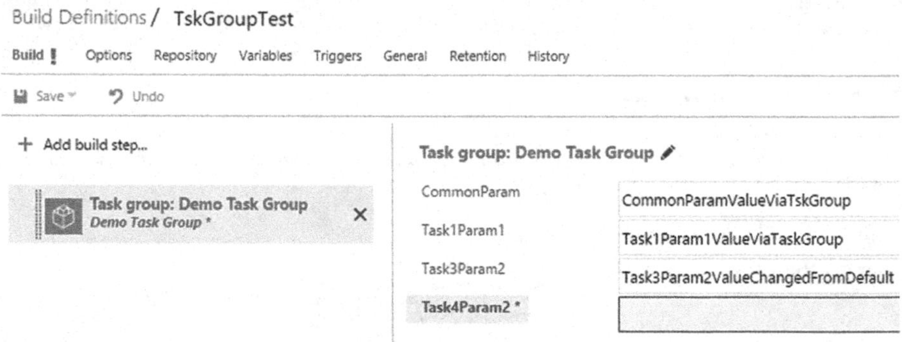

Build Definitions / TskGroupTest

Build ❗ Options Repository Variables Triggers General Retention History

🖫 Save ▾   ⤺ Undo

╋ Add build step...

Task group: Demo Task Group
Demo Task Group *	✕

Task group: Demo Task Group ✎

CommonParam	CommonParamValueViaTskGroup
Task1Param1	Task1Param1ValueViaTaskGroup
Task3Param2	Task3Param2ValueChangedFromDefault
Task4Param2 *	

Figure 7-19. New parameter in task group is required in the build definition that is using the task group

7. Provide the value **Task4Param2ValueviaBuild** in the build
    definition, save, and queue a build to verify. See Figure 7-20.

```
Author       : Microsoft Corporation
Help         : [More Information](https://go.microsoft.com/fwlink/?LinkID=613736)
================================================================================
. 'C:\Users\buildguest\AppData\Local\Temp\e3f7c637-e9bf-4ff8-bd98-1f396ae084fe.ps1'
Task 3 CommonParam Value: CommonParamValueViaTskGroup
Task 3 TaskParam1 Value: Task3FixedValueforParam1
Task 3 TaskParam2 Value: Task4Param2ValueviaBuild
********************************************************************************
Finishing: PowerShell Script 4
********************************************************************************
```

Figure 7-20. *New parameter value shown in build log*

You learned how to manage an existing task group in this lesson. Do further
experiments by modifying the task group in order to understand more about them.

Lesson 7.04 – Organize Folders to Group Builds

When you have multiple build definitions in a team project, you might find at times it is
not easy to locate a given build definition. To group or categorize your build definitions,
you can use folders, as shown in the following steps.

1. In the Builds tab, go to All Definitions and click Manage
    Folders. See Figure 7-21.

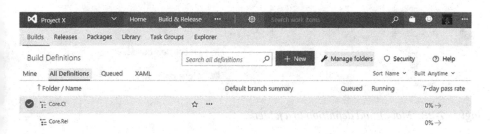

Figure 7-21. *Manage folders for grouping build definitions*

2. Click on Create new folder, provide a name, and click OK. See Figure 7-22.

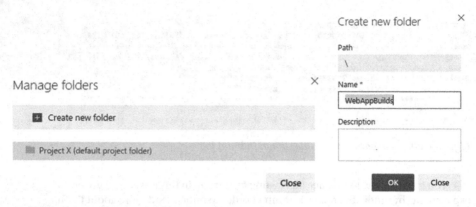

Figure 7-22. *Creating new folder*

3. Then, click on the menu link for a build and choose Move definition. See Figure 7-23.

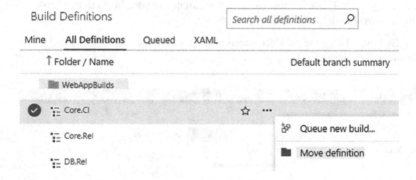

Figure 7-23. *Move build definition to a folder*

4. Select the folder and click OK, as shown in Figure 7-24.

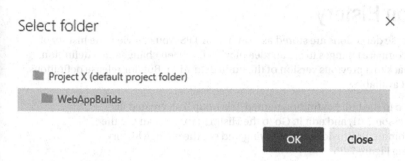

Figure 7-24. Selecting a folder for build definition

5. This way, you can group your build definitions into folders to organize them properly. See Figure 7-25.

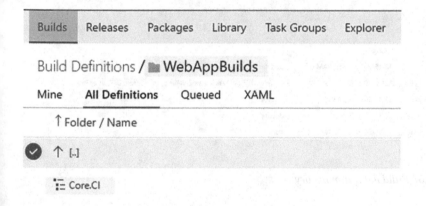

Figure 7-25. Build definition moved to folder

You can use folders to group your build definitions in order to keep them organized and categorized in your team project.

Lesson 7.05 – Track Build/Release Definition History

Build and release definitions are stored as json files in TFS. You can view the history of updates and compare changes to get an idea of what has been changed in a definition. You can roll back to a previous version of the build definition. But, for release definitions, rollback is not available.

1. Go to the build definition named TskGroupTest, created in Lesson 7.01, and edit it. Go to the History tab. You can see the comments provided while saving and see the change history. See Figure 7-26.

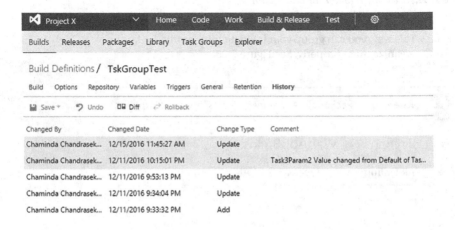

Figure 7-26. *Build definition history*

2. You can view the differences by selecting two versions and clicking on Diff, as shown in Figure 7-27.

Figure 7-27. Build definition version comparison

3. In the build definition history, you can select a version and click on Rollback to go back to that version of the build. See Figure 7-28.

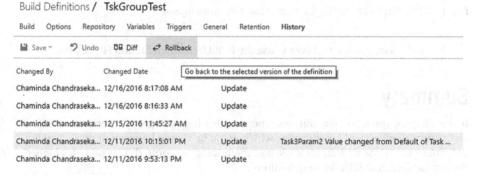

Figure 7-28. Rollback build definition

4. In the new build editor layout (explained in Chapter 1), you can see the rollback option and comparison of definitions via a menu link. **Rollback** is available as **Revert Definition,** and **Diff** is available as **Compare difference**. See Figure 7-29.

Builds	Releases	Packages	Library	Task Groups	Explorer		

🏗 TskGroupTest   🖫 Save

	Tasks	Variables	Triggers	Options	Retention	History
✓	Changed By			Change Type		Changed Date
	Chaminda Chandrasekara			Update		12/16/2016 8:17:08 AM
	Chaminda Chandrasekara			Update		12/16/2016 8:16:33 AM
✓	Chaminda Chandrasekara		•••	Update		12/15/2016 11:45:27 AM
	Chaminda Chandrasekara		🔢 Compare Difference			12/11/2016 10:15:01 PM
	Chaminda Chandrasekara		↩ Revert Definition			12/11/2016 9:53:13 PM
	Chaminda Chandrasekara			Update		12/11/2016 9:34:04 PM
	Chaminda Chandrasekara			Add		12/11/2016 9:33:32 PM

Figure 7-29. *Rollback and Diff in new build definition layout*

In this lesson, you learned how to use the build/release definition History tab.

Summary

In this chapter, you learned about task groups. These help you group a common set of tasks into a single unit of functionality, which could be shared between multiple build definitions or release definitions while parameterizing as required. This provides higher maintainability in build/release definitions.

Organizing builds using folders allows you to maintain a proper structure and to categorize your builds. This is useful if you are using a large team project with multiple teams, or applications with multiple builds.

The build and release history allows you to track changes made to a definition. Rollback of build definitions lets you go back to the previous versions easily if you made any mistakes in an update. This would be a really nice feature to have for release definitions as well, and will eventually be available in the future.

In the next chapter, you will learn how to build source code in external repositories using Team Services build.

CHAPTER 8

■ ■ ■

Building with External Repositories and Other Platform Builds

In this chapter, you will learn how to use Team Services builds to build code in GitHub and how to build Java code with Team Services builds. Using a similar mechanism which you will use for GitHub, you will be able to build code in other repositories, such as Subversion.

Lesson 8.01 – Create a Console App and Commit It to GitHub

Prerequisites: You have signed up for a GitHub account (https://github.com/), and you have a Team Services account (https://www.visualstudio.com/team-services/).

Let's create a simple console application in Visual Studio and commit it to GitHub.

1. Open GitHub in your browser and click on the Start a project button, as shown in Figure 8-1.

Learn Git and GitHub without any code!

Using the Hello World guide, you'll create a repository, start a branch, write comments, and open a pull request.

Read the guide   Start a project

Figure 8-1. *Start a project in GitHub*

2. Type in TFS.Build.Demo for the repository name and create a repository. A public repository will allow anyone to see it, but you can control who is allowed to commit code to it. A private one allows you to control who can see the repository as well. If you select the "Initialize this repository" option you will be allowed to clone the repository to your computer immediately. Do not select this option, since it will be cloned in a later step using Visual Studio. See Figure 8-2.

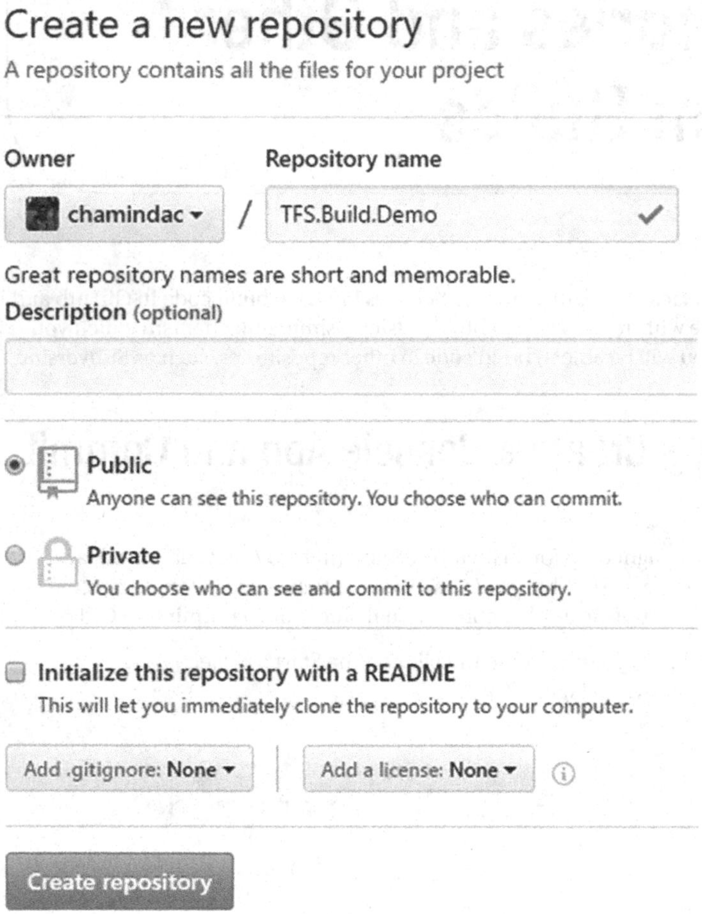

Figure 8-2. *Create GitHub repository*

3. Make sure you have installed GitHub Extension for Visual Studio. If not, install it in Visual Studio by clicking on Tools ➤ Extensions and Updates. Then, search for GitHub Extension in the popup window. Install it to Visual Studio by clicking Download and following the steps in the popup installation window. For Visual Studio 2017, the default behavior is that the installation will be started once you close Visual Studio. See Figure 8-3.

Figure 8-3. *Installing GitHub Extensions for Visual Studio*

4. Open Team Explorer in Visual Studio. On the Connect page, click on Manage Connections and select "Connect to GitHub" from the dropdown list, as shown in Figure 8-4.

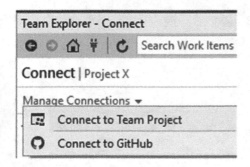

Figure 8-4. *Connect to GitHub*

5. Provide the credentials to the GitHub account and click Login. See Figure 8-5.

Figure 8-5. *Login to GitHub*

6. Once logged in, in the Team Explorer you can see an option to clone GitHub repositories (see Figure 8-6). Click it.

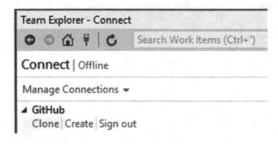

Figure 8-6. *Clone GitHub repositories*

7.   The popup window shows the repositories available to clone
     in the GitHub account. Select the TFS.Build.Demo repository
     and provide a local path for the repository. Then, clone the
     repository by clicking Clone. See Figure 8-7.

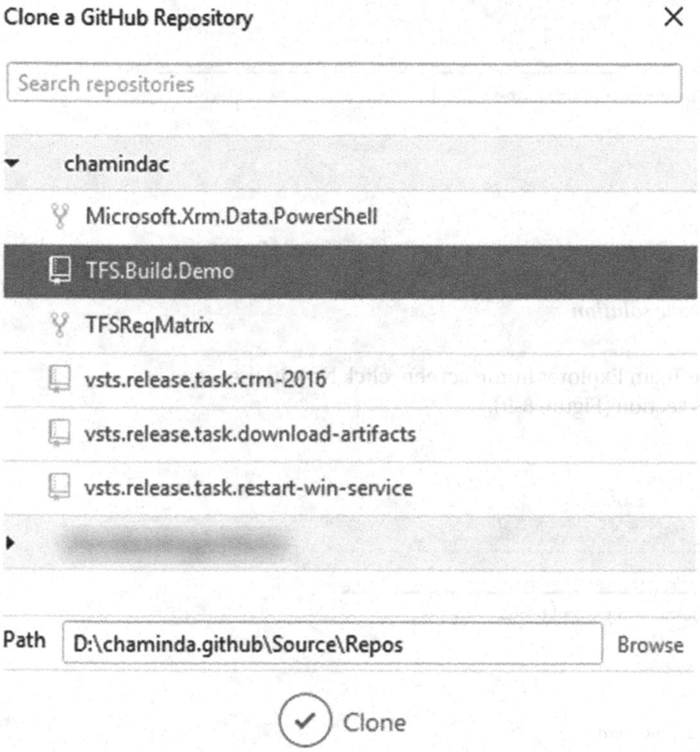

Figure 8-7. *Clone GitHub repository*

8. Create a new solution using the "Create a new project or solution" link. See Figure 8-8.

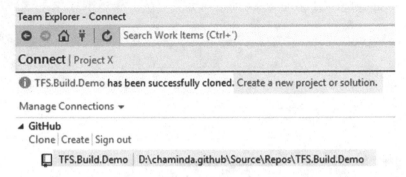

Figure 8-8. *Creating new solution*

Or, on the Team Explorer home screen, click New in the Solutions section (Figure 8-9).

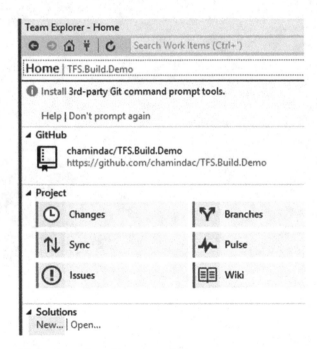

Figure 8-9. *Creating a new solution*

9. Create an empty solution by selecting the Blank Solution template in the popup window. Name the solution "GitHubSolution" and add a console application named "ConsoleApp" to it by right clicking on the solution in the Solution Explorer. See Figure 8-10.

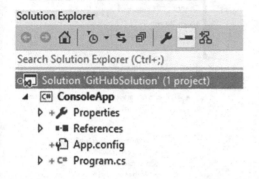

Figure 8-10. *Console application added to solution*

10. On the Team Explorer home screen, click on Changes to commit the changes to the local repository. See Figure 8-11.

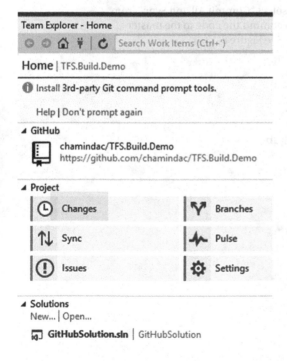

Figure 8-11. *Pending changes*

11.   Let Git save the user details if prompted. See Figure 8-12.

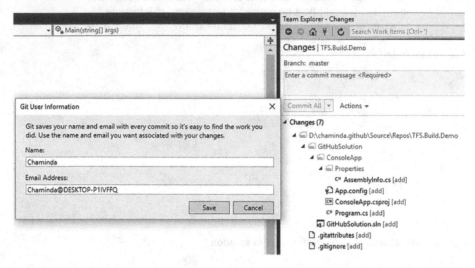

Figure 8-12. Saving username for Git

12.   Provide a comment and select "Commit All and Sync" from the dropdown options to commit the code to the master branch of the repository. See Figure 8-13.

Figure 8-13. Commit the changes

13. The solution will be synchronized with the GitHub repository. See Figure 8-14.

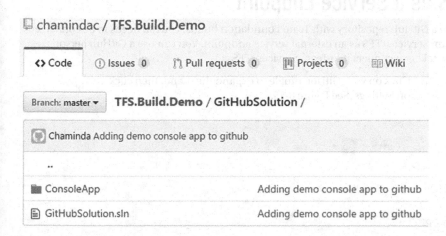

Figure 8-14. *GitHub updated with the changes*

You created a solution and a console application and committed it to GitHub. This code from GitHub can be built with TFS/Team Services builds, as explained in a future lesson of this chapter.

Lesson 8.02 – Link GitHub with Team Services/ TFS as a Service Endpoint

To use a GitHub repository with Team Foundation builds, GitHub needs to be connected to Team Services/TFS as an external service endpoint. You can use a GitHub personal access token to connect it to Team Services/TFS.

1. Click on your GitHub profile to expand the menu, then click on Settings. See Figure 8-15.

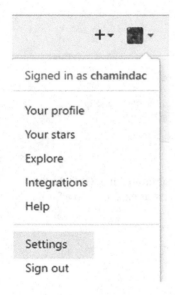

Figure 8-15. *Select GitHub account settings*

2. Click on the Generate new token button in the **Personal access tokens** tab on the Settings page. See Figure 8-16.

Personal access tokens

Generate new token   Revoke all

Figure 8-16. *Generate token in GitHub*

3. Type TFSLink as the description of the token and select the scopes: **repo, admin:repo_hook,** and **user**. Click the Generate token button as shown in Figure 8-17.

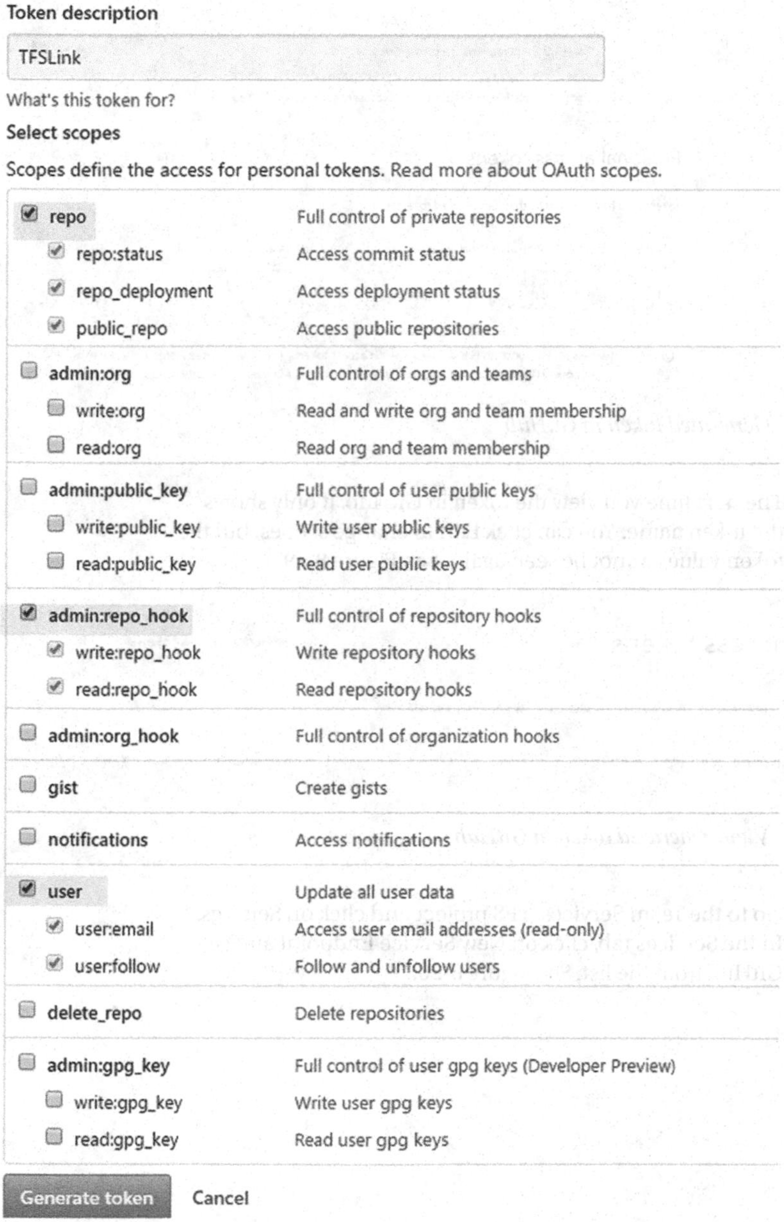

Token description

TFSLink

What's this token for?

Select scopes

Scopes define the access for personal tokens. Read more about OAuth scopes.

☑ **repo**	Full control of private repositories
☑ repo:status	Access commit status
☑ repo_deployment	Access deployment status
☑ public_repo	Access public repositories
☐ **admin:org**	Full control of orgs and teams
☐ write:org	Read and write org and team membership
☐ read:org	Read org and team membership
☐ **admin:public_key**	Full control of user public keys
☐ write:public_key	Write user public keys
☐ read:public_key	Read user public keys
☑ **admin:repo_hook**	Full control of repository hooks
☑ write:repo_hook	Write repository hooks
☑ read:repo_hook	Read repository hooks
☐ **admin:org_hook**	Full control of organization hooks
☐ **gist**	Create gists
☐ **notifications**	Access notifications
☑ **user**	Update all user data
☑ user:email	Access user email addresses (read-only)
☑ user:follow	Follow and unfollow users
☐ **delete_repo**	Delete repositories
☐ **admin:gpg_key**	Full control of user gpg keys (Developer Preview)
☐ write:gpg_key	Write user gpg keys
☐ read:gpg_key	Read user gpg keys

Generate token   Cancel

Figure 8-17. Scopes for token in GitHub

4.   The generated token only appears once in GitHub. You should copy it and save it in a notepad or some other text document. Keep the token securely somewhere so it can be accessed when required. See Figure 8-18.

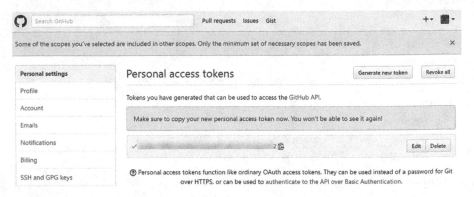

Figure 8-18. *Generated token in GitHub*

5.   The next time you view the token in GitHub, it only shows the token name. You can click Edit to change scopes, but the token value cannot be seen again. See Figure 8-19.

Figure 8-19. *View generated token in GitHub*

6.   Go to the Team Services/TFS project and click on Settings. In the Services tab, click on New Service Endpoint and select GitHub from the list. See Figure 8-20.

Figure 8-20. *Creating GitHub service endpoint*

7. Select the "Personal access token" option in the popup window, provide a name for the GitHub link, provide the personal access token generated previously and click OK. See Figure 8-21.

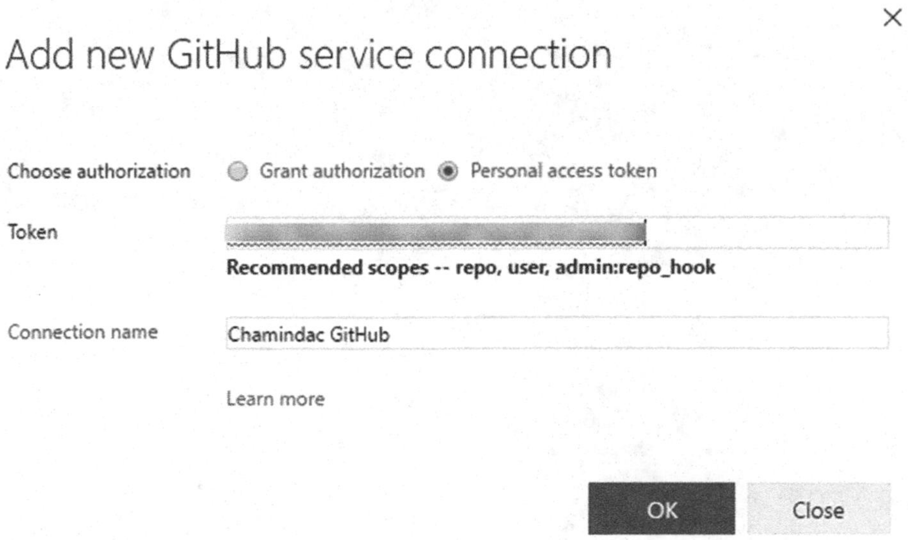

×

Add new GitHub service connection

Choose authorization	○ Grant authorization ● Personal access token	
Token		
	Recommended scopes -- repo, user, admin:repo_hook	
Connection name	Chamindac GitHub	
	Learn more	

OK   Close

Figure 8-21. *Creating GitHub service endpoint with personal access token*

8. The GitHub service endpoint is added to the Team Services/ TFS project. See Figure 8-22.

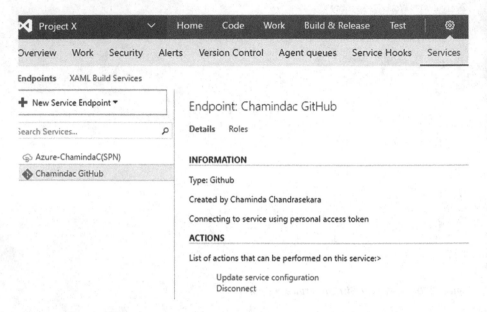

Figure 8-22. *GitHub service endpoint*

In this lesson, you created a GitHub service endpoint in TFS/VSTS to enable access to code in GitHub from VSTS/TFS builds.

Lesson 8.03 – Build GitHub Code in Team Foundation Build

Let's create a new build definition with which to build the solution created and submitted to GitHub previously.

1. Create a new build definition with an empty template and select GitHub as the repository (you can change the repository type after creating the definition in the Repository tab of the build definition). See Figure 8-23.

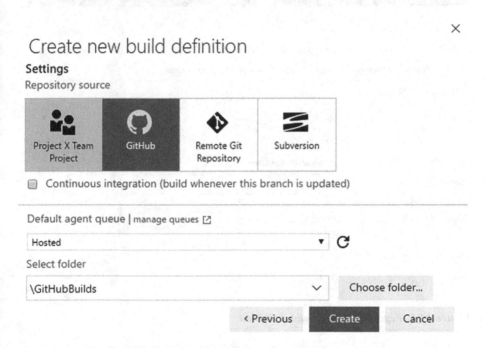

Figure 8-23. *New build definition with GitHub as the repository*

2. Go to the Repository tab and make sure GitHub is selected as the repository type. Select the service endpoint that was created in the previous lesson as the Connection (you can use the Manage link to go to Settings, then to the Services tab, to create an external service endpoint). Select the TFS. Build.Demo repository and select the master branch, since you committed the solution to the master branch in the first lesson in this chapter. See Figure 8-24.

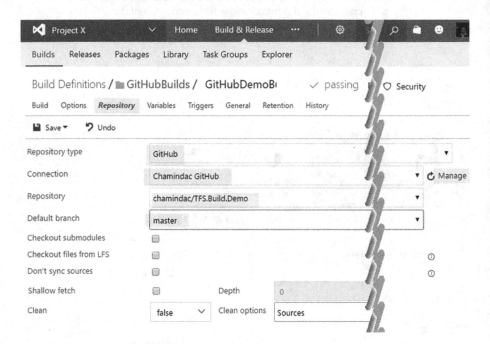

Figure 8-24. Repository tab of build definition

3. In the Build tab, add a Visual Studio Build step and select the GitHub solution to build with this build definition. See Figure 8-25.

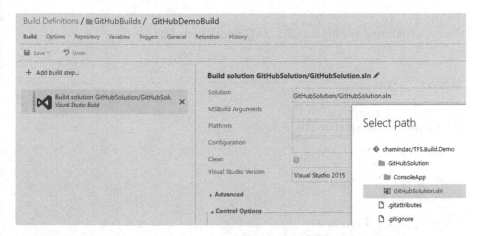

Figure 8-25. *Selecting GitHub solution to build in the Visual Studio Build step of the build definition*

4. Queue a new build to verify. See Figure 8-26.

Figure 8-26. *GitHub solution is built with TFS build*

5. Go to Edit build definition and, in the Trigger tab, set each check-in to build by selecting the "Continuous integration" box. This will allow you to verify whether a build can be triggered for a commit to the GitHub repository. See Figure 8-27.

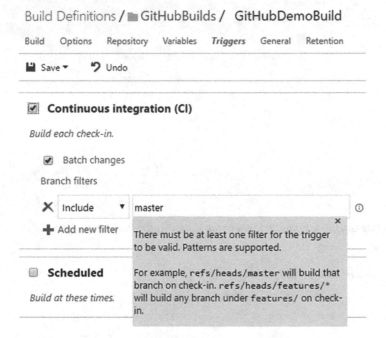

Figure 8-27. Continuous integration using GitHub

6. Do a code change and select Commit and Sync. You will see that a new build is triggered automatically. See Figure 8-28.

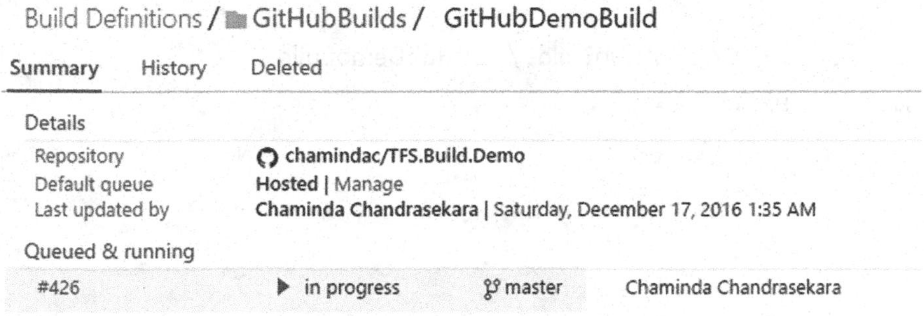

Build Definitions / GitHubBuilds / GitHubDemoBuild
Summary
History
Deleted
Details
Repository
chamindac/TFS.Build.Demo
Default queue
Hosted | Manage
Last updated by
Chaminda Chandrasekara | Saturday, December 17, 2016 1:35 AM
Queued & running
#426
in progress
master
Chaminda Chandrasekara

Figure 8-28. *Continuous integration build in progress*

7. You can see in Figure 8-29 that this build is marked with an icon to denote as a continuous integration build.

Builds
Releases
Packages
Library
Task Groups
Explorer
Build 426
Build
Initialize Agent
Get Sources
Build solution GitHubSolution/GitH...
Post Job Cleanup
GitHubDemoBuild / Build 426
Edit build definition
Cancel
Queue new build...
Download all logs as zip
Build Started
Build 426
Running for 77 seconds (Hosted)
Summary
Timeline
Code coverage*
Tests
Build details
Definition
GitHubDemoBuild (edit)
Source
master
Source version
b450435
Requested by
[chamindac]\Project Collection Service Accounts on behalf of Chaminda Chandrasekara
Queued
Saturday, December 17, 2016 1:36 AM
Started
Saturday, December 17, 2016 1:36 AM
Finished
Associated work items
No associated work items found for this build
Associated changes
b450435 Authored by Chaminda
Commit to test CI

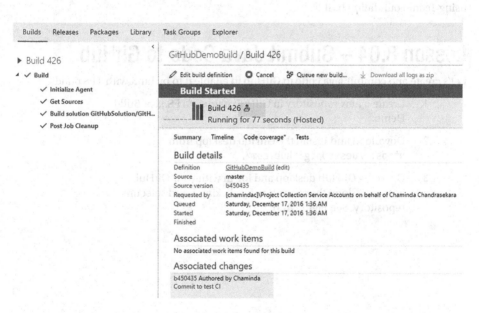

Figure 8-29. *Continuous integration build completed*

This confirms that the commit to the GitHub repository allows TFS/VSTS to trigger a build, as shown (batched continuous integration) in Figure 8-30.

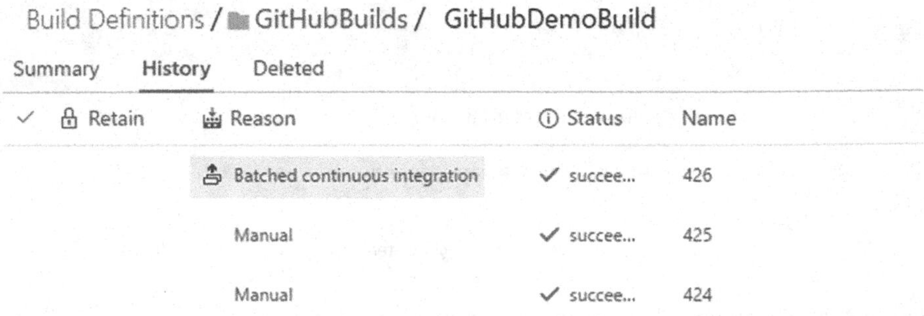

Build Definitions / ■ GitHubBuilds / GitHubDemoBuild

✓	🔒 Retain	⚒ Reason	ⓘ Status	Name
		🔼 Batched continuous integration	✓ succee...	426
		Manual	✓ succee...	425
		Manual	✓ succee...	424

Figure 8-30. *Continuous integration build with GitHub code repository*

You created a build definition with which to build .NET code committed to GitHub using Team Foundation builds.

Lesson 8.04 – Submit Java Code to GitHub

Let's create and commit Java code to GitHub to enable it to be built with TFS builds.

1. Create a new repository in GitHub named "TFS.Java.Build. Demo."

2. Download and install the GitHub desktop from `https://desktop.github.com/`.

3. Open the GitHub desktop and log in with your GitHub account. Clone the repository by clicking + and selecting the repository. See Figure 8-31.

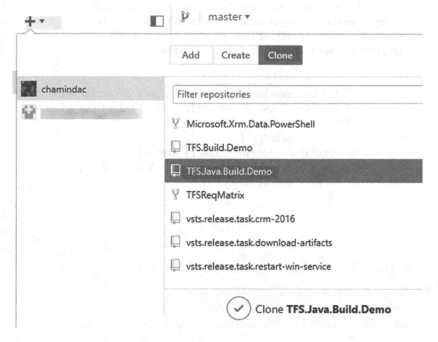

Figure 8-31. *Clone repository with GitHub desktop*

4. After cloning, click on the repository name and click "open this repository" to open the Windows Explorer folder of the repository. See Figure 8-32.

Figure 8-32. *Open Windows Explorer folder with GitHub desktop*

5. Create a folder called "JavaDemo" in the repository folder and create a DemoX.java file with the following code. This code is available at `https://docs.oracle.com/javase/tutorial/getStarted/cupojava/win32.html`. See Figure 8-33.

```
/**
        * The HelloWorldApp class implements an application that
        * simply prints "Hello World!" to standard output.
        */
       classHelloWorldApp {
       publicstaticvoidmain(String[] args) {
       System.out.println("Hello World - TFS Builds!");
       // Display the string.
          }
       }
```

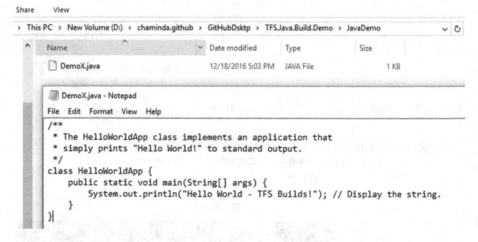

Figure 8-33. *"Hello World" Java code*

6. In the repository folder, create a file named build.xml and add the following XML content. Make sure the src.dir property has value JavaDemo (name of folder holding the Java code). You can find the original code at https://ant.apache.org/manual/tutorial-HelloWorldWithAnt.html. See Figure 8-34.

```xml
<project name="HelloWorld" basedir="." default="main">

    <property name="src.dir"     value="JavaDemo"/>

    <property name="build.dir"   value="build"/>
    <property name="classes.dir" value="${build.dir}/classes"/>
    <property name="jar.dir"     value="${build.dir}/jar"/>

    <property name="main-class"  value="HelloWorldApp"/>

    <target name="clean">
        <delete dir="${build.dir}"/>
    </target>

    <target name="compile">
        <mkdir dir="${classes.dir}"/>
        <javac srcdir="${src.dir}" destdir="${classes.dir}"/>
    </target>

    <target name="jar" depends="compile">
        <mkdir dir="${jar.dir}"/>
        <jar destfile="${jar.dir}/${ant.project.name}.jar"
basedir="${classes.dir}">
            <manifest>
                <attribute name="Main-Class"
                value="${main-class}"/>
            </manifest>
        </jar>
    </target>

    <target name="run" depends="jar">
        <java jar="${jar.dir}/${ant.project.name}.jar"
        fork="true"/>
    </target>

    <target name="clean-build" depends="clean,jar"/>

    <target name="main" depends="clean,run"/>

</project>
```

323

Figure 8-34. Build.xml

7. Using the GitHub desktop, commit the changes to the repository. See Figure 8-35.

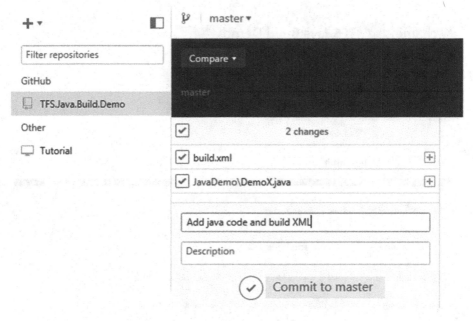

Figure 8-35. *Commit the Java code and build.xml to master branch*

8. Then, publish them to GitHub, as seen in Figure 8-36.

Figure 8-36. *Publish to GitHub*

9. GitHub gets updated with the Java code and the build.xml file. See Figure 8-37.

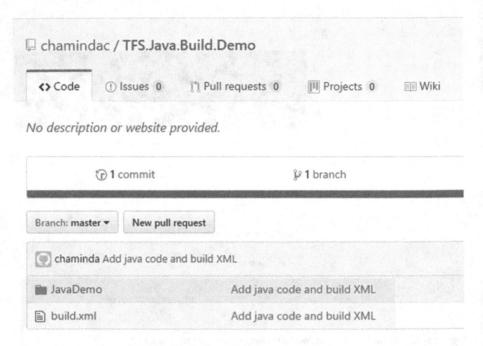

Figure 8-37. *Code and XML published to GitHub*

You created a "Hello World" Java code and a build.xml file and submitted them to GitHub.

Lesson 8.05 – Build Java Code in GitHub with Team Foundation Build

Let's create a build definition in TFS/VSTS with which to build the Java code committed to GitHub in the previous lesson.

1. As explained in Lesson 8.02 – Link GitHub with Team Services/TFS as a Service Endpoint, set up a link to GitHub with the team project.

2. Create a new build definition and select TFS.Java.Build.Demo as the repository. See Figure 8-38.

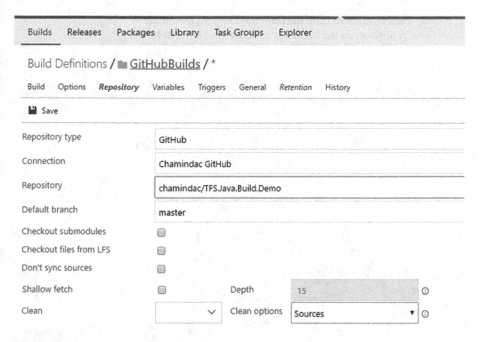

Figure 8-38. Repository tab of build definition

3. Add the Ant build step to the definition from the Task Catalog, as shown in Figure 8-39.

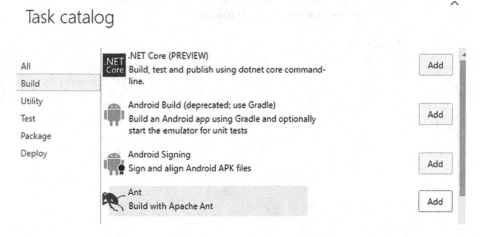

Figure 8-39. Ant build task

4. Select the build.xml file from the TFS.Java.Demo.Build
    repository as the build file, as shown in Figure 8-40.

Figure 8-40. *Select build.xml in Ant build task*

5. Add a Copy Publish Artifact step to the build from the Task
    Catalog. Set the content to copy as follows:

```
**/*.class
**/*.jar
```

Provide information for the Artifact Name let's say
"AntOutput" and for Artifact Type select Server, as seen in
Figure 8-41.

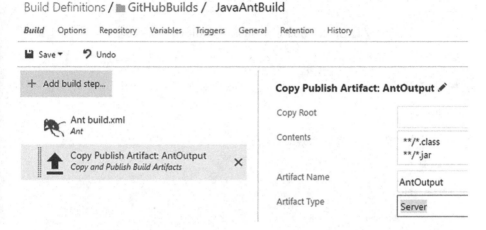

Figure 8-41. *Task to publish built Java code*

6. Use the hosted build agent to build the Java code with the Ant
   build task. (If you are using on-premises TFS, you have to set
   up a build server with Ant, as explained here: http://ant.
   apache.org/manual/install.html.) See Figure 8-42.

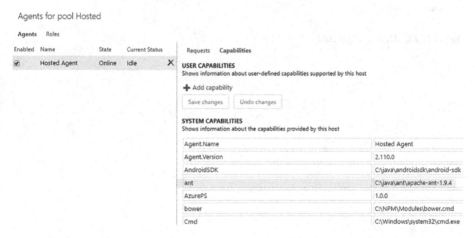

Figure 8-42. *Hosted build agent has Ant capability*

7. In the General tab of the build definition, add a demand for the agent to look for Ant within itself (see Figure 8-43).

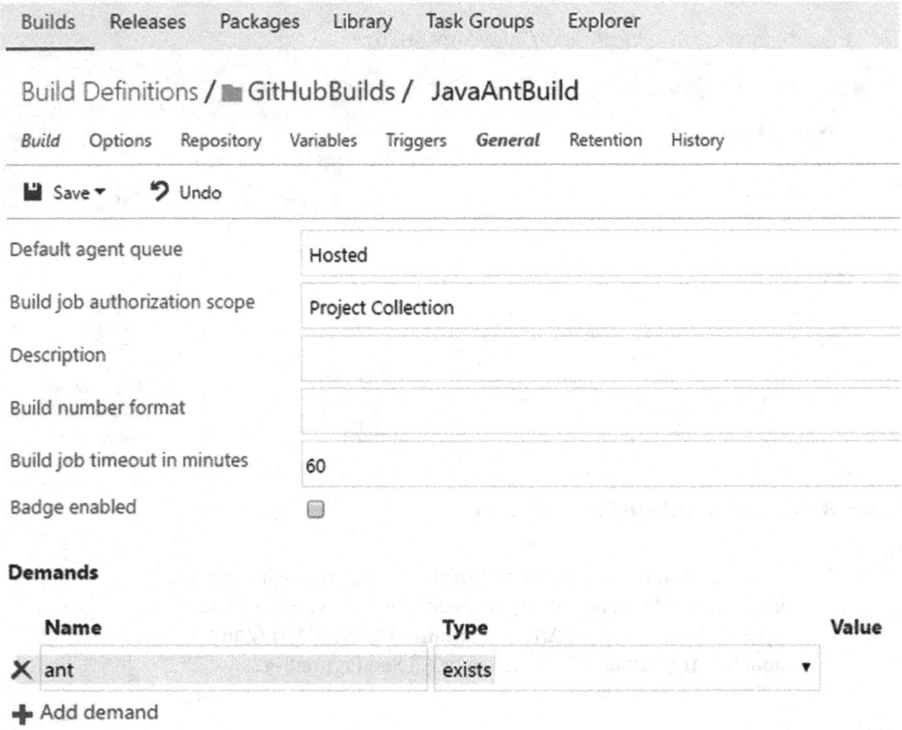

Builds	Releases	Packages	Library	Task Groups	Explorer

Build Definitions / ■ GitHubBuilds / JavaAntBuild

Build	Options	Repository	Variables	Triggers	*General*	Retention	History

💾 Save ▾   🔁 Undo

Default agent queue	Hosted
Build job authorization scope	Project Collection
Description	
Build number format	
Build job timeout in minutes	60
Badge enabled	☐

Demands

Name	Type	Value
✕ ant	exists ▾	

➕ Add demand

Figure 8-43. *Demand for Ant*

8. Queue a build, and it should build the .class and .jar files and make them available as output. See Figure 8-44.

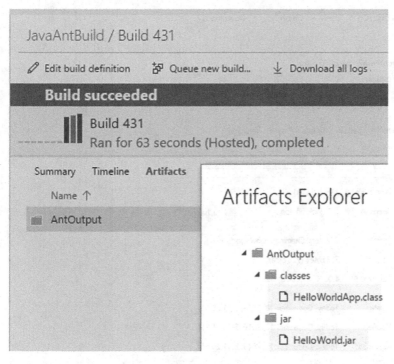

Figure 8-44. Build output

9. Download the .jar file, open the properties of the downloaded file, and unblock it. See Figure 8-45.

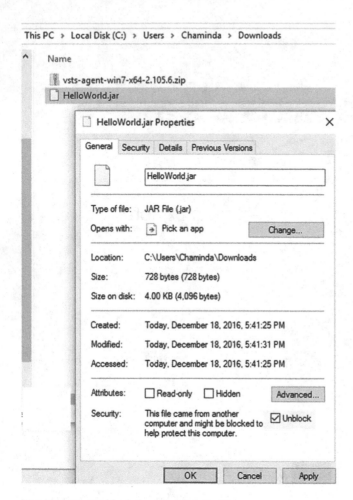

Figure 8-45. *Unblock downloaded .jar file*

10. Execute the .jar file with the following Java command to verify the Java code built with TFS build (Java Runtime required). See Figure 8-46.

```
Command Prompt

C:\Users\Chaminda\Downloads>java -jar HelloWorld.jar
Hello World - TFS Builds!

C:\Users\Chaminda\Downloads>
```

Figure 8-46. *Running the downloaded .jar file*

In this lesson, you created a build definition with which to build Java code committed to GitHub.

Summary

In this chapter, you learned how to link GitHub to Team Services/TFS to enable building the code available in GitHub using Team Foundation builds. Similarly, you can integrate it with source code repositories such as Remote Git repositories and Subversion.

Java code can be built using Ant and Maven. This chapter covered very basic Java code build using Ant builds. Experimentation with more-complex Java projects is required to gain more experience in this area.

In the next chapter, you will learn how to use, test automation capabilities with build and release management with TFS.

CHAPTER 9

Test Automation with Build and Release

This chapter will give you an overview of test automation, as well as of the capabilities of Team Foundation build and release management to run automated tests with build and deployment processes. Hands-on lessons will guide you step-by-step on unit test integration, functional test integration, and cloud-based load-test execution with TFS and Team Services.

Test Automation

Test automation has become a buzz word in modern software development. This enthusiasm is the result of test automation's vitality to the software delivery process. No software delivery company can afford to test their software using manpower alone. Manual testing requires a lot of time and could introduce human errors. A small bug fix of a software product manually taken through a full system test or smoke test costs more time and money to a software development organization than an automated process does. Hence, such companies must have the capability to run tests faster and with less human involvement. This could lead to dramatic savings in the effort and cost required for a delivery cycle, which in turn provides a competitive advantage to the software vendor.

It is essential to have automated builds and deployments integrated with the automated tests to get the maximum productivity outcome in the delivery cycle of a software. Visual Studio Team Services and TFS have built-in capabilities, to integrate with automated tests written using Visual Studio, Selenium, and so forth. In the following lessons, we will look at a few types of tests that can be automated and integrated with TFS build and release management.

Lesson 9.01 – Write Unit Tests and Integrate with Build

Let's look at how to automate the running of unit tests with TFS builds in order to validate code checked in to a given repository.

1. Create a Visual Studio solution and add a class library project to it.

2. In the class, write two simple methods as follows. (The code is available at https://github.com/chamindac/Book-Beginning-Build-ReleaseManagement-/blob/master/Chapter09/UnitTestDemo/Lib/Class1.cs.)

```
public class Class1
{
public int Add(int num1, int num2)
        {
return num1 + num2;
        }

public int Substract(int num1, int num2)
        {
return num1 - num2;
        }
}
```

3. In the Visual Studio Solution Explorer, right click on the solution and select New Project to add a unit test project to the solution. In the pop up window select "Unit Test Project" and provide a name for the project, then click OK. See Figure 9-1.

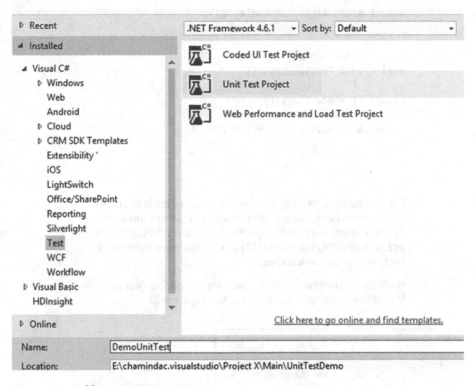

Figure 9-1. Adding a unit test project

4. Add a reference to class library project from the unit
   test project. Then, add two unit test methods to test
   the Add and Subtract methods (the code is available
   at https://github.com/chamindac/Book-Beginning-
   Build-ReleaseManagement-/blob/master/Chapter09/
   UnitTestDemo/DemoUnitTest/UnitTest1.cs).

```
using System;
using Microsoft.VisualStudio.TestTools.UnitTesting;
using Lib;

namespace DemoUnitTest
{
    [TestClass]
public class UnitTest1
    {
        [TestMethod]
public void TestAdd()
        {
Class1 c1 = new Class1();
```

337

```
Assert.AreEqual(10, c1.Add(4, 6));
    }

    [TestMethod]
public void TestSubstract()
    {
Class1 c1 = new Class1();

Assert.AreEqual(2, c1.Substract(6, 4));
    }
  }
}
```

Discussing advanced topics related to unit testing is out of the scope of this book. Refer to articles such as the one found at https://msdn.microsoft.com/en-us/library/hh549175.aspx?f=255&MSPPError=-2147217396 to learn more about topics such as Fakes for unit testing.

5. Build the solution and execute the tests in Test Explorer in Visual Studio to verify the solution. See Figure 9-2.

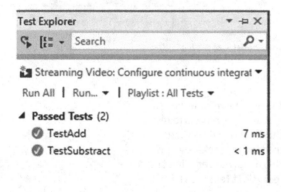

Figure 9-2. Executing unit tests in Visual Studio

6. Check the solution in to the source control repository.

7. Create a new build definition and set the repository to the Solution folder. Creating a build definition is explained in Chapter 3. See Figure 9-3.

Build Definitions / **UnitTestDemoBuild**

Build   Options   **Repository**   Variables   Triggers   General   Retention   History

💾 Save ▾   ⟳ Undo

Repository type	Team Foundation Version Control
Repository name	Project X
Label sources	Don't label sources
Clean	false ∨ Clean options Sources ▾ ⓘ

Mappings

	Type	Server Path
✕	Map ▾	$/Project X/Main/UnitTestDemo
✚	Add mapping	

Figure 9-3. *Map unit test project in build definition*

    8.   Add BuildPlatform and BuildConfiguration variables in the
            Variables tab and set their values to any cpu and release,
            respectively, as shown in Figure 9-4.

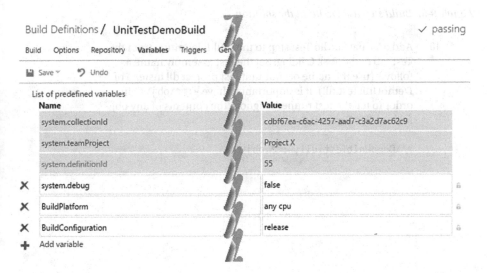

Figure 9-4. *Build variables*

9. Add a Visual Studio build step and select the UnitTestDemo.
    sln file to build. See Figure 9-5.

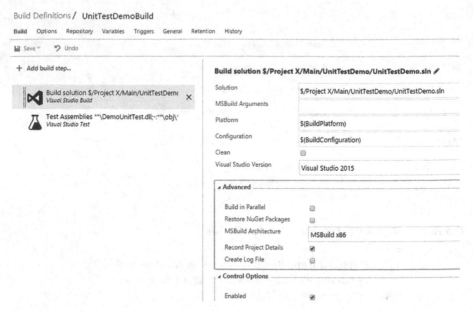

Figure 9-5. *Build step used to build the solution*

10. Add a Visual Studio Test step to the build definition from the
    Test tab of the Task Catalog. Set the test assembly name as
    follows (use the name of your unit test project dll instead of
    DemoUnitTest.dll). It is important to have -:**\obj** in
    order to tell the test runner to ignore the contents of any obj
    folders. See Figure 9-6.

```
**\DemoUnitTest.dll;-:**\obj\**
```

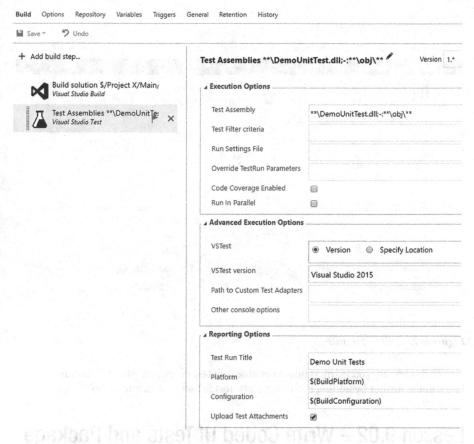

Figure 9-6. *Build step to run unit tests*

11.   Queue a new build. You can see the test results in the Tests tab of the build details screen. See Figure 9-7.

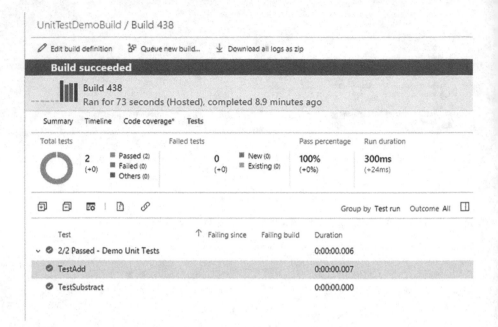

Figure 9-7. *Unit test results*

In this lesson, you learned how to enable unit test execution with TFS builds. Experiment further by adding more unit tests, test fail scenarios, and so on.

Lesson 9.02 – Write Coded UI Tests and Package with Build

To automate functional tests, you can use coded UI tests in Visual Studio. The following steps describe how to create a coded UI test and how to package it using TFS builds.

1. Create a Visual Studio solution named "CodedUIDemo."

2. Add a new Coded UI Test Project to the solution and name it "DemoCodedUI." See Figure 9-8.

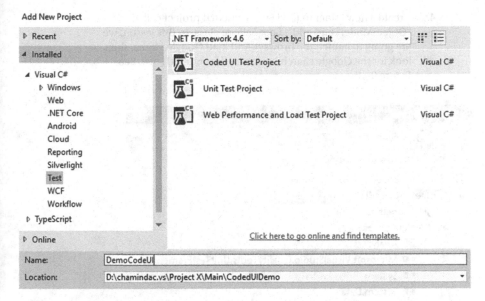

Figure 9-8. Adding Coded UI Test Project

3. A popup window appears that will allow you to generate code. Click the Cancel button to close that window, since we are going to write the coded UI test manually in this lesson. See Figure 9-9.

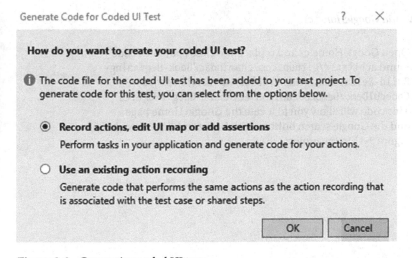

Figure 9-9. Generating coded UI tests

4. Create a new folder in the DemoCodedUI project called "ObjectModel" and add a GoogleHome class. In this lesson, we are going to launch the browser and load Google Home, then look for the Google search button as the coded UI test. See Figure 9-10.

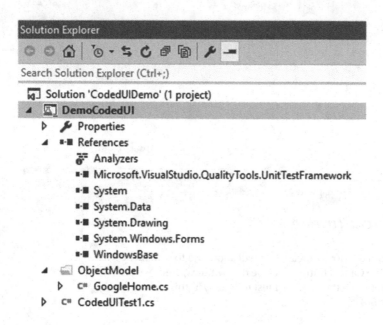

Figure 9-10. *Add GoogleHome.cs*

5. Open GoogleHome.cs and replace the class code with code found at https://github.com/chamindac/Book-Beginning-Build-ReleaseManagement-/blob/master/Chapter09/CodedUIDemo/DemoCodedUI/ObjectModel/GoogleHome.cs. This code will allow you to locate the Google Home page and the Google search button. Add the assemblies shown in Figure 9-11 to the project.

```
  Solution 'CodedUIDemo' (1 project)
  ▲ a ▦ DemoCodedUI
    ▷ a ⚙ Properties
    ▲ ■-■ References
        ▓ Analyzers
        ■-■ Microsoft.VisualStudio.QualityTools.CodedUITestFramework
        ■-■ Microsoft.VisualStudio.QualityTools.UnitTestFramework
        ■-■ Microsoft.VisualStudio.TestTools.UITest.Common
        ■-■ Microsoft.VisualStudio.TestTools.UITest.Extension
        ■-■ Microsoft.VisualStudio.TestTools.UITesting
        ■-■ System
        ■-■ System.Data
        ■-■ System.Drawing
        ■-■ System.Windows.Forms
        ■-■ UiaComWrapper
        ■-■ WindowsBase
```

Figure 9-11. *Add reference assemblies*

6. Open the default added CodedUITest1.cs and replace the code with the code found at https://github.com/chamindac/ Book-Beginning-Build-ReleaseManagement-/blob/master/ Chapter09/CodedUIDemo/DemoCodedUI/CodedUITest1.cs. Five passing test methods and two failing test methods (purposely failing for learning purposes) are written in this code. You must make sure you have added the assemblies shown in the previous figure. Sample passing and failing test methods are shown here:

```
[TestMethod]
public void SampleCodedUIPassTestMethod()
{
    BrowserWindow browser = BrowserWindow.Launch(new System.
Uri("http://www.google.com"));
    GoogleHome gh = new GoogleHome(browser);

    HtmlInputButton uIGoogleSearchButton = gh.GoogleSearchButton;
    Assert.AreEqual("Google Search", uIGoogleSearchButton.
ValueAttribute);
}

[TestMethod]
public void SampleCodedUIFailTestMethod()
{
    BrowserWindow browser = BrowserWindow.Launch(new System.
Uri("http://www.google.com"));
    GoogleHome gh = new GoogleHome(browser);
```

345

```
HtmlInputButton uIGoogleSearchButton = gh.GoogleSearchButton;
Assert.AreEqual("Google1 Search", uIGoogleSearchButton.
ValueAttribute);

}
```

7. Build the solution in Visual Studio and execute all the tests in Test Explorer to verify. You will notice five tests pass and two fail. See Figure 9-12.

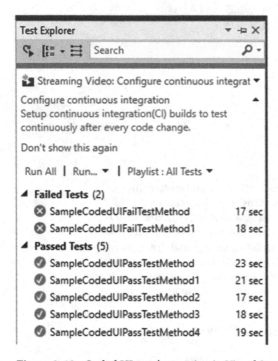

Figure 9-12. *Coded UI tests' execution in Visual Studio*

8. Check all the code in to the source control repository.

9. Create a new empty build definition. Name it "CodedUIDemoBuild."

10. In the Repository tab, set the CodedUIDemo solution path, as shown in Figure 9-13.

Builds   Releases   Packages   Library   Task Groups   Explorer

Build Definitions / **CodeUIDemoBuild**

Build   Options   **Repository**   Variables   Triggers   General   Retention   History

💾 Save ▾   ↩ Undo

Repository type	Team Foundation Version Control
Repository name	Project X
Label sources	Don't label sources

Clean | false ∨ | Clean options | Sources ▾ | ⓘ

Mappings

	Type		Server Path
✕	Map ▾		$/Project X/Main/CodedUIDemo
✚	Add mapping		

Figure 9-13. Map the coded UI project in the build definition

11.   Add BuildPlatform and BuildConfiguration variables with values of any cpu and release, respectively.

12.   Add a Visual Studio Build step and select the CodedUIDemo solution to build. See Figure 9-14.

Figure 9-14. Build step to build the coded UI demo solution

13. Add the Copy Publish Artifact step and set contents to **/
bin/**/DemoCodedUI.dll. This will publish the build artifacts
once the build is executed. See Figure 9-15.

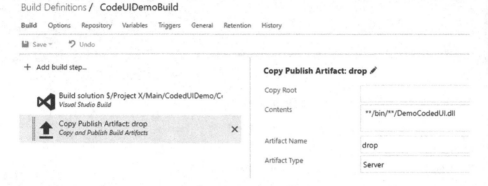

Figure 9-15. *Build step to publish artifacts*

14. Save and queue a new build. The build should create the
DemoCodedUI.dll as the output/artifacts of the completed
build. See Figure 9-16.

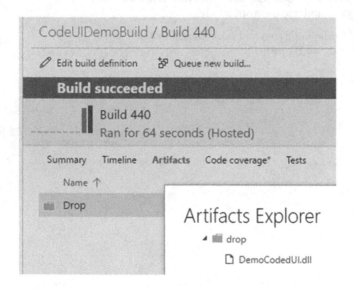

Figure 9-16. *Built coded UI test dll*

You created the Coded UI Test Project with a few tests and then created a build to
package it. This can be used to execute functional tests using Team Foundation release
management.

Lesson 9.03 – Run Functional Tests with TFS/VSTS Release

Prerequisites: Set up a TFS build/release agent on a machine. Then, set up a machine or virtual machine to be used as a test client machine with OS Window 8.1 or 10. The agent machine should have line of sight to the test client machine. Refer to Chapter 2 to understand the TFS build and release agents.

Let's look at the steps required to execute functional tests with Team Foundation release management.

1. In the machine setup as the **test client**, create a user named "adminuser" and add it to the Administrator group. Log on to the test client machine using "adminuser" at least once. See Figure 9-17.

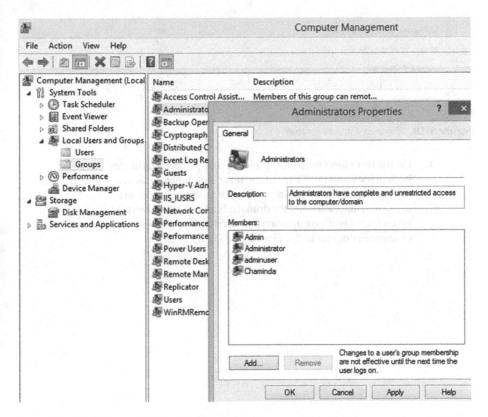

Figure 9-17. *Adding user to Administrator group*

2. Create another user named "testsvcuser" to run the test agent
   service. See Figure 9-18.

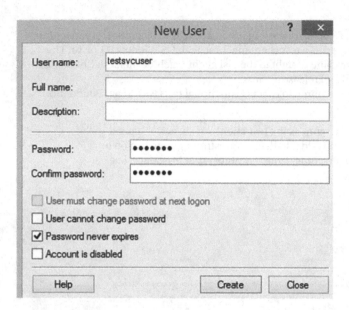

Figure 9-18. *Creating test service user*

3. On the **test client** machine, allow file and printer sharing for
   both private and public use if the test client machine is in a
   work group. If it is in the same domain as the build/release
   agent machine, allowing for domain is okay. The screenshots
   taken from a work group machine used as **test client** so you
   cannot see domain in the Figure. See Figure 9-19.

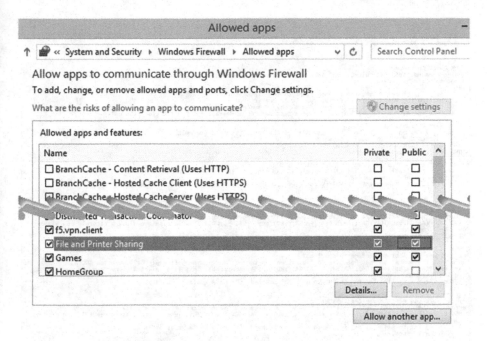

Figure 9-19. *Allow file and printer sharing in test client*

4. Set up test client machine with WinRM (https://msdn. microsoft.com/en-us/library/aa384372(v=vs.85).aspx) if not already installed. (WinRM is automatically installed with all currently supported versions of the Windows operating system.)

5. Enable PowerShell remoting on the **test client** machine by executing the following command in the Administrative PowerShell window. See Figure 9-20.

```
Enable-PSRemoting
```

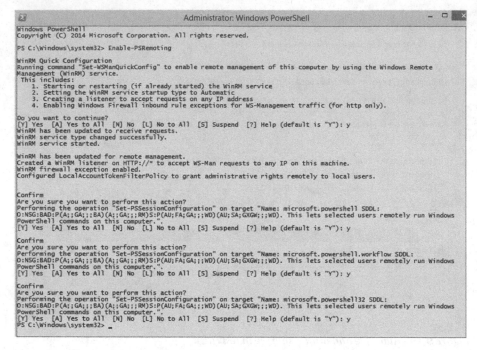

Figure 9-20. *Enable PowerShell remoting*

Note This may throw an error that is a bit misleading and does not provide enough information if your virtual machine is not in a domain. More details are explained here: https://4sysops.com/archives/enable-powershell-remoting-on-a-standalone-workgroup-computer/

This can be fixed by running the command with a –SkipNetworkProfileCheck switch.

Enable-PSRemoting –SkipNetworkProfileCheck

---

6. If your test client machine is not in the same domain as the build/release agent, then allow public access to WinRM by enabling the firewall rule shown in Figure 9-21 (it is by default not enabled).

Inbound Rules					
Name	Group	Profile	Enabled	Action	^
BranchCache Content Retrieval (HTTP-In)	BranchCache - Content Retr...	All	No	Allow	
Media Center Extenders - WMDRM-ND/R...	Media Center Extenders	All	No	Allow	
Core Networking - Dynamic Host Config...	Core Networking	All	Yes	Allow	
Windows Remote Management (HTTP-In)	Windows Remote Manage...	Public	No	Allow	
Windows Remote Management (HTTP-In)	Windows Remote Manage...	Domai...	Yes	Allow	
Media Center Extenders - RTSP (TCP-In)	Media Center Extenders	All	No	Allow	

Figure 9-21. Remote management public firewall rule

7. Verify PowerShell remoting access from the build/release agent machine by entering into a remote PowerShell session to the test client machine from the build/release agent machine. It could throw an error, as shown in Figure 9-22.

```
Enter-PSSession –ComputerName<remotemachinenameorip>
-Credential <remotemachineadminuser>
```

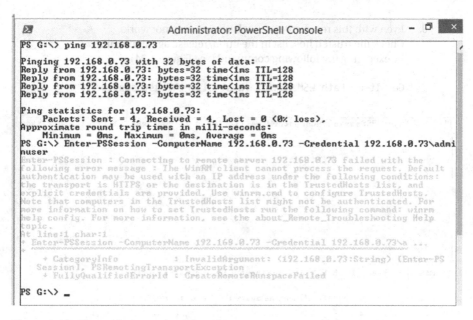

Figure 9-22. Error when entering PS session

8. If WinRM is not set up in the build/release agent machine, run the following command to set it up (see Figure 9-23):

```
winrm qc
```

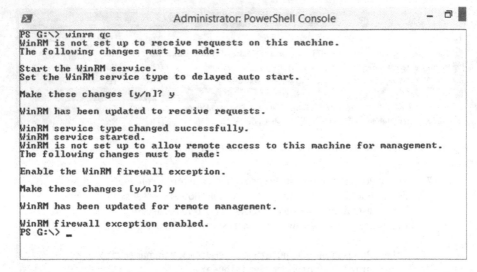

Figure 9-23. *Setting up WinRM in build/release agent machine*

9. Even with this remote PowerShell session may not work.
   Check the trusted host list in the build/release agent machine
   by executing the following command (see Figure 9-24).

```
Get-Item -Path WSMan:\localhost\Client\TrustedHosts
```

```
PS G:\> Enter-PSSession -ComputerName 192.168.0.73 -Credential 192.168.0.73\admi
nuser
Enter-PSSession : Connecting to remote server 192.168.0.73 failed with the
following error message : The WinRM client cannot process the request. Default
authentication may be used with an IP address under the following conditions:
the transport is HTTPS or the destination is in the TrustedHosts list, and
explicit credentials are provided. Use winrm.cmd to configure TrustedHosts.
Note that computers in the TrustedHosts list might not be authenticated. For
more information on how to set TrustedHosts run the following command: winrm
help config. For more information, see the about_Remote_Troubleshooting Help
topic.
At line:1 char:1
+ Enter-PSSession -ComputerName 192.168.0.73 -Credential 192.168.0.73\a ...
+ CategoryInfo          : InvalidArgument: (192.168.0.73:String) [Enter-PS
Session], PSRemotingTransportException
+ FullyQualifiedErrorId : CreateRemoteRunspaceFailed

PS G:\> get-Item -Path WSMan:\localhost\Client\TrustedHosts


   WSManConfig: Microsoft.WSMan.Management\WSMan::localhost\Client

Type           Name                            SourceOfValue   Value
----           ----                            -------------   -----
System.String  TrustedHosts
```

Figure 9-24. *Get trusted hosts*

10. To add the test client machine as a trusted host, execute the
    following command (see Figure 9-25).

    ```
    Set-Item -Path WSMan:\localhost\Client\TrustedHosts -Value
    <remotemachinenameorip>
    ```

```
PS G:\> get-Item -Path WSMan:\localhost\Client\TrustedHosts

   WSManConfig: Microsoft.WSMan.Management\WSMan::localhost\Client

Type            Name                        SourceOfValue   Value
----            ----                        -------------   -----
System.String   TrustedHosts

PS G:\> set-Item -Path WSMan:\localhost\Client\TrustedHosts -Value 192.168.0.73

WinRM Security Configuration.
This command modifies the TrustedHosts list for the WinRM client. The computers
 in the TrustedHosts list might not be authenticated. The client might send
credential information to these computers. Are you sure that you want to modify
 this list?
[Y] Yes  [N] No  [S] Suspend  [?] Help (default is "Y"): y
PS G:\> get-Item -Path WSMan:\localhost\Client\TrustedHosts

   WSManConfig: Microsoft.WSMan.Management\WSMan::localhost\Client

Type            Name                        SourceOfValue   Value
----            ----                        -------------   -----
System.String   TrustedHosts                                192.168.0.73
```

Figure 9-25. *Adding test client machine to trusted hosts in build/release agent machine*

11. Then, retry obtaining a remote PowerShell session and create
    a folder on the test client machine from the build/release
    agent machine to confirm the session access. See Figure 9-26.

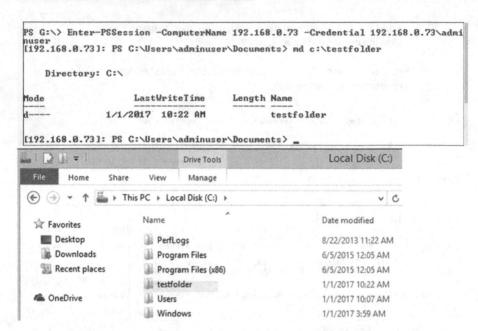

Figure 9-26. *Create folder with PowerShell remotely*

12. Create a new release definition with an empty template and set the linked artifact to the build (CodedUIDemoBuild) created in Lesson 9.02. See Figure 9-27.

Figure 9-27. *Linked artifacts*

13. Add variables with the usernames and passwords for the test client machine in the first environment 1, which is added by default to the release definition. Make sure to add the adminuser without the machine name, as shown in Figure 9-28—just the username only. However, if it is a domain username, add it as domain\username. For the test service user, input machineip\username.

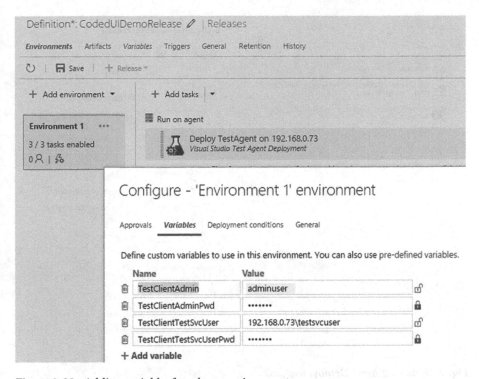

Figure 9-28. Adding variables for release environment

14. Set the agent to run as the release agent. Add a Visual Studio Test Agent Deployment task from the Task Catalog. For machines, provide the IP address (or FQDN if in a domain) of the test client machine. Use the variables defined for the admin user and the test service user. Select HTTP as the protocol. Make sure to run the task as an interactive process to enable the execution of functional UI tests on the test client machine. See Figure 9-29.

Figure 9-29. *Test Agent Deployment task*

15. Add a Windows Machine File Copy task to the release environment. This allows coded UI test assemblies and any other required files to be copied to the test client machine, so the UI tests can be executed in the test client. Select the source file or folder from the build output. Set the test client machine IP as the machine to copy files to. Provide defined variables for the admin user credentials of the test client machine and set a local folder path destination (local folder will be created automatically on the test client machine). See Figure 9-30.

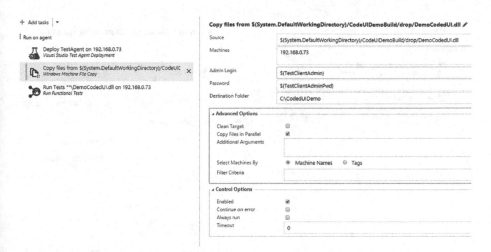

Figure 9-30. *Copy files task*

16. To execute the tests on the test client, add a Run Functional Tests task from the Task Catalog. Define the IP of the test client machine and set the test drop location to be the local destination folder path specified in the previous task (Windows Machine File Copy). Set the Test Selection field to Test Assembly and provide **\DemoCodedUI.dll as the value of the Test Assemble field. Make sure to check "Continue on error." This will allow the release environment to proceed, with partially completed state, despite individual test failures. If this option is not selected, the environment will fail even if a single test fails. See Figure 9-31.

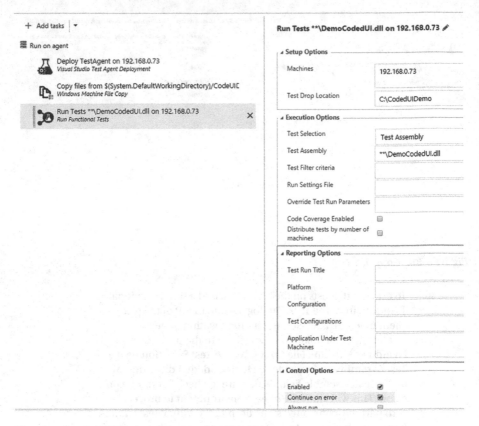

Figure 9-31. *Run Functional Tests task*

17. Create a new release using the build completed in Lesson
9.02. You will see that the environment completes as Partially
Succeeded. This is because we have intentionally set some test
methods to fail to demonstrate how it works. See Figure 9-32.

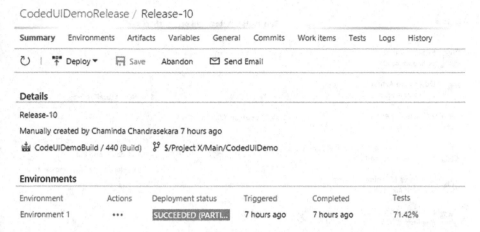

Figure 9-32. *Release summary*

18. In the Test tab of the release, you can see the details of the tests passed and failed. Failure information is available, including screenshots and assert fail details. See Figure 9-33.

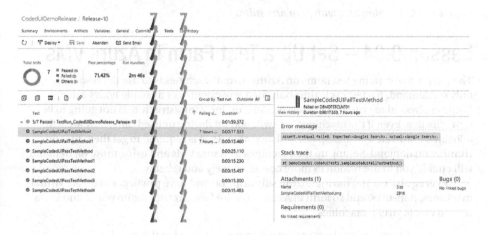

Figure 9-33. *Test run details*

This is simplest demo of functional test execution. You can introduce run settings files and do more experiments. You can generate test cases from the test assembly by following the instructions described at https://msdn.microsoft.com/en-us/library/dd465191%28v=vs.110%29.aspx?f=255&MSPPError=-2147217396. Then, add them to a Test Plan and Test Suites. You can use the Test Plan and Test Suites in the Run Functional Tests task. Experiment with these to learn more. See Figure 9-34.

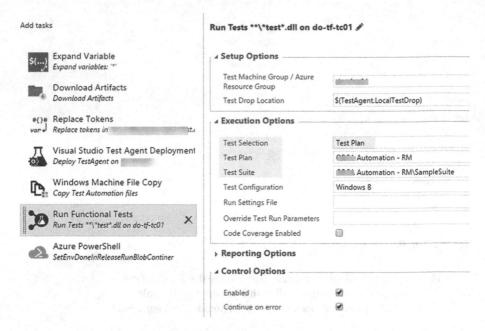

Figure 9-34. Test Run task with plan and suites

Lesson 9.04 – Set Up a Test Farm in Azure VMs

The purpose of creating test farms on Azure virtual machines is to use the resources only on demand. If a test cycle runs only for a few minutes or a couple hours a day, keeping physical or virtual machines running on local infrastructure is not going to be cost effective. Even if the machines are switched off during unused time, they are still allocated hardware like disk space, and available RAM is required to get them up and running on demand. Setting up the machines as Azure VMs and using those on demand will enable you to use resources more cost effectively and reliably.

Prerequisites: You have an Azure subscription and have privileges to create virtual machines, networks, and so forth in Azure. You are familiar with Azure portal and know how to create virtual machines.

1. Create a virtual network in Azure portal following the instructions found at https://docs.microsoft.com/en-us/ azure/virtual-network/virtual-networks-create-vnet- arm-pportal.

   Create a Windows 8.1 virtual machine as the admin machine that will keep the TFS agents running. Name it "testFarmAdmin." See Figure 9-35.

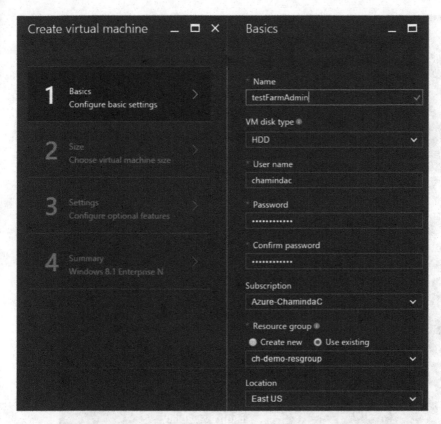

Figure 9-35. *Test farm admin machine*

2.   Choose a size for the machine and select the virtual network
     created in step one of this lesson. See Figure 9-36.

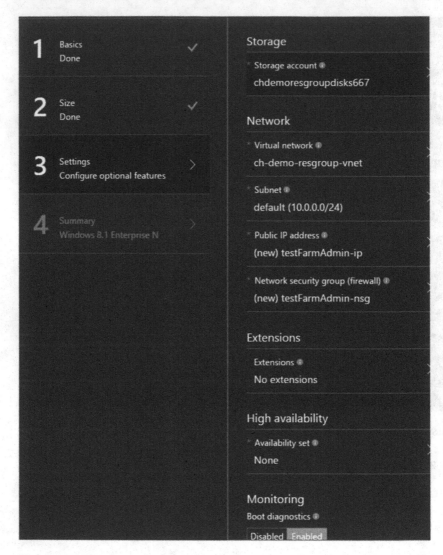

Figure 9-36. *Test farm admin machine settings*

3. In the summary review, click Create to create the virtual machine.

4. Create another two Windows 8.1 virtual machines (testClient01 and testClient02) to use as test clients, then add them to the same virtual network. See Figure 9-37.

Figure 9-37. *Test--farm machines*

5. For each of the three machines, go to Settings ➤ Network interfaces. Click on the network interface, then Settings ➤ IP configurations. Click on "IP configuration." Then set the Private IP address settings to Static, as shown in Figure 9-38. Save.

Figure 9-38. *Test farm machines to use internal static IP*

6. Log on to both test client machines and create a user, testsvcuser, to run the test service as an interactive process. See Figure 9-39.

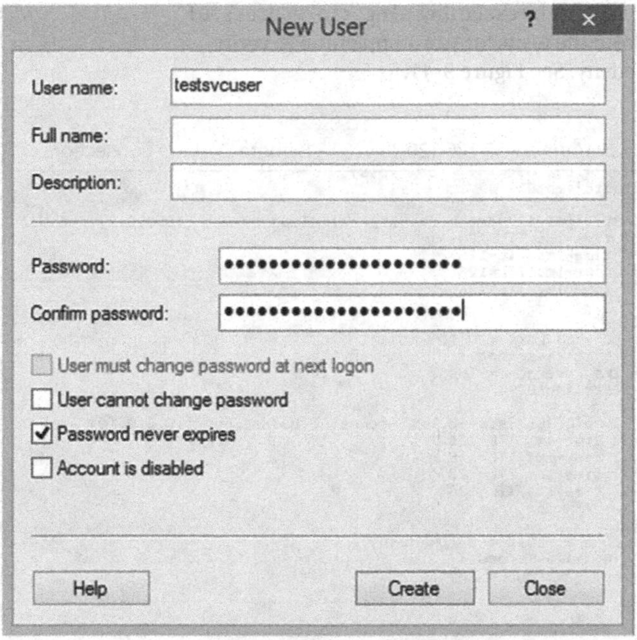

Figure 9-39. Test service user on test client machines

7. Enable File and Printer Sharing for Private and Public networking on both test client machines. See Figure 9-40.

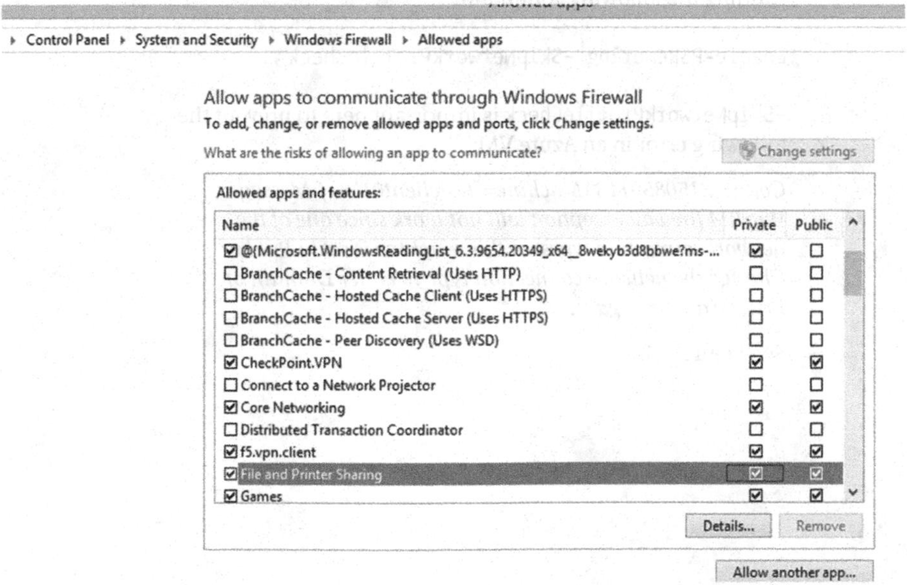

Figure 9-40. File and Printer Sharing on test client machines

8. Ping the two test clients by executing ping <ip address of test client> from the testfarmAdmin machine to verify network connectivity. See Figure 9-41.

```
                    testFarmAdmin - 52.186.120.34:3389 - Remote Desktop Connection
     Packets: Sent = 4, Received = 0, Lost = 4 (100% loss),
PS C:\Users\chamindac> ping testclient01

Pinging testclient01.mj4ikxjm3yiulgn2y13lscr43b.bx.internal.cloudapp.net [10.0.0.9] with 32
Reply from 10.0.0.9: bytes=32 time=2ms TTL=128
Reply from 10.0.0.9: bytes=32 time<1ms TTL=128
Reply from 10.0.0.9: bytes=32 time=1ms TTL=128
Reply from 10.0.0.9: bytes=32 time=1ms TTL=128

Ping statistics for 10.0.0.9:
    Packets: Sent = 4, Received = 4, Lost = 0 (0% loss),
Approximate round trip times in milli-seconds:
    Minimum = 0ms, Maximum = 2ms, Average = 1ms
PS C:\Users\chamindac> ping testclient02

Pinging testclient02.mj4ikxjm3yiulgn2y13lscr43b.bx.internal.cloudapp.net [10.0.0.10] with 32
Reply from 10.0.0.10: bytes=32 time=4ms TTL=128
Reply from 10.0.0.10: bytes=32 time=1ms TTL=128
Reply from 10.0.0.10: bytes=32 time=1ms TTL=128
Reply from 10.0.0.10: bytes=32 time=1ms TTL=128

Ping statistics for 10.0.0.10:
    Packets: Sent = 4, Received = 4, Lost = 0 (0% loss),
Approximate round trip times in milli-seconds:
    Minimum = 1ms, Maximum = 4ms, Average = 1ms
PS C:\Users\chamindac> _
```

Figure 9-41. Ping test client machines from test farm admin machine

9. Enable PowerShell remoting in both test client machines by running the following command:

Enable-PSRemoting –SkipNetworkProfileCheck

–SkipNetworkProfileCheck is important here to prevent the following error in an Azure VM:

Code="2150859113" Machine="testclient01"><f:Message> WinRM firewall exception will not work since one of the networkconnection types on this machine is set to Public. Change the network connection type to either Domain or Private and try again.

See Figure 9-42.

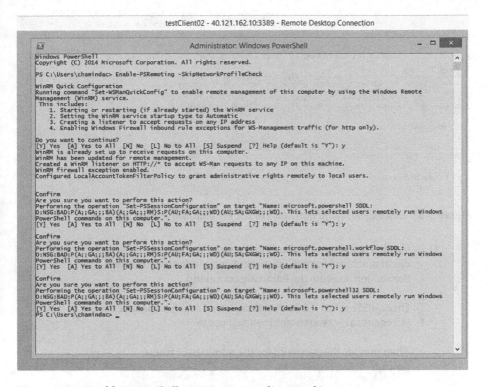

Figure 9-42. *Enable PowerShell remoting in test client machines*

10. On the testfarmAdmin machine, add the two test client machine names to the trusted host with the following command (both machine names are provided as a single string with a comma separating machine names). See Figure 9-43.

```
Set-Item -Path WSMan:\localhost\Client\TrustedHosts
-Value <remotemachinenameorip>
```

```
Set-Item -Path WSMan:\localhost\Client\TrustedHosts
-Value "testclient01,testclient02"
```

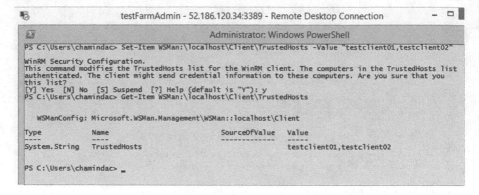

Figure 9-43. *Adding test client machines to test farm admin trusted hosts list*

11. Verify that a remote session can be obtained to each of the test client machines from the testfarmAdmin machine. To obtain the session, execute the following command.

```
Enter-PSSession –ComputerName<remotemachinenameorip>
–Credential <remotemachineadminuser>
```

Then provide the password for the admin user when prompted. See Figure 9-44.

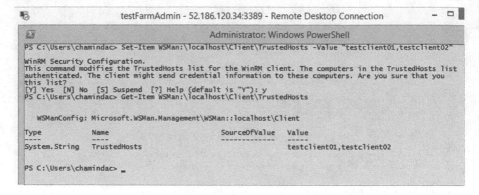

Figure 9-44. *Entering a PS session*

In each test client machine, create a folder using a remote
PowerShell session from the test farm admin machine, to
verify the accessibility via remote PowerShell. See Figure 9-45.

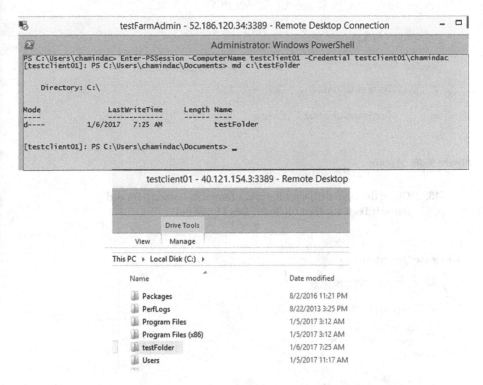

Figure 9-45. Creating folder to verify PS remoting access

12. Download and set up two build/release agents on the
testFarmAdmin machine. Chapter 2 has information on
how to set up an agent on a Windows machine. Extract the
downloaded agent zip file to two different folders and set up
two agents to run agent service using the admin account of
the machines. Two agents are required since we have two test
client machines to monitor in parallel. Make sure to register
the agents to a pool that is accessible by the team project
that contains the release definition created in Lesson 9.03,
"Running Functional Tests with TFS15/VSTS Release." See
Figure 9-46.

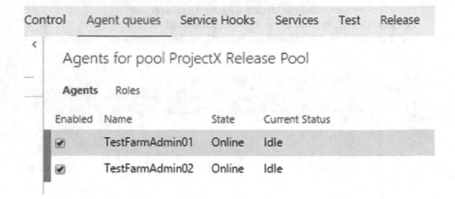

Figure 9-46. *Agents*

13. Clone the CodedUIDemoRelease created in Lesson 9.03 and name it TestFarmDemoRelease. See Figure 9-47.

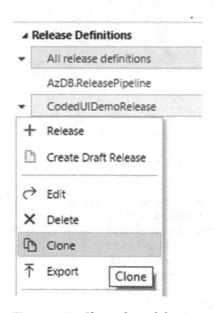

Figure 9-47. *Clone release definition*

14. Change the existing environment name to "Test Client 01," and in the **Run on agent** screen set a demand to Agent.Name with a value of TestFarmAdmin01. Make sure to select correct agent queue name (same as agent pool name) containing the agent in test farm admin machine. See Figure 9-48.

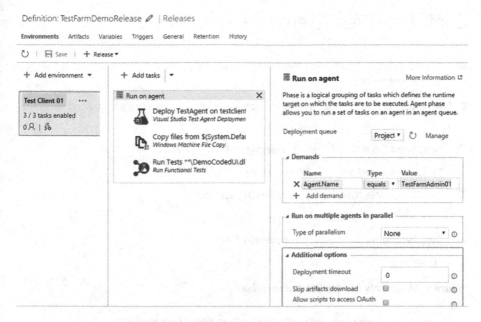

Figure 9-48. *Run on TestFarmAdmin01 agent*

15. Go to the environment variables and create variables
for TestClientAdmin's username and password,
TestClientTestSvcUser username and password, and a new
variable for TestClientName. Use the admin username used
for the Test Client and Test Farm Admin machines as the
TestFarm admin user. Use TestClientTestSvcUser (variable
name) as the test service user (created on both test client
machines as a local user). Use it as testclientmachinename\
testserviceuser, as shown in Figure 9-49, to allow the use of
the user created locally on each test client machine.

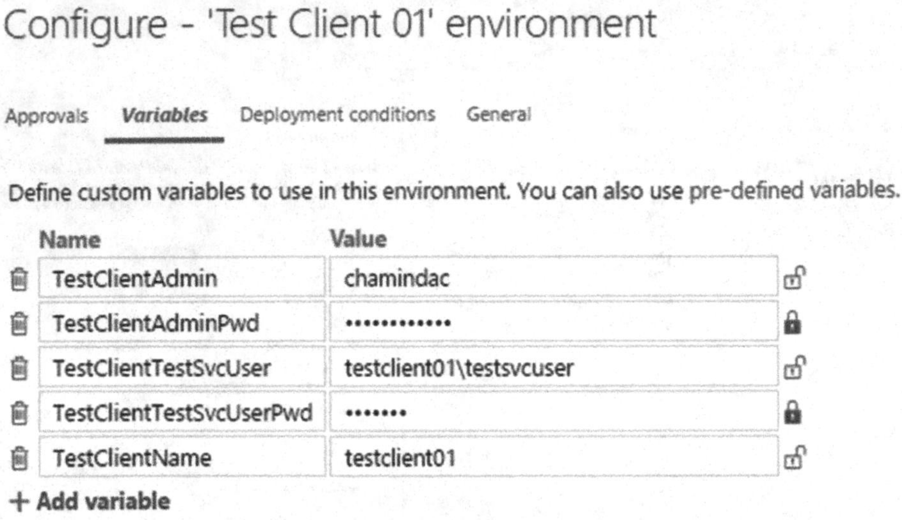

Configure - 'Test Client 01' environment

Approvals   *Variables*   Deployment conditions   General

Define custom variables to use in this environment. You can also use pre-defined variables.

	Name	Value	
🗑	TestClientAdmin	chamindac	🔓
🗑	TestClientAdminPwd	••••••••••••	🔒
🗑	TestClientTestSvcUser	testclient01\testsvcuser	🔓
🗑	TestClientTestSvcUserPwd	••••••••	🔒
🗑	TestClientName	testclient01	🔓

+ Add variable

Figure 9-49. *Test client environment variables*

16. Use these variables in the Deploy Test Agent task available in the environment. See Figure 9-50.

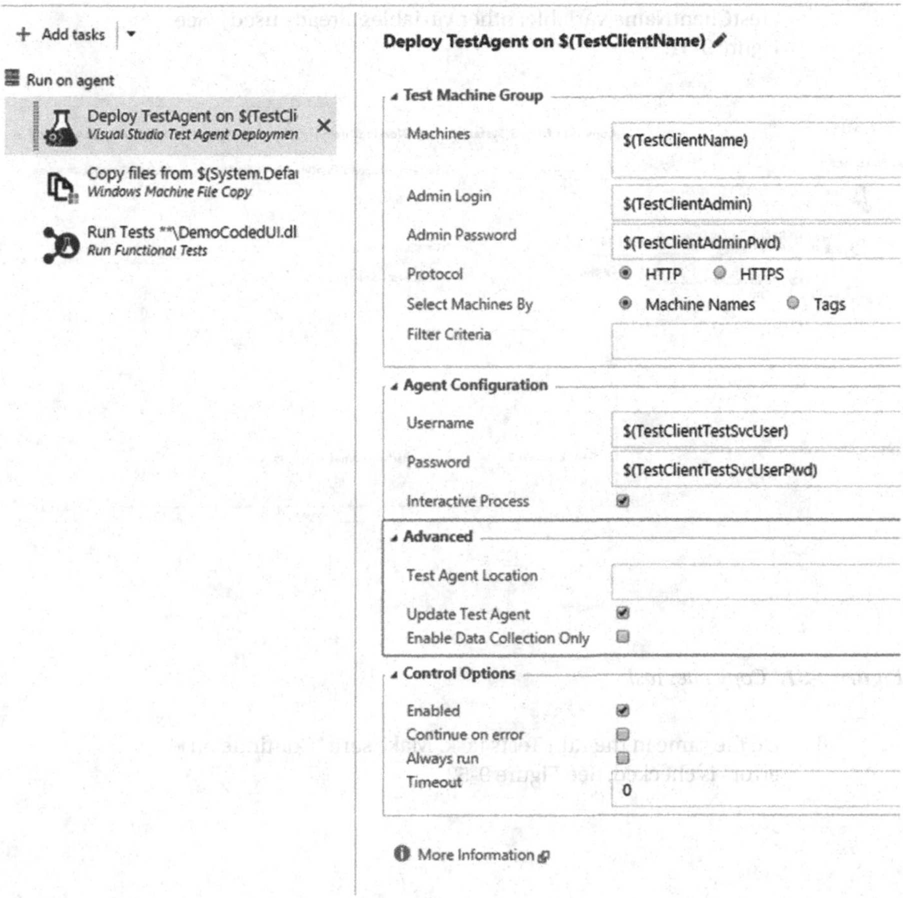

Figure 9-50. *Deploy TestAgent task*

17. Modify the Copy Files task to use the variables (TestClientName variable; other variables already used). See Figure 9-51.

Figure 9-51. *Copy Files task*

18. Do the same in the Run Tests task. Make sure "Continue on error" is checked. See Figure 9-52.

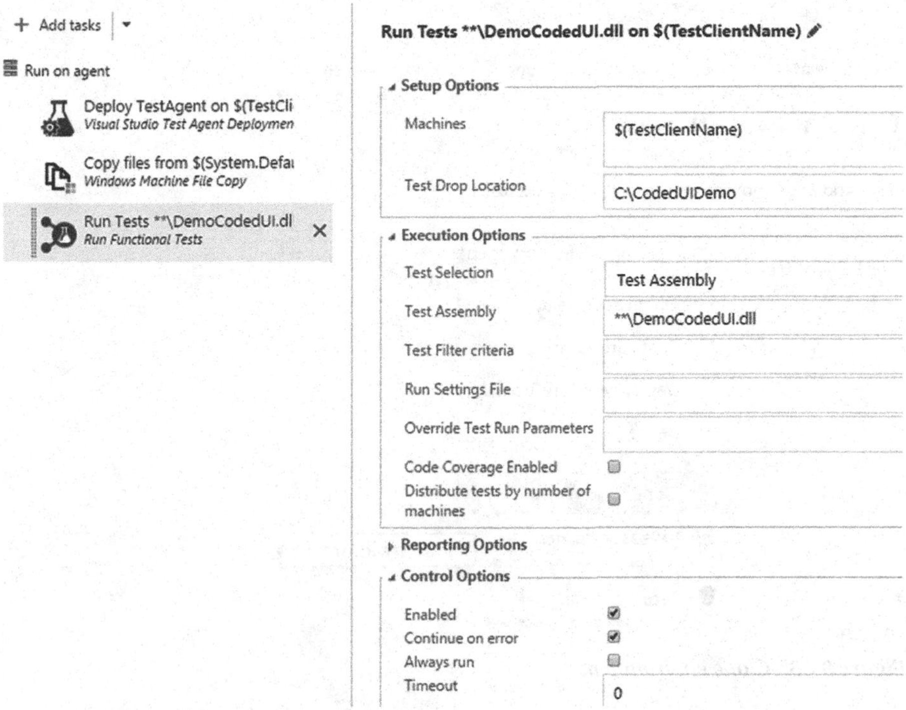

+ Add tasks ▾

▦ Run on agent

    Deploy TestAgent on $(TestCli
    Visual Studio Test Agent Deploymen

    Copy files from $(System.Defaι
    Windows Machine File Copy

    Run Tests **\DemoCodedUI.dl ✕
    Run Functional Tests

Run Tests **\DemoCodedUI.dll on $(TestClientName) ✏

⊿ **Setup Options**

Machines	$(TestClientName)
Test Drop Location	C:\CodedUIDemo

⊿ **Execution Options**

Test Selection	**Test Assembly**
Test Assembly	**\DemoCodedUI.dll
Test Filter criteria	
Run Settings File	
Override Test Run Parameters	
Code Coverage Enabled	☐
Distribute tests by number of machines	☐

▸ **Reporting Options**

⊿ **Control Options**

Enabled	☑
Continue on error	☑
Always run	☐
Timeout	0

***Figure 9-52.** Run Functional Tests task*

19. Save the definition and clone the Test Client 01 environment. See Figure 9-53.

Figure 9-53. *Clone environment*

20. In the popup widow, uncheck the Trigger option to deploy automatically once the Test Client 01 environment is done, as we are setting triggers later. See Figure 9-54.

×

Add new environment ⓘ

Tasks, parameters and configuration settings from the environment Test Client 01 will be copied to the new environment. Values for encrypted variables shall not be copied.

Pre-deployment approval

Select the users who can approve or reject deployments to the new environment

◉ Automatically approve

◯ Specific users

Trigger

☐ Deploy automatically whenever a deployment to the environment Test Client 01 is successful

Queue

Select an agent queue | manage queues ↗

ProjectX Release Pool	▼	↻

Create   Cancel

Figure 9-54. Cloning environment

21. Name the cloned environment "Test Client 02" and set it to run on agent TestFarmAdmin02. See Figure 9-55.

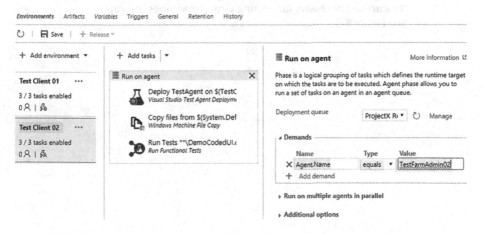

Figure 9-55. Run on TestFarmAdmin02

22. Open the Configure Variables window for the Test Client 02 environment. Set the TestClientName and TestServiceUserName values to reflect test client machine 02.

Configure - 'Test Client 02' environment

Approvals   *Variables*   Deployment conditions   General

Define custom variables to use in this environment. You can also use pre-defined variables.

	Name	Value	
🗑	TestClientAdmin	chamindac	🔓
🗑	TestClientAdminPwd	••••••••••••	🔒
🗑	TestClientTestSvcUser	testclient02\testsvcuser	🔓
🗑	TestClientTestSvcUserPwd	••••••••	🔒
🗑	TestClientName	testclient02	🔓

+ **Add variable**

Figure 9-56. *Test environment 02 variables*

23. Save the definition and add a new environment to the top of Test Client 01 environment. Name the new environment "Test Farm Start." Set it to run on a hosted agent if you are using VSTS. If TFS is used, set up a different local agent that Azure PowerShell is installed on (this agent should not be an agent running on the Azure machine created as the test farm admin). Select the "Skip downloading artifacts" option, since they are not necessary for starting virtual machines in Azure. See Figure 9-57.

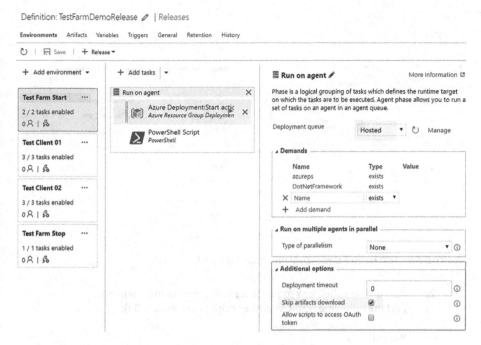

Figure 9-57. Test Farm Start, Run on agent

24. Add an Azure Resource Group Deployment task to the Test
Farm Start environment and select Azure Resource Manager
from the Azure Connection Type dropdown. Then, select
linked Azure RM Subscription, as shown in Figure 9-58.
Linking the Azure subscription is covered in Chapter 3
(Lesson 3.03.1). Select Start Virtual Machines from the Action
dropdown and select the resource group (ch-demo-resgroup
contains all the Azure virtual machines - you should use your
resource group name) that has the test farm machines.

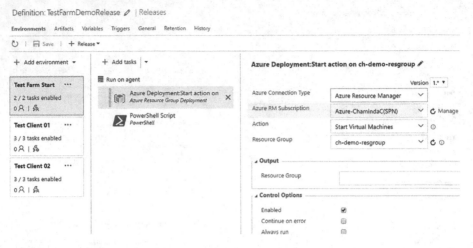

Figure 9-58. *Test Farm Start, Azure machine start task*

25. Add a PowerShell task to the Test Farm Start environment and add the following script as inline script (see Figure 9-59):

```
Param(
[Parameter(mandatory=$true)]
[int]$EnvReadyWait
)
sleep -Seconds $EnvReadyWait
```

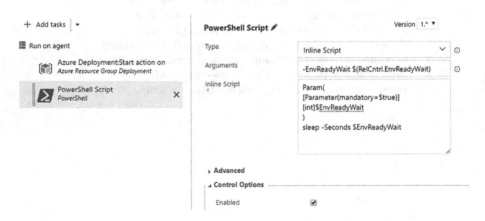

Figure 9-59. *Test Farm Start, Wait for machines to start*

26. Pass wait time as a parameter and set up a variable in the release definition to provide the wait time for virtual machines to be ready after start. See Figure 9-60.

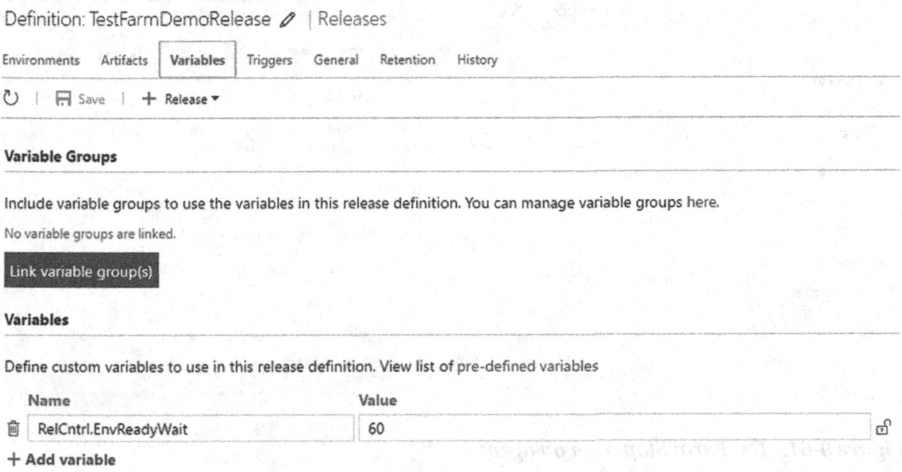

Definition: TestFarmDemoRelease ✎ | Releases

Environments   Artifacts   **Variables**   Triggers   General   Retention   History

↻ | 🖫 Save | ╋ Release ▾

Variable Groups

Include variable groups to use the variables in this release definition. You can manage variable groups here.

No variable groups are linked.

Link variable group(s)

Variables

Define custom variables to use in this release definition. View list of pre-defined variables

Name	Value	
🗑 RelCntrl.EnvReadyWait	60	🔓

╋ **Add variable**

Figure 9-60. *Environment ready wait time variable*

27. Add another environment named Test Farm Stop to the end of the release definition. Set this to run on the hosted agent (for VSTS) or on a separate on-premises agent that has Azure PowerShell. This agent cannot be an agent on the Test Farm Admin machine, since that also will be stopped by the tasks in this environment. Skip the downloading of artifacts, since artifacts are not required for this environment. See Figure 9-61.

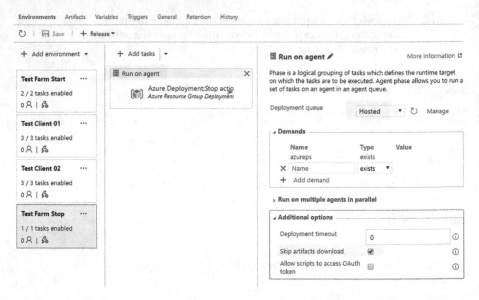

Figure 9-61. *Test Farm Stop, Run on agent*

28. Add an Azure Resource Group Deployment task and select Stop Virtual Machines from the Action dropdown. Select the same Azure RM subscription used in Test Farm Start. See Figure 9-62.

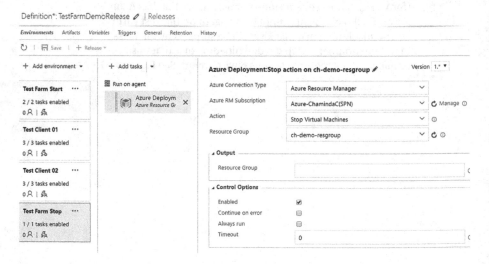

Figure 9-62. *Test Farm Stop, Stop virtual machines*

29. Save the release definition. In the Triggers tab of the release definition, set up environment triggers. Test Farm Start should run immediately after release creation. Test Client 01 and Test Client 02 should start once Test Farm Start has successfully completed. Test Farm Stop should start only once Test Client 01 and Test Client 02 have both completed. See Figure 9-63.

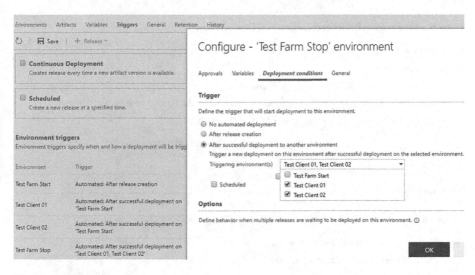

Figure 9-63. *Test Farm triggers*

30. Make sure to select "Also trigger for partially succeeded deployment(s)" in the Test Farm Stop environment deployment conditions to ensure Test Farm Stop runs even in a situation where tests fail and test client environments have only partially succeeded. See Figure 9-64.

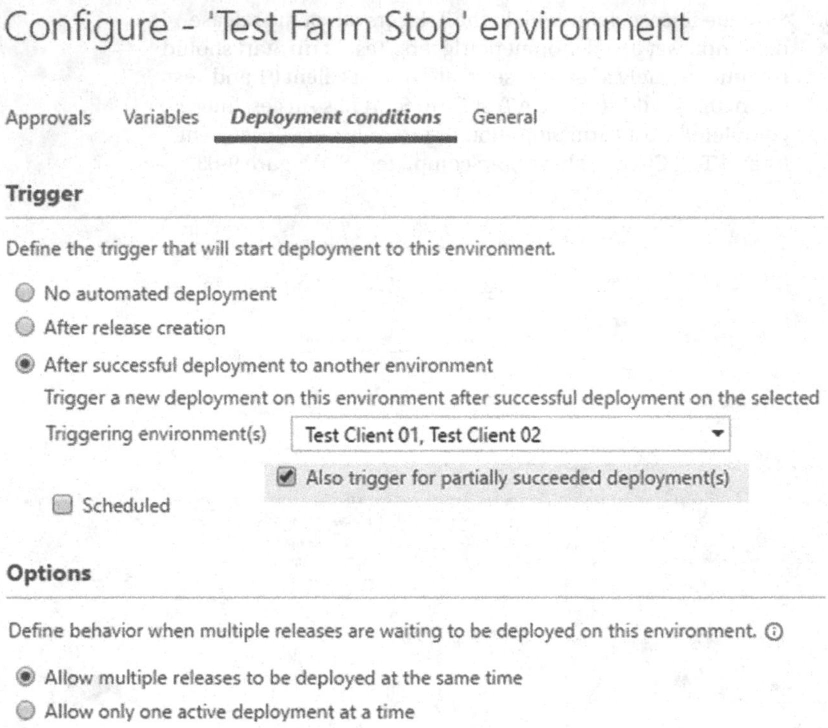

Configure - 'Test Farm Stop' environment

Approvals   Variables   ***Deployment conditions***   General

Trigger

Define the trigger that will start deployment to this environment.

○ No automated deployment

○ After release creation

◉ After successful deployment to another environment

Trigger a new deployment on this environment after successful deployment on the selected

Triggering environment(s) | Test Client 01, Test Client 02   ▼ |

☑ Also trigger for partially succeeded deployment(s)

☐ Scheduled

Options

Define behavior when multiple releases are waiting to be deployed on this environment. ⓘ

◉ Allow multiple releases to be deployed at the same time

○ Allow only one active deployment at a time

Figure 9-64. *Test Farm Stop trigger*

31. In Azure portal, stop the test farm virtual machines. This allows you to experience the virtual machines getting started on demand, when Test Farm start environment executed with the release management. See Figure 9-65.

Figure 9-65. *Stop all VMs*

32. Create a new release. You will see the warning in Figure 9-66, since the agents on the test farm admin machine are offline. This is OK because Test Farm Start will initiate the test farm admin virtual machine.

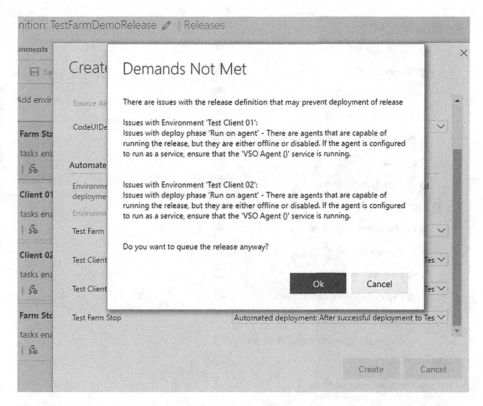

Figure 9-66. Release-creation warning

33. You will notice in the release definition log that the Test Client 01 and Test Client 02 environments execute the tests in parallel. See Figure 9-67.

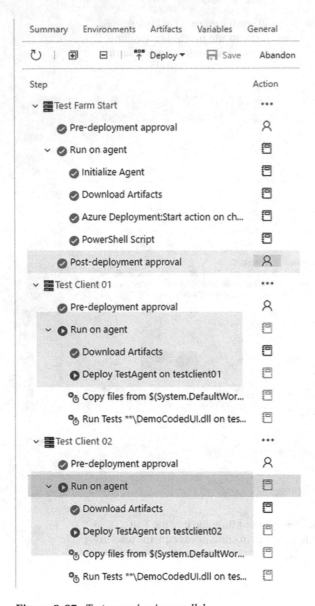

Figure 9-67. *Tests running in parallel*

34. Once the execution has completed, the release definition summary shows that the test clients have only partially succeeded. This is because we set a few tests to fail for demo purposes. See Figure 9-68.

Figure 9-68. *Release summary*

35. The Test tab of the definition can be used to analyze the results of the test run in the release definition. See Figure 9-69.

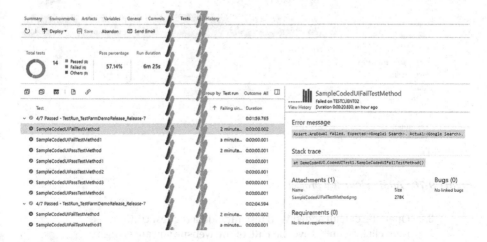

Figure 9-69. *Test run information in release definition*

You can use test plans and suites to a run different set of tests for each test client. This way, you can achieve fast execution time in your test automation by running different test suites in parallel. The benefit of using test automation with release definitions is that you can deploy to a given target environment and then have the test automation running. This allows you to achieve build, deploy, and test the workflow in a fully automated way, saves time, and is cost-effective, all good things for the software delivery process. Azure's on-demand test farm reduces costs further by using resources only when required.

Lesson 9.05 – Run Cloud-Based Load Tests with Release Management

Cloud-based load tests allow you to run load tests on a website without setting up any infrastructure. You can set up a Team Services release to run cloud-based load tests on an environment after a deployment. Let's look at a very simple scenario where we set up a load test for the home page of a basic ASP.NET website deployed to Azure.

Prerequisites: You have followed the Chapter 2 lessons and deployed a basic ASP. NET MVC 5 website to the Azure app service, or you have a different simple site with an anonymous, accessible home page. You have set up a VSTS account.

1. Connect Visual Studio to a VSTS team project.

2. Create a new solution in Visual Studio and add a Web Performance and Load Test project. See Figure 9-70.

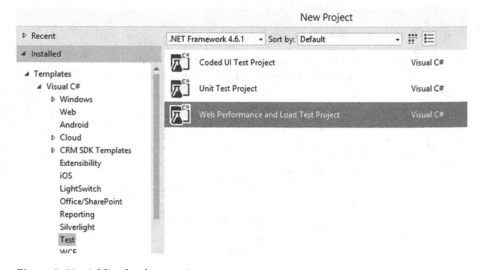

Figure 9-70. Adding load test project

3. Open the default added WebTest and add a request URL by right clicking on it. Give the URL of the website you are going to load test. See Figure 9-71.

Figure 9-71. *Setting URL in web test*

4. Right click on the project and select Add New Item. Then, select Load Test in the popup window and click Add. See Figure 9-72.

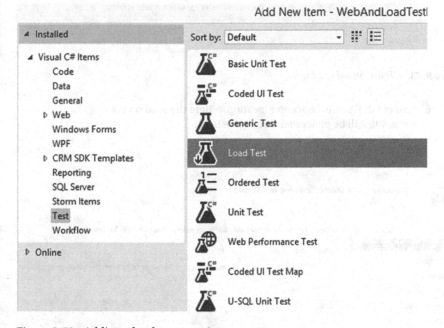

Figure 9-72. *Adding a load test to project*

5. Select the cloud-based load test option in the popup window and click Next. Your VSTS account is selected by default. However, this can be set to run with a different VSTS account if required when running with release management. See Figure 9-73.

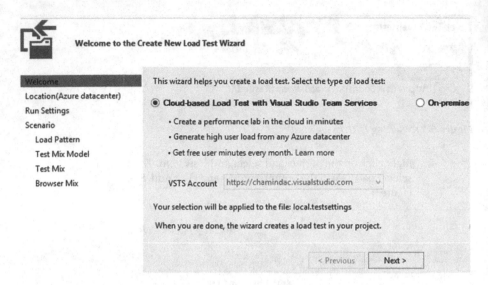

Figure 9-73. *Cloud-based load test*

6. Select the Azure datacenter location, where the load on your website will be generated. See Figure 9-74.

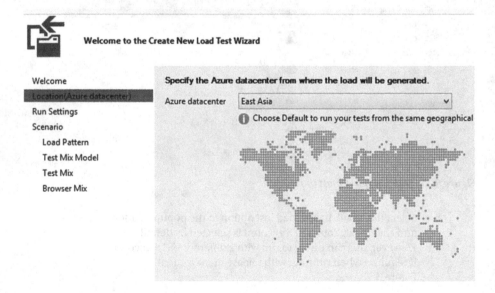

Figure 9-74. *Select datacenter*

7. Set the load test run settings. Set the warmup time to ten seconds and the test run time to one minute, as shown in Figure 9-75.

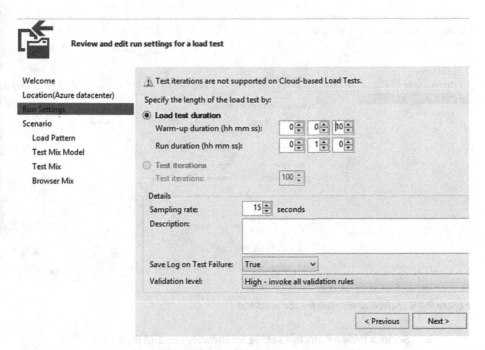

Figure 9-75. *Run settings for the load test*

8. Click on Test Mix and select the WebTest, as in Figure 9-76.

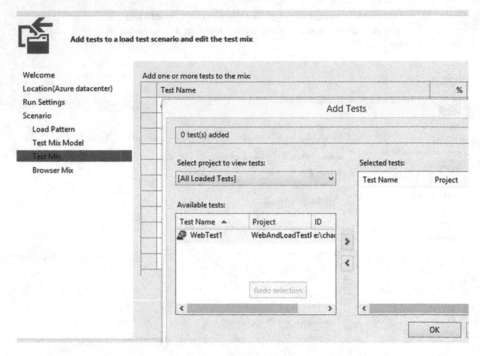

Figure 9-76. *Selecting web test for the load test*

9. Set up a browser mix by clicking on Browser Mix and then selecting from the browsers listed in the dropdowns. Click OK to complete setting up the load test. See Figure 9-77.

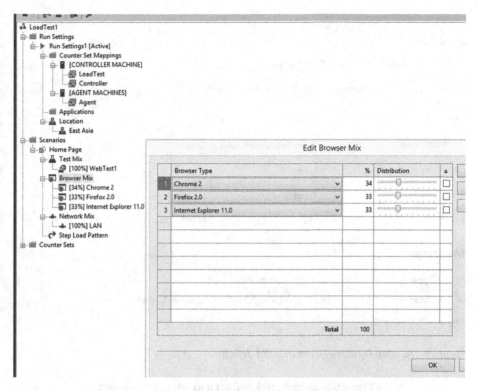

Figure 9-77. Browser mix

10. You can build and run the load test from Visual Studio to check if it is executing as expected. This will start a cloud-based load test. To get it running with Team Services/TFS release management, you need to build the load test project with TFS builds. Create a new empty build definition and set the repository path (Server Path) to the load test's solution folder. See Figure 9-78.

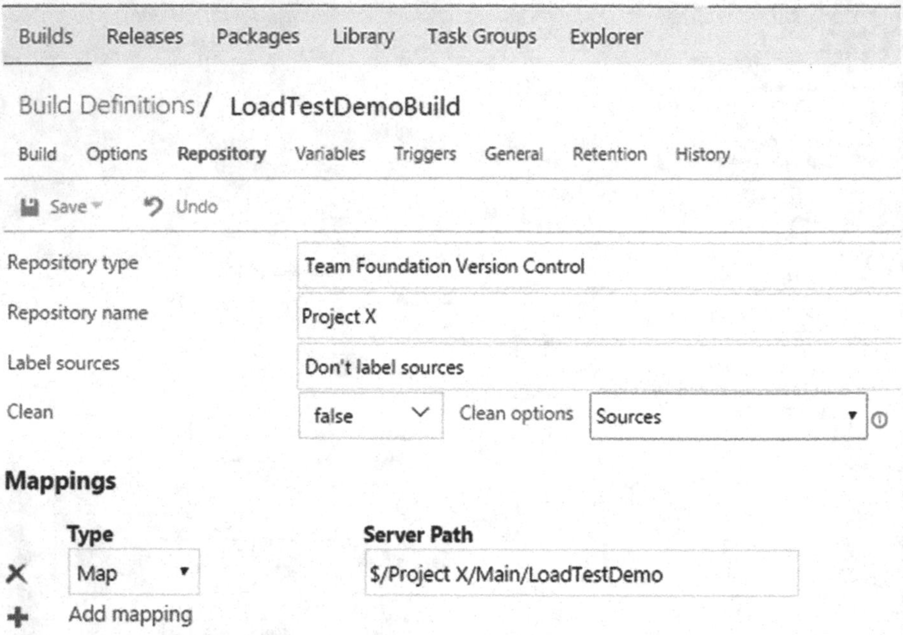

Builds	Releases	Packages	Library	Task Groups	Explorer

Build Definitions / **LoadTestDemoBuild**

Build	Options	**Repository**	Variables	Triggers	General	Retention	History

💾 Save ▾   ↺ Undo

Repository type	Team Foundation Version Control
Repository name	Project X
Label sources	Don't label sources
Clean	false ∨ Clean options Sources ▾ ⓘ

Mappings

	Type	**Server Path**
✕	Map ▾	$/Project X/Main/LoadTestDemo
✚	Add mapping	

Figure 9-78. *Map LoadTestDemo in build definition*

11. Add a Visual Studio Build task and set it to select the solution and build. Set the build argument to /p:OutDir="$(build. stagingDirectory) (see Figure 9-79).

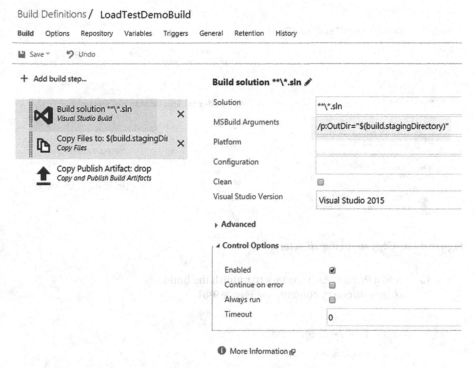

Figure 9-79. Build LoadTest solution

12. Add a Copy File step to copy the test settings file to the build staging directory (this is the local path on the build agent to which any artifacts are copied before being pushed to their destination). More information can be found at https://www.visualstudio.com/en-us/docs/build/define/variables. See Figure 9-80.

Figure 9-80. *Copy to staging directory*

13. Add a Publish Artifacts task to publish the build. stagingdirectory content. See Figure 9-81.

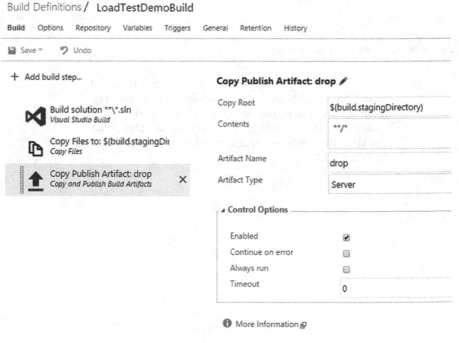

Figure 9-81. *Publish artifacts*

14. Save and queue a build and verify the artifacts in the build summary page by clicking Explore in the Artifacts tab.

15. Go to the settings screen of the team project. In the Services tab, add a generic service endpoint with the Team Services account's URL. You can use the same Team Services account that your team project is in (self-referencing to the same Team Services account). This service endpoint to Team Services account is created to use with cloud-based load test release tasks. This way, even on-premises TFS can run cloud-based load tests by connecting to a Team Services account. Creating a token (PAT, or Personal Access Token) is described in Chapter 2. See Figure 9-82.

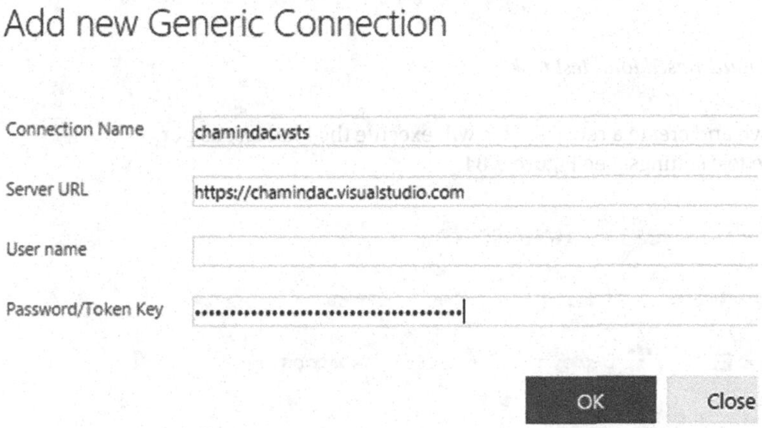

Add new Generic Connection

Connection Name	chamindac.vsts
Server URL	https://chamindac.visualstudio.com
User name	
Password/Token Key	••••••••••••••••••••••••••••••••••••

OK   Close

Figure 9-82. *Link Team Services account*

16. Create a new release definition and link the load test build. Then, add a cloud-based load test task from the Test tab in the Task Catalog. Select the created generic connection to the Team Services account (can be self-referencing to the same Team Services account) as the "Registered connection". Select the correct test settings file for the "Test settings file" feild, then select the artifacts location that contains the load test built files as the "Load test files folder". Provide the load test file name in the "Load test file" field. Set the test to automatically provision an agent for running load tests. See Figure 9-83.

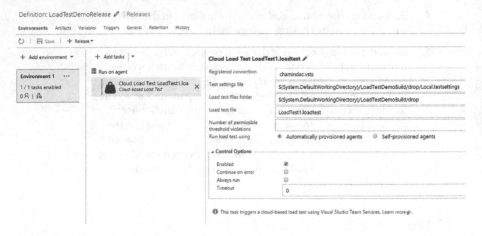

Figure 9-83.   *Cloud-based load test task*

17.   Save and create a release. This will execute the load test as per the test settings. See Figure 9-84.

LoadTestDemoRelease / Release-1

Summary   Environments   Artifacts   Variables   General

↻ | 🔲 🔳 | ⬆ Deploy ▾   🔲 Save   Abandon

Step	Action
∨ 🗄 Environment 1	•••
✔ Pre-deployment approval	R
∨ ✔ Run on agent	🗐
✔ Initialize Agent	🗐
✔ Download Artifacts	🗐
✔ Cloud Load Test LoadTest1.loadtest	🗐
✔ Post-deployment approval	R

Figure 9-84.   *Running cloud-based load tests*

18.   You can view the load test results in the VSTS account's Test tab under "load tests." See Figure 9-85.

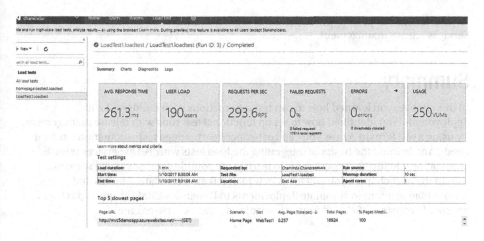

Figure 9-85. Load test results summary

19. You can view charts, compare test runs, and so forth. See Figure 9-86.

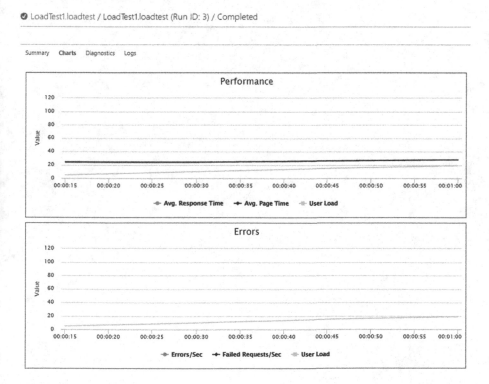

Figure 9-86. Load test results charts

In this lesson, you created a cloud-based load test and executed it using Team Services release management.

Summary

In this chapter, you learned how to run test automations with builds and with deployments. You identified how to set up functional test runs with release management. By using a test farm in Azure, you can cost-effectively manage test automation hardware needs. You learned the basics of integrating the load tests with Team Services release automation. Do further experiments to learn more complex and advanced scenarios.

In the next chapter, you will learn how to use Team Foundation builds and release management to automate deployments to Dynamics CRM (https://partner.microsoft.com/en-US/Solutions/microsoft-dynamics-crm-online).

■■■

CHAPTER 10

Dynamics CRM Deployments with TFS/VSTS Release

Streamlining Dynamics CRM deployments is always a challenging task because there is less support from development environments. In this chapter, you will get hands-on lessons on Dynamics CRM 2016/CRMOnline, customizations source controlling, and build and deployment with TFS. This chapter can be skipped if you are not familiar with Dynamics CRM development. For more information on Dynamics CRM visit https://partner.microsoft.com/en-US/Solutions/microsoft-dynamics-crm-online.

Prerequisites: You are familiar with customizing CRM and developing plugins, workflows, and so on with Dynamics CRM. Set up two CRM organizations—one to do development and the other to use as a deployment target. If required, you can set up two organizations in CRM online. To set up CRM online (for a trial), go to https://www.microsoft.com/en-us/dynamics/free-crm-trial.aspx.

Lesson 10.01 – Install SDK Template for Visual Studio

To enable developing for Dynamics CRM with Visual Studio, you need to install the required SDK templates as described in the following steps:

1. Download CRM sdk from https://www.microsoft.com/en-us/download/details.aspx?id=50032.

2. Run the exe and extract the SDK to a local folder.

3. Install the CRM SDK template for Visual Studio from the templates folder in the SDK. See Figure 10-1.

© Chaminda Chandrasekara 2017
C. Chandrasekara, *Beginning Build and Release Management with TFS 2017 and VSTS*,
DOI 10.1007/978-1-4842-2811-1_10

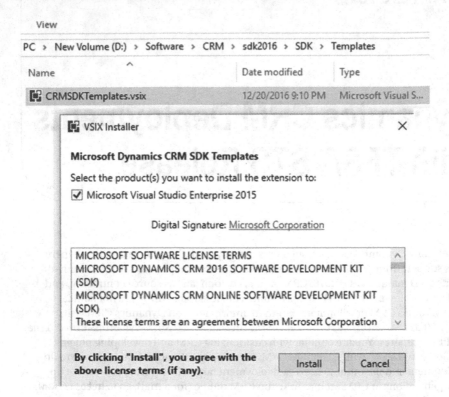

Figure 10-1. Install CRM SDK templates for Visual Studio

4.   CRM templates will be available in Visual Studio, as shown in Figure 10-2.

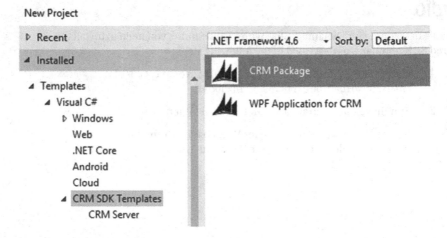

Figure 10-2. CRM project templates

You are now ready with the prerequisites to follow the other lessons in this chapter.

Lesson 10.02 – Create CRM Customization Solution and Plugin

Let's create a CRM solution in your new development CRM organization, which has already been created as a prerequisite of this chapter. You will then add a few entities, along with plugin code to work with them, in this lesson.

1. Go to Settings ➤ Solutions in your development CRM organization. See Figure 10-3.

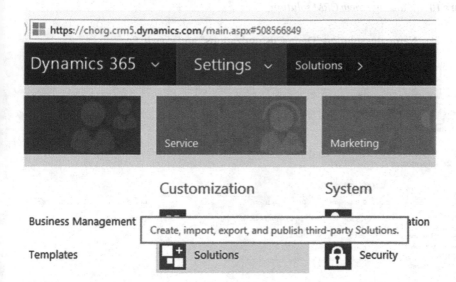

Figure 10-3. *CRM solutions*

2. Click on New under Solutions. See Figure 10-4.

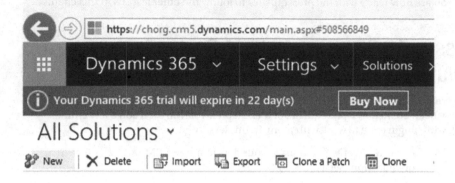

Figure 10-4. Adding a new CRM solution

3. Name the solution "DemoCustomizations" and save it. See Figure 10-5.

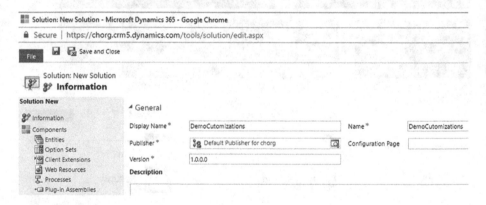

Figure 10-5. New CRM Solution

4. Click on Entities ➤ New Entity and create Demo Entity 1 by filling in the mandatory fields, as shown in Figure 10-6. Save the entity by clicking Save, and then click **Fields** in the left-hand menu.

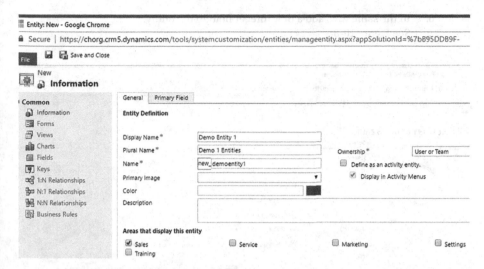

Figure 10-6. *New entity in CRM*

5. In the Fields tab's action toolbar click **New** to add a new string field to the entity. Fill in the details for the string field as shown in Figure 10-7 and click Save.

| Field: New for Demo Entity 1 - Google Chrome |

🔒 Secure | https://chorg.crm5.dynamics.com/tools/systemcustomization/attributes/manageAttribute.aspx?appSolutionId

File 💾 📑 Save and Close 📇

Field
New for Demo Entity 1

Common	General
Information	**Schema**
Business Rules	

Display Name*	string feild1	Field Requirement*	Optional
Name*	new_stringfeild1	Searchable	Yes
Field Security	○ Enable ● Disable		

⚠ Enabling field security? <u>What you need to know</u>

Auditing*   ● Enable ○ Disable

⚠ This field will not be audited until you enable auditing on the entity.

Description

Appears in global filter in interactive experience ☐   Sortable in interactive experience dashboard ☐

For information about how to interact with entities and fields programmatically, see the <u>Microsoft Dynamics 365 SDK</u>

Type

Data Type*	Single Line of Text ▼
Field Type*	Simple ▼
Format*	Text
Maximum Length*	100
IME Mode*	auto

Figure 10-7. *New string field*

6. In the same way, add a new integer field to the entity.
    See Figure 10-8.

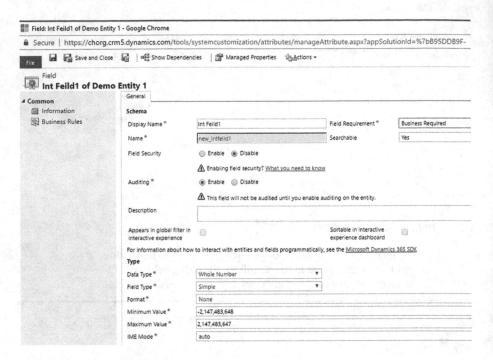

Figure 10-8. New integer field

7. Add another field with name Int Field 2, but let the type of the
    field be a single line of text. See Figure 10-9.

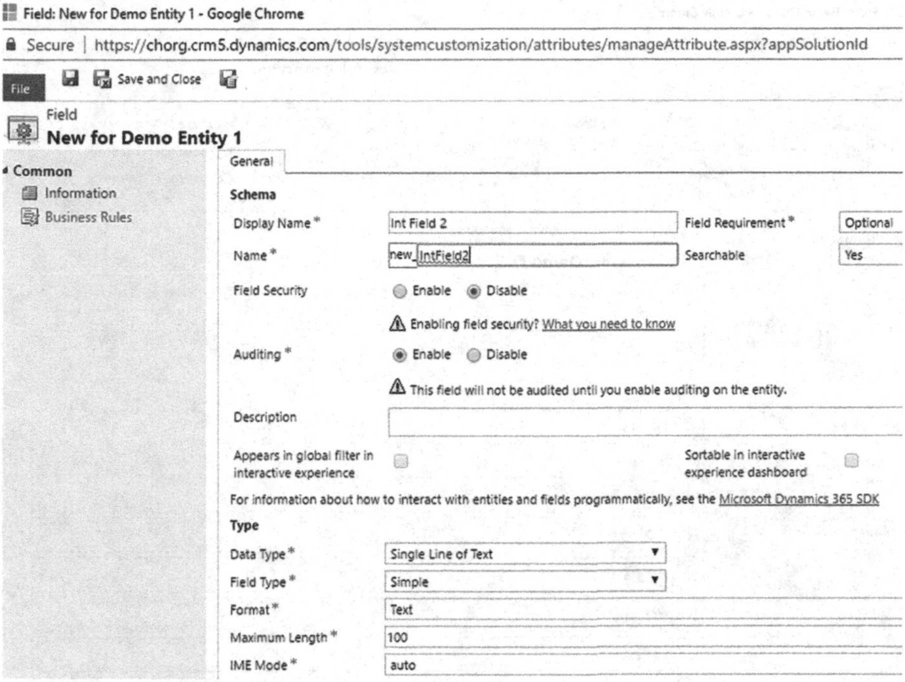

Figure 10-9. New string field with name IntField2

8. Save the fields and then open the main form in the Forms tab. Add the new fields to it and save. See Figure 10-10.

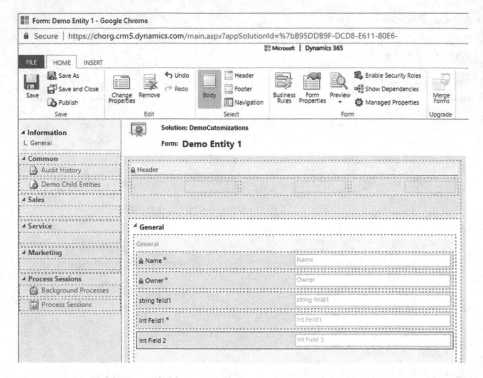

Figure 10-10. *Adding new fields to main form*

9. Add another entity with a few fields, adding the fields to the main form of that entity. Save and publish all customizations in the solution. Figure 10-11.

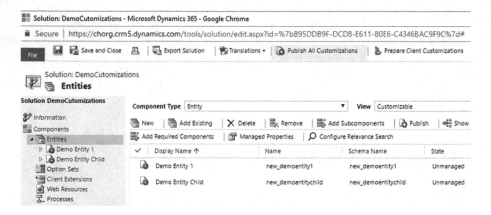

Figure 10-11. *Publish all customizations*

10. Create a blank Visual Studio solution named "CRMDemo" and add a project named "PluginDemo" using the CRM plugin template. See Figure 10-12.

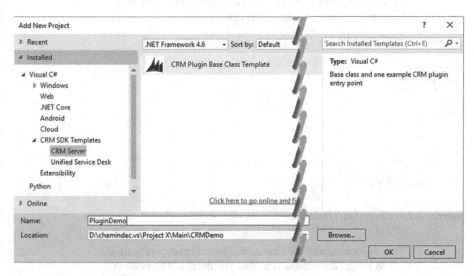

Figure 10-12. Plugin project

11. Right click on the solution and in the pop up menu, click Restore NuGet packages and build the solution. This will add the required NuGet packages, while missing dll warnings will go away and the build will succeed. See Figure 10-13.

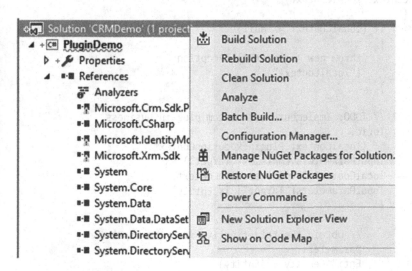

Figure 10-13. Restore NuGet

411

12. Open the PluginEntryPoint.cs file that was added with
    the project and replace the code with the code from
    https://github.com/chamindac/Book-Beginning-Build-
    ReleaseManagement-/blob/master/Chapter10/CRMDemo/
    PluginDemo/PluginEntryPoint.cs.

    See Figure 10-14.

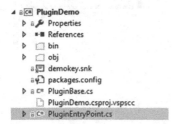

Figure 10-14. *PluginEntryPoint.cs*

The required assemblies are added with the project template
(CRM Plugin Base Class Template) by default. The code in
https://github.com/chamindac/Book-Beginning-Build-
ReleaseManagement-/blob/master/Chapter10/CRMDemo/
PluginDemo/PluginEntryPoint.cs contains the following
ExecuteCRMPlugin method:

```
protected override void ExecuteCrmPlugin(LocalPlugin
Context localContext)
{
    if (localContext == null)
    {
        throw new ArgumentNullException
        ("localContext");
    }

    // TODO: Implement your custom plug-in business
    logic.
    if (localContext.PluginExecutionContext.
    InputParameters.Contains("Target") &&
    localContext.PluginExecutionContext.
    InputParameters["Target"] is Entity)
    {

        // Obtain the target entity from the input
        parameters.
        Entity entity = (Entity)
        localContext.PluginExecutionContext.
        InputParameters["Target"];
```

```
int f1val = (int)entity.Attributes
["new_intfeild1"];

if (entity.Attributes.Contains
("new_intfield2"))
{
    entity.Attributes["new_intfield2"] =
    (f1val*2).ToString();

}
else
{
    entity.Attributes.Add("new_intfield2",
    (f1val * 2).ToString());

}
}

}
```

13. The preceding plugin code will work with Demo Entity 1 and multiply the value of intfield1 by two. Then, it will add that result as a string to intField2 since its field type is a single line of text. With the preceding code, make sure to use the exact field names you created previously. (CRM development is out of the scope of this book, which assumes the reader is experienced with CRM development. This is just a basic plugin to demonstrate deployment with TFS release management).

14. Build the solution.

15. Open the plugin registration tool in SDK as shown in Figure 10-15.

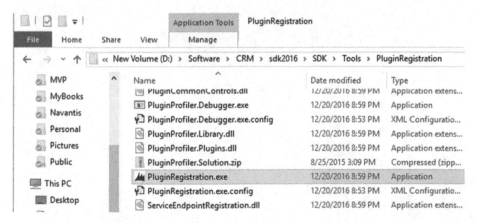

Figure 10-15. Plugin registration tool

16. Connect to your development CRM organization and register the plugin dll built with Visual Studio. See Figure 10-15.

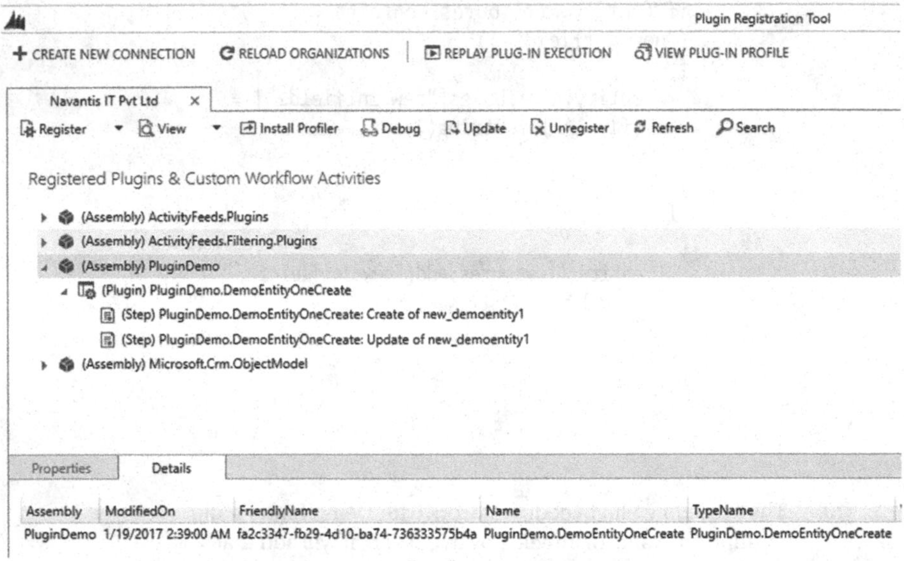

Figure 10-16. Register plugin

17. Add steps to update and create messages of Demo Entity 1, so the plugin steps are wired to the create and update actions of the entity.

The Create step should be set up like in Figure 10-17.

Update Existing Step

General Configuration Information

Message	Create
Primary Entity	new_demoentity1
Secondary Entity	none
Filtering Attributes	Message does not support Filtered Attributes
Event Handler	(Plugin) PluginDemo.DemoEntityOneCreate ⌄
Step Name	PluginDemo.DemoEntityOneCreate: Create of new_demoentity1
Run in User's Context	Calling User ⌄
Execution Order	1
Description	PluginDemo.DemoEntityOneCreate: Create of new_demoentity1

Event Pipeline Stage of Execution   Execution Mode   Deployment

○ Pre-validation   ◉ Asynchronous   ☑ Server

◉ Pre-operation   ◉ Synchronous   ☐ Offline

○ Post-operation

☐ Delete AsyncOperation if StatusCode = Successful

Figure 10-17. Create step

415

18. The Update step should be set up as shown in Figure 10-18.

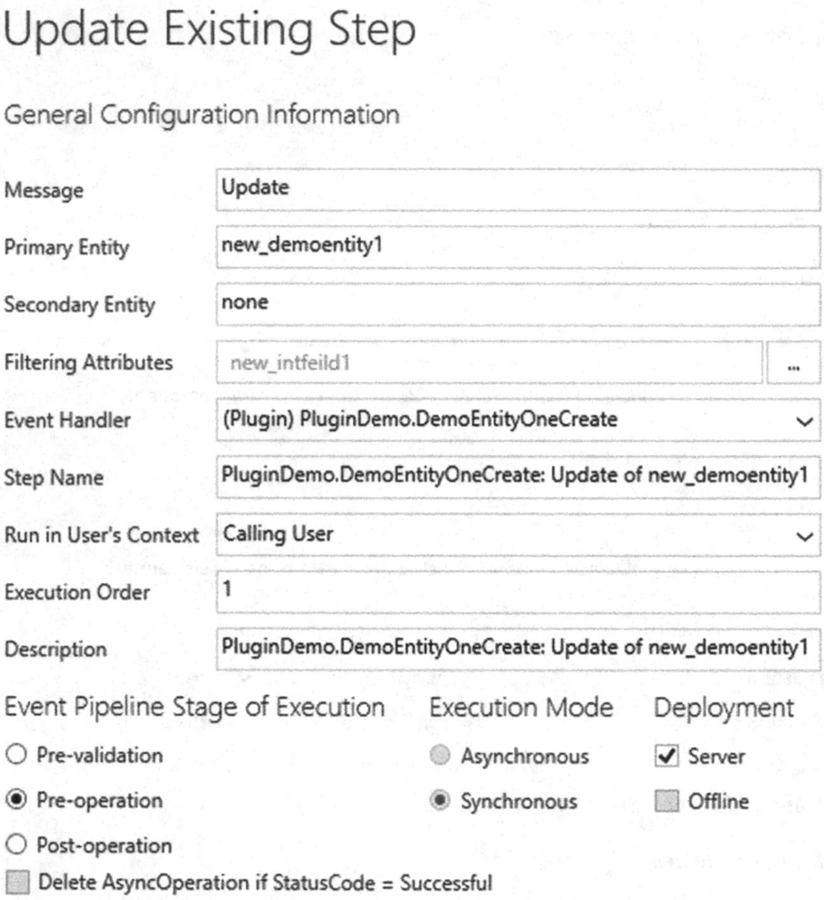

Update Existing Step

General Configuration Information

Message	Update
Primary Entity	new_demoentity1
Secondary Entity	none
Filtering Attributes	new_intfeild1 ...
Event Handler	(Plugin) PluginDemo.DemoEntityOneCreate ⌄
Step Name	PluginDemo.DemoEntityOneCreate: Update of new_demoentity1
Run in User's Context	Calling User ⌄
Execution Order	1
Description	PluginDemo.DemoEntityOneCreate: Update of new_demoentity1

Event Pipeline Stage of Execution   Execution Mode   Deployment

- ○ Pre-validation   ○ Asynchronous   ☑ Server
- ◉ Pre-operation   ◉ Synchronous   ☐ Offline
- ○ Post-operation

☐ Delete AsyncOperation if StatusCode = Successful

Figure 10-18.   *Update step*

19. Try creating a new entity record for Demo Entity 1. You will notice intfield2 will be auto-updated with double the value of intfield1 via plugin. See Figure 10-19.

DEMO ENTITY 1 : INFORMATION

test

⊿ General

Name *	test
Owner *	👤 Chaminda Chandrasekara
string feild1	test
Int Feild1 *	6
Int Field 2	12

Figure 10-19. *Entity created*

You created a CRM solution and added two entities and a plugin in this lesson. In the next lesson, you will be adding these customizations to the source control repository to enable packaging them with Team Foundation build.

Lesson 10.03 – Source Control CRM Customizations

Source control of CRM customization solutions can be done in three different ways:

- Export customizations zip file and check in/submit the zip file as it is to the source control repository.

- Export customizations zip file, extract it, and check in/submit extracted files.

- Export customizations zip file and unpack it using SolutionPackager.exe, available with the SDK. This gives individual-entity, relationship, form, and view levels of granularity. However, it is a more complex process for the development team, and at times some teams find this process is causing unwanted delays in progress of work and in return results in less productivity.

Out of these three, the first option does not provide any valuable information in the source control history because comparing zip files is not possible. The most feasible option for many teams is the second one. It involves just unzipping the exported customizations solution zip file and checking it into source control. This way you can compare the customization XML of the solution with previous versions and have a simple check-in model. In this book, we will only discuss the second option for the check-in of CRM customizations and how to package them back with TFS builds. We will use PowerShell scripts and this available open source PowerShell module: `https://github.com/seanmcne/Microsoft.Xrm.Data.PowerShell`.

417

1. Create a folder called "DevScripts" in the solution. Add the script from https://github.com/chamindac/Book-Beginning-Build-ReleaseManagement-/blob/master/Chapter10/CRMDemo/DevScripts/DownloadCRMSolutions.ps1to the folder. See Figure 10-20.

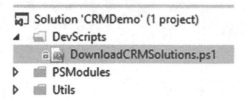

Solution 'CRMDemo' (1 project)
▲ 🗀 DevScripts
   🔒📄 DownloadCRMSolutions.ps1
▷ 📁 PSModules
▷ 📁 Utils

Figure 10-20. *Download CRMSolutions.ps1*

2. Use the PSModules folder available at https://github.com/chamindac/Book-Beginning-Build-ReleaseManagement-/tree/master/Chapter10/CRMDemo/PSModulesand add its content to the solution, as shown in Figure 10-21. The Microsoft.Xrm.Data.PowerShell module is an open source PowerShell module capable of handling many functionalities with CRM 2016 and CRM online. Use the content from https://github.com/chamindac/Book-Beginning-Build-ReleaseManagement-/tree/master/Chapter10/CRMDemo/PSModules/Microsoft.Xrm.Data.PowerShell, as it is slightly modified from the original files available at https://github.com/seanmcne/Microsoft.Xrm.Data.PowerShell.

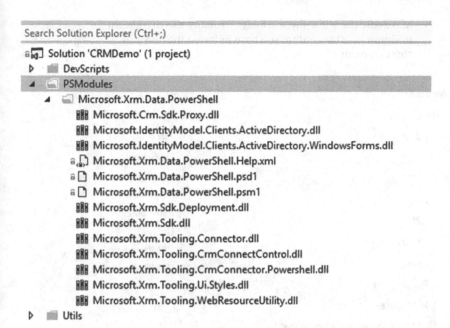

Figure 10-21. *Microsoft.Xrm.Data.PowerShell*

3. Create a folder called "Utils" and add the CommonFunctions. ps1from https://github.com/chamindac/Book-Beginning-Build-ReleaseManagement-/blob/master/Chapter10/CRMDemo/Utils/CommonFunctions.ps1to it. This script contains common functions required to work with CRM solutions. See Figure 10-22.

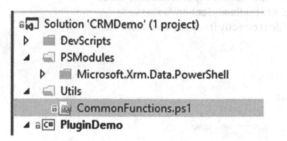

Figure 10-22. *CommonFunctions.ps1*

4. Make sure there is a physical folder structure like that shown in Figure 10-23 to confirm you have followed the previous steps correctly.

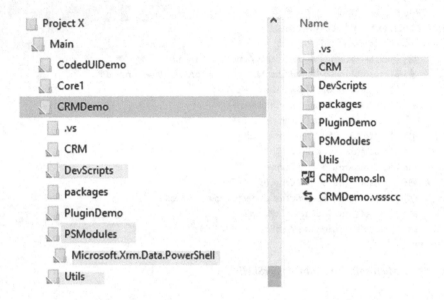

Figure 10-23. *CRMDemo folder structure*

5. Check in the solution, along with the DevScripts, PSModules, and Utils folder contents to the source control repository.

6. Execute the DownloadCRMSolutions script with the DevScripts folder using PowerShell. You can add the Run with PowerShell Visual Studio Extension (https://marketplace.visualstudio.com/items?itemName=JochenVanGasse.RunWithPowerShell) to do it directly from the Visual Studio. See Figure 10-24.

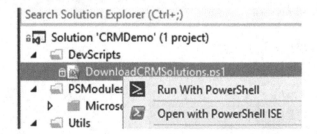

Figure 10-24. *Run PowerShell from Visual Studio*

You might encounter run restrictions in PowerShell. You can allow the scripts to run from VS by going to your system drive path (C:\Windows\SysWOW64\WindowsPowerShell\v1.0), as shown in Figure 10-25, and set execution policy as remote signed.

Run PowerShell.exe in the path as Administrator. Note that running PowerShell from the start menu and setting execution policy will not allow scripts to run from Visual Studio.

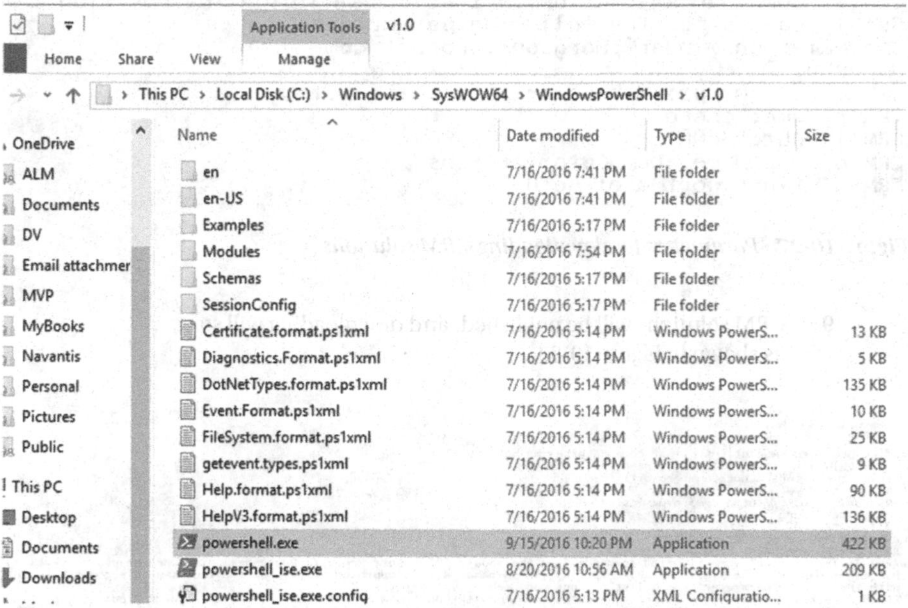

Figure 10-25. *SysWOW64 PowerShell*

7. Set the execution policy to be remote signed. See Figure 10-26.

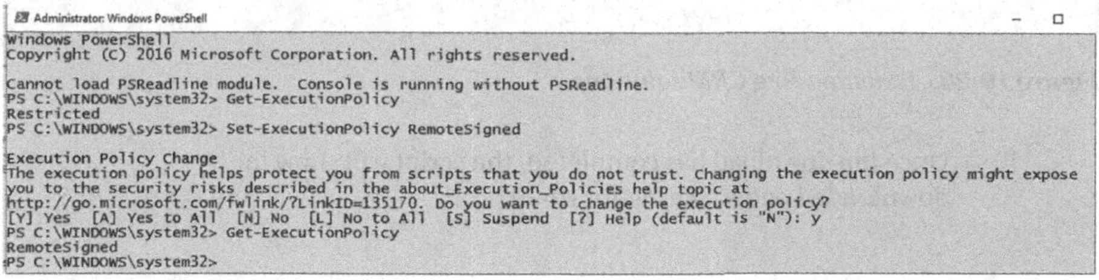

Figure 10-26. *Set execution policy*

8. The DownloadCRMSolutions script will prompt for parameters for CRM URL, organization name, credentials, and solution name. Timeout is in seconds. Provide the details of the development CRM organization and solution. Set ExportMode as **Both** in order to download both managed and unmanaged solutions. See Figure 10-27.

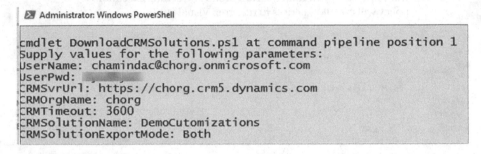

Figure 10-27. *Parameters for downloading CRM solutions*

9. CRM solutions will be published, and downloading will start, as shown in Figure 10-28.

```
Administrator: Windows PowerShell                                          —   □   ×

cmdlet DownloadCRMSolutions.ps1 at command pipeline position 1
Supply values for the following parameters:
UserName: chamindac@chorg.onmicrosoft.com
UserPwd: Ayodhyal
CRMSvrUrl: https://chorg.crm5.dynamics.com
CRMOrgName: chorg
CRMTimeout: 3600
CRMSolutionName: DemoCutomizations
CRMSolutionExportMode: Both
WARNING: The names of some imported commands from the module 'Microsoft.Xrm.Data.PowerShell' include unapproved verbs
that might make them less discoverable. To find the commands with unapproved verbs, run the Import-Module command again
 with the Verbose parameter. For a list of approved verbs, type Get-Verb.
VERBOSE: Verbose output log file: 'C:\Users\Chaminda\AppData\Roaming\Microsoft Corporation\Microsoft® Windows®
Operating System\10.0.14393.0\Microsoft.Xrm.Tooling.CrmConnector.Powershell-2017-01-18-1.log'
VERBOSE: Connection Complete
VERBOSE: Using the supplied single filter of uniquename 'like' DemoCutomizations
VERBOSE: Solution found with version# 1.0.0.0
VERBOSE: Solution path: D:\chamindac.vs\Project X\Main\CRMDemo\CRM\Solutions\tmp\DemoCutomizations.zip
VERBOSE: ExportSolutionRequests may take several minutes to complete execution.
VERBOSE: Using solution file to path: $path
VERBOSE: Successfully wrote file

VERBOSE: Using the supplied single filter of uniquename 'like' DemoCutomizations
VERBOSE: Solution found with version# 1.0.0.0
VERBOSE: Solution path: D:\chamindac.vs\Project X\Main\CRMDemo\CRM\Solutions\tmp\DemoCutomizations_managed.zip
VERBOSE: ExportSolutionRequests may take several minutes to complete execution.
```

Figure 10-28. *Downloading CRM solutions*

10. Once the download has completed, the script will show the downloaded paths. See Figure 10-29.

```
WARNING: The names of some imported commands from the module 'Microsoft.Xrm.Data.PowerShell' include unapproved verbs
that might make them less discoverable. To find the commands with unapproved verbs, run the Import-Module command again
 with the Verbose parameter. For a list of approved verbs, type Get-Verb.
VERBOSE: Verbose output log file: 'C:\Users\Chaminda\AppData\Roaming\Microsoft Corporation\Microsoft® Windows®
Operating System\10.0.14393.0\Microsoft.Xrm.Tooling.CrmConnector.Powershell-2017-01-18.log'
VERBOSE: Connection Complete
VERBOSE: Using the supplied single filter of uniquename 'like' DemoCutomizations
VERBOSE: Solution found with version# 1.0.0.0
VERBOSE: Solution path: D:\chamindac.vs\Project X\Main\CRMDemo\CRM\Solutions\tmp\DemoCutomizations.zip
VERBOSE: ExportSolutionRequests may take several minutes to complete execution.
VERBOSE: Using solution file to path: $path
VERBOSE: Successfully wrote file

VERBOSE: Using the supplied single filter of uniquename 'like' DemoCutomizations
VERBOSE: Solution found with version# 1.0.0.0
VERBOSE: Solution path: D:\chamindac.vs\Project X\Main\CRMDemo\CRM\Solutions\tmp\DemoCutomizations_managed.zip
VERBOSE: ExportSolutionRequests may take several minutes to complete execution.
VERBOSE: Using solution file to path: $path
VERBOSE: Successfully wrote file
ExportSolutionResponse                                  SolutionPath
----------------------                                  ------------
Microsoft.Crm.Sdk.Messages.ExportSolutionResponse D:\chamindac.vs\Project X\Main\CRMDemo\CRM\Solutions\tmp\DemoCutom...
Microsoft.Crm.Sdk.Messages.ExportSolutionResponse D:\chamindac.vs\Project X\Main\CRMDemo\CRM\Solutions\tmp\DemoCutom...
```

Figure 10-29. *Downloaded CRM solution*

11. DownloadCRMSolutions will connect to specified CRM
organization and will download the specified solution. Then,
it will extract the CRM solution into a folder hierarchy, as
shown in Figure 10-30, inside the Visual Studio solution.

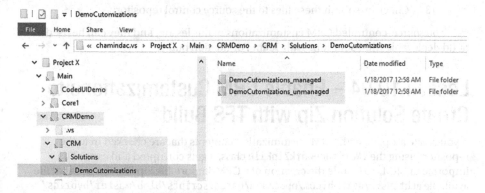

Figure 10-30. *Downloaded managed and unmanaged CRM solutions*

12. Managed and unmanaged solution folders will contain the
customization files. See Figure 10-31.

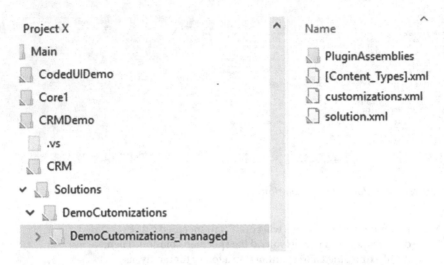

Figure 10-31. *Contents of CRM solution*

13. Check in/submit these files to the source control repository.

You source-controlled CRM customizations in this lesson, and they can be used to build deployable CRM solutions with Team Foundation builds.

Lesson 10.04 – Enable CRM Customizations to Create Solution Zip with TFS Build

If you create a zip file with CRM customization contents that are checked in to the repository using the .NetframeworkZipFile class, it gets corrupted and cannot be imported to CRM. To enable the creation of a CRM-importable zip file, the zipjs.bat file available at https://github.com/npocmaka/batch.scripts/blob/master/hybrids/jscript/zipjs.bat should be used.

1. Create a folder called "BuildScripts" (in the screenshots provided the BuildScripts folder is misspelled as BuidScripts - keep a note of it while following the lessons in this Chapter) inside the Solution folder in Source Control Explorer.

2. Download the zipjs.bat file from https://github.com/npocmaka/batch.scripts/blob/master/hybrids/jscript/zipjs.bat or https://github.com/chamindac/Book-Beginning-Build-ReleaseManagement-/blob/master/Chapter10/CRMDemo/BuidScripts/zipjs.bat. Download PackageCRMSolutions.ps1 provided at https://github.com/chamindac/Book-Beginning-Build-ReleaseManagement-/blob/master/Chapter10/CRMDemo/BuidScripts/PackageCRMSolutions.ps1 and add them to the BuildScripts folder. See Figure 10-32.

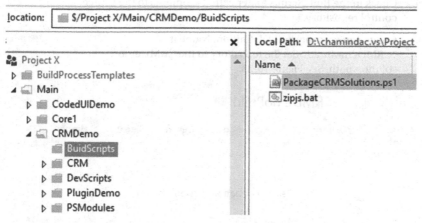

Figure 10-32. zipjs/bat and PackageCRMSolutions.ps1

3. PackageCRMSolutions.ps1 contains the following PowerShell
   script, and it will package the CRM solution's extracted files
   back to a CRM-importable zip file.

```
param(
$CRMSolutionsRootPath,
$CRMSolutionName
)

$ErrorActionPreference = "Stop"

#resolve path to make sure no VB script errors
$CRMSolutionsRootPath = Resolve-Path $CRMSolutionsRootPath

$SolutionContainerPath = Join-Path $CRMSolutionsRootPath
$CRMSolutionName
$SolutionContainerPathInfo = New-Object System.IO.DirectoryInfo
$SolutionContainerPath
$SolutionDirectories = $SolutionContainerPathInfo.
GetDirectories();

foreach($SolutionDirName in $SolutionDirectories)
{

    $zipFileName = "$CRMSolutionsRootPath\$SolutionDirName.zip"
    $foldertozip = "$SolutionContainerPath\$SolutionDirName"

    #& CScript  zip.vbs $foldertozip $zipFileName | out-null
    & $PSScriptRoot\zipjs.bat zipDirItems -source $foldertozip
-destination $zipFileName -keep yes -force no | out-null
}
```

4. Check in the BuildScripts folder with its contents to the source control repository.

5. Create a new empty build definition. Name it "CRMDemoBuild." Set the repository to the CRMDemo solution path. See Figure 10-33.

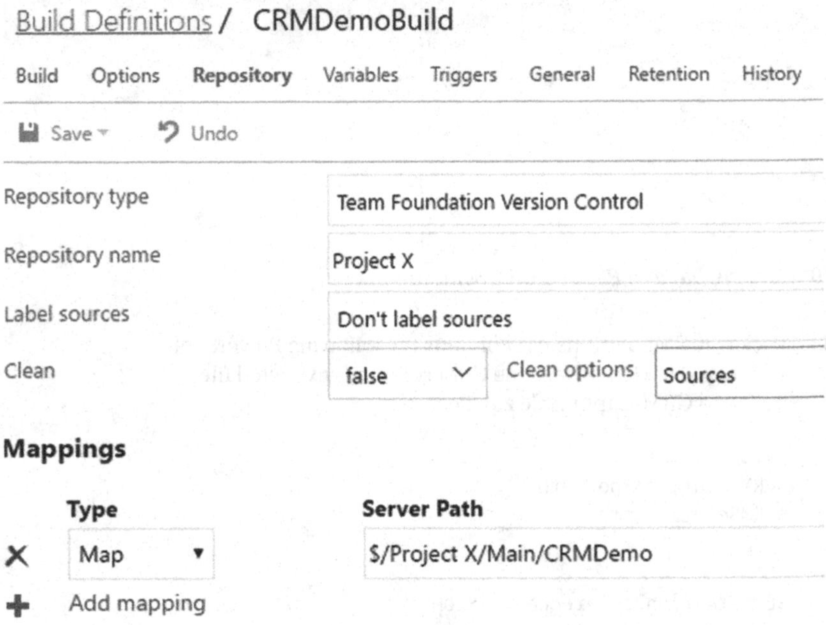

Build Definitions / CRMDemoBuild

| Build | Options | **Repository** | Variables | Triggers | General | Retention | History |

💾 Save ▾   🔄 Undo

Repository type	Team Foundation Version Control
Repository name	Project X
Label sources	Don't label sources
Clean	false ⌄ Clean options Sources

Mappings

	Type	**Server Path**
✗	Map ▾	$/Project X/Main/CRMDemo
➕	Add mapping	

Figure 10-33. Map CRMDemo path

6. Add a PowerShell task to the build definition and select the script PackageCRMSolutions.ps1. This script will package the checked in CRM cutomizations (extracted files are checked-in in the previous lesson) as zip files when the build is executing. Provide the following arguments to the script:

```
-CRMSolutionsRootPath $(Build.SourcesDirectory)\CRM\
Solutions -CRMSolutionNameDemoCustomizations
```

See Figure 10-34.

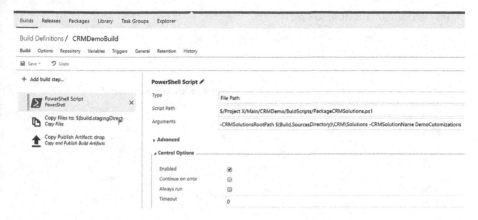

Figure 10-34. Package CRM solutions

7. Add a Copy Files task to the build definition. Keep the source folder empty to allow selecting from the root of the repository recursively matching the provided pattern. Provide contents (file pattern) as follows to allow the copying of all CRM solution zip files to the build staging directory which will be published as output/artifacts of the build in the next step.

    `**\CRM\Solutions\*.zip`

    Set the target folder to the build-staging directory. See Figure 10-35.

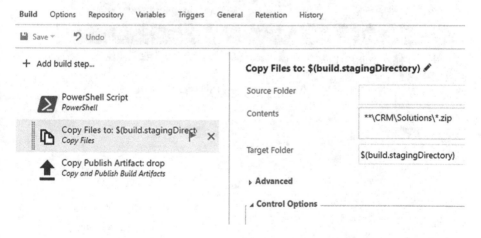

Figure 10-35. Copy Files step

8. As the last step of the build definition, add a Copy Publish Artifact task. Set the copy root as a build-staging directory and contents as * to copy all. Type "drop" in the Artifact Name field and "Server" in the Artifact Type field. See Figure 10-36.

Figure 10-36. *Publish Artifacts step*

9. Queue a new build and verify the output with the CRM solution zip files in the Build Artifacts explorer. See Figure 10-37.

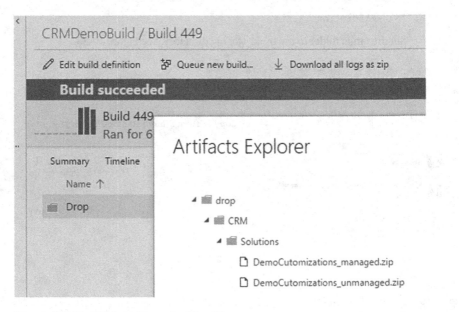

Figure 10-37. *CRM zip files as build artifacts*

In this lesson, you have packaged CRM solutions using Team Foundation builds. These solutions can be used to deploy to a target CRM organization.

Lesson 10.05 – Deploy CRM Solution with TFS Release

There is an extension created to allow CRM solution deployment and to activate CRM workflows after deployment. This extension is available at `https://marketplace.visualstudio.com/items?itemName=chamindac.chamindac-vsts-release-task-crm-2016`. This extension can only run on a build/release agent that is created on-premises (private agent). Hosted agents are currently not supported. You can use this extension with Visual Studio Team Services by using an agent set up as an on-premises agent. Instructions on installing Marketplace extensions are available in Chapter 2.

Prerequisites: You have an on-premises build release agent set up for VSTS or TFS. You have installed the Chamindac.vsts.release.task.crm-2016 file from Visual Studio Marketplace (`https://marketplace.visualstudio.com/items?itemName=chamindac.chamindac-vsts-release-task-crm-2016`) to your Team Services or TFS. Chapter 2 describes the installation of extensions from Marketplace to Team Services or TFS.

1. Create an empty release definition.

2. Link the build CRMDemoBuild to the release. See Figure 10-38.

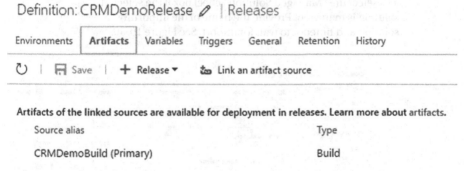

Figure 10-38. *Linked artifacts*

3. In the Environment 1 that was added by default, set Run on agent to an on-premises (private agent). See Figure 10-39.

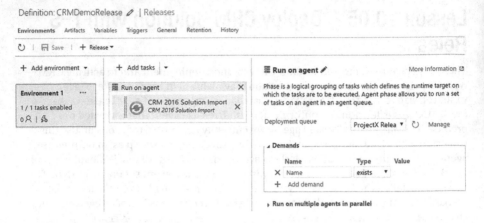

Figure 10-39. *Run on agent*

4. Add a CRM 2016 Solution Import task to the release definition environment 1. Set the target CRM organization URL and credentials. Select the solution to deploy from the build drop and select the "Managed Solution" checkbox if the selected solution is managed. Provide the name of the importing solution and timeout to wait for import. See Figure 10-40.

Figure 10-40. *CRM Solution Import task*

5. Save the release definition and create a release. It deploys to the target CRM. See Figure 10-41.

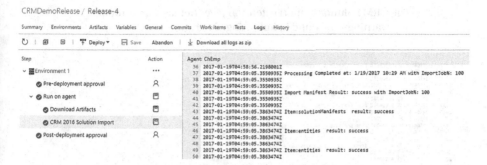

Figure 10-41. CRM Solution deployed with release management

6. CRM entities and plugins work as expected in the target CRM organization. See Figure 10-42.

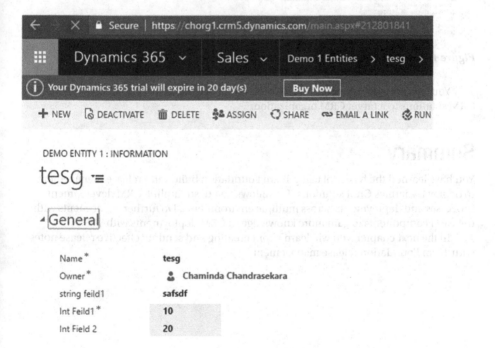

Figure 10-42. CRM customizations available in target CRM

7. The CRM Solution Import extension gives details if an error or any warnings are found in importing. See Figure 10-43.

```
40  2017-01-19T04:59:05.3550935Z Import Manifest Result: success with ImportJob%: 100
41  2017-01-19T04:59:05.3550935Z
42  2017-01-19T04:59:05.3550935Z
43  2017-01-19T04:59:05.3863474Z Item:solutionManifests  result: success
44  2017-01-19T04:59:05.3863474Z
45  2017-01-19T04:59:05.3863474Z
46  2017-01-19T04:59:05.3863474Z Item:entities  result: success
47  2017-01-19T04:59:05.3863474Z
48  2017-01-19T04:59:05.3863474Z
49  2017-01-19T04:59:05.3863474Z Item:entities  result: success
50  2017-01-19T04:59:05.3863474Z
51  2017-01-19T04:59:05.3863474Z
52  2017-01-19T04:59:05.4019588Z Item:SolutionPluginAssemblies  result: success
53  2017-01-19T04:59:05.4019588Z
54  2017-01-19T04:59:05.4019588Z
55  2017-01-19T04:59:05.4019588Z Item:SdkMessageProcessingSteps  result: warning
56  2017-01-19T04:59:05.4019588Z
57  2017-01-19T04:59:05.4019588Z
58  2017-01-19T04:59:05.4019588Z errorcode: 0x80045043 errortext: The original sdkmessageprocessingstep has been disabled and replaced. more details:
59  2017-01-19T04:59:05.4019588Z
60  2017-01-19T04:59:05.4019588Z
61  2017-01-19T04:59:05.4019588Z Item:SdkMessageProcessingSteps  result: success
62  2017-01-19T04:59:05.4019588Z
63  2017-01-19T04:59:05.4019588Z
64  2017-01-19T04:59:05.4019588Z Item:SdkMessageProcessingSteps  result: success
65  2017-01-19T04:59:05.4019588Z
66  2017-01-19T04:59:05.4019588Z
67  2017-01-19T04:59:05.4019588Z Item:SdkMessageProcessingSteps  result: warning
68  2017-01-19T04:59:05.4019588Z
69  2017-01-19T04:59:05.4019588Z
70  2017-01-19T04:59:05.4019588Z errorcode: 0x80045043 errortext: The original sdkmessageprocessingstep has been disabled and replaced. more details:
71  2017-01-19T04:59:05.4019588Z
72  2017-01-19T04:59:05.4019588Z
```

Figure 10-43. *CRM Solution Import task logs*

You created a release definition in Team Foundation release management to deploy CRM solutions to a target CRM organization.

Summary

You have learned the basics of using Team Foundation builds and release management to deploy Dynamics CRM solutions. This allows you to streamline CRM development processes and deployments across multiple environments. Do further experiments with the CRM components to gain more knowledge of CRM deployments with TFS.

In the next chapter, you will learn about creating and sending effective release notes with Team Foundation release management.

CHAPTER 11

███

Effective Release Notes with TFS Release

Release notes, generated based on the target deployment environment, are important as they identify what work (requirements, bug fixes etc.) are getting delivered to the target environment. This provides visibility and traceability from inception of the requirements through to delivery and then production. Lessons in this chapter will give you guidance in generating automated release notes based on the work getting delivered.

Prerequisites: You need to have a working knowledge of TFS/VSTS work items, Kanban boards, Iterations, and so forth. These topics are out of the scope of this book, but a brief explanation will be provided in the lessons while using them.

What Is an Effective Release Note?

An effective release note clearly communicates what work (requirements, bug fixes etc.) are getting delivered with the software package to the target environment. It contains other information, like who reviewed, when to release, and what work-items are associated with this release. Let's have a look at an example to understand this.

Consider the release pipeline (created with a release definition having four target environments) shown in Figure 11-1. It has four stages. DevInt (developer integration), QA, UAT, and production.

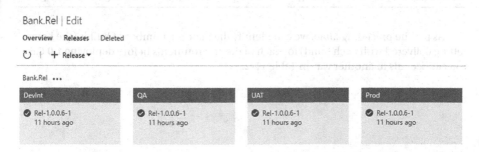

Figure 11-1. *Release pipeline with four stages*

© Chaminda Chandrasekara 2017
C. Chandrasekara, *Beginning Build and Release Management with TFS 2017 and VSTS*,
DOI 10.1007/978-1-4842-2811-1_11

The environments have been deployed with several builds using this pipeline. The current deployment sent to all the environments was done with build 1.0.0.6, as shown in Figure 11-2.

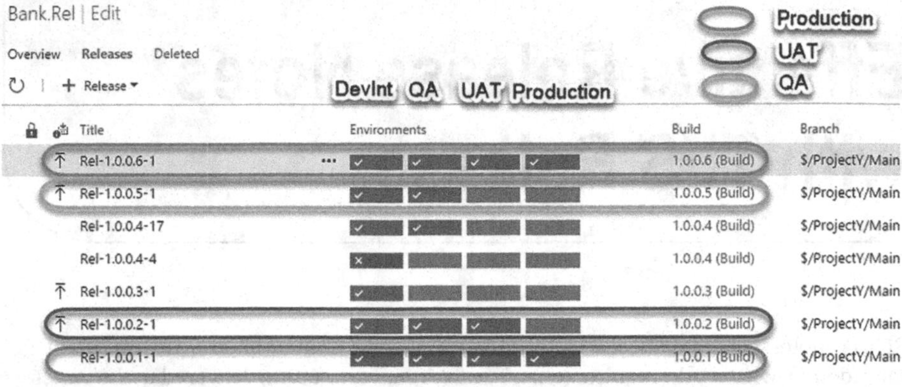

Figure 11-2. Release history

The previous build to reach the production environment was 1.0.0.1. The last build to reach UAT before 1.0.0.6 was 1.0.0.2. The last build to reach QA and DevInt before 1.0.0.6 was 1.0.0.5. Table 11-1 explains what the state of each target environment was before build 1.0.0.6 was deployed. With this, we can determine the gap between builds for each target.

Table 11-1. Release and Builds — Deploy Status for Environment

	1.0.0.1	1.0.0.2	1.0.0.3	1.0.0.4	1.0.0.5	1.0.0.6
DevInt	Deployed	Deployed	Deployed	Deployed	Deployed	Pending
QA	Deployed	Deployed	Deployed	Deployed	Deployed	Pending
UAT	Deployed	Deployed	Pending	Pending	Pending	Pending
Production	Deployed	Pending	Pending	Pending	Pending	Pending

As per the preceding table, we can identify the pending number of builds (the items getting delivered with each build) for each of the environments before deploying 1.0.0.6. You can see this in another way in Table 11-2.

Table 11-2. *Environment Deployed Builds*

Environment	Builds Pending Deployment
DevInt	1.0.0.6
QA	1.0.0.6
UAT	1.0.0.3, 1.0.04, 1.0.0.5, 1.0.0.6
Production	1.0.0.2, 1.0.0.3, 1.0.04, 1.0.0.5, 1.0.0.6

This means the DevInt and QA environments should get a release note along with those requirement/fixes getting delivered with build 1.0.0.6 only. See Figure 11-3.

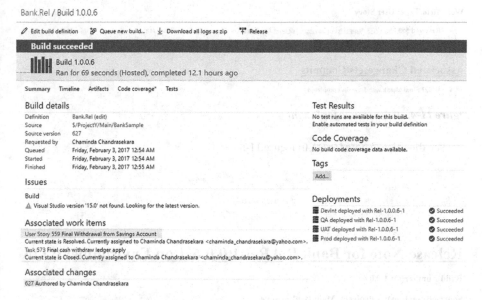

Figure 11-3. *Associated work items in build 1.0.0.6*

Task work items can be ignored, as they explain development or testing activities for achieving a requirement or bug fix.

1.0.0.6 has User Story 559, which should be available in both the QA and UAT release notes.

See the release note for DevInt in Figure 11-4.

⊖ Reply ⊖ Reply All ⊖ Forward
vstsdemo.chamindac@gmail.com   Chaminda Chandrasekara
Release Note for Bank.Rel Rel-1.0.0.6-1 on Environment: DevInt

Release Note for Bank.Rel Rel-1.0.0.6-1 on Environment: DevInt

Build Number(s): 1.0.0.6

Source Branch(es): $/ProjectY/Main/BankSample

Associated Work Items

Work Item Type: User Story

- Resolved 559 Final Withdrawal from Savings Account Assigned To: Chaminda Chandrasekara

Associated Changesets/Commits

- ID 627 Final chask withdraw SA completed

Figure 11-4. *Release note for DevInt*

See the release note for QA in Figure 11-5.

⊖ Reply ⊖ Reply All ⊖ Forward
vstsdemo.chamindac@gmail.com   Chaminda Chandrasekara
Release Note for Bank.Rel Rel-1.0.0.6-1 on Environment: QA

Release Note for Bank.Rel Rel-1.0.0.6-1 on Environment: QA

Build Number(s): 1.0.0.6

Source Branch(es): $/ProjectY/Main/BankSample

Associated Work Items

Work Item Type: User Story

- Resolved 559 Final Withdrawal from Savings Account Assigned To: Chaminda Chandrasekara

Associated Changesets/Commits

- ID 627 Final chask withdraw SA completed

Figure 11-5. *Release note for QA*

For the UAT environment, requirements and fixes delivered with builds 1.0.0.6, 1.0.0.5, 1.0.0.4, and 1.0.0.3 are all accumulated and get delivered with build 1.0.0.6. The release note should consider all of those builds to be associated work.

Build 1.0.0.5's associated work items are shown in Figure 11-6.

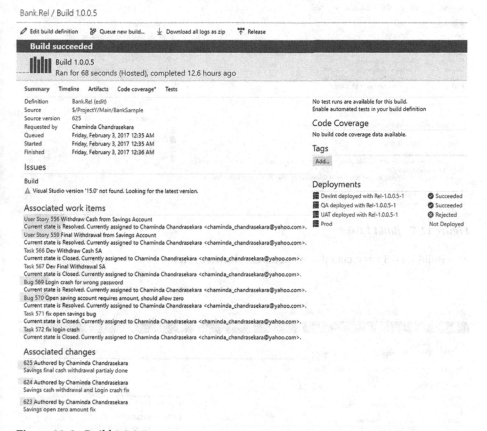

Figure 11-6. *Build 1.0.0.5*

Build 1.0.0.4's associated work items are shown in Figure 11-7.

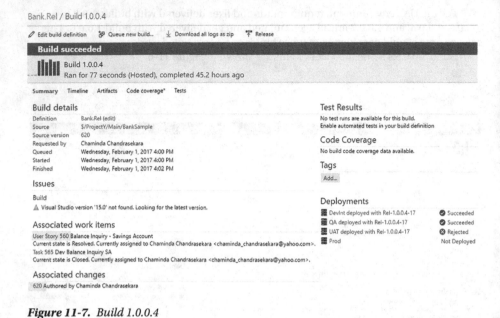

Figure 11-7. *Build 1.0.0.4*

Build 1.0.0.3's associated work items are shown in Figure 11-8.

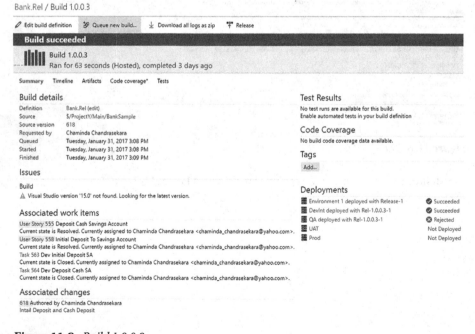

Figure 11-8. *Build 1.0.0.3*

For the release note to UAT, the work items in Table 11-3 from each build should be added.

Table 11-3. *UAT Environment Build and Work Items Pending Deployment*

Build	Work Items
1.0.0.6	User Story 559
1.0.0.5	User Stories 559(partial), 556 and Bugs 569, 570
1.0.0.4	User Story 560
1.0.0.3	User Stories 558, 555

A release not going to UAT would look like that shown in Figure 11-9.

🖃 Reply 🖃 Reply All 🖃 Forward

vstsdemo.chamindac@gmail.com   Chaminda Chandrasekara
Release Note for Bank.Rel Rel-1.0.0.6-1 on Environment: UAT

Release Note for Bank.Rel Rel-1.0.0.6-1 on Environment: UAT

Build Number(s): 1.0.0.3 1.0.0.4 1.0.0.5 1.0.0.6

Source Branch(es): $/ProjectY/Main/BankSample $/ProjectY/Main/BankSample $/ProjectY/Main/BankSample $/ProjectY/Main/BankSample

Associated Work Items

Work Item Type: Bug

- Resolved 569 Login crash for wrong password Assigned To: Chaminda Chandrasekara
- Resolved 570 Open saving account requires amount, should allow zero Assigned To: Chaminda Chandrasekara

Work Item Type: User Story

- Resolved 555 Deposit Cash Savings Account Assigned To: Chaminda Chandrasekara
- Resolved 556 Withdraw Cash from Savings Account Assigned To: Chaminda Chandrasekara
- Resolved 558 Initial Deposit To Savings Account Assigned To: Chaminda Chandrasekara
- Resolved 559 Final Withdrawal from Savings Account Assigned To: Chaminda Chandrasekara
- Resolved 560 Balance Inquiry - Savings Account Assigned To: Chaminda Chandrasekara

Associated Changesets/Commits

- ID 618 Intail Deposit and Cash Deposit
- ID 620
- ID 625 Savings final cash withdrawal partialy done
- ID 624 Savings cash withdrawal and Login crash fix
- ID 623 Savings open zero amount fix
- ID 627 Final chask withdraw SA completed

Figure 11-9. *UAT release note with build 1.0.0.6*

Note that the release note does not show duplicates of the same work item 559 that was seen in the previous note. It has completely finished by the time build 1.0.0.6 is getting delivered. In the release note of build 1.0.0.5, it is shown as an active item since it is only partially done. This informs us it is incomplete. See Figure 11-10.

Reply   Reply All   Forward
vstsdemo.chamindac@gmail.com | Chaminda Chandrasekara
Release Note for Bank.Rel Rel-1.0.0.5-1 on Environment: DevInt

Release Note for Bank.Rel Rel-1.0.0.5-1 on Environment: DevInt

Build Number(s): 1.0.0.5

Associated Work Items

Work Item Type: Bug

- Resolved <u>569 Login crash for wrong password</u> Assigned To: Chaminda Chandrasekara
- Resolved <u>570 Open saving account requires amount, should allow zero</u> Assigned To: Chaminda Chandrasekara

Work Item Type: User Story

- Resolved <u>556 Withdraw Cash from Savings Account</u> Assigned To: Chaminda Chandrasekara
- Active <u>559 Final Withdrawal from Savings Account</u> Assigned To: Chaminda Chandrasekara

Associated Changesets/Commits

- ID 625 Savings final cash withdrawal partialy done
- ID 624 Savings cash withdrawal and Login crash fix
- ID 623 Savings open zero amount fix

Figure 11-10. *Release note with incomplete work*

The release note for the Production environment should contain the work items of build 1.0.0.2 in addition to the following (see Table 11-4), which were available in the UAT release note.

Table 11-4. *UAT Environment Deployed Build and Work Items*

Build	Work Items
1.0.0.6	User Story 559
1.0.0.5	User Stories 559(partial), 556 and Bugs 569,570
1.0.0.4	User Story 560
1.0.0.3	User Stories 558, 555

Build 1.0.0.2's associated work items are shown in Figure 11-11.

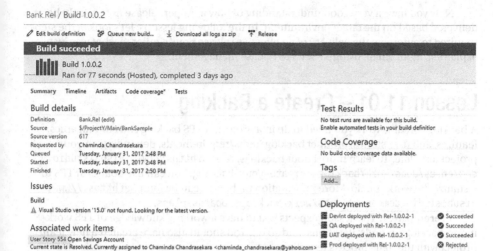

Figure 11-11. *Build 1.0.0.2*

The release note for production is shown in Figure 11-12.

Release Note for Bank.Rel Rel-1.0.0.6-1 on Environment: Prod

Build Number(s): 1.0.0.2 1.0.0.3 1.0.0.4 1.0.0.5 1.0.0.6

Source Branch(es): $/ProjectY/Main/BankSample $/ProjectY/Main/BankSample $/ProjectY/Main/BankSample $/ProjectY/Main/BankSample $/ProjectY/Main/BankSample

Associated Work Items

Work Item Type: Bug

- Resolved <u>569 Login crash for wrong password</u> Assigned To: Chaminda Chandrasekara
- Resolved <u>570 Open saving account requires amount, should allow zero</u> Assigned To: Chaminda Chandrasekara

Work Item Type: User Story

- Resolved <u>554 Open Savings Account</u> Assigned To: Chaminda Chandrasekara
- Resolved <u>555 Deposit Cash Savings Account</u> Assigned To: Chaminda Chandrasekara
- Resolved <u>556 Withdraw Cash from Savings Account</u> Assigned To: Chaminda Chandrasekara
- Resolved <u>558 Initial Deposit To Savings Account</u> Assigned To: Chaminda Chandrasekara
- Resolved <u>559 Final Withdrawal from Savings Account</u> Assigned To: Chaminda Chandrasekara
- Resolved <u>560 Balance Inquiry - Savings Account</u> Assigned To: Chaminda Chandrasekara

Associated Changesets/Commits

- ID 617 Open savings account
- ID 618 Intall Deposit and Cash Deposit
- ID 620
- ID 625 Savings final cash withdrawal partialy done
- ID 624 Savings cash withdrawal and Login crash fix
- ID 623 Savings open zero amount fix
- ID 627 Final chask withdraw SA completed

Figure 11-12. *Production environment release note*

Now you have a very good understanding of how a proper release note should be delivered based on the target environment. In the following lessons, let's look at the steps required to automate the delivery of an effective release note, similar to what was just explained, as an email, using TFS/VSTS release management.

Lesson 11.01 – Create a Backlog

A backlog contains work you need to do in a project. A TFS backlog can contain epics, features, and user stories/product backlog items/requirements, depending on your project template. To learn more about backlogs, refer to https://www.visualstudio.com/en-us/docs/work/backlogs/create-your-backlog. You can use boards in TFS to visualize the work you do. More information on boards can be found at https://www.visualstudio.com/en-us/docs/work/backlogs-boards-plans.

Prerequisites: This lesson expects you to have a working knowledge of TFS work items, backlogs, boards, iterations, and so on. You should also have created a new team project with the Agile process template.

1. In the new team project, go to the **Work** tab and click on Backlogs. Then, click on Stories. Next, click on the backlog settings icon at the top right. See Figure 11-13.

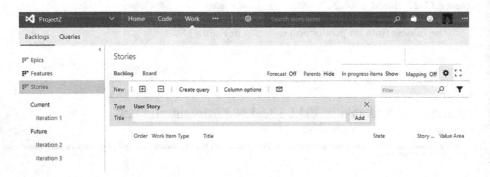

Figure 11-13. *Work tab backlog settings*

2. On the Settings page, select "Working with bugs" at the left-hand side, then select the "Bugs appear on the backlogs and boards with requirements" option and click Save. See Figure 11-14.

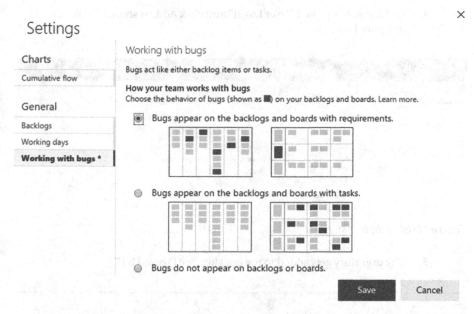

Figure 11-14. Bugs in backlog with requirements setting

3. Now, you will be able to add user story and bug work items to the backlog. See Figure 11-15.

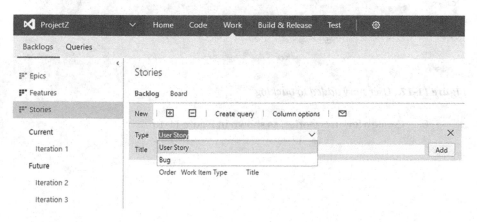

Figure 11-15. Bugs and user stories in backlog

4. Add a user story titled "User Login" and click Add, as shown in Figure 11-16.

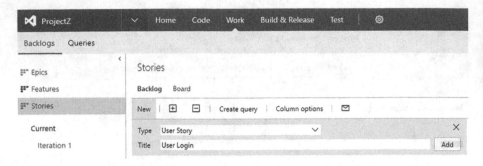

Figure 11-16. *Add user story*

5. The user story gets added to the backlog. See Figure 11-17.

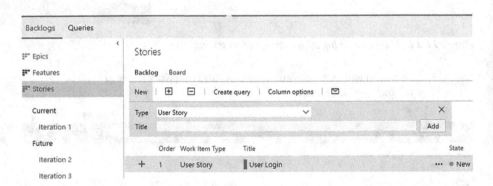

Figure 11-17. *User story added to backlog*

6. Create a few user stories, as shown in Figure 11-18.

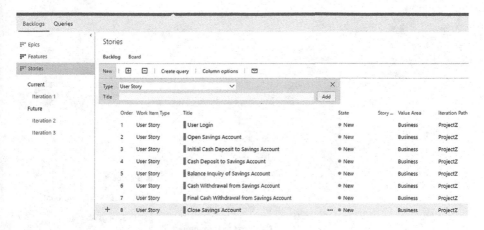

Figure 11-18. *User stories added to backlog*

Note that we have just created a set of user stories with only titles. A proper user story should contain a lot more information so as to provide enough details to the team to do the implementation. Backlog management is out of the scope of this book. We have just fulfilled the minimum requirements in order to demonstrate a release note generation.

7. Highlight the first six user stories, right click, and move them to Iteration 1 (you can drag and drop). An iteration is a short period of work at the end of the period you are trying to deliver a shippable product version to the client. For more information visit `https://www.visualstudio.com/en-us/docs/work/scrum/define-sprints`. See Figure 11-19.

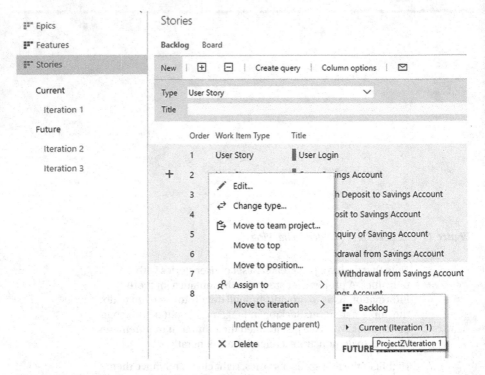

Figure 11-19. *Moving user stories to Iteration 1*

8. In Iteration 1, go to the Board tab and click on New Item for each story to add a new task. Provide a title, such as "Develop User Login." See Figure 11-20.

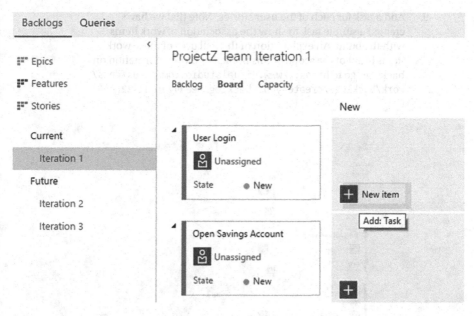

Figure 11-20. *Adding task to a user story*

You can chage the task of the user story in the board itself, as shown in Figure 11-21.

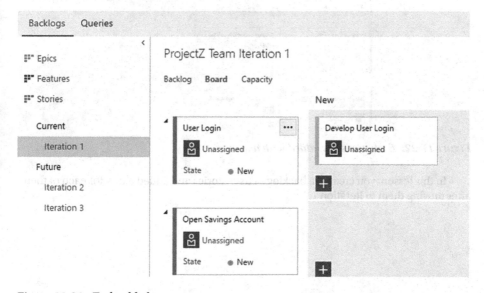

Figure 11-21. *Task added to a user story*

9. Add a task for each of the user stories. Note that we have created a simple task to show the association of work items with the build. An explanation of the real uses of these work items is out of the scope of this book. For more information on backlogs, go to https://www.visualstudio.com/en-us/docs/work/backlogs/create-your-backlog. See Figure 11-22.

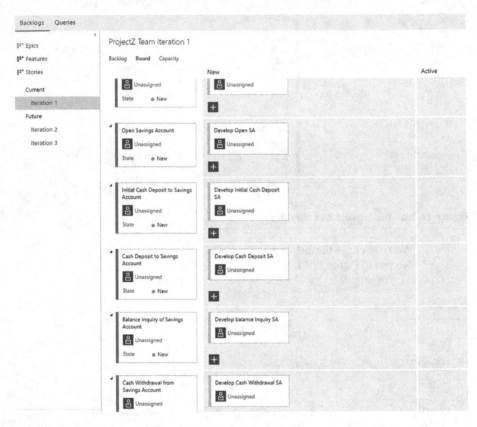

Figure 11-22. Each user story added with a task

In this lesson, you created a backlog of user stories and added a task for each of them after moving them to Iteration 1.

Lesson 11.02 – Submit Work and Create a Build

Now that you have a backlog, let's create a small application and associate work items with it.

1.   Create a Visual Studio solution and add a console application project to it after connecting to the same team project for which you created a backlog in the previous lesson. See Figure 11-23.

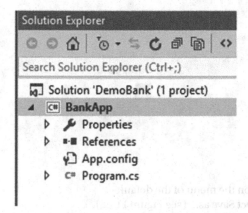

Figure 11-23. *Solution and the console application*

This will show as pending changes in the Source Control Explorer (see Figure 11-24).

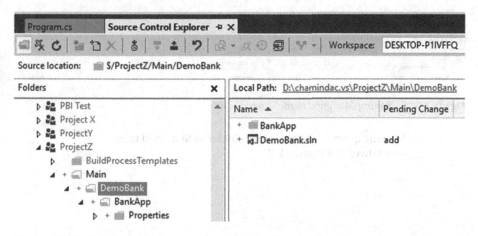

Figure 11-24. *Solution and the console application as pending changes*

2. Go to the iteration backlog board in the TFS web portal and activate the **User Login** user story and its development task. Assign them to yourself. See Figure 11-25.

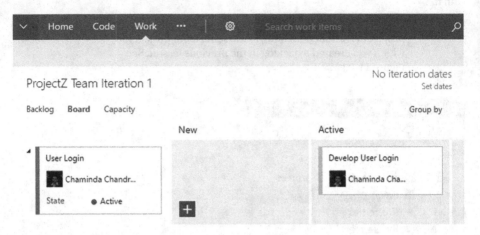

Figure 11-25. Activate user story and task

3. Go to the Queries tab and click on the menu of the default "Assigned to me" query and select Save as... (see Figure 11-26).

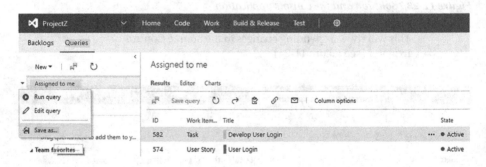

Figure 11-26. Saving "Assigned to me" query

4. Save the query in the My Queries folder as "Assigned to me and active." See Figure 11-27.

Save query as

×

Name

Assigned to me and active

Folder

My Queries

OK	Cancel

Figure 11-27. *Save "Assigned to me" query in My Queries folder*

5. Add a new clause to the query to filter active work items. Save the query. See Figure 11-28.

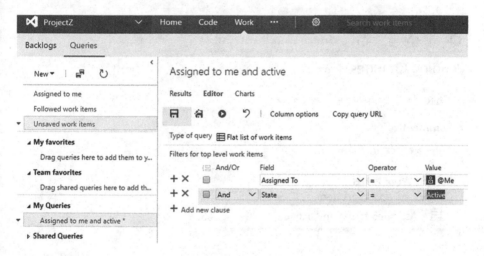

Figure 11-28. *Filter for active work items assigned to me*

6. Open the program.cs file in the Visual Studio console application you created and add the following code to it.

```
using System;
using System.Collections.Generic;
using System.Linq;
using System.Text;
using System.Threading.Tasks;
```

```
namespace BankApp
{
    class Program
    {
        static void Main(string[] args)
        {
            Console.WriteLine("User login");

            Console.ReadLine();
        }
    }
}
```

7. Go to the Pending Changes screen in Team Explorer and click on Queries. Then, click on "Assigned to me and active." See Figure 11-29.

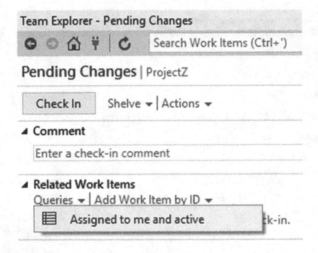

Figure 11-29. *Open query from Visual Studio*

8. In the opened query, you can see the active items assigned to you: the user login user story and the development task for it. Drag them both to the Pending Changes screen in Team Explorer under Related Work Items. See Figure 11-30.

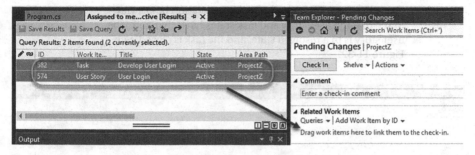

Figure 11-30. Associating work items with pending changes

9. Check in the solution and the console application, being sure to provide an appropriate comment. Let the work items resolve with the check-in. See Figure 11-31.

Figure 11-31. Pending changes

10. Once check-in completes, refresh the iteration board view to see that the user story and task states have changed. The user story is in a resolved state, and the task is closed. See Figure 11-32.

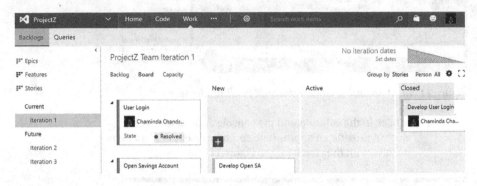

Figure 11-32. *Resolved user story and closed task*

11. Create a new empty build definition named "Bank.Rel" and set the repository to the DemoBank solution folder path, as shown in Figure 11-33.

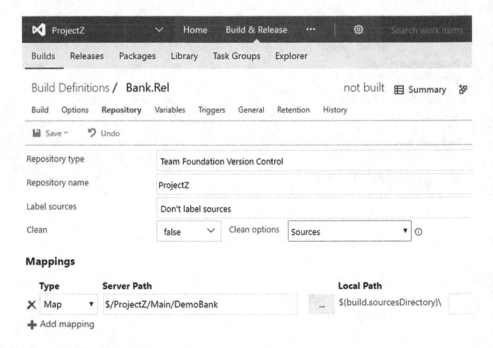

Figure 11-33. *Map solution path*

12. Add the Visual Studio Build step and select the DemoBank solution to build. See Figure 11-34.

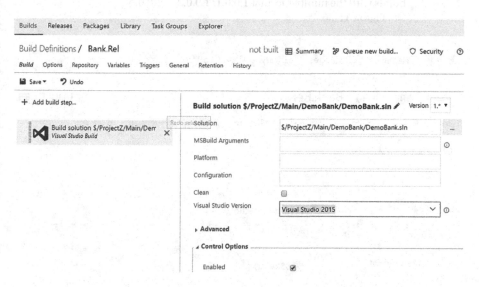

Figure 11-34. *Visual Studio Build step*

13. Add a Copy Publish Artifact step and set the content to be ***. exe in order to copy the console app. Name the artifact drop. Select Server as the Artifact Type. See Figure 11-35.

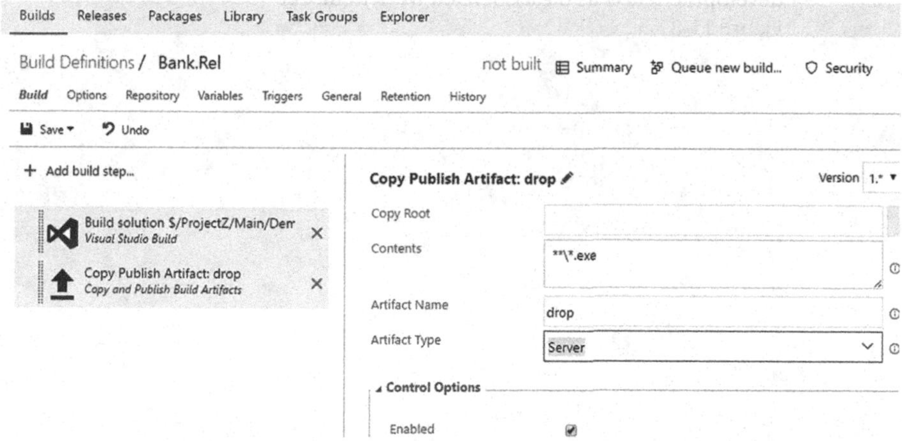

Figure 11-35. *Copy Publish Artifact step*

14. In the General tab of the build definition, provide the value "1.0.0$(rev:.r)" for the build number format. This will create builds with the number format 1.0.0.1, 1.0.0.2 ... 1.0.0.*N*. See Figure 11-36.

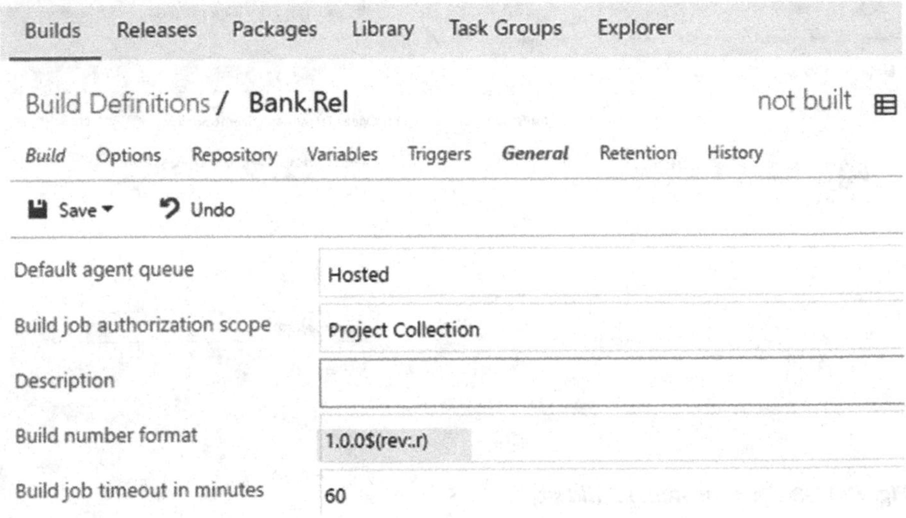

| Builds | Releases | Packages | Library | Task Groups | Explorer |

Build Definitions / **Bank.Rel**   not built ▦

Build Options Repository Variables Triggers *General* Retention History

💾 Save ▾   ↩ Undo

Default agent queue	Hosted
Build job authorization scope	Project Collection
Description	
Build number format	1.0.0$(rev:.r)
Build job timeout in minutes	60

Figure 11-36. *Set build number format*

15. Save the build definition and queue a new build. The completed build will have a User Login work item and its development task as the associated work item. See Figure 11-37.

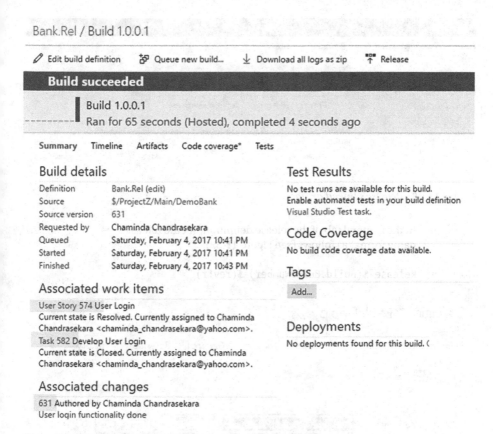

Figure 11-37. Completed build associated with work items

In this lesson, you created a small application and associated it with the work items while checking it in to the source control repository. Then, you created a build definition with which to build the source code; it contains the associated work items completed by the time when a build is executed.

Lesson 11.03 – Create a Release Pipeline with Release Note Capability

Using the build created in the previous lesson, let's create a release pipeline that has release notes.

1. Create an empty release definition and select the Bank.Rel build as the linked artifact. See Figure 11-38.

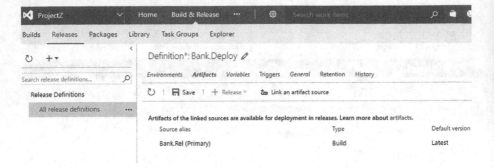

Figure 11-38. Release's linked artifacts

2. In the General tab of the release definition, set the release's name format as follows (see Figure 11-39):

```
Release-$(Build.BuildNumber)-$(rev:r)
```

Definition*: Bank.Deploy ✎

Environments   Artifacts   Variables   Triggers   **General**   Retention   History

↺ | 🖫 Save | ➕ Release ▾

Release name format | Release-$(Build.BuildNumber)-$(rev:r) | ⓘ

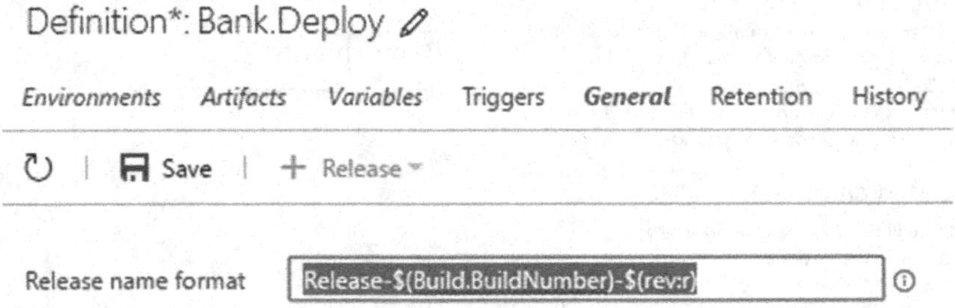

Figure 11-39. Release name format

3. In the Variables tab, add the following variables and values. The SMTP details are for sending email. You can use a Gmail account as the SMTP. ReleaseNoteMD defines the markdown (usage of this file explained in next steps) file path that will be used to generate a release note. ReleaseEmail. SkipTaskWIT specifies whether to include the Task work item in the release note. You can move any of these variables to the release definition's environment level if you want to have environment-specific values (SMTP settings and so on). See Table 11-5.

Table 11-5. *Variables for Release Definition*

Variable Name	Value
ReleaseNotePath	$(System.DefaultWorkingDirectory)\$(Build.DefinitionName)_$(Build.BuildNumber)_ReleaseNote
ReleaseNoteMD	$(ReleaseNotePath).md
SMTP.User	SMTP User Email
SMTP.UserPwd	SMTP User Password
SMTP.Server	SMTP Server
SMTP.Port	SMTP Port
ReleaseEmail.SkipTaskWIT	True
ReleaseEmail.Subject	Release Note for $(Release.DefinitionName) $(Release.ReleaseName) on Environment: $(Release.EnvironmentName)
ReleaseEmail.Recipients	Email addresses of recipients separated by semi-colon (there should be no space between email addresses).

These variables should be defined as shown in Figure 11-40.

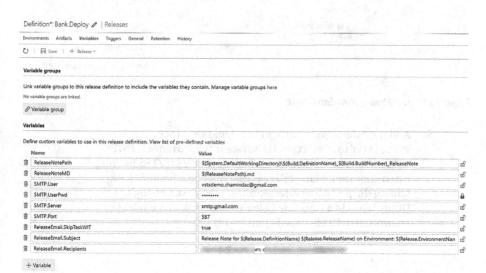

Figure 11-40. *Release variables*

4. Rename the default added environment to "DevInt" (Dev Integration environment) and add a PowerShell task to it. Select it as an inline script and add the following script to it:

```
param ([String]$EnvName)
Write-Host "Deploying Build - $EnvName"
```

As arguments to the script, pass

```
-EnvName $(Release.EnvironmentName)
```

This is just to simulate a build getting deployed. An actual deployment is not performed, as this lesson's goal is to learn the release note–generation aspect of the process. See Figure 11-41.

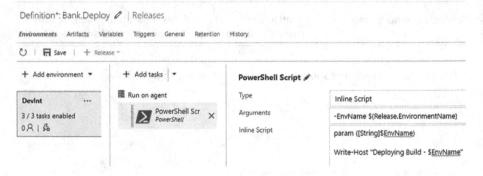

Figure 11-41. *Deploy simulated task*

5. Add the extension found at `https://marketplace.visualstudio.com/items?itemName=richardfennellBM.BM-VSTS-GenerateReleaseNotes-Task` to your VSTS/TFS (adding extensions from Marketplace is described in Chapter 2). After adding the preceding extension, from the Task Catalog's Utility tab, add a Generate Release Notes task to the release environment DevInt. See Figure 11-42.

Task catalog

Figure 11-42. *Generate release note task*

6. In the Generate Release Notes task, specify $(ReleaseNoteMD)
    as the output file. This variable contains the path and name
    for the release note.md (mark down) file. Release note
    generate task will create a release note in mark down format,
    using the generated release note mark down content, in the
    provided mark down file path. For the Template Location,
    select "InLine," and provide the following as the Template
    (available at https://github.com/chamindac/Book-
    Beginning-Build-ReleaseManagement-/blob/master/
    Chapter11/ReleaseNoteDemo/ReleaseNoteTemplate.txt).
    Also see Figure 11-43.

```
#Release notes for build $defname
**Build Number(s)**  : $($build.buildnumber)
**Source Branch(es)** : $($build.sourceBranch)

###Associated work items
@@WILOOP@@
* **$($widetail.fields.'System.WorkItemType') $($widetail.id)**
[$($widetail.fields.'System.State')] [$($widetail.fields.'System.Title')]
($($widetail._links.html.href)) [Assigned To: $($widetail.fields.'System.
AssignedTo')]
@@WILOOP@@

###Associated change sets/commits
@@CSLOOP@@
* **ID $($csdetail.changesetid)$($csdetail.commitid)** $($csdetail.comment)
@@CSLOOP@@
```

Figure 11-43. Generate release note task fields

Make sure to uncheck "Generate for only this Release" (this is checked by default) in Advanced settings, as shown in Figure 11-43. This allows you to generate release notes that consider the last successful deployment made to the environment. The release note provides all work items associated with any builds after the last deployed build to a given environment,

7. Add this extension from Marketplace to the TFS/ VSTS: https://marketplace.visualstudio.com/ items?itemName=petergroenewegen.PeterGroenewegen-Xpirit-Vsts-Build-InlinePowershell. The default PowerShell task does not allow longer scripts to be used as inline scripts (script that you type in the task itself). However, this extension has an Inline PowerShell task that allows a longer script to be an inline one. Add it to the release environment DevInt. See Figure 11-44.

Task catalog

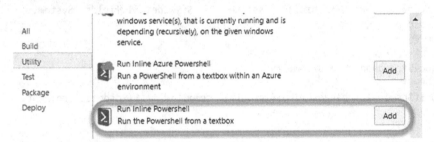

Figure 11-44. Inline PowerShell task

8. In the Run Inline PowerShell task, provide the PowerShell script contents from https://github.com/chamindac/ Book-Beginning-Build-ReleaseManagement-/blob/master/ Chapter11/ReleaseNoteDemo/ReleaseNoteFromMD.ps1.This script is written based on the .md (mark down) template provided. It converts a generated release note mark-down file via the Generate Release Notes task, into HTML content and sends an email. Note that if you are altering the mark-down template this script should be adjusted accordingly (the string replaces sections).

Arguments for the PowerShell are as follows:

```
-mdfilePath "$(ReleaseNoteMD)"
-SMTPServer $(SMTP.Server)
-SMTPPort $(SMTP.Port)
-Username $(SMTP.User)
-Password $(SMTP.UserPwd)
-EmailTo "$(ReleaseEmail.Recipients)"
-EmailSubject "$(ReleaseEmail.Subject)"
-SkipTasks $(ReleaseEmail.SkipTaskWIT)
```

See Figure 11-45.

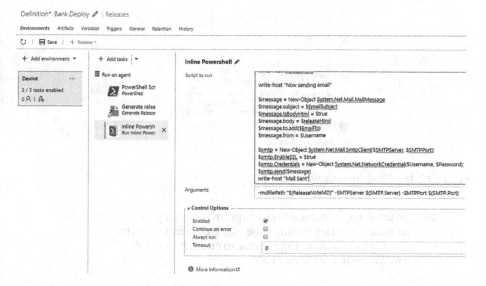

Figure 11-45. *Release note converting to HTML and email task*

9. Click on Clone environment for DevInt, as shown in
   Figure 11-46.

Figure 11-46. Clone the environment

10. In the popup window, select an approver (select your username) and set cloning to be triggered after the DevInt environment is done. Click Create to create the cloned environment. See Figure 11-47.

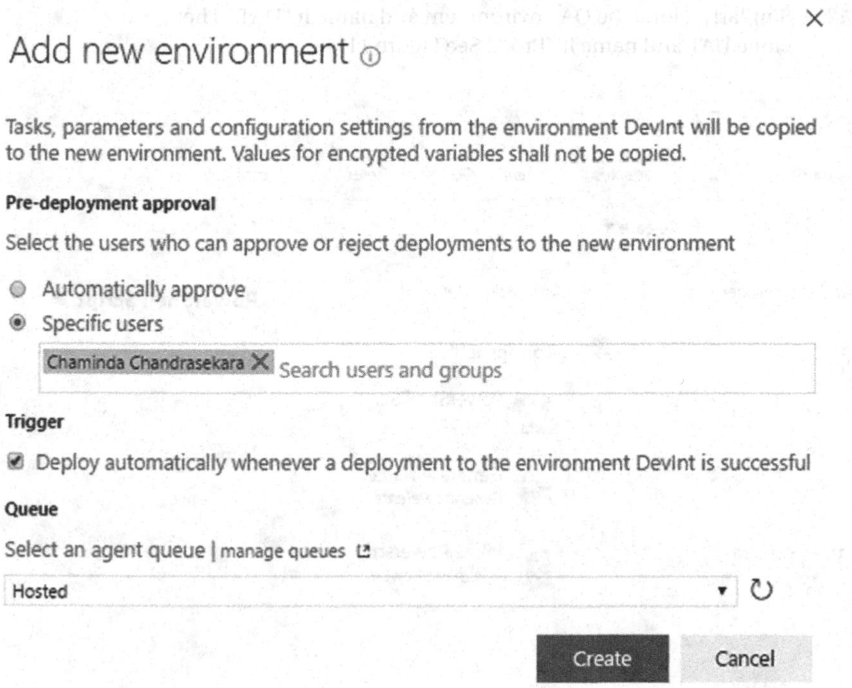

Add new environment ⓘ

×

Tasks, parameters and configuration settings from the environment DevInt will be copied to the new environment. Values for encrypted variables shall not be copied.

Pre-deployment approval

Select the users who can approve or reject deployments to the new environment

○ Automatically approve

⦿ Specific users

> Chaminda Chandrasekara ✕ Search users and groups

Trigger

☑ Deploy automatically whenever a deployment to the environment DevInt is successful

Queue

Select an agent queue | manage queues ↙

> Hosted ▾   ↻

Create   Cancel

Figure 11-47. Providing parameters for the cloned environment

> 11.   Rename the cloned environment "QA." See Figure 11-48.

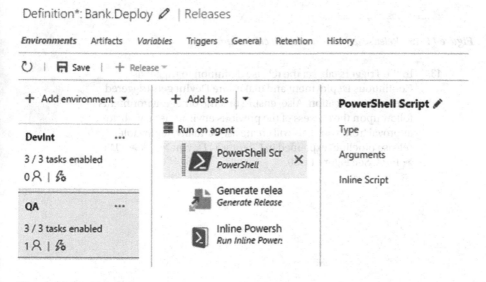

Figure 11-48. QA environment

12. Similarly, clone the QA environment and name it "UAT." Then, clone UAT and name it "Prod." See Figure 11-49.

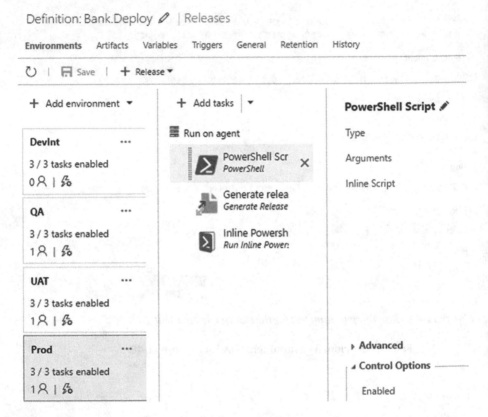

Figure 11-49. Release definition with all environments

13. In the Triggers tab, set the release definition to trigger as Continuous Deployment and make sure DevInt gets triggered after release creation. Also, ensure that the other environments follow upon the success of the previous environment, with an approval from you. This will create asquantially deployable release pipeline (explained in Chapter 1) DevInt ➤ QA ➤ UAT ➤ Prod. See Figure 11-50.

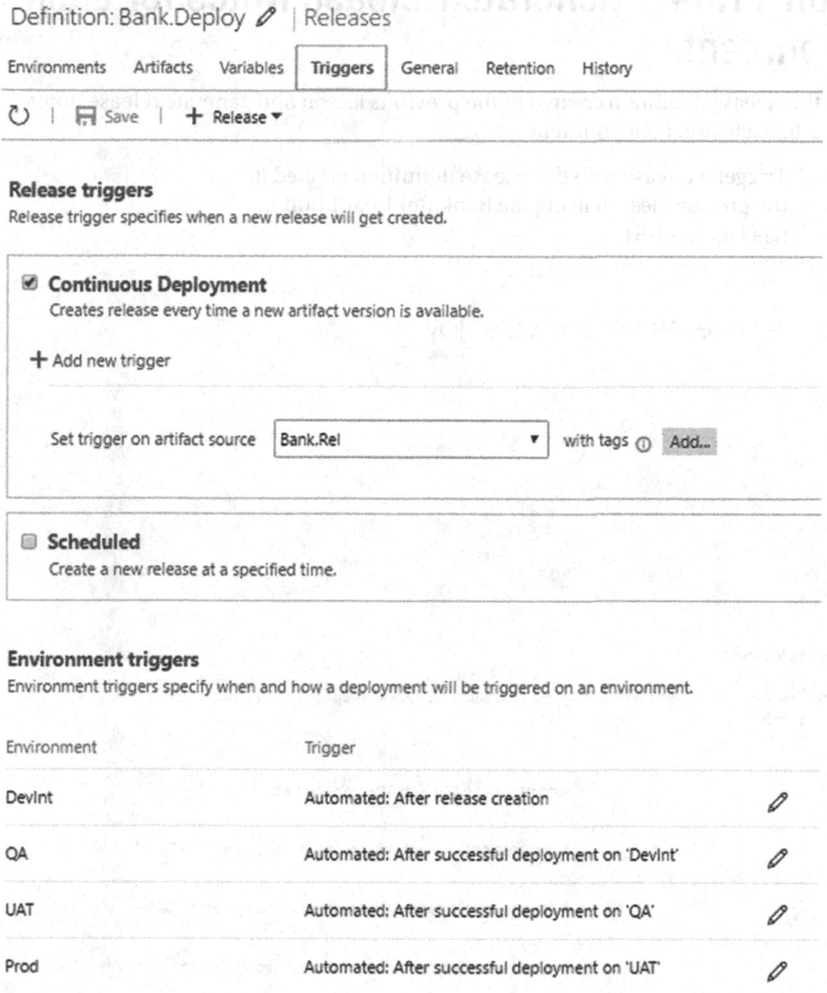

Definition: Bank.Deploy ✎ | Releases

Environments   Artifacts   Variables   **Triggers**   General   Retention   History

↻ | 💾 Save | ➕ Release ▾

Release triggers

Release trigger specifies when a new release will get created.

☑ **Continuous Deployment**
  Creates release every time a new artifact version is available.

➕ Add new trigger

Set trigger on artifact source | Bank.Rel   ▼ | with tags ⓘ   Add...

☐ **Scheduled**
  Create a new release at a specified time.

Environment triggers

Environment triggers specify when and how a deployment will be triggered on an environment.

Environment	Trigger	
DevInt	Automated: After release creation	✎
QA	Automated: After successful deployment on 'DevInt'	✎
UAT	Automated: After successful deployment on 'QA'	✎
Prod	Automated: After successful deployment on 'UAT'	✎

Figure 11-50. *Release definition triggers*

You created a release definition in this lesson to simulate deployments to different environments and to generate and email release notes.

Lesson 11.04 – Generate Release Notes for Each Environment

Let's use the release definition created in the previous lesson and generate release notes applicable to each target environment.

1. Trigger a release with the release definition created in the previous lesson using the Bank.Rel 1.0.0.1 build. See Figure 11-51.

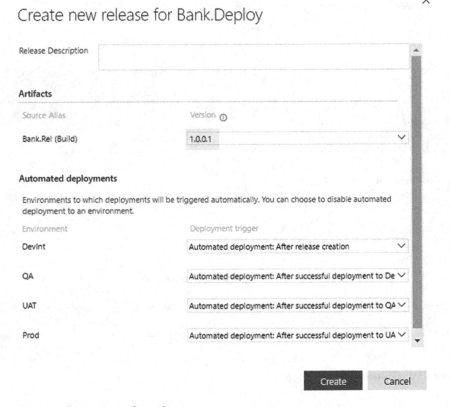

Figure 11-51. *Create first release*

2. The release is deployed to DevInt and waits for approval in QA. See Figure 11-52.

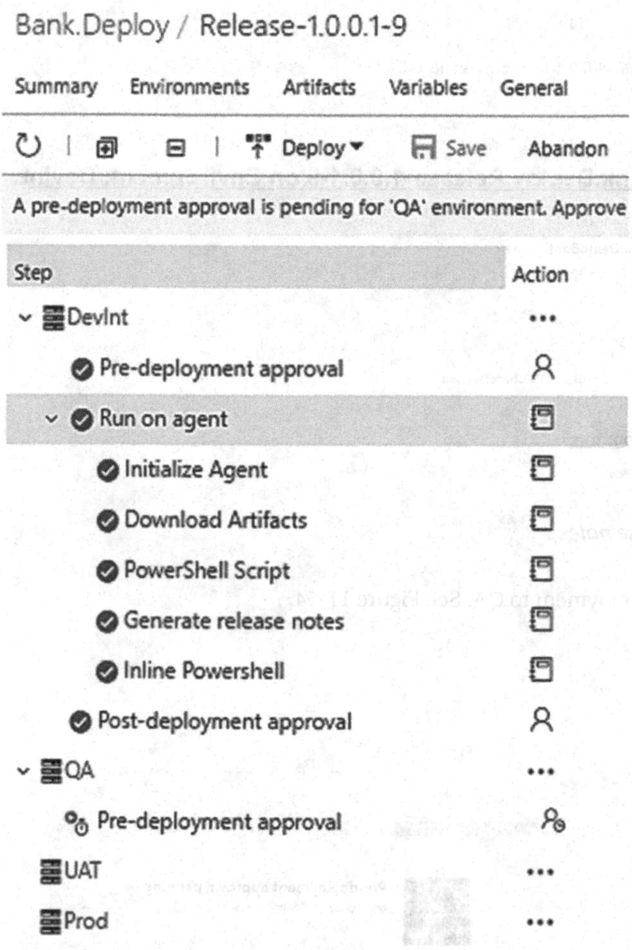

Bank.Deploy / Release-1.0.0.1-9

Summary   Environments   Artifacts   Variables   General

○ | ⊞   ⊟ | ⊤ Deploy ▼   ⊟ Save   Abandon

A pre-deployment approval is pending for 'QA' environment. Approve

Step	Action
∨ ▤ DevInt	•••
✓ Pre-deployment approval	八
∨ ✓ Run on agent	▤
✓ Initialize Agent	▤
✓ Download Artifacts	▤
✓ PowerShell Script	▤
✓ Generate release notes	▤
✓ Inline Powershell	▤
✓ Post-deployment approval	八
∨ ▤ QA	•••
⚙ Pre-deployment approval	八⚙
▤ UAT	•••
▤ Prod	•••

Figure 11-52.   Waiting for approval

3.   The release note for the DevInt environment is delivered to
     the mail recipient with the **User Login** user story. Task work
     items are automatically filtered and are not included in the
     release note because tasks done by each developer are not
     valuable information in a release note. See Figure 11-53.

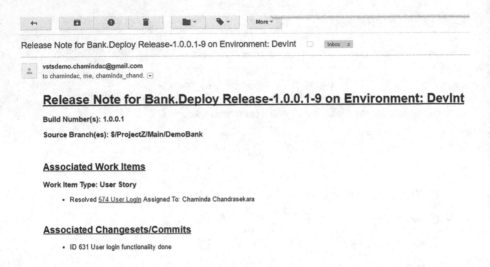

Figure 11-53. *DevInt release note*

4. Approve the deployment to QA. See Figure 11-54.

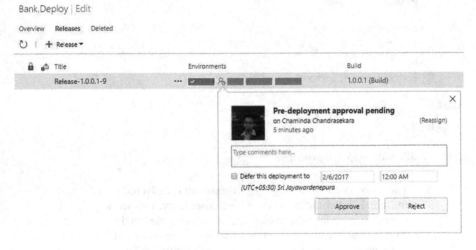

Figure 11-54. *Approve release to QA*

5. The deployment completes for QA, and the QA release note with the User Login user story gets delivered. Figure 11-55.

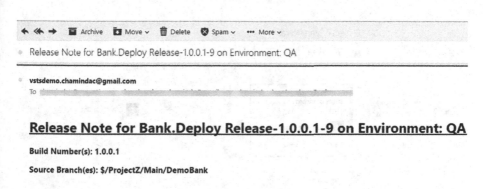

Figure 11-55. QA release note

6. Let's say QA reported a bug that must be fixed. It is added to the iteration. See Figure 11-56.

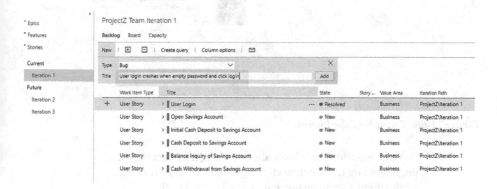

Figure 11-56. New bug

7. Add a Task work item to fix the bug. Activate bug and assign to yourself. Activate the Bug Fix Task work item. See Figure 11-57.

Figure 11-57. *Bug and Task activated*

8. Now that the release has a bug in QA, reject the release from deploying to UAT. See Figure 11-58.

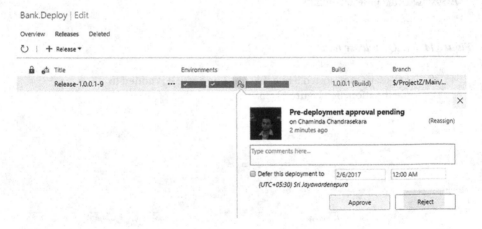

Figure 11-58. *Reject UAT deployment*

9. You can abandon the release after rejecting it by clicking on the release menu and then clicking Abandon, since further deployment should be prevented. See Figure 11-59.

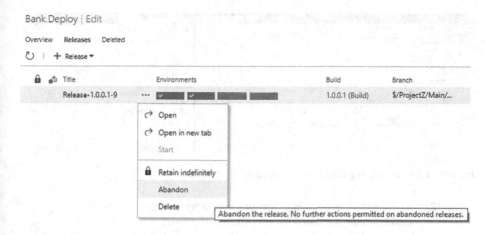

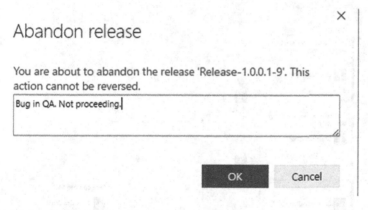

Figure 11-59. *Abandoning release*

10. Provide a reason for abandoning the release in the popup window and click OK to abandon the release. See Figure 11-60.

Figure 11-60. *Release abandonment reason*

11. Add the following code line to the BankAppProgram.cs file and check the file in to source control, being sure to associate with it the bug to fix and its task, setting them to resolve. This is done to simulate a bug fixing activity. See Figure 11-61.

```
Console.WriteLine("Fix user login crash");
```

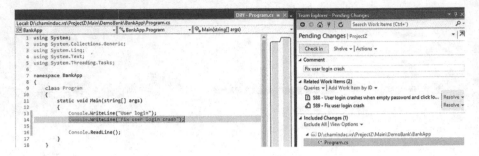

Figure 11-61. Fixing bug and submitting code to repository

> 12. Activate the Open Savings Account user story and its development task. See Figure 11-62.

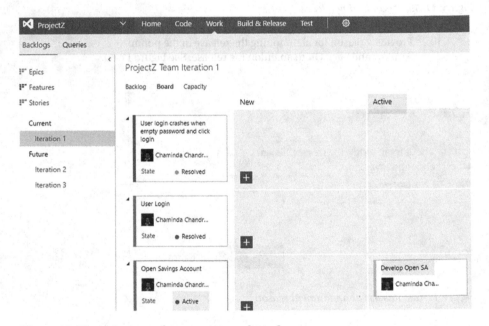

Figure 11-62. Activate another user story and a task

> 13. Add the following code line to BankAppProgram.cs and check the file in to source control while associating and resolving the user story "Open Savings Account" and its task work item. See Figure 11-63.

```
Console.WriteLine("Open savings account");
```

Figure 11-63. *Completing another user story*

14. Queue a new build (1.0.0.2) with the Bank.Rel build definition, and it will automatically trigger a deployment to the DevInt environment once the build completes. See Figure 11-64.

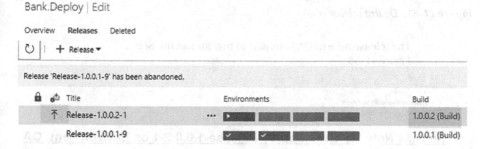

Figure 11-64. *Deploying build 1.0.0.2*

15. Approve deployment to QA as well.

16. This build, 1.0.02, contains the bug fix and the Open Savings Account user story.

    The release note to DevInt includes these. See Figure 11-65.

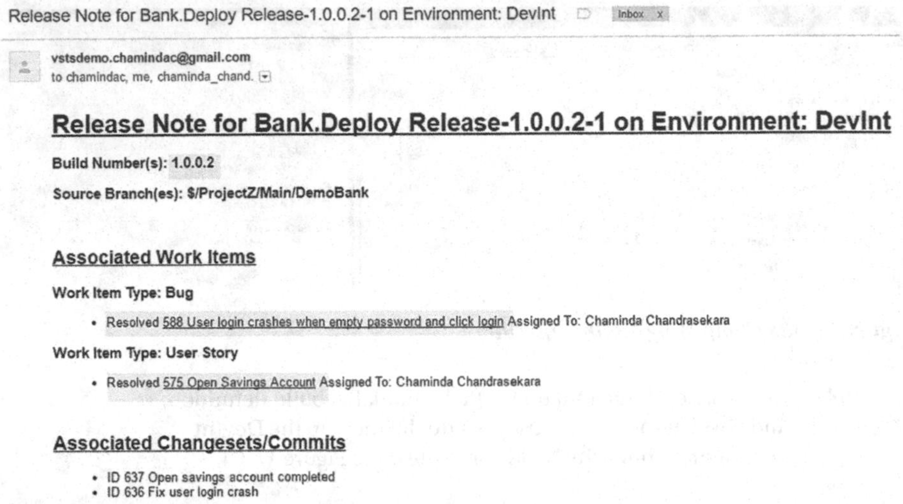

Release Note for Bank.Deploy Release-1.0.0.2-1 on Environment: DevInt 　▷　 Inbox　x

vstsdemo.chamindac@gmail.com
to chamindac, me, chaminda_chand. ▾

Release Note for Bank.Deploy Release-1.0.0.2-1 on Environment: DevInt

Build Number(s): 1.0.0.2

Source Branch(es): $/ProjectZ/Main/DemoBank

Associated Work Items

Work Item Type: Bug

- Resolved 588 User login crashes when empty password and click login Assigned To: Chaminda Chandrasekara

Work Item Type: User Story

- Resolved 575 Open Savings Account Assigned To: Chaminda Chandrasekara

Associated Changesets/Commits

- ID 637 Open savings account completed
- ID 636 Fix user login crash

Figure 11-65. *DevInt release note*

The release note to QA is similar to that for DevInt. See
Figure 11-66.

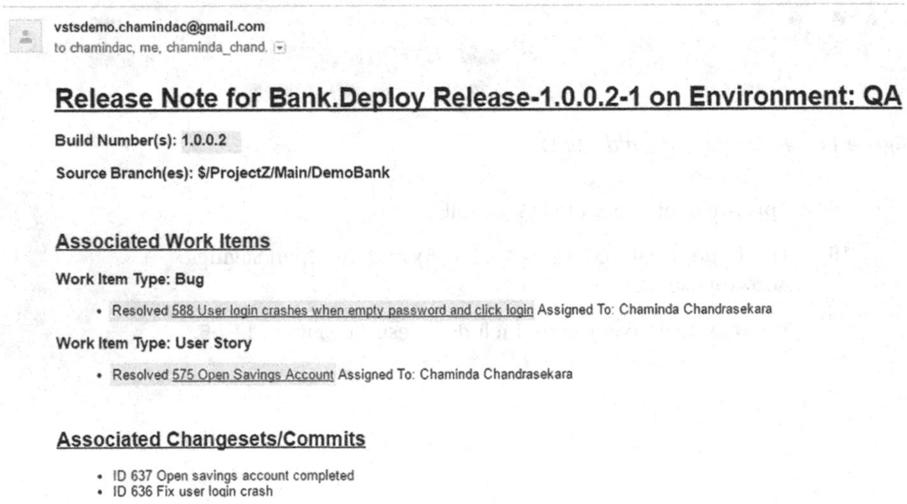

vstsdemo.chamindac@gmail.com
to chamindac, me, chaminda_chand. ▾

Release Note for Bank.Deploy Release-1.0.0.2-1 on Environment: QA

Build Number(s): 1.0.0.2

Source Branch(es): $/ProjectZ/Main/DemoBank

Associated Work Items

Work Item Type: Bug

- Resolved 588 User login crashes when empty password and click login Assigned To: Chaminda Chandrasekara

Work Item Type: User Story

- Resolved 575 Open Savings Account Assigned To: Chaminda Chandrasekara

Associated Changesets/Commits

- ID 637 Open savings account completed
- ID 636 Fix user login crash

Figure 11-66. *QA release note*

17. Now, proceed with deployment to UAT by approving it for pre-deployment in UAT. The release note to UAT should include work items from builds 1.0.01 and 1.0.0.2, since UAT has not been deployed with both builds. When 1.0.0.2 gets deployed to UAT, it has the code changes that came in 1.0.0.1 as well. See Figure 11-67.

Bank.Deploy | Edit
Overview Releases Deleted
Release
Release 'Release-1.0.0.1-9' has been abandoned.
Title
Environments
Build
Branch
Created
Created By
Description
Release-1.0.0.2-1
1.0.0.2 (Build)
$/ProjectZ/Main/...
11 minutes ago
Chaminda Chand...
Triggered by Bank.Rel 1.0.0.2.
Release-1.0.0.1-9
1.0.0.1 (Build)
$/ProjectZ/Main/...
an hour ago
Chaminda Chand...

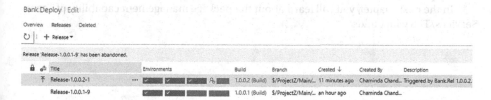

Figure 11-67. Deploying to UAT

The UAT release note includes builds 1.0.0.1 and 1.0.0.2, as shown in Figure 11-68.

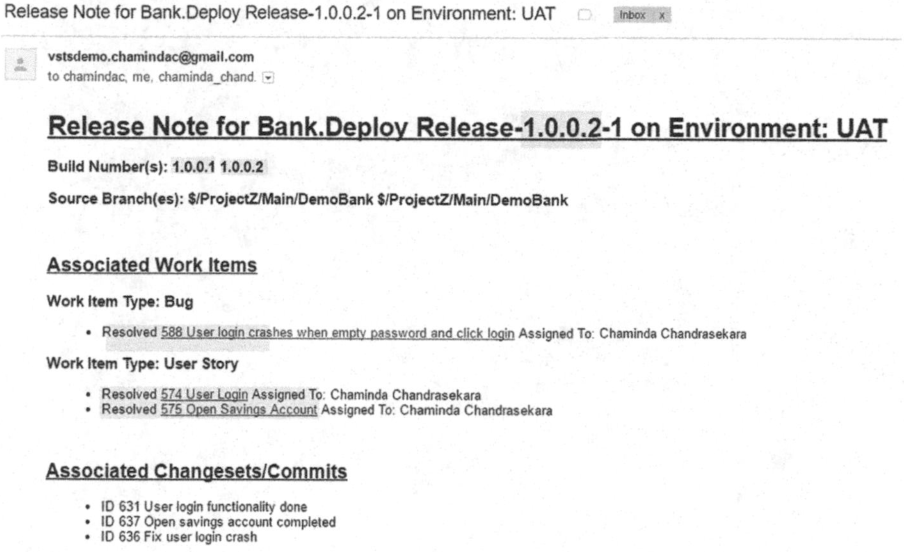

Release Note for Bank.Deploy Release-1.0.0.2-1 on Environment: UAT
Inbox x
vstsdemo.chamindac@gmail.com
to chamindac, me, chaminda_chand.
Release Note for Bank.Deploy Release-1.0.0.2-1 on Environment: UAT
Build Number(s): 1.0.0.1 1.0.0.2
Source Branch(es): $/ProjectZ/Main/DemoBank $/ProjectZ/Main/DemoBank
Associated Work Items
Work Item Type: Bug
• Resolved 588 User login crashes when empty password and click login Assigned To: Chaminda Chandrasekara
Work Item Type: User Story
• Resolved 574 User Login Assigned To: Chaminda Chandrasekara
• Resolved 575 Open Savings Account Assigned To: Chaminda Chandrasekara
Associated Changesets/Commits
• ID 631 User login functionality done
• ID 637 Open savings account completed
• ID 636 Fix user login crash

Figure 11-68. UAT release note

Now you have a working release pipeline with auto-generated release notes. Do further check-ins with associated work items, queue builds, and deployment approvals to various stages to see the effective release notes.

Summary

In this chapter, you learned how to generate effective release notes using Marketplace extensions and emailing with a custom PowerShell script task. Release notes based on the target deployment environment, help teams and clients to track the requirements to delivery. This enhances the capability of the continuous delivery process, paving the way to DevOps (software **DEV**elopment and information technology **OP**eration**S**).

In the next chapter, you will learn about the package management capability of Team Services/TFS with builds.

CHAPTER 12

■ ■ ■

Package Management

This chapter will guide you in creating NuGet packages and then using a feed with TFS/VSTS to store the packages so that they can be shared within your organization. Hands-on lessons will give you instructions for creating feeds for packages and restoring, building, and deploying packages with TFS/VSTS.

Prerequisites: You have TFS/VSTS accounts with the package management feature. Install the Package Management extension, available at https://marketplace.visualstudio.com/items?itemName=ms.feed, to enable package management features. You are using Visual Studio 2015, and you have installed productivity power tools for VS 2015 (https://marketplace.visualstudio.com/items?itemName=VisualStudioProductTeam.ProductivityPowerTools2015) in your Visual Studio environment.

Lesson 12.01 – Create a NuGet Package

Let's create a NuGet package by following these steps:

1. Download nuget.exe from https://dist.nuget.org/index.html and copy it to a local folder. Add the nuget.exe path to the Path environment variable. See Figure 12-1.

© Chaminda Chandrasekara 2017
C. Chandrasekara, *Beginning Build and Release Management with TFS 2017 and VSTS*,
DOI 10.1007/978-1-4842-2811-1_12

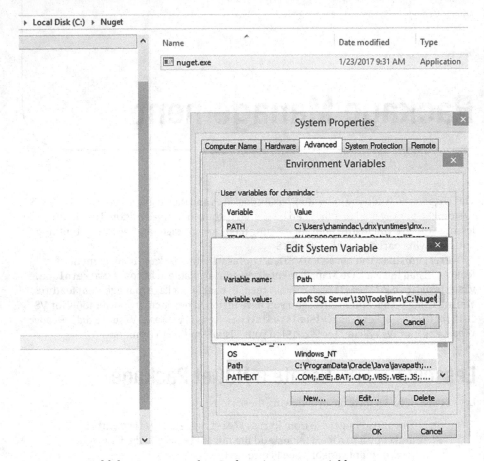

Figure 12-1. *Add the nuget.exe path to Path environment variable*

2. Once you do this, NuGet is recognized as a command in the system. See Figure 12-2.

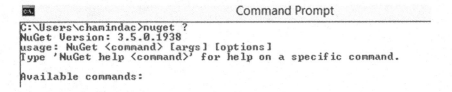

Figure 12-2. *NuGet command*

3. Create a new Visual Studio solution named "PkgMgmtDemo."
   Add a class library project named "NugetPackageDemo" to it.
   See Figure 12-3.

Figure 12-3. *Class library project*

4. Rename the default added Class1.cs to DemoPackage.cs
   and add the following code to the class file. Then, build the
   solution in Visual Studio to verify it compiles.

```csharp
using System;
using System.Collections.Generic;
using System.Linq;
using System.Text;
using System.Threading.Tasks;

namespace NugetPackageDemo
{
    public class DemoPackage
    {
        public string HelloWorldNugetDemo()
        {
            return "Hello world! Welcome to nuget packages!";
        }
    }
}
```

481

5.   Right click on the NugetPackageDemo project and open the
     command prompt from the Power Commands menu (this
     is available if you have installed productivity power tools).
     Or, open a command prompt and change the directory to
     the folder where NugetPackageDemo.csproj is located. See
     Figure 12-4.

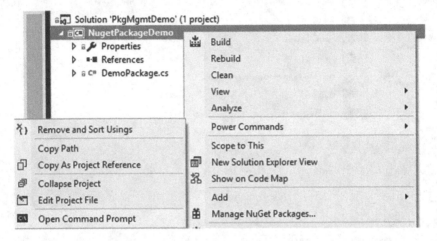

Figure 12-4. Open the command prompt from Visual Studio

6.   Run the nuget spec command to generate the
     NugetPackageDemo.nuspec file. See Figure 12-5.

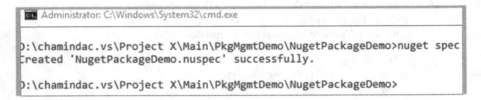

Figure 12-5. Generating the nuspec file

7.   Click the "show all files" icon in Solution Explorer after
     selecting the NugetPackageDemo project. This will show the
     nuspec file in Solution Explorer, as shown in Figure 12-6.

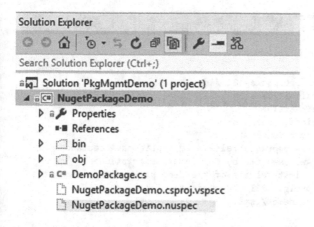

Figure 12-6. nuspec file in Solution Explorer

8. Double click on the nuspec file to open it in Visual Studio. See Figure 12-7.

```
NugetPackageDemo.nuspec ⊕ X  Source Control Explorer
 1    <?xml version="1.0"?>
 2  ☐<package >
 3  ☐  <metadata>
 4      <id>$id$</id>
 5      <version>$version$</version>
 6      <title>$title$</title>
 7      <authors>$author$</authors>
 8      <owners>$author$</owners>
 9      <licenseUrl>http://LICENSE_URL_HERE_OR_DELETE_THIS_LINE</licenseUrl>
10      <projectUrl>http://PROJECT_URL_HERE_OR_DELETE_THIS_LINE</projectUrl>
11      <iconUrl>http://ICON_URL_HERE_OR_DELETE_THIS_LINE</iconUrl>
12      <requireLicenseAcceptance>false</requireLicenseAcceptance>
13      <description>$description$</description>
14      <releaseNotes>Summary of changes made in this release of the package.</releaseNotes>
15      <copyright>Copyright 2017</copyright>
16      <tags>Tag1 Tag2</tags>
17    </metadata>
18  </package>
```

Figure 12-7. Generated nuspec file

9. Edit the nuspec file in Visual Studio and add an ID, author name, owner name, and description, as shown in Figure 12-8. Leave the version and title as they are for the time being, since they will be updated later to use with builds. Remove licenseUrl, projectUrl, and iconUrl. Leave requireLicenceAcceptance as false.

483

```
NugetPackageDemo.nuspec ⇅ X  Source Control Explorer
 1    <?xml version="1.0"?>
 2  ⊟<package >
 3  ⊟    <metadata>
 4        <id>chamindac.demo.package01</id>
 5        <version>$version$</version>
 6        <title>$title$</title>
 7        <authors>chamindac</authors>
 8        <owners>chamindac</owners>
 9        <requireLicenseAcceptance>false</requireLicenseAcceptance>
10        <description>Awesome demo by Chaminda</description>
11        <releaseNotes>First release of the demo package.</releaseNotes>
12        <copyright>Copyright 2017</copyright>
13        <tags>chamindac demo</tags>
14     </metadata>
15  </package>
```

Figure 12-8. *Edited nuspec file*

10. Execute the following command from the folder holding the
.csproj and .nuspec files. This will generate a NuGet package.
See Figure 12-9.

```
nuget pack NugetPackageDemo.csproj
```

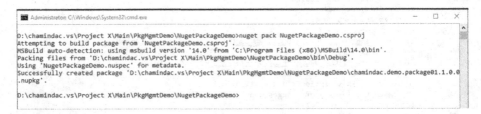

Figure 12-9. *Generating NuGet package*

11. The generated package will be available in the project folder.
See Figure 12-10.

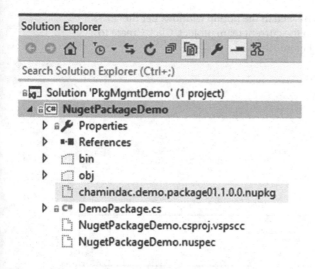

Figure 12-10. *Generated NuGet package*

In this lesson, you created a simple NuGet package using nuget.exe.

Lesson 12.02 – Create a Feed and Publish Package in the Feed

A feed is used as a container for packages. A package is consumed or published with a given feed. Let's look at how we can create a feed with TFS/VSTS package management.

1. Go to Team Project ➤ Build & Release ➤ Packages tab. Click on New feed. See Figure 12-11.

Figure 12-11. *New feed in team project*

485

2. Provide a name for the feed in the popup window. Let the feed be visible only to the current team project. Click Create to create the feed. See Figure 12-12.

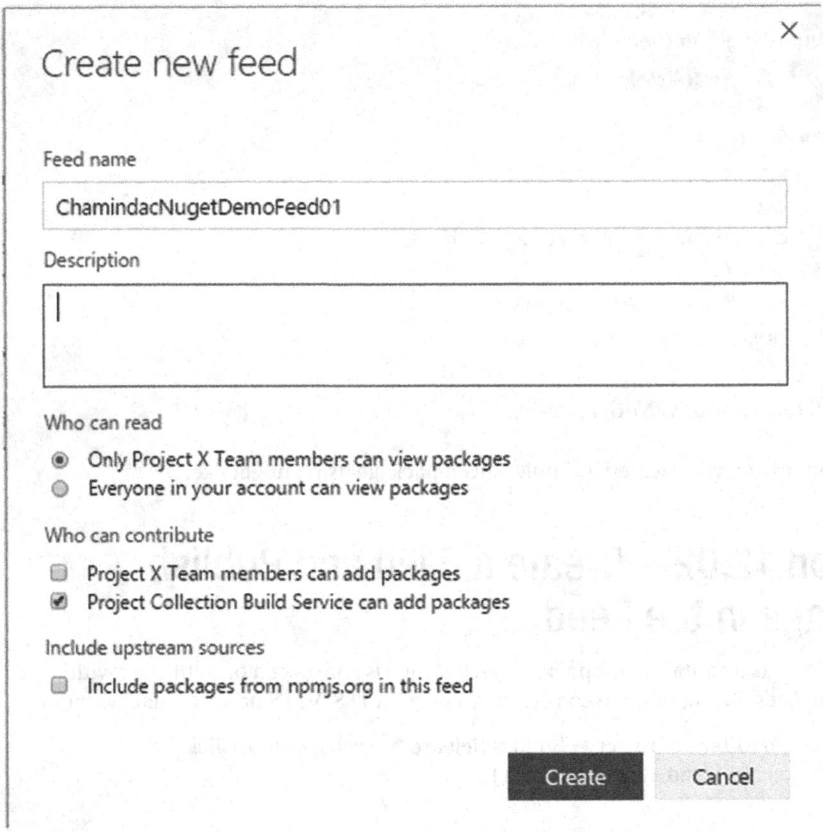

Figure 12-12. *Creating a new feed*

3. The created feed can be edited by selecting Edit from the menu of the feed, which is available in the Packages tab. See Figure 12-13.

New feed
Feeds
ChamindacNugetDemoFeed01
Edit
Delete
Edit

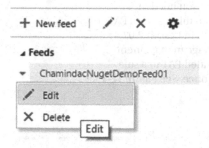

Figure 12-13. *Edit feed*

4. You can change the options, such as the permissions of the feed, once you are in the Edit window. After editing, click Save. See Figure 12-14.

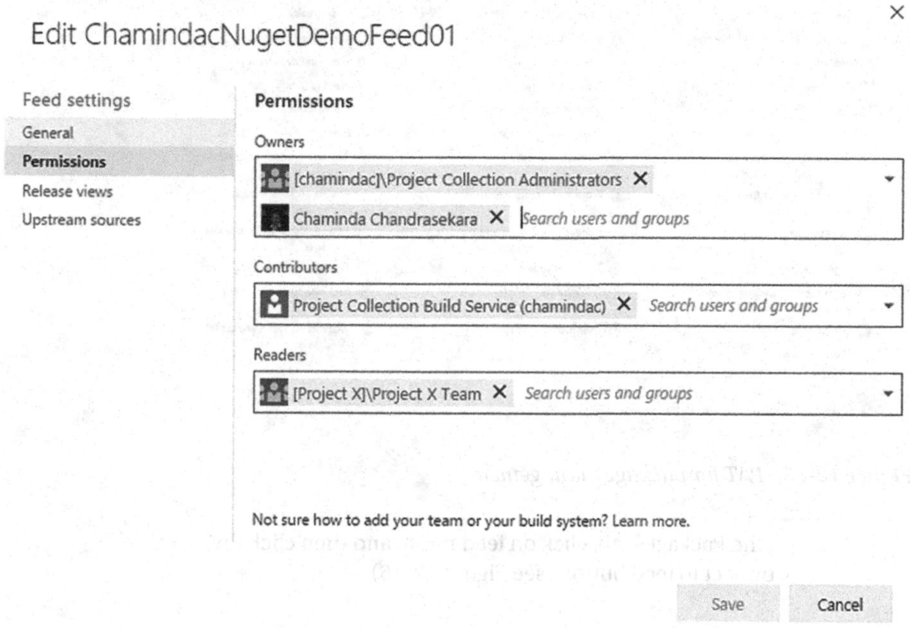

Edit ChamindacNugetDemoFeed01
Feed settings
General
Permissions
Release views
Upstream sources
Permissions
Owners
[chamindac]\Project Collection Administrators
Chaminda Chandrasekara
Search users and groups
Contributors
Project Collection Build Service (chamindac)
Search users and groups
Readers
[Project X]\Project X Team
Search users and groups
Not sure how to add your team or your build system? Learn more.
Save
Cancel

Figure 12-14. *Editing feed*

5. To publish a package to the created feed, you need to authenticate when using nuget.exe. To do this, create a PAT (Personal Access Token; covered in detail in Lesson 2.02.4 of Chapter 2). Setting the scope for package management is sufficient for this PAT. Copy the generated PAT to a safe location, since it will only be displayed once. See Figure 12-15.

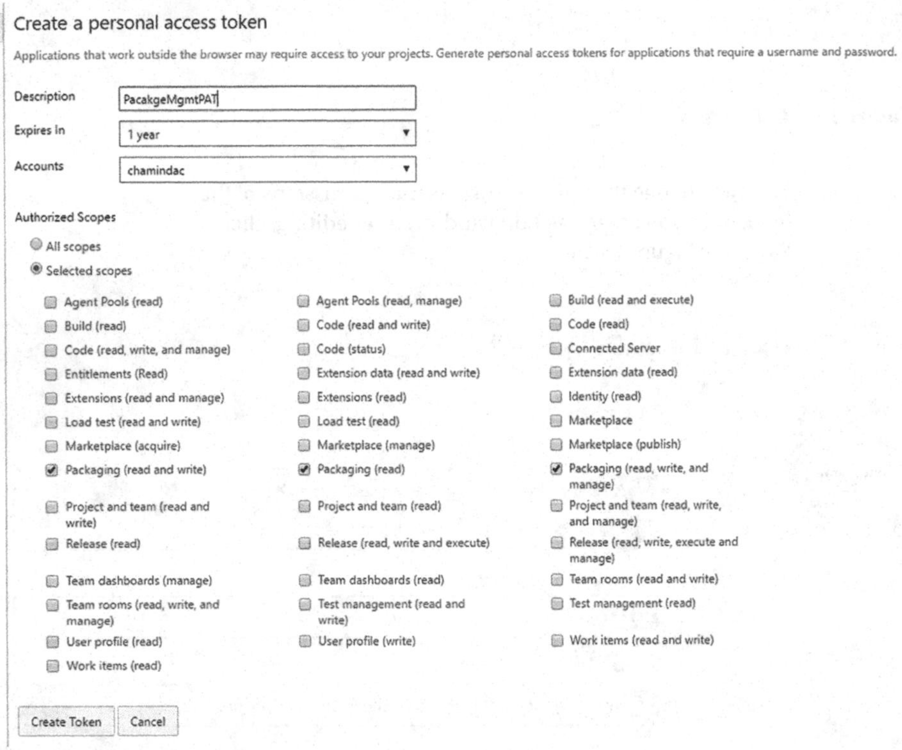

Create a personal access token

Applications that work outside the browser may require access to your projects. Generate personal access tokens for applications that require a username and password.

Description: PacakgeMgmtPAT

Expires In: 1 year ▼

Accounts: chamindac ▼

Authorized Scopes
○ All scopes
● Selected scopes

☐ Agent Pools (read)	☐ Agent Pools (read, manage)	☐ Build (read and execute)
☐ Build (read)	☐ Code (read and write)	☐ Code (read)
☐ Code (read, write, and manage)	☐ Code (status)	☐ Connected Server
☐ Entitlements (Read)	☐ Extension data (read and write)	☐ Extension data (read)
☐ Extensions (read and manage)	☐ Extensions (read)	☐ Identity (read)
☐ Load test (read and write)	☐ Load test (read)	☐ Marketplace
☐ Marketplace (acquire)	☐ Marketplace (manage)	☐ Marketplace (publish)
☑ Packaging (read and write)	☑ Packaging (read)	☑ Packaging (read, write, and manage)
☐ Project and team (read and write)	☐ Project and team (read)	☐ Project and team (read, write, and manage)
☐ Release (read)	☐ Release (read, write and execute)	☐ Release (read, write, execute and manage)
☐ Team dashboards (manage)	☐ Team dashboards (read)	☐ Team rooms (read and write)
☐ Team rooms (read, write, and manage)	☐ Test management (read and write)	☐ Test management (read)
☐ User profile (read)	☐ User profile (write)	☐ Work items (read and write)
☐ Work items (read)		

[Create Token] [Cancel]

Figure 12-15. *PAT for package management*

6. In the Packages tab, click on feed name and then click the Connect to feed button (see Figure 12-16).

ChamindacNugetDemoFeed01

Connect to feed

Start sharing packages with your team

Connect to feed

Learn more about Package Management

Figure 12-16. Connect to feed

7. The popup widow has two important commands. The first one
    can be used to add the feed authentication. The second one can
    be used to push a package to the feed. See Figure 12-17.

Figure 12-17. *Feed commands*

8. Copy the **"Add this feed"** command (shown in Figure 12-17) to a notepad and add two additional parameters, -username and –password, to the end of the copied command in the notepad. Username can be any value, while the password must be PAT-scoped to manage packages. An example is shown here:

```
nuget.exe sources Add -Name "ChamindacNugetDemoFeed01"
-Source "https://chamindac.pkgs.visualstudio.com/_packaging/
ChamindacNugetDemoFeed01/nuget/v3/index.json" -username
"cc" -password <PATvalue>
```

9. Execute the preceding command in a command window from the project folder that contains the NuGet package generated in the previous lesson. See Figure 12-18.

Figure 12-18. *Add feed authentication*

10. Then, copy the **"Push a package"** command from Figure 12-17 and change the package name to your package name. From a folder where your package is available, execute the following push command:

```
nuget.exe push -Source "ChamindacNugetDemoFeed01"
-ApiKey VSTS my_package.nupkg
```

See Figure 12-19.

```
D:\chamindac.vs\Project X\Main\PkgMgmtDemo\MyPackage>nuget.exe push -Source "ChamindacNugetDemoFeed01" -ApiKey VSTS cham
indac.demo.package01.1.0.0.nupkg
Pushing chamindac.demo.package01.1.0.0.nupkg to 'https://chamindac.pkgs.visualstudio.com/_packaging/e5f87ae0-a6c8-4508-a
07a-4af3c916634e/nuget/v2/'...
  PUT https://chamindac.pkgs.visualstudio.com/_packaging/e5f87ae0-a6c8-4508-a07a-4af3c916634e/nuget/v2/
  Accepted https://chamindac.pkgs.visualstudio.com/_packaging/e5f87ae0-a6c8-4508-a07a-4af3c916634e/nuget/v2/ 6471ms
Your package was pushed.

D:\chamindac.vs\Project X\Main\PkgMgmtDemo\MyPackage>
```

Figure 12-19. *Push a package to the feed*

11. Your package is now available in the feed. See Figure 12-20.

Figure 12-20. *NuGet package available in the feed*

You created a feed in the team project and pushed the NuGet package to the feed using the command line.

Lesson 12.03 – Build and Publish Packages with TFS Builds and Release

In this lesson, let's look at how to build NuGet packages with TFS/VSTS builds and deploy them to a package management feed with TFS/VSTS release.

1. Create a new build definition and set the repository to the PkgMgmtDemo solution folder. Save the build definition with the name "PkgMgmtBuildDemo." See Figure 12-21.

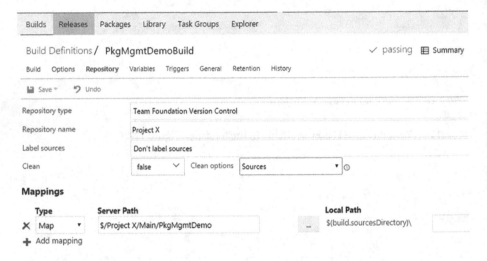

Figure 12-21. *Map the solution folder*

2. Add BuildConfiguration and BuildPlatform variables with values of release and any cpu, respectively. Add another two variables, Package.title and Package.version. Set the Package. title value as NugetPackageDemo and Package.version as $(Build.BuildNumber), which will get the current build number. See Figure 12-22.

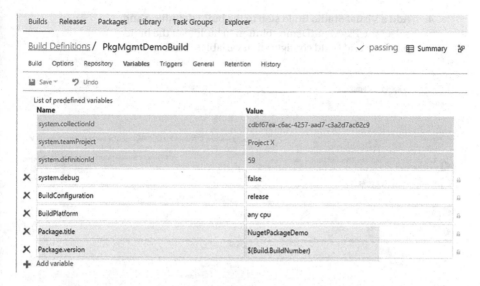

Figure 12-22. *Build variables*

3. Open the .nuspec file in the PkgMgmtDemo solution in Visual Studio and change the version and title to the following values. Then, check in the .nuspec file to the source control repository. See Figure 12-23.

```
<version>$Package.version$</version>
<title>$Package.title$</title>
```

```
NugetPackageDemo.nuspec ⌗ ✕ Source Control Explorer
  1    <?xml version="1.0"?>
  2    <package >
  3      <metadata>
  4        <id>chamindac.demo.package01</id>
  5        <version>$Package.version$</version>
  6        <title>$Package.title$</title>
  7        <authors>chamindac</authors>
  8        <owners>chamindac</owners>
  9        <requireLicenseAcceptance>false</requireLicenseAcceptance>
 10        <description>Awesome demo by Chaminda</description>
 11        <releaseNotes>First release of the package.</releaseNotes>
 12        <copyright>Copyright 2017</copyright>
 13        <tags>chamindac demo</tags>
 14      </metadata>
 15    </package>
```

Figure 12-23. *nuspec file updated to support build variables*

4.   Add a Visual Studio Build step to the build definition and
     select the PkgMgmtDemo solution to build. Set the build
     platform and build configuration variables. See Figure 12-24.

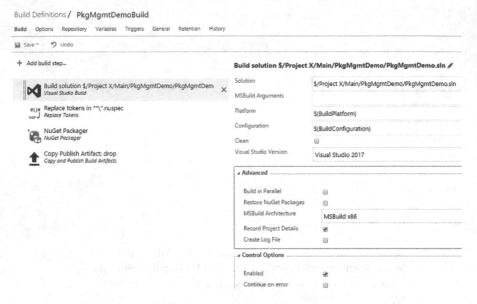

Figure 12-24. *Build step to build the solution*

5.   Add a Replace Token task to the build definition (this task
     comes with the extension found at https://marketplace.
     visualstudio.com/items?itemName=qetza.replacetokens,
     and instructions to add Marketplace extensions to TFS can be
     found in Chapter 2). Set $ as the value of both the token prefix
     and the token suffix. Keep the Root directory field empty to
     allow files to be located in the root folder of the repository and
     in all child folders recursively. Target file should be set as ***.
     nuspec. This will apply the Package.title variable value and
     the build number as the version (using the Package.version
     build variable) to the .nuspec file. See Figure 12-25.

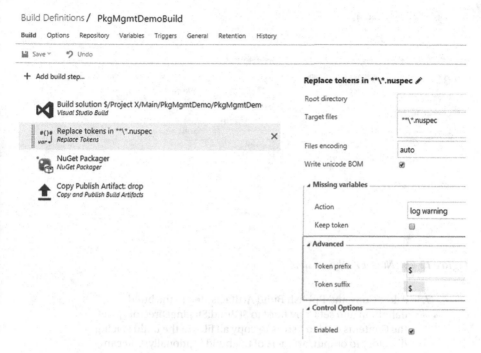

Build Definitions / PkgMgmtDemoBuild

Build Options Repository Variables Triggers General Retention History

💾 Save ▾   🔄 Undo

+ Add build step...

Build solution $/Project X/Main/PkgMgmtDemo/PkgMgmtDem
Visual Studio Build

Replace tokens in ***.nuspec
Replace Tokens   ×

NuGet Packager
NuGet Packager

Copy Publish Artifact: drop
Copy and Publish Build Artifacts

Replace tokens in ***.nuspec ✏

Root directory

Target files   ***.nuspec

Files encoding   auto

Write unicode BOM   ☑

⊿ **Missing variables**

Action   log warning

Keep token   ☐

⊿ **Advanced**

Token prefix $

Token suffix $

⊿ **Control Options**

Enabled   ☑

Figure 12-25. *Replace Tokens step*

6. Add the NuGet Packager task from the Task Catalog's
    Package tab. Select NugetPackageDemo.csproj (do not select
    the .nuspecfile, as it will be auto-loaded when the project
    file is specified). Set the Package Folder field to $(build.
    StagingDirectory) and the Configuration to Package field as
    $(BuildConfiguration). See Figure 12-26.

Figure 12-26. *NuGet Packager step*

7. Add a Copy and Publish Build Artifacts step to the build definition and set Copy Root to $(Build.StagingDirectory). Set the Contents field to * so as to copy all files in the build staging directory to output/artifacts of the build (optionally, you can set it as *.nupkg to filter NuGet packages). Set Artifact Name as drop and select Server as the Artifact Type. See Figure 12-27.

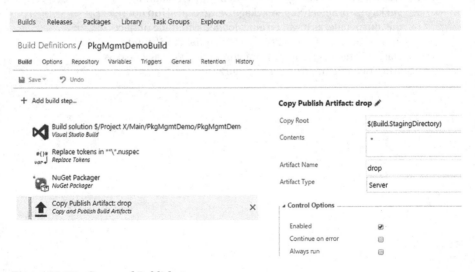

Figure 12-27. *Copy and Publish step*

8. Queue a build, and it will package a .nupkg with the build version number as the package's version number. In the following example, build version 1.0.0.7 is applied to NuGet package chamindac.demo.package01. See Figure 12-28.

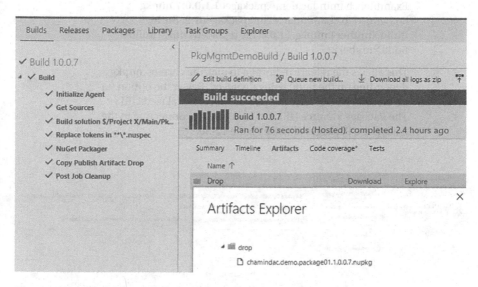

Figure 12-28. Build generated a NuGet package

9. Go to the Release tab of the team project and create a new release definition. Name it "pkgmgmtDemo.Release." In the Artifacts tab, select PkgMgmtDemoBuild as the linked artifact. See Figure 12-29.

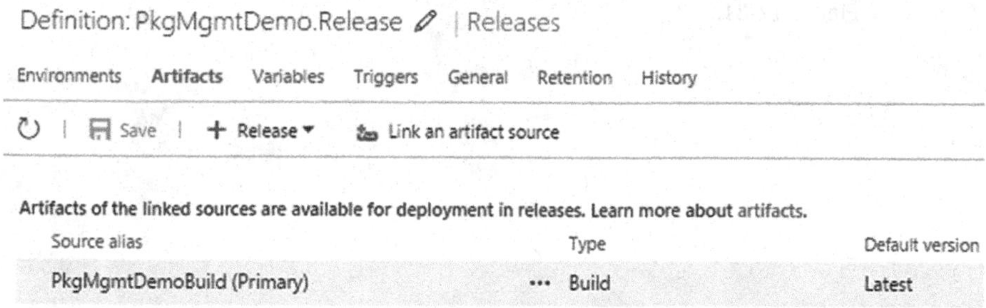

Definition: PkgMgmtDemo.Release ✎ | Releases

Environments   **Artifacts**   Variables   Triggers   General   Retention   History

↻ | 💾 Save | ＋ Release ▾   ⤸ Link an artifact source

Artifacts of the linked sources are available for deployment in releases. Learn more about artifacts.

Source alias		Type	Default version
PkgMgmtDemoBuild (Primary)	•••	Build	Latest

Figure 12-29. Release definition's linked artifacts

10. Add a NuGet Publisher task to the release definition Environment 1 from the Package tab of the Task Catalog. Select the .nupkg from the artifacts and change the version number part of the path to $(Build.BuildNumber).

Example: chamindac.demo.package01.**1.0.0.7**.nupkg is changed to chamindac.demo.package01.**$(Build. BuildNumber)**.nupkg. (**1.0.0.7** is replaced with $(Build. BuildNumber).

This allows the release definition to pick the correct .nupkg depending on the build being deployed. Select the option for an internal NuGet feed and provide the internal feed URL. The Package's source URL can be found by connecting to the feed in the Packages tab. See Figure 12-30.

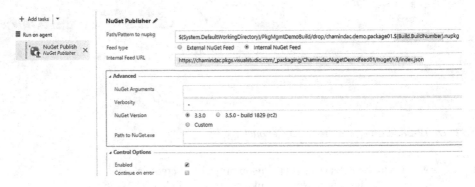

Figure 12-30. *NuGet Publisher task*

11. Create a release; it deploys the package to the feed. See Figure 12-31.

Figure 12-31. *NuGet package published to feed*

12. The package version built with TFS will be available in the feed after deployment. See Figure 12-32.

Figure 12-32. *NuGet package version available in the feed*

In this lesson, you created a build and a release definition to create a NuGet package and deploy it to a feed in the team project.

Lesson 12.04 – Consume Package in Internal Feed in Visual Studio & TFS Builds

In this lesson, you will learn how to consume a package published to an internal feed in a Visual Studio project. As the next step, restoring a NuGet package in the internal feed with TFS builds is explained.

1. Open Visual Studio 2015 and click on Tools ➤ Options. Expand the NuGet Package Manger and select Package Sources. Click on the green + to add a new package source. See Figure 12-33.

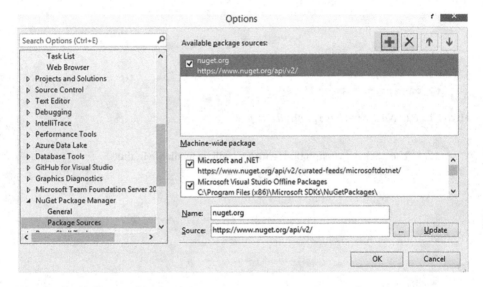

Figure 12-33. *New package source*

2. Connect to the feed in the Packages tab of the team project web portal and copy the package source URL. See Figure 12-34.

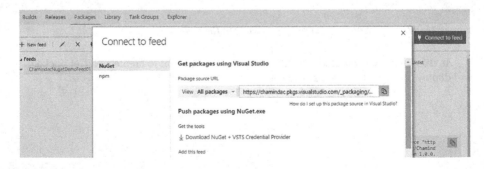

Figure 12-34. *Package source URL*

3. Provide the copied package source URL in the Source field and provide a name to the package. Click on Update, and you will now see the new package source below the default nuget. org package source. Click OK to close the options window. See Figure 12-35.

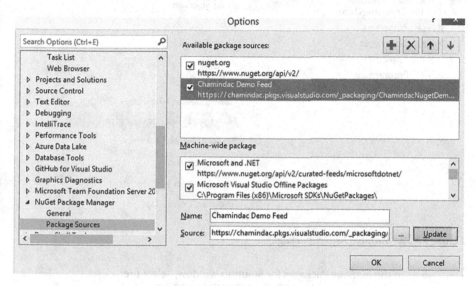

Figure 12-35. Package source added to Visual Studio

4. Create a new Visual Studio solution called "ConsumePkgDemo2015" in Visual Studio 2015 after connecting to the same team project which we created the NuGet package in a previous lesson. Add a console application to it named "PkgConsumeDemoApp." Right click on the solution and then click on "Manage NuGet Packages for Solution". See Figure 12-36.

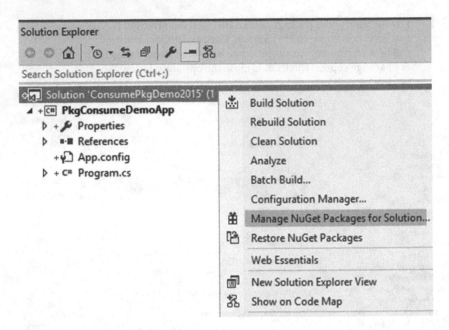

Figure 12-36. Manage NuGet packages

> 5. In the Manage Packages for Solution window, select the package source added in Step 3. See Figure 12-37.

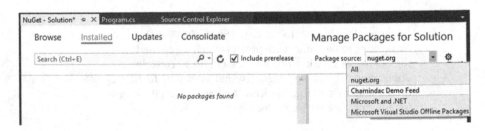

Figure 12-37. Selecting the package source

> 6. In the popup window, provide the credentials to your Team Services or Team Foundation Server account. See Figure 12-38.

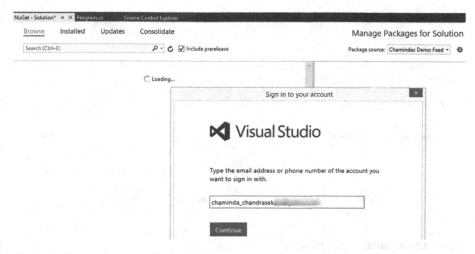

Figure 12-38. *Authorizing the feed usage*

7. In the Browse tab, the package from the internal feed will be visible. Select PkgConsumeDemoApp and click Install. See Figure 12-39.

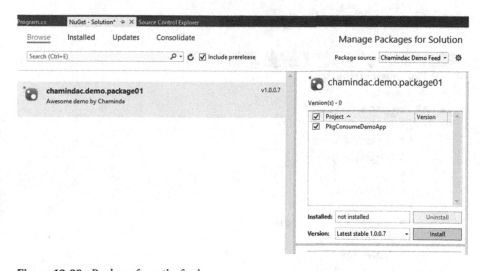

Figure 12-39. *Package from the feed*

8. Confirm the installation by clicking OK in the popup window. See Figure 12-40.

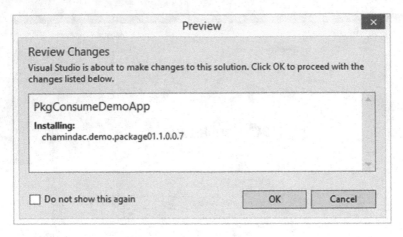

Figure 12-40. *Installing the package*

9. NugetPackageDemo is added to the console application as a reference, and packages.config is added. See Figure 12-41.

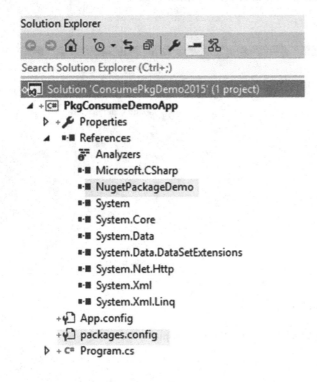

Figure 12-41. *Package installed*

10. Add the following code to console application Program. cs's file. This code uses the package and displays the return message from the package object DemoPackage.

```
using System;
usingSystem.Collections.Generic;
usingSystem.Linq;
usingSystem.Text;
usingSystem.Threading.Tasks;

namespacePkgConsumeDemoApp
{
classProgram
    {
staticvoid Main(string[] args)
        {
NugetPackageDemo.DemoPackagedemoPkg = newNugetPackageDemo.
DemoPackage();

Console.WriteLine(demoPkg.HelloWorldNugetDemo());

Console.ReadLine();

        }
    }
}
```

11. Build and run the project to verify all is well, and you will see the message from the package is displayed (package code created in Lesson 12.1). See Figure 12-42.

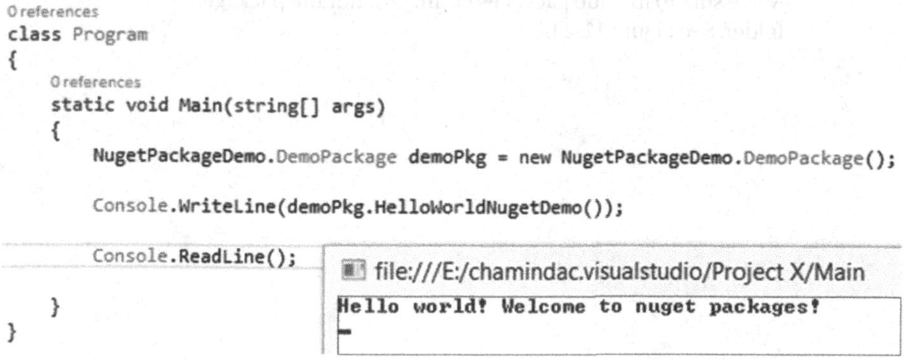

```
0 references
class Program
{
    0 references
    static void Main(string[] args)
    {
        NugetPackageDemo.DemoPackage demoPkg = new NugetPackageDemo.DemoPackage();

        Console.WriteLine(demoPkg.HelloWorldNugetDemo());

        Console.ReadLine();

    }
}
```

▓ file:///E:/chamindac.visualstudio/Project X/Main

Hello world! Welcome to nuget packages!

Figure 12-42. Using the package

12. Before checking in/submitting the ConsumePkgDemo2015
    solution to the repository, go to Source Control Explorer and
    undo the packages folder added. It is not a good practice to
    submit packages to the source control repository. Adding
    packages folder increase TFS database sizes unnecessarily
    while those packages are readily available to download on
    demand. Instead, the packages should be restored during
    the build. See Figure 12-43.

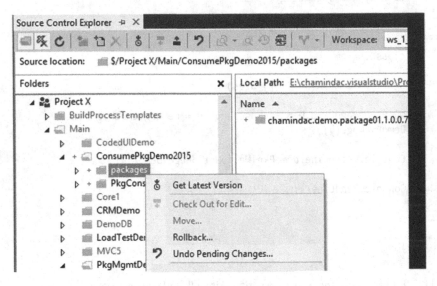

Figure 12-43. Undo adding packages to the repository

13. Check in/submit the solution and the console application.
    Make sure to include packages.config but not the packages
    folder. See Figure 12-44.

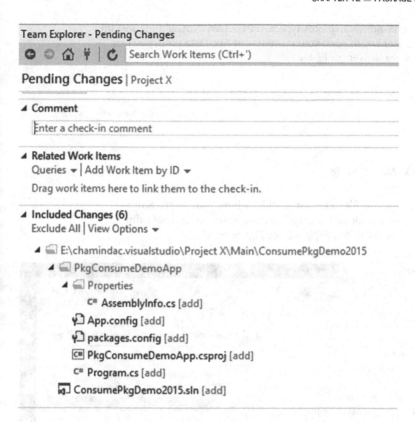

Team Explorer - Pending Changes

⊙ ⊙ ⌂ ⫟ | ⟳ Search Work Items (Ctrl+')

Pending Changes | Project X

◢ Comment

Enter a check-in comment

◢ Related Work Items
Queries ▾ | Add Work Item by ID ▾

Drag work items here to link them to the check-in.

◢ Included Changes (6)
Exclude All | View Options ▾

◢ ⊟ E:\chamindac.visualstudio\Project X\Main\ConsumePkgDemo2015
◢ ⊟ PkgConsumeDemoApp
◢ ⊟ Properties
C# AssemblyInfo.cs [add]
🗋 App.config [add]
🗋 packages.config [add]
C# PkgConsumeDemoApp.csproj [add]
C# Program.cs [add]
🔧 ConsumePkgDemo2015.sln [add]

Figure 12-44. *Check in to source control repository*

14. You need to make sure that the internal package source can be found in TFS builds. It is required that you provide the package source information. This is available in NuGet.Config in the %APPDATA%\NuGet path. See Figure 12-45.

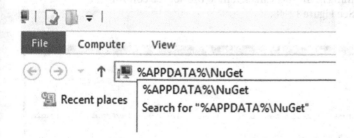

File   Computer   View

⊙ ⊙ ▾ ↑ | 💻 %APPDATA%\NuGet

🖳 Recent places

%APPDATA%\NuGet
Search for "%APPDATA%\NuGet"

Figure 12-45. *Locating NuGet.config*

507

15. In Windows Explorer, type %APPDATA%\NuGet and press the Enter key to open your current user AppData path; you can see a NuGet.config file.

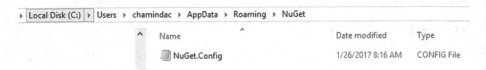

Figure 12-46. NuGet.config

16. Copy this file to the same folder where your Visual Studio solution file is. Then, add that file to source control using Source Control Explorer. See Figure 12-47.

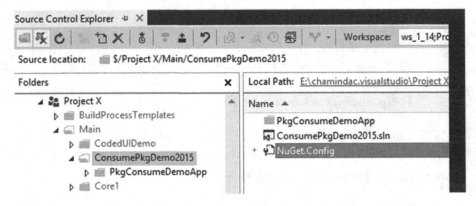

Figure 12-47. NuGet.config added to repository

17. If you open the Nuget.config file in Visual Studio, you can see the available internal feed information. Do not change anything in the file. Check it in to the source control repository. See Figure 12-48.

```
E:\chamindac.visu...o2015\NuGet.Config   ⇌ ×  Source Control Explorer
 1   <?xml version="1.0" encoding="utf-8"?>
 2   <configuration>
 3     <packageRestore>
 4       <add key="enabled" value="True" />
 5       <add key="automatic" value="True" />
 6     </packageRestore>
 7     <packageSources>
 8       <add key="nuget.org" value="https://www.nuget.org/api/v2/" />
 9       <add key="Chamindac Demo Feed" value="https://chamindac.pkgs.visualstudio.com/_packaging/ChamindacNugetDemoFeed01/nuget/v3/index.json
10     </packageSources>
11     <activePackageSource>
12       <add key="nuget.org" value="https://www.nuget.org/api/v2/" />
13     </activePackageSource>
14   </configuration>
```

Figure 12-48. NuGet.config content

508

18. Create a new empty build definition and set the repository (server path) to the ConsumepkgDemo2015 solution. See Figure 12-49.

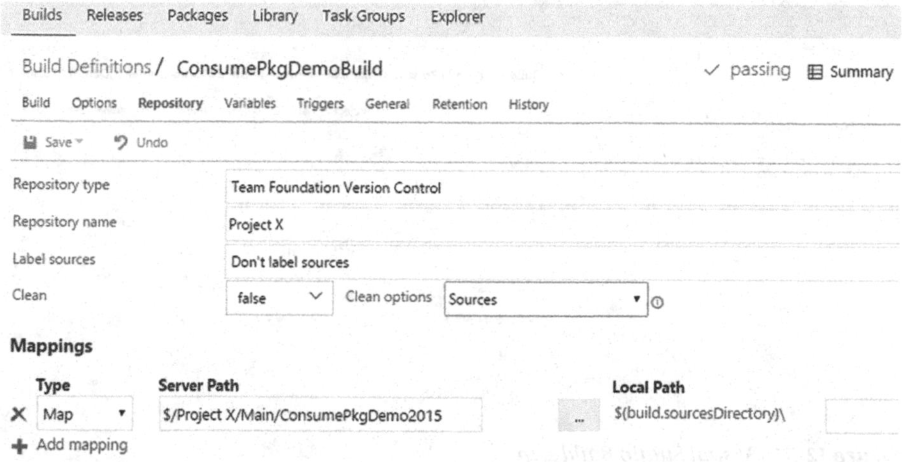

Figure 12-49. Map solution path

19. Add a NuGet Installer step to the build definition and select the ConsumePkgDemo2015 solution as the path to solution. Select the NuGet.config file checked in previously as the path to NuGet.config. Set Installation Type to Restore. See Figure 12-50.

Figure 12-50. NuGet restore step using NuGet.config

20. Add a Visual Studio build step and select the ConsumePkgDemo2015 solution to build. See Figure 12-51.

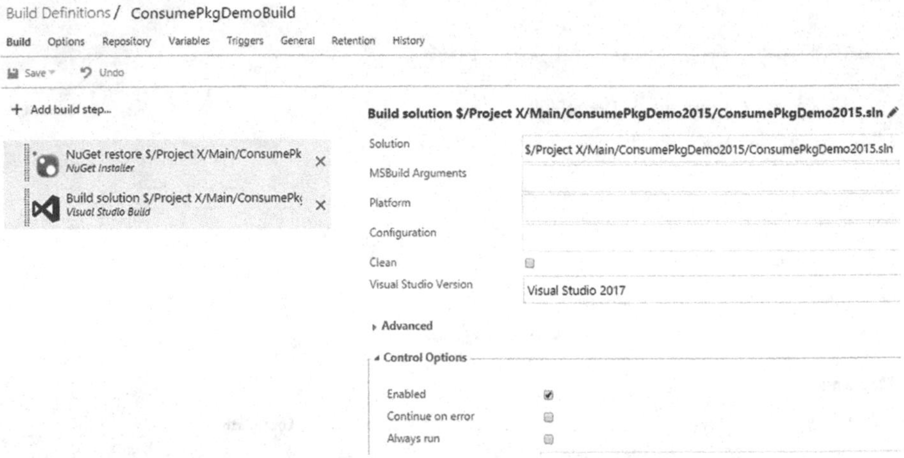

Figure 12-51. *Visual Studio Build step*

21. Save and queue a build. You can see internal packages getting restored, and the project builds successfully. See Figure 12-52.

Figure 12-52. *Restore NuGet package from internal feed*

In this lesson, you created a solution and a project that would consume the NuGet package from the internal feed. Then, you used the internal package feed in a Team Foundation build successfully.

Summary

In this chapter, you created identified package management features available with Team Services and TFS. Package management will allow you to share common code as packages using internal feeds. A feed can be shared to all in the organization or to just a project team in the organization. This chapter only covered NuGet packages, but you can use npm packages as well with package management. Do experiments on npm packages to improve your knowledge.

In the next chapter, you will learn how to extend build and release management tasks so as to enhance the build/release features of Team Services or Team Foundation Server.

CHAPTER 13

■ ■ ■

Extending Build and Release Tasks on Your Own

You will learn how to set up your Visual Studio environment to enable extension development for VSTS/TFS. Developing a build and release task and publishing and using it in build/release will give you the capability to add your own functional components to TFS build and release management.

Prerequisites: You have Visual Studio 2015 and VSTS/TFS. In your Visual Studio environment, npm is available. If not, get npm from https://www.npmjs.com/get-npm and set up Node.js and npm.

Lesson 13.01 – Update npm and Add Visual Studio Project Templates for TFS Extensions

Let's prepare the Visual Studio environment for developing extensions for Team Services and TFS build and release management.

1. Open a command prompt as administrator and run the following command to update npm to the latest version (see Figure 13-1):

    npm install npm@latest-g

```
Administrator: Command Prompt                                              —     □

C:\Windows\System32>npm install npm@latest -g
C:\Users\Chaminda\AppData\Roaming\npm\npm -> C:\Users\Chaminda\AppData\Roaming\npm\node_modules\npm\bin\npm-cli.js
C:\Users\Chaminda\AppData\Roaming\npm
`-- npm@4.1.2
```

Figure 13-1. *Update npm*

© Chaminda Chandrasekara 2017
C. Chandrasekara, *Beginning Build and Release Management with TFS 2017 and VSTS*,
DOI 10.1007/978-1-4842-2811-1_13

2. Get the TFS Cross Platform Command Line Interface (tfx-cli) by using this npm command (see Figure 13-2).

```
npmi -g tfx-cli
```

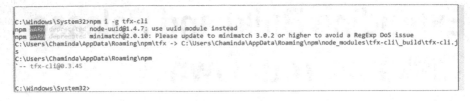

Figure 13-2. Get tfx-cli

3. Close all Visual Studio instances and download the VSTS Extension Project Templates from https://marketplace. visualstudio.com/items?itemName=JoshGarverick. VSTSExtensionProjectTemplates (see Figure 13-3).

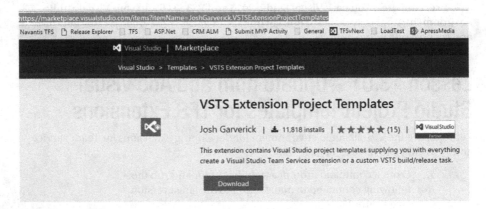

Figure 13-3. Download VSTS Extension Project Templates

4. Install the downloaded .vsix (VSOExtensionPackage.3.0.vsix) file. See Figure 13-4.

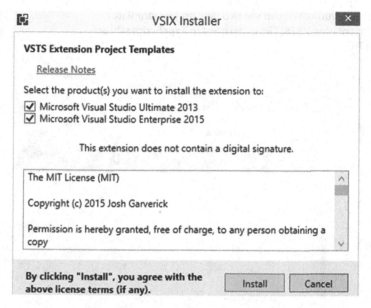

Figure 13-4. *Installing VSTS Extension Project Templates*

Installation should add templates to all compatible Visual Studio versions. See Figure 13-5.

Figure 13-5. *Completed VSTS Extension Project Templates installation*

5. Open Visual Studio. You can see two new project templates. One is for creating VSTS/TFS extensions in TypeScript tab. See Figure 13-6.

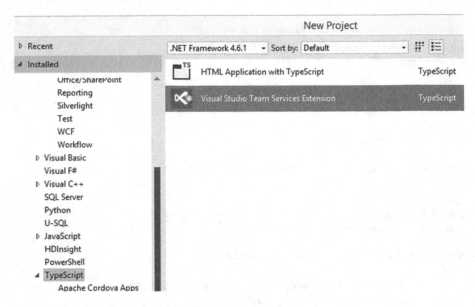

Figure 13-6. *TypeScript-based VSTS extension template*

6. The other one is found in the PowerShell section and is used to create VSTS/TFS Build Release extensions. This is the extension we are going to discuss in this chapter. See Figure 13-7.

Figure 13-7. *PowerShell-based VSTS extension template*

You have set up your Visual Studio environment to develop extensions for TFS/VSTS in this lesson.

Lesson 13.02 – Develop a Build/Release Extension and Packaging

Let's develop a build and release extension using the new templates and package it for upload to Marketplace (https://marketplace.visualstudio.com/vsts).

1. Create a Visual Studio solution named "BuildReleaseExtensionDemo" and add a project named "DemoBuildReleaseTask" to it with the template Visual Studio Team Services Build Task, found in the PowerShell section. See Figure 13-8.

Figure 13-8. *Build Task project template*

2. The project is created with an Example Task template. See Figure 13-9.

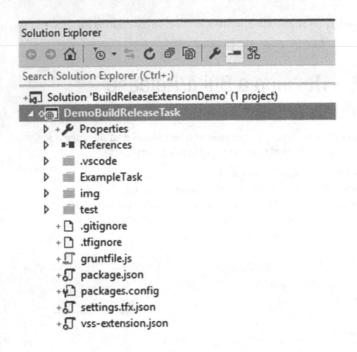

Figure 13-9. *Build Task project*

3. In Task Runner Explorer in Visual Studio, the Gruntfile.js file will show as "failed to load" for few seconds until node_modules and VstsTaskSdk have loaded as specified in Gruntfile.js. See Figure 13-10.

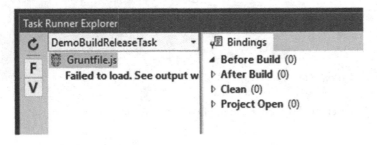

Figure 13-10. *Task runner showing error*

4. After few seconds, the Task Runner Explorer shows that node_modules have loaded and the VstsTaskSdk has been copied to ExampleTask\ps_modules. See Figure 13-11.

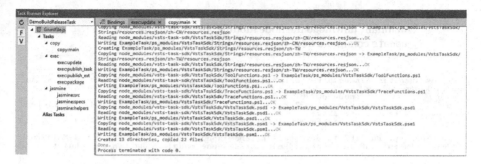

Figure 13-11. *Task runner loading modules*

5. This should add node_modules and VstsTaskSdk, as shown in the Solution Explorer in Figure 13-12.

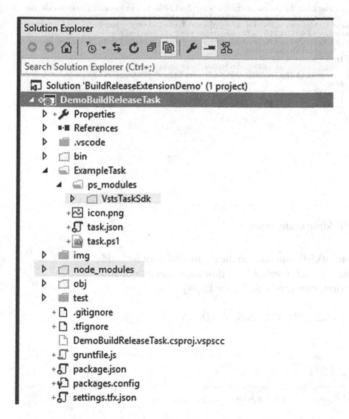

Figure 13-12. *VstsTaskSdk and node_modules added*

1. If this does not work automatically for some reason, you can manually download the node modules by running the npm update command from the project folder. See Figure 13-13.

```
E:\chamindac.visualstudio\Project X\Main\BuildReleaseExtensionDemo\DemoBuildRele
aseTask>npm update
npm WARN deprecated node-uuid@1.4.7: use uuid module instead
npm WARN deprecated minimatch@2.0.10: Please update to minimatch 3.0.2 or higher
 to avoid a RegExp DoS issue
npm WARN prefer global coffee-script@1.10.0 should be installed with -g

> phantomjs-prebuilt@2.1.14 install E:\chamindac.visualstudio\Project X\Main\Bui
ldReleaseExtensionDemo\DemoBuildReleaseTask\node_modules\phantomjs-prebuilt
> node install.js

PhantomJS not found on PATH
Downloading https://github.com/Medium/phantomjs/releases/download/v2.1.1/phantom
js-2.1.1-windows.zip
Saving to C:\Users\CHAMIN~1\AppData\Local\Temp\phantomjs\phantomjs-2.1.1-windows
.zip
Receiving...
 [=========================================] 99%
Received 17767K total.
Extracting zip contents
Removing E:\chamindac.visualstudio\Project X\Main\BuildReleaseExtensionDemo\Demo
BuildReleaseTask\node_modules\phantomjs-prebuilt\lib\phantom
Copying extracted folder C:\Users\CHAMIN~1\AppData\Local\Temp\phantomjs\phantomj
s-2.1.1-windows.zip-extract-1485512198596\phantomjs-2.1.1-windows -> E:\chaminda
c.visualstudio\Project X\Main\BuildReleaseExtensionDemo\DemoBuildReleaseTask\nod
e_modules\phantomjs-prebuilt\lib\phantom
Writing location.js file
Done. Phantomjs binary available at E:\chamindac.visualstudio\Project X\Main\Bui
ldReleaseExtensionDemo\DemoBuildReleaseTask\node_modules\phantomjs-prebuilt\lib\
phantom\bin\phantomjs.exe
@0.0.0 E:\chamindac.visualstudio\Project X\Main\BuildReleaseExtensionDemo\DemoBu
ildReleaseTask
+-- @types/jquery@2.0.39
+-- @types/q@0.0.32
+-- grunt@1.0.1
+-- grunt-contrib-copy@1.0.0
+-- grunt-contrib-jasmine@1.1.0
+-- grunt-exec@1.0.1
+-- jasmine@2.5.3
+-- rimraf@2.5.4
+-- tfx-cli@0.3.45
+-- typescript@2.1.5
`-- vsts-task-sdk@0.6.4
```

Figure 13-13. Manually adding node_modules

2. To get the VstsTaskSdk manually to the ps_modules folder inside the task folder, open a PowerShell window as administrator and run the following command (see Figure 13-14):

```
Save-Module -Name VstsTaskSdk -Path .\
```

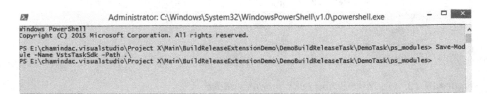

Administrator: C:\Windows\System32\WindowsPowerShell\v1.0\powershell.exe

```
Windows PowerShell
Copyright (C) 2015 Microsoft Corporation. All rights reserved.

PS E:\chamindac.visualstudio\Project X\Main\BuildReleaseExtensionDemo\DemoBuildReleaseTask\DemoTask\ps_modules> Save-Mod
ule -Name VstsTaskSdk -Path .\
PS E:\chamindac.visualstudio\Project X\Main\BuildReleaseExtensionDemo\DemoBuildReleaseTask\DemoTask\ps_modules>
```

Figure 13-14. Manually adding VstsTaskSdk

3. But, if you download VstTaskSdk manually, make sure to move all contents from the version-numbered folder to the VstsTaskSdk folder. See Figure 13-15.

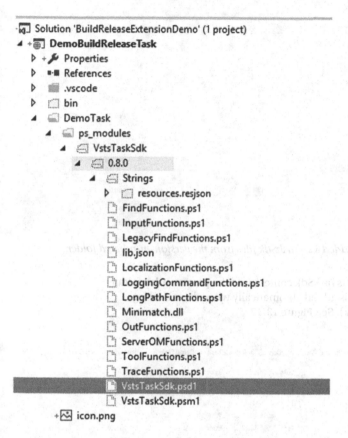

Figure 13-15. Manually added VstsTaskSdk in a version-numbered folder

4. Cut the files from the version-numbered folder in Windows Explorer. See Figure 13-16.

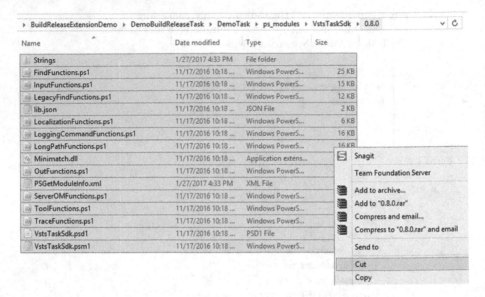

Figure 13-16. *Cut the added VstsTaskSdk files from the version-numbered folder*

5. Paste the VstsTaskSdk content into the **ps_ modules** folder (this folder is added automatically when downloading VstsTaskSdk). See Figure 13-17.

Name	Date modified	Type	Size
0.8.0	1/27/2017 4:42 PM	File folder	
Strings	1/27/2017 4:33 PM	File folder	
FindFunctions.ps1	11/17/2016 10:18 ...	Windows PowerS...	25 KB
InputFunctions.ps1	11/17/2016 10:18 ...	Windows PowerS...	15 KB
LegacyFindFunctions.ps1	11/17/2016 10:18 ...	Windows PowerS...	12 KB
lib.json	11/17/2016 10:18 ...	JSON File	2 KB
LocalizationFunctions.ps1	11/17/2016 10:18 ...	Windows PowerS...	6 KB
LoggingCommandFunctions.ps1	11/17/2016 10:18 ...	Windows PowerS...	16 KB
LongPathFunctions.ps1	11/17/2016 10:18 ...	Windows PowerS...	16 KB
Minimatch.dll	11/17/2016 10:18 ...	Application extens...	18 KB
OutFunctions.ps1	11/17/2016 10:18 ...	Windows PowerS...	4 KB
PSGetModuleInfo.xml	1/27/2017 4:33 PM	XML File	22 KB
ServerOMFunctions.ps1	11/17/2016 10:18 ...	Windows PowerS...	26 KB
ToolFunctions.ps1	11/17/2016 10:18 ...	Windows PowerS...	4 KB
TraceFunctions.ps1	11/17/2016 10:18 ...	Windows PowerS...	5 KB
VstsTaskSdk.psd1	11/17/2016 10:18 ...	PSD1 File	2 KB
VstsTaskSdk.psm1	11/17/2016 10:18 ...	Windows PowerS...	7 KB

Figure 13-17. *Paste the VstsTaskSdk files into the ps_modules folder*

6. Remove the version-numbered folder so that the folder structure looks as shown in Figure 13-18.

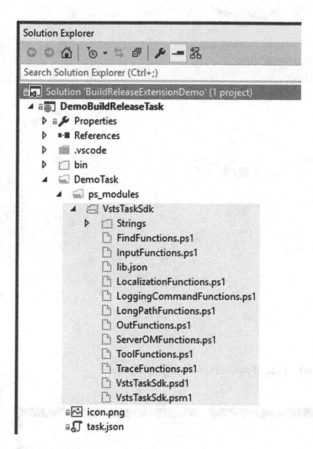

Figure 13-18. VstsTaskSdk files

6. Let's rename the task as "DemoTask." First, change the folder name to "DemoTask," as shown in Figure 13-19.

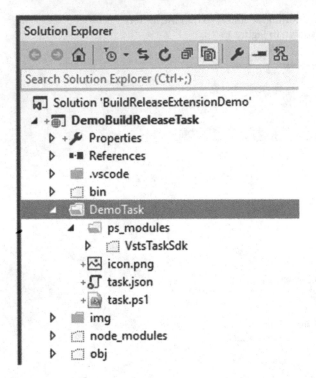

Figure 13-19. *Rename task*

7. Open gruntfile.js and replace Exampletask with DemoTask. See Figure 13-20.

```
gruntfile.js ⇄ X  Source Control Explorer
module                                                                    ▼  {} exports(grunt)
  4    Click here to learn more. http://go.microsoft.com/fwlink/?LinkID=513275&clcid=0x409
  5   */
  6  ☐module.exports = function (grunt) {
  7  ☐   grunt.initConfig({
  8           pkg: grunt.file.readJSON("package.json"),
  9           settings: grunt.file.readJSON("settings.tfx.json"),
 10  ☐        exec: {
 11  ☐            update: {
 12                   command: "npm up --save-dev",
 13                   stdout: true,
 14                   stderr: true
 15               },
 16  ☐            publish_task: {
 17                   command: "tfx build tasks upload --token <%= settings.publish.token %> --auth-type pat --task-path ./DemoTask --service-url <%=
 18                   stdout: true,
 19                   stderr: true
 20               },
 21  ☐            publish_ext: {
 22                   command: "tfx extension publish --token <%= settings.publish.token %> --auth-type pat --service-url <%= settings.serviceUrl %>"
 23                   stdout: true,
 24                   stderr: true
 25               },
 26  ☐            package: {
 27                   command: "tfx extension create --manifest-globs <%= settings.package.manifestGlobs %>",
 28                   stdout: true,
 29                   stderr: true
 30               }
 31           },
 32  ☐        copy: {
 33  ☐            main: {
 34  ☐                files: [
 35                       { expand: true, cwd: 'node_modules/vsts-task-sdk/', src: ['VstsTaskSdk/**'], dest: 'DemoTask/ps_modules' }]
 36               }
 37           },
 38  ☐        jasmine: {
```

Figure 13-20. *Update gruntfile.js with new task name*

524

8. Open task.json in the DemoTask folder and change the values, as shown in Figure 13-21. Provide name as DemoTask and set the same value to InstanceNameFormat. Provide a **friendlyName** and a description. Change the two variables available by default to have the YourName variable as a string and ShowWarningMsg and ShowErrorMsgandFail as Boolean variables. Visibility indicates whether it is available for build or release or both (for both option you need to specify Build and Release seperated by a comma).

```
gruntfile.js    task.json  ₽ X  task.ps1    vss-extension.json    Source Control Explorer
hema: <No Schema Selected>
 1   ⊟{
 2         "id": "0e8e79db-252f-40d0-9cfa-a539cf9e576e",
 3         "name": "DemoTask",
 4         "friendlyName": "Demo Task",
 5         "description": "VSTS/TFS Demo Build Release Task",
 6         "helpMarkDown": "[More Information](https://url.to/yourmarkdown)",
 7         "category": "Utility",
 8   ⊟     "visibility": [
 9             "Build",
10             "Release"
11         ],
12         "author": "",
13   ⊟     "version": {
14             "Major": 1,
15             "Minor": 0,
16             "Patch": 11
17         },
18   ⊟     "demands": [
19         ],
20         "minimumAgentVersion": "1.83.0",
21   ⊟     "groups": [
22
23         ],
24   ⊟     "inputs": [
25   ⊟         {
26                 "name": "YourName",
27                 "type": "string",
28                 "label": "Your Name",
29                 "defaultValue": "",
30                 "required": true
31             },
32   ⊟         {
33                 "name": "ShowWarningMsg",
34                 "type": "boolean",
35                 "label": "Show Warning Message",
36                 "defaultValue": "false",
37                 "required": true,
38                 "helpMarkDown": "Shows a warning message if this is checked."
39             },
40   ⊟         {
41                 "name": "ShowErrorMsgandFail",
42                 "type": "boolean",
43                 "label": "Show Error Message",
44                 "defaultValue": "false",
45                 "required": true,
46                 "helpMarkDown": "Shows an error message and fail the task and build if this is checked."
47             }
         ],
         "instanceNameFormat": "DemoTask",
   ⊟     "execution": {
   ⊟         "PowerShell3": {
                 "target": "$(currentDirectory)\\task.ps1",
                 "argumentFormat": "",
                 "workingDirectory": "$(currentDirectory)"
             }
         }
   [}]
```

Figure 13-21. *task.json*

9. Open task.ps1 in the DemoTask folder and replace the
    PowerShell code with the following (or download from
    https://github.com/chamindac/Book-Beginning-
    Build-ReleaseManagement-/blob/master/Chapter13/
    BuildReleaseExtensionDemo/DemoBuildReleaseTask/
    DemoTask/task.ps1).

```
#
# DemoTask.ps1
#
[CmdletBinding(DefaultParameterSetName = 'None')]
param()

Write-Host "Starting DemoTask"
Trace-VstsEnteringInvocation $MyInvocation

try {

    $YourName              = Get-VstsInput -Name
                             YourName -Require
    $ShowWarningMsg        = Get-VstsInput -Name
                             ShowWarningMsg
        $ShowErrorMsgandFail   = Get-VstsInput -Name
                                 ShowErrorMsgandFail

    $compName = $env:COMPUTERNAME;

    Write-Host ("Hello from {0}, {1}"
    -f $compName, $YourName);

    if($ShowWarningMsg.ToLower() -eq "true")
    {
            Write-Warning ("Warnig message you
            requested from {0}, {1}"
            -f $compName, $YourName);
    }

    if($ShowErrorMsgandFail.ToLower() -eq
    "true")
    {
            Write-Error ("Error message you
            requested from {0}, {1}" -f
            $compName, $YourName);
    }
```

```
    } catch {
            throw;
    } finally {
            Trace-VstsLeavingInvocation $MyInvocation
    }

    Write-Host "Ending DemoTask"
```

10. Open the vss-extension.json file and change the ID, version, name, description, and publisher. The publisher name should be the name you intend to use in Marketplace (https:// marketplace.visualstudio.com). The extension is not yet ready for the public. Keep it false. How to make an extension public is discussed later in this chapter. Leave the links as they are for the time being. See Figure 13-22.

Figure 13-22. vss-extension.json

11. Change the file path and name of the contribution to DemoTask (task folder name must be used for these two items). Change the contribution ID to be demo-task. Save vss-extension.json with the changes. See Figure 13-23.

527

```
 gruntfile.js      task.json       task.ps1        vss-extension.json  ↴ ✕
hema: <No Schema Selected>
 26    ⊟       getstarted": {
 27              "uri": "https://bit.ly"
 28            },
 29    ⊟     "learn": {
 30              "uri": "https://bit.ly"
 31            },
 32    ⊟     "support": {
 33              "uri": "https://bit.ly"
 34            },
 35    ⊟     "repository": {
 36              "uri": "https://bit.ly"
 37            },
 38    ⊟     "issues": {
 39              "uri": "https://bit.ly"
 40            }
 41          },
 42    ⊟     "branding": {
 43            "color": "rgb(220, 235, 252)",
 44            "theme": "light"
 45          },
 46    ⊟     "files": [
 47    ⊟        {
 48              "path": "DemoTask"
 49            },
 50    ⊟        {
 51                "path": "node_modules/vss-web-extension-sdk/lib",
 52                "addressable": true,
 53                "packagePath": "lib"
 54            }
 55
 56          ],
 57    ⊟     "categories": [
 58            "Build and release"
 59          ],
 60    ⊟     "contributions": [
 61    ⊟        {
 62              "id": "demo-task",
 63    ⊟        "targets": [
 64              "ms.vss-distributed-task.tasks"
 65            ],
 66            "type": "ms.vss-distributed-task.task",
 67    ⊟        "properties": {
 68              "name": "DemoTask"
 69            }
 70          }
 71          ]
 72    }
 73
```

Figure 13-23. *vss-extension.json*

12. The vss-web-extension-sdk module is required in order to
     package the extension. This should be available in node_
     modules, since vss-extension.json is set to look for it in there.
     See Figure 13-24.

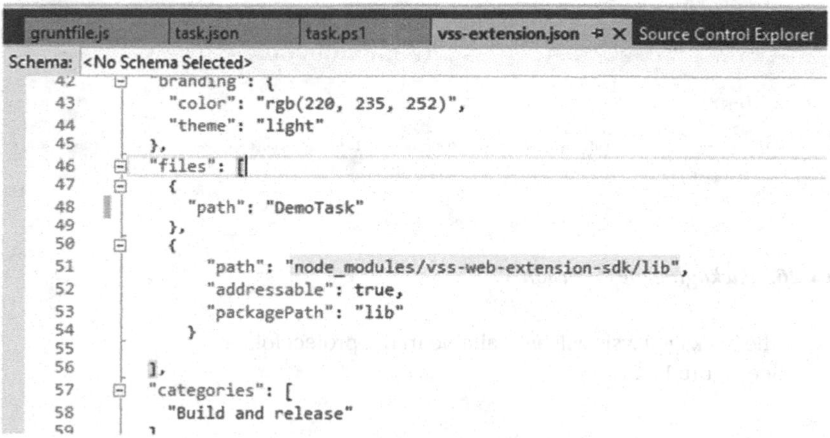

```
 gruntfile.js       task.json         task.ps1        vss-extension.json  ⌐ ×  Source Control Explorer
Schema: <No Schema Selected>
   42    ⊟    "branding": {
   43             "color": "rgb(220, 235, 252)",
   44             "theme": "light"
   45          },
   46    ⊟    "files": [
   47    ⊟       {
   48                "path": "DemoTask"
   49             },
   50    ⊟       {
   51                "path": "node_modules/vss-web-extension-sdk/lib",
   52                "addressable": true,
   53                "packagePath": "lib"
   54             }
   55
   56          ],
   57    ⊟    "categories": [
   58             "Build and release"
   59          ]
```

Figure 13-24. Setting vss-web-extension-sdk/lib.

13. To download vss-web-extension-sdk to node_modules, execute the following command from the project folder (see Figure 13-25):

```
npm install vss-web-extension-sdk
```

```
 Administrator: Command Prompt                                                                          —

D:\chamindac.vs\Project X\Main\BuildReleaseExtensionDemo\DemoBuildReleaseTask>npm install vss-web-extension-sdk
@0.0.0 D:\chamindac.vs\Project X\Main\BuildReleaseExtensionDemo\DemoBuildReleaseTask
`-- vss-web-extension-sdk@2.109.1
  +-- @types/jqueryui@1.11.32
  +-- @types/knockout@3.4.39
  +-- @types/react@0.14.57
  `-- @types/requirejs@2.1.28

D:\chamindac.vs\Project X\Main\BuildReleaseExtensionDemo\DemoBuildReleaseTask>
```

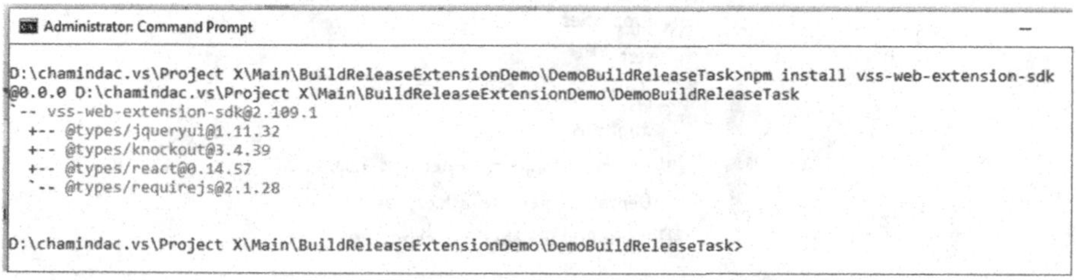

Figure 13-25. Downloading vss-web-extension-sdk

14. To package the Demo extension, execute the following command from the project folder (see Figure 13-26):

```
tfx extension create --manifest-globs vss-extension.json
```

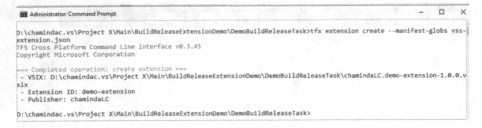

Figure 13-26. Packaging the extension

15. The packaged .vsix will be available in the project folder. See Figure 13-27.

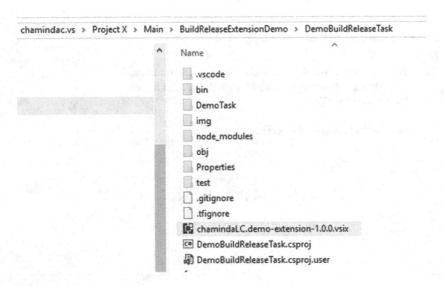

Figure 13-27. Packaged .vsix file

In this lesson, you created an extension to build and release and packaged it to get it ready for deployment.

Lesson 13.03 – Sign Up for Publishing Extensions in Marketplace and Publish Extension

You need to sign up in Visual Studio Marketplace to publish extensions.

1. Go to https://marketplace.visualstudio.com and click on the Publish Extensions link in the footer of the page. See Figure 13-28.

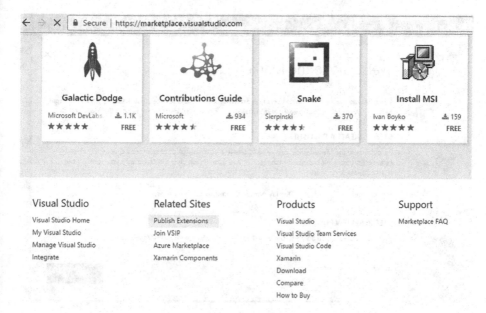

Figure 13-28. Publish Extensions link

2. Sign in with your Microsoft account that has a VSTS account to test the extension.

3. After signing in with your Microsoft account, in the popup window, provide your publisher ID. It is the same value used for Publisher in vss-extension.json. Provide a display name and click Create. See Figure 13-29.

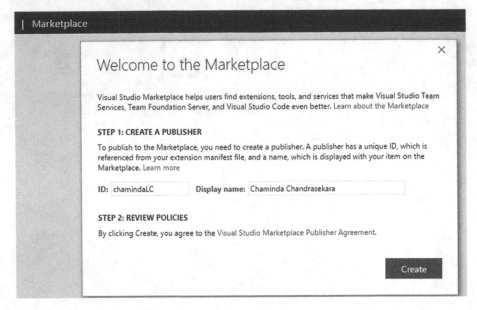

Figure 13-29. *Create a publisher*

4. This will allow you to upload extensions to share privately (publishing extensions publically is discussed later in this chapter). Click on the Upload new extension button, shown in Figure 13-30.

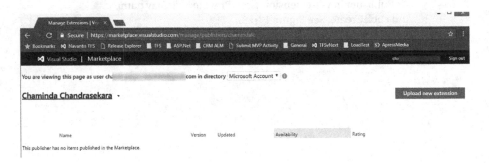

Figure 13-30. *Publisher*

5. In the popup window, click the Browse button and select the extension packaged in the previous lesson. See Figure 13-31.

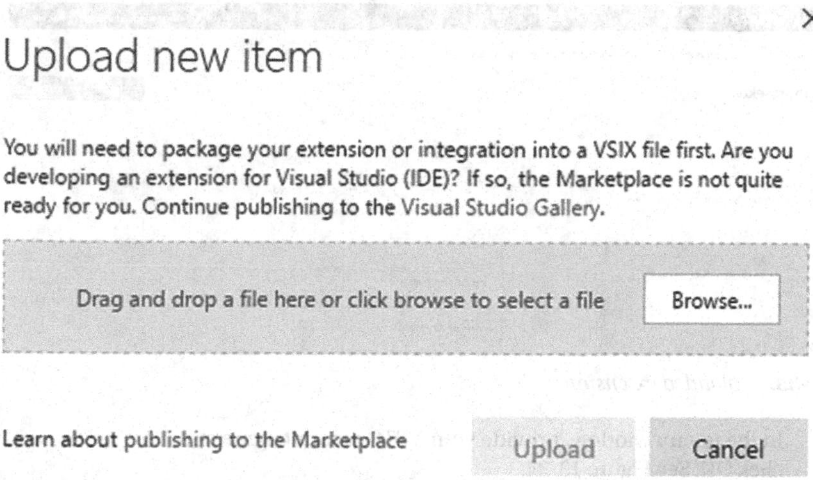

✕

Upload new item

You will need to package your extension or integration into a VSIX file first. Are you developing an extension for Visual Studio (IDE)? If so, the Marketplace is not quite ready for you. Continue publishing to the Visual Studio Gallery.

Drag and drop a file here or click browse to select a file   Browse...

Learn about publishing to the Marketplace   Upload   Cancel

Figure 13-31. Browsing extension

6. Click on Upload after selecting the extension .vsix. See Figure 13-32.

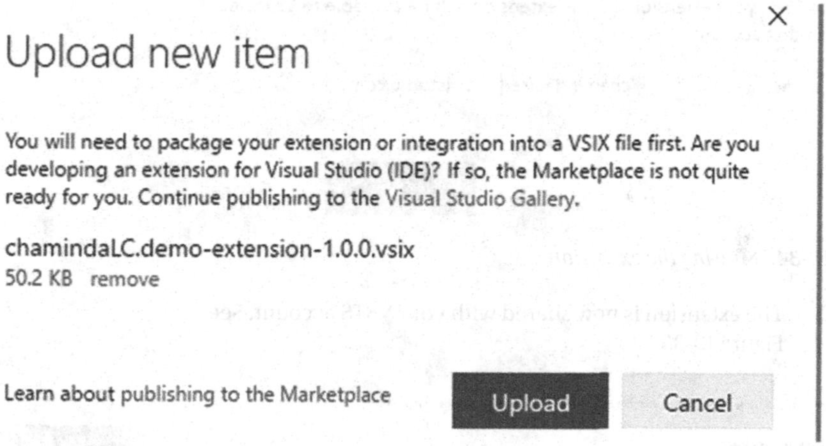

✕

Upload new item

You will need to package your extension or integration into a VSIX file first. Are you developing an extension for Visual Studio (IDE)? If so, the Marketplace is not quite ready for you. Continue publishing to the Visual Studio Gallery.

chamindaLC.demo-extension-1.0.0.vsix
50.2 KB   remove

Learn about publishing to the Marketplace   Upload   Cancel

Figure 13-32. Uploading the extension .vsix

7. The extension uploads, and it is not yet shared to any VSTS/ TFS account since it is private. To share it, click on the Share button. See Figure 13-33.

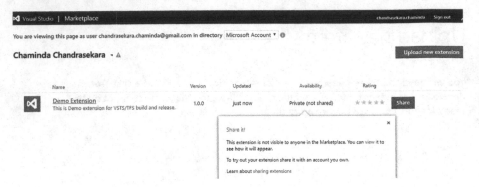

Figure 13-33. Uploaded extension

8. In the popup window, provide your VSTS account name and click OK. See Figure 13-34.

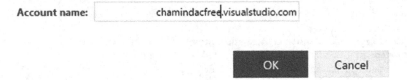

Figure 13-34. Sharing the extension

9. The extension is now shared with your VSTS account. See Figure 13-35.

Figure 13-35. Shared extension

534

You created a publisher, uploaded the extension to Marketplace, and shared it with your Team Services account.

Lesson 13.04 – Install Privately Shared Extension

Let's install a shared extension to the Team Services account.

1. Go to your VSTS account and click on Manage extensions. See Figure 13-36.

Figure 13-36. *Manage extensions*

2. The shared extension is available to install. Click on Demo Extension Name. See Figure 13-37.

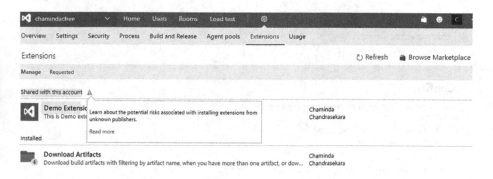

Figure 13-37. *Extension available to install*

3. The Marketplace extension page will be opened. Install the extension into your VSTS account by clicking Install. See Figure 13-38.

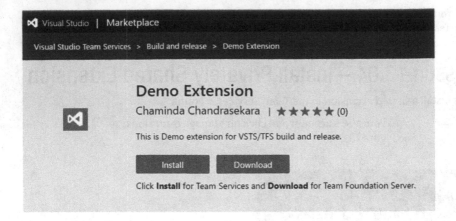

Figure 13-38. *Install extension*

4. Select your Team Services account in the popup window and click Confirm. See Figure 13-39.

Demo Extension
by Chaminda Chandrasekara

Account

Select a Visual Studio Team Services account where you would like to install this extension.

chamindacfree ⌄

Confirm

The extension will be granted these permissions:

- Work items (read and write)
- Work items (read)

This extension is offered to you for your use by a third party, not Microsoft. By clicking Confirm, you agree to the publisher's terms, if any, for this extension.

Confirm   Cancel

Figure 13-39. *Select Team Services account in which to install extension*

5. The extension will be installed in your VSTS account. See Figure 13-40.

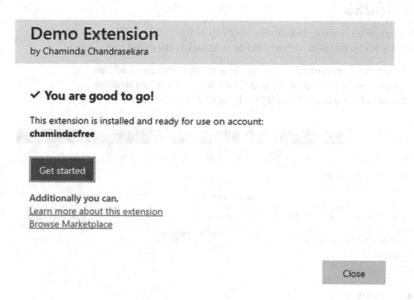

Figure 13-40. Extension installed

6. Refresh the Manage Extensions page, and you will see the extension is now installed. See Figure 13-41.

Figure 13-41. Extension available

You have installed a privately shared extension to your Team Services account.

Lesson 13.05 – Use the Extension in the Build/Release

After installing a privately shared extension to VSTS or uploaded and installed it to on-premises TFS, it can be used with a build or release (as specified in the task).

1. Create a folder named "Dummy" in a team project and add an empty text file, dummy.txt, and check it in. This is just to allow the build to have a repository path. See Figure 13-42.

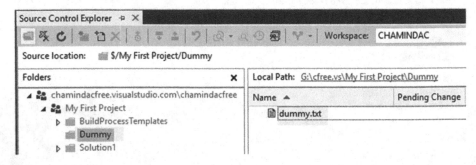

Figure 13-42. *Dummy*

2. Create a new empty build definition and set the repository to Dummy. See Figure 13-43.

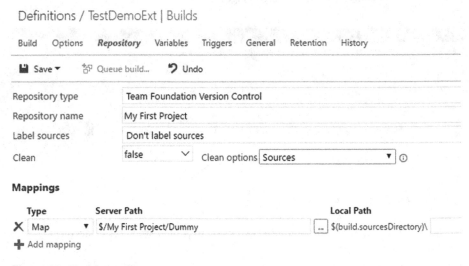

Figure 13-43. *Map to Dummy*

3. Click Add build step in the Build tab of the build definition. In the pop up Task Catalog window Utility tab, you will find the new "Demo Task" added with the new extension. Add it to the definition. See Figure 13-44.

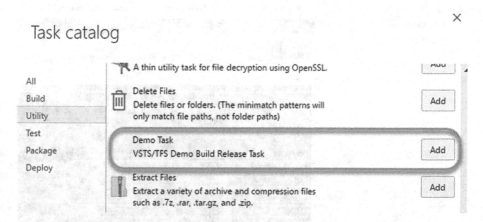

Figure 13-44. Add Demo task

4. In the Demo task, provide a value for the Your Name field and select Show Warning Message. See Figure 13-45.

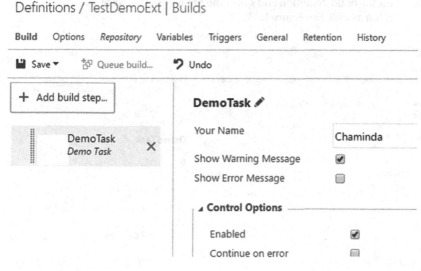

Figure 13-45. Demo task

5.   Queue a new build. The Demo task displays a message and warning message, and the build succeeds. See Figure 13-46.

Figure 13-46. *Demo task running with warning*

6.   Edit the build definition and select the Show Error Message option as well. See Figure 13-47.

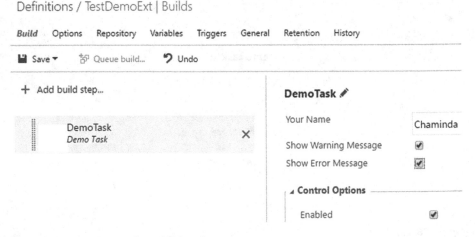

Figure 13-47. *Demo task enabled to show error*

7. Queue a build. The Demo task will show an error message and fail both the task and the build. With this, you have learned how to create a build release task and run it. It shows warnings, and on errors it knows how to fail a task. See Figure 13-48.

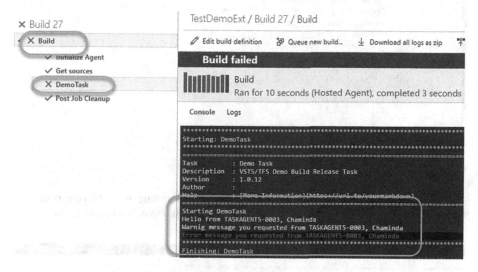

Figure 13-48. *Demo task failing with error*

In this lesson, you used the extension installed to the Team Services/TFS with a build definition.

What Else Is Possible with Build/Release Extensions?

You have learned how to add new build/release tasks to the Task Catalog. You have created a publisher account, but you could not share your extensions publicly. In order to make the extension available publicly in Marketplace, it should have useful functionality and should work with Visual Studio/Visual Studio code or Team Services/TFS. You have to follow the instructions found at https://www.visualstudio.com/en-us/docs/integrate/extensions/publish/publicize to become a verified publisher.

Once you have done so, you can make your extensions public by changing the vss-extension.json public setting to true. See Figure 13-49.

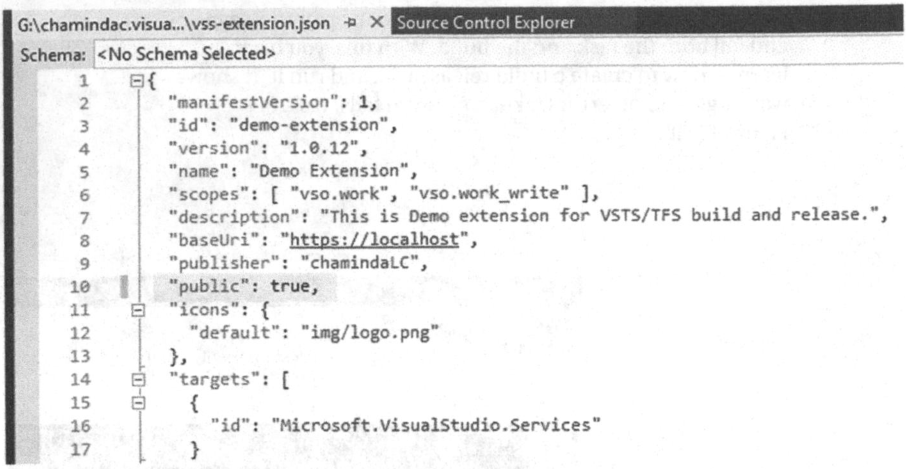

```
G:\chamindac.visua...\vss-extension.json  ⊣□ ✕  Source Control Explorer
Schema: <No Schema Selected>
    1   ⊟{
    2        "manifestVersion": 1,
    3        "id": "demo-extension",
    4        "version": "1.0.12",
    5        "name": "Demo Extension",
    6        "scopes": [ "vso.work", "vso.work_write" ],
    7        "description": "This is Demo extension for VSTS/TFS build and release.",
    8        "baseUri": "https://localhost",
    9        "publisher": "chamindaLC",
   10        "public": true,
   11   ⊟    "icons": {
   12          "default": "img/logo.png"
   13        },
   14   ⊟    "targets": [
   15   ⊟      {
   16            "id": "Microsoft.VisualStudio.Services"
   17          }
```

Figure 13-49. Making an extension public

Your extensions will be public once you package and update them. Make sure to increase the version number for each update to make it effective. See Figure 13-50.

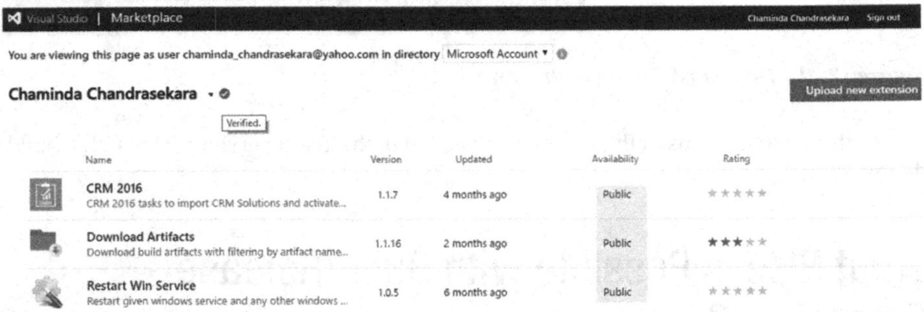

Figure 13-50. Public extensions

You have seen that the Demo task we created had a blank icon and default logo, and that its page in Marketplace had no documentation. Before you make your extensions public, you need to improve these.

- You can replace the icon.png file in your task folder with an image named "icon." There is no need to reference this file from task. json or anywhere. It will be automatically displayed as the icon of the task as long as it is in the folder of the task.

- You can replace logo.png in the img folder of the extension template. This is referred to in the vss-extension.json icons section as follows:

```
"icons": {
    "default": "img/logo.png"
  },
```

- Add a folder called "screenshots" to the img folder; you can add screenshots of your extension for the documentation. See Figure 13-51.

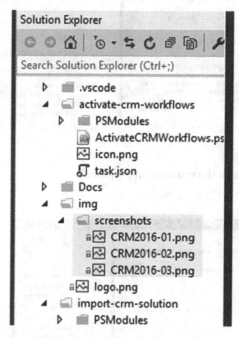

Figure 13-51. *Screenshots for extension*

This should be referred to in vss-extension.json as shown here:

```
"screenshots": [
    {
      "path": "img/screenshots/CRM2016-01.png"
    },
    {
      "path": "img/screenshots/CRM2016-02.png"
    },
```

```
{
  "path": "img/screenshots/CRM2016-03.png"
}
],
```

- Adding license text is required for a public extension. See Figure 13-52.

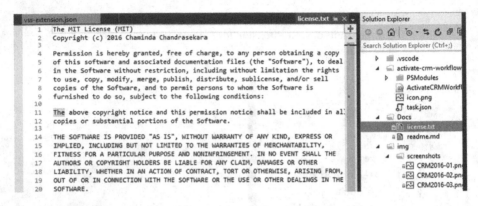

***Figure 13-52.** License for extension*

- The readme.md file can be added for documentation purposes. See Figure 13-53.

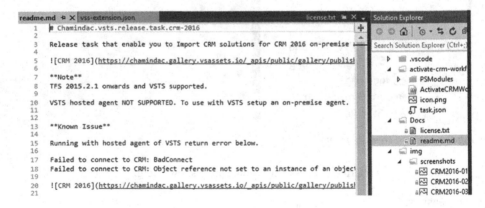

***Figure 13-53.** Readme file for the extension*

Refer to these files in vss-extension.json as follows:

```
"content": {
  "details": {
    "path": "Docs/readme.md"
  },
  "license": {
    "path": "Docs/license.txt"
  }
},
```

You can update the extension with screenshots once it is in Marketplace.
You have to put screenshot URLs in the readme.md file, then package and update again.
See Figure 13-54.

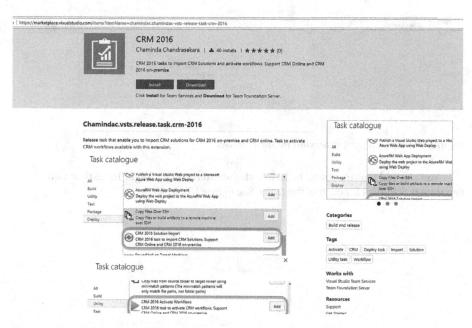

Figure 13-54. *Using screenshots in documentation*

To package an update to an extension, execute the package command with
--rev-version. This will auto-increment the version of the generated .vsix by updating
the vss-extension.json automatically. See Figure 13-55.

Figure 13-55. *Packaging extension with version increment*

To update an extension in Marketplace, click on the dropdown menu and select Update. Then, browse for the updated package and update it. See Figure 13-56.

Figure 13-56. *Updating extension in Marketplace*

You can add multiple build tasks in a single extension package. To do that, add separate task folders for each of the tasks. See Figure 13-57.

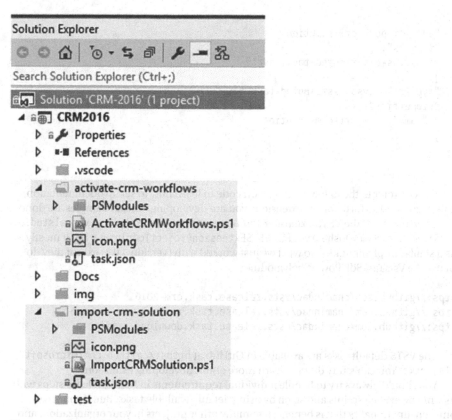

Figure 13-57. Multiple tasks in extension

In the vss-extension.json file, define contributions for each of the tasks in order to enable multiple tasks in a single extension package, as follows:

```
"contributions": [
  {
    "id": "activate-crm-workflows",
    "type": "ms.vss-distributed-task.task",
    "targets": [
      "ms.vss-distributed-task.tasks"
    ],
    "properties": {
      "name": "activate-crm-workflows"
    }
  },
```

```
{
  "id": "import-crm-solution",
  "targets": [
    "ms.vss-distributed-task.tasks"
  ],
  "type": "ms.vss-distributed-task.task",
  "properties": {
    "name": "import-crm-solution"
  }
}
]
```

You can refer to the following extension code to learn how to set up documentation, icons, logos, and so forth for the extensions you are developing. These examples are done on the version 2.4 of the VSTS Extension Template (https://marketplace.visualstudio.com/items?itemName=JoshGarverick.VSTSExtensionProjectTemplates), but it mostly has a similar implementation to what we just worked with (version 3.0.2) except they do not use the VstsTaskSdk PowerShell module.

https://github.com/chamindac/vsts.release.task.crm-2016
https://github.com/chamindac/vsts.release.task.restart-win-service
https://github.com/chamindac/vsts.release.task.download-artifacts

The VSTS default tasks are available in GitHub at https://github.com/Microsoft/vsts-tasks. You can study them to learn more about developing extensions.

You should always try to handle individual requirements in builds/release steps with custom PowerShell scripts and so on by using default available tasks. But, if you have common functionality that is beneficial to many other projects in your organization, and to other organizations, you can use the extending capability of Team Services/TFS build/release tasks.

Summary

In this book, you have learned how Visual Studio Team Services/TFS Build & Release management can help you enable continuous delivery so that you can achieve DevOps. Many concepts are covered, and the role Team Foundation Services Build & Release can play is explained in the book. Concepts such as using agent pools and queues, the security aspect of them, and setting up prerequisites for builds and release are explained via walkthrough lessons that even cover setting up in the Linux platform and building .NET source code in external repositories such as GitHub.

Several lessons allowed you to explore the deployment capabilities of Team Foundation Build & Release to Microsoft cloud platform Azure. You have been given detailed practical guidance on automating deployments of websites in the Azure app service, doing database deployments to Azure platform, micro-services deployments in Azure Service Fabric, docker-enabled ASP.NET Core web app deployments, and more using Team Foundation build and release management.

Hands-on lessons gave you experience in automating the generation of effective release notes with each deployment in a given target environment (QA, UAT, Production, and so forth) to empower your teams to achieve DevOps by enabling the requirement to production delivery traceability. Walkthroughs for deploying to and using packages from Team Services package management feeds with build and release management have given all the required guidance to use Team Services Package Management for internal NuGet and npm package sharing.

Dynamics CRM Solution deployment lessons have given you hands-on experience automating deployments for CRM with Team Services/TFS. Walkthroughs for CRM deployments could be followed by anyone who has minimal knowledge of Microsoft Dynamics CRM.

Test automation lessons on how to integrate the automated tests into builds and deployments have covered all essentials required in order for you to gain practical knowledge of challenges in test automation and overcoming them. The hands-on lessons even include guidance on setting up an on-demand test farm using Azure virtual machines to effectively reduce implementation costs.

Several hands-on lessons in the book allowed you to understand how to optimize the build release management definitions by using capabilities such as task groups. Knowledge in diagnosing and fixing issues in automated builds and deployments has been given via practical walkthroughs. Information on enhancing the capability of TFS Build & Release Management by using Team Services/TFS Marketplace extensions and writing your own extensions for any missing functionality was provided with hands-on lessons.

Index

■ B

Get the eBook for only $5!

Why limit yourself?

With most of our titles available in both PDF and ePUB format, you can access your content wherever and however you wish—on your PC, phone, tablet, or reader.

Since you've purchased this print book, we are happy to offer you the eBook for just $5.

To learn more, go to http://www.apress.com/companion or contact support@apress.com.

Apress®

Printed in the United States
By Bookmasters